Shifting Shape,
Shaping Text

Shifting Shape, Shaping Text

Philosophy and Folklore in the Fox Kōan

Steven Heine

University of Hawai'i Press
HONOLULU

© 1999 University of Hawai'i Press
All rights reserved
Printed in the United States of America

04 03 02 01 00 99   5 4 3 2 1

Library of Congress Cataloging-in-Publication Data

Heine, Steven 1950–
    Shifting shape, shaping text : philosophy and folklore in the Fox kōan
/ Steven Heine.
        p.   cm.
    Includes bibliographical references and index.
    ISBN 0–8248–2150–5 (alk. paper). — ISBN 0–8248–2197–1 (paper :
alk. paper)
    1. Koan.   2. Hui-hai, 720–814.   3. Zen meditations.   4. Zen
Buddhism—Folklore.   5. Karma.   I. Title.
BQ9289.5.H44   1999
294.3'927—dc21   99–24368
                                                                      CIP

University of Hawai'i Press books are printed on acid-free
paper and meet the guidelines for permanence and
durability of the Council on Library Resources.

Designed by Northeastern Graphic Services, Inc.

Printed by The Maple-Vail Book Manufacturing Group

Contents

Preface

It takes a fox to know a fox.
—*Ts'ung-jung lu,* case 24

This book draws on my fascination with the complex varieties and multiple meanings of the shape-shifting wild fox—a symbol of liminality in East Asian folklore—in order to analyze the theory and practice of Ch'an/Zen Buddhism in its formative period in China and Japan. The book develops a wide range of implications about early Zen by examining a specific example of the kōan tradition known as "Pai-chang (J. Hyakujō) and the wild fox" or "Pai-chang's wild fox kōan," which is included as the second case in the *Wu-men kuan* and numerous other collections. While most interpretations comment on the philosophy of causality, my aim is to show how the fox kōan deals with the doctrine of karma in terms of a generally overlooked folklore narrative of fox-spirit possession and exorcism borrowed from Buddhist morality tale literature (often labeled *setsuwa bungaku*). The kōan thus serves as a lens for examining the intersection in Zen of philosophical discussions on cause-and-effect and popular religious approaches to karmic retribution and release. The relation between these interlocking discursive perspectives is discussed in light of the image of Master Pai-chang as a strict disciplinarian who advocates an ethic of "no work, no food"—an ethic reflected in his monastic rules text, the *Ch'an-men kuei-shih* (J. *Zenmon kishiki*), which also stresses the need to banish rogue or miscreant members of the *saṃgha*.

Thus the book deals with the relation between a triad of issues: a philosophical debate about the paradoxical identity of causality and its antithesis noncausality; a folkloric expression of retribution and repentance conveyed by the kōan's exorcism narrative; and Pai-chang's monastic rules and recorded sayings texts. The book demonstrates that Pai-chang's rules and records articulate a sense of monastic order and moral stability that combats the criticism of Buddhism as an antinomian, antisocial, "wild fox" religious lifestyle in a way that dovetails with the ritual elimination of an intruding vulpine spirit that is performed in the kōan record.

Chapter 1 introduces the text and context of the fox kōan and evaluates Zen's ambiguous (or duplicitous) attitude about supernatural beliefs and diverse uses of the rhetoric of the wild fox—either as a criticism of rogue monks who violate rules or as praise of morally superior patriarchs who transcend the need for regulations. This chapter analyzes various kinds of syncretism incorporating indigenous fox-cult worship that encompasses the poles of the fox portrayed as positive/protective and as negative/destructive—even while Zen rhetoric cloaks itself in an aura of iconoclastic repudiation of animism. Chapter 2 explores the methodological issue of examining the connection between philosophy and folklore while attempting to overcome the conventional two-tiered model of great and little traditions. The underlying theme in the examination of ambivalent approaches to the fundamentally bivalent vulpine imagery in Part One is that fox transfiguration represents the crossing of boundaries and the possibility of conquering illusion during times of transition and transformation—especially in moral crises when conventional reality is challenged, undermined, or otherwise called into question. Throughout the book there are citations of literary and artistic expressions of fox folklore in relation to Zen thought.

In Part Two, Chapter 3 focuses on philosophical interpretations of the doctrine of causality and explores the debate between a literal reading of the kōan, which emphasizes a strict adherence to the law of karma, and the mainstream paradoxical reading, which embraces an identity of causality and noncausality. Chapter 4 deals extensively with the contradictory interpretations of the fox kōan presented in two fascicles of Dōgen's *Shōbōgenzō* and related writings. It also considers the controversy in contemporary scholarship, particularly Critical Buddhism, about whether it is possible to appropriate Dōgen's apparent change of heart—expressed in an exclusive emphasis on the literal reading of the kōan in his later period—to illumine socioethical problems in Buddhism's interaction with modern society. Chapter 5, citing examples of fox folklore from a variety of *setsuwa* sources, shows that one must understand how folklore motifs provide a literary and conceptual underpinning of the fox kōan's approach to the experience of repentance if one is to interpret the philosophical level of the case. Chapter 6 returns to the hermeneutic issue of overcoming the two-tiered model. In this chapter I assess recent attempts by leading scholars to deal with the role of popular religions in the Zen tradition and then propose an alternative model based on a theory of intertextuality—that is, the interconnectedness of diverse textual materials.

The appendixes contain two sets of translations. Appendix I presents the standard *Wu-men kuan* edition and an alternative early edition of the fox kōan from the *T'ien-sheng kuang-teng lu,* including a detailed comparison of the two versions, as well as the edition of the kōan in the *Ts'ung-jung lu* kōan collection and two verses contained in Dōgen's *Eihei kōroku juko* collection. Appendix II presents a translation of Pai-chang's rules, the *Ch'an-men kuei-shih,* which was first included as an appendix to the biography of Pai-chang in the *Ching-te ch'uan-teng lu* ("transmission of the lamp" text) of 1004. Additional translations of prose and poetic commentaries on the kōan appear throughout the book.

Acknowledgments

The major source of funding for the research for this book was a fellowship awarded by the National Endowment of the Humanities (1996–1997). Other funding sources include Florida International University DSRT funding (1997–1998), the Northeast Asia Council of the Association for Asian Studies (1996), the American Academy of Religion (1996), the Pennsylvania State University Liberal Arts Research and Graduate Studies Office (1994 and 1996) as well as the Institute for Arts and Humanistic Studies (1995), the Indiana University East Asian Studies Program (1995), and the University of Chicago East Asian Studies Program (1996).

Some of the material first appeared in "Putting the 'Fox' Back in the 'Wild Fox Kōan': The Intersection of Philosophical and Popular Religious Elements in the Ch'an/Zen Kōan Tradition," *Harvard Journal of Asiatic Studies* 56(2) (1996):257–317. Additional material was incorporated from the following two articles: "Sōtō Zen and the Inari Cult: Symbiotic and Exorcistic Trends in Buddhist–Folk Religious Amalgamations," *Pacific World* 10 (1994):71–95; and "Critical Buddhism *(Hihan Bukkyō)* and the Debate Concerning the 12-Fascicle and 75-Fascicle *Shōbōgenzō* Texts," *Japanese Journal of Religious Studies* 21(1) (1994):37–72. Various versions of the paper on the fox kōan were presented at the Harvard University Buddhist Studies Forum (1994), the American Academy of Religion's annual national meeting (1994) and Mid-Atlantic annual regional meeting (1996), the Fuse Lecture Series of the University of Tokyo Department of Indian and Buddhist Philosophy (1996), the Princeton University East Asian Studies Department (1997), and the Miami-Dade CC Honors Program (1998). I thank Yoshizu Yoshihide and Ishii Shūdō of Komazawa University and Sueki Fumihiko of Tokyo University for helpful advice and suggestions that guided my research in Zen theories and practices. Thanks also to Patricia Crosby and the staff of University of Hawai'i Press for their support. Special thanks also to David Olson, Soho Machida, Dale Wright, Bernard Faure, Jackie Stone, and Karen Smyers, among other foxy friends.

Figures 11 and 12 showing inscribed stones from Pai-chang's temple in Kiangsi province in China—including what is said to be the original "wild fox rock" where the discovery of the vulpine corpse and funeral took place according to the kōan narrative—are presented courtesy of Ishii Shūdō. Thanks also to Stephen Addiss for permission to reprint two photos (Figures 2 and 14) from his collection and to the Idemitsu Museum of Art for Figure 1.

Notes on Transliteration

This book uses the term "Zen" to refer to both Ch'an Buddhism in China and Zen Buddhism in Japan (except in quotations from scholars who do otherwise). Wade-Giles romanization is used throughout the book, again with the exception of quotations from scholars who use pinyin. Asian names are given family name first, except in instances that cite an author's works in English.

Abbreviations

CCL	*Ching-te ch'uan-teng lu* (J. *Keitoku dentōroku*, 1004), 30 *chüan*, in *T* 51, 2076.
CLEAR	Chinese Literature: Essays, Articles, Reviews
CMKS	*Ch'an-men kuei-shih* (J. *Zenmon kishiki*, 1004), in *CCL*, in *chüan* 6.
CSLT	*Ch'an-tsung sung-ku lien-chu-t'ung chi* (J. *Zenshū juko renshutsū shū*, 1392), in *HTC* 115.
CYCK	*Ch'an-yüan ch'ing-kuei* (J. *Zen'en shingi*, 1103), in *Yakuchū Zen'en shingi*, eds. Kagamishima Genryū, Satō Tatsugen, and Kosaka Kiyū (Tokyo: Sōtōshū shūmuchō, 1972).
DZZ	*Dōgen zenji zenshū*, ed. Kagamishima Genryū et al., 7 vols. (Tokyo: Shunjūsha, 1988–1993).
EK	*Eihei kōroku* (1236–1253), in *DZZ*, vols. 3–4.
HCKL	*Hung-chih kuang-lu* (J. *Wanshi kōroku*, 1201), 10 *chüan*, in *T* 48, 2001.
HTC	*Hsü tsang ching* (J. *Nihon zoku zōkyō*), 150 vols. (Taipei: Shin wen fang, n.d.).
IBK	Indogaku Bukkyōgaku *kenkyū*
JCYL	*Ju-ching yü-lu* (J. *Nyojō goroku*, 1228), in *Tendō Nyojō zenji no kenkyū*, ed. Kagamishima Genryū (Tokyo: Shunjūsha, 1983).

JSS	*Jūnikanbon Shōbōgenzō no shomondai,* ed. Kagamishima Genryū and Suzuki Kakuzen (Tokyo: Daizō shuppan, 1991).
KDBR	*Komazawa Daigaku Bukkyōgakubu ronshū*
KKMJ	*Kokonchomonjū* (1254), in *NKBT,* vol. 84.
KM	*Konjaku monogatari* (ca. 1100), in *NKBT,* vols. 22–26.
LL	*Lin-chi lu* (J. *Rinzai roku,* 1144), in *T* 47, 1985; and in *RR.*
MS	*Mana Shōbōgenzō* (also known as: *Shinji Shōbōgenzō; Shōbōgenzō sanbyakusoku;* 1235), in *DZZ,* vol. 5.
NKBT	*Nihon koten bungaku taikei,* ed. Yamada Yoshio et al., 100 vols. (Tokyo: Iwanami shoten, 1961–1963).
PCYL	*Pai-chang yü-lu* (J. *Hyakujō goroku,* 1144), in *HTC* 119.
PYL	*Pi-yen lu* (J. *Hekiganroku,* 1128), in *T* 48, 2003.
RR	*Rinzai roku,* ed. Iriya Yoshitaka (Tokyo: Iwanami shoten, 1991).
SK	*Shōbōgenzō* (1223–1253), in *DZZ,* vols. 1–2.
SKSC	*Sung kao-seng chuan,* in *T* 50, 2061.
SSC	*Sou-shen chi* (335–349), ed. Wang Shao-ying (Beijing: Chung-hua shu-chü, 1979).
SZ	*Shōbōgenzō zuimonki* (1236), in *DZZ,* vol. 7.
T	*Taishō shinshū daizōkyō,* ed. Takakusu Junjirō and Watanabe Kaigyoku, 100 vols. (Tokyo: Taishō issaikyō kankōkai, 1924–1932).
TJL	*Ts'ung-jung lu* (J. *Shōyōroku,* 1224), in *T* 48, 2004.
TKL	*T'ien-sheng kuang-teng lu* (J. *Tenshō kōtōroku,* 1036), in *HTC* 135.
TLH	*Tsung-men lien-teng hui-yao* (J. *Shūmon rentōeyō,* 1183), in *HTC* 136.
TNHT	*Tsung-men nien-ku hui-chi* (J. *Shūmon nenko ishū,* 1664), in *HTC* 115.
TPKC	*T'ai-p'ing kuang-chi* (978), ed. Wang Meng'ou (Beijing: Chung-hua shu-chü, 1981).
TTC	*Tsu-t'ang chi* (J. *Sōdōshū,* 952), in *Sōdōshū,* ed. Yanagida Seizan (Kyoto: Chūbun shuppansha, 1974).

TTY   *Tsung-men t'ung-yao chi* (J. *Shūmon tōyōshū*, 1093), Tōyō Bunka edition, photo-facsimile edition in Komazawa University Library.

WMK   *Wu-men kuan* (J. *Mumonkan*, 1228), in *T* 48, 2005.

WTH   *Wu-teng hui-yüan* (J. *Gotō egen*, 1253), in *HTC* 138.

Location of Mt. Pai-chang in Kiangsi Province

Part One

Shape-Shifting

1 · Putting the Fox Back in the Fox Kōan

Ah, the emotions of supernatural beings reflect the meaning of human existence!
> —*Jen-shih chuan* ("The Tale of Miss Jen"), a T'ang folktale

Thirteen days seems like thirteen years . . .
> —*Konjaku monogatari*

The "wild fox kōan" is one of the most elusive and enigmatic records in the vast repertoire of medieval Ch'an/Zen anecdotes and dialogues. Although it is found in dozens of sources, it is probably best known for its inclusion as the second case in the *Wu-men kuan* (J. *Mumonkan*, 1228), a collection of prose and verse commentary on kōans. The kōan (C. *kung-an*) deals with the mysterious presence in the *saṃgha* of a wild fox (C. *yeh-hu;* J. *yako*) appearing in human form. (See Appendix I for a complete translation and discussion of textual history).[1]

The Kōan: Text and Context

According to the case record, on hearing a sermon delivered by Abbot Pai-chang Huai-hai (J. Hyakujō Ekai, 749–814),[2] the fox confesses to being an anomalous apparition or "nonhuman" (C. *fei-jen;* J. *hinin*), a term typically used in East Asian spirit-possession folklore. The term also commonly appears in Buddhist literature on the entities of the six realms of transmigration. The fox/monk claims that he was once a master of the

3

same temple who has been suffering karmic retribution lasting five hundred lifetimes for having misunderstood and denied the impact of the law of moral causation. In responding to a disciple's query during the era of Kāśyapa, the sixth of the seven primordial buddhas culminating in Śākyamuni,[3] he maintained that enlightenment lies beyond (or does not fall into) the inexorable effects of causality (C. *pu-lo yin-kuo;* J. *furaku inga;* literally "not falling into or no bondage to causality"). The fox/monk—referred to in some commentaries as the "former Pai-chang" since masters took their names from the location of their temples—beseeches the help of the abbot, the current Pai-chang. He is liberated from the punishment by the "pivot (or turning) word" (C. *i-chüan-yü;* J. *ittengo*) proffered by the abbot, which affirms the universality of karmic causality even for the enlightened. According to Pai-chang's alteration of a single character in a four-character phrase, there is no escape from (or obscuring of bondage to) karma, which continues after awakening (C. *pu-mei yin-kuo;* J. *fumai inga;* "not obscuring or remaining subject to causality" or seeing that "causality is obviously apparent").

Now spiritually liberated, the vulpine corpse of the ancient monk, as he predicts just before his demise, is discovered by Pai-chang under a large rock behind the gates of the temple compound. Pai-chang instructs the rector (Skt. *karmadāna;* C. *wei-na;* J. *ino*)—the registrar charged by Zen monastic codes with the supervision of the Monks' Hall—to announce that a proper clerical cremation and funeral for the deceased monk will take place after the noon meal. This ceremony accords with the last request of the fox/monk, who seeks posthumous recognition. But the other monks in the assembly had not been aware of his presence, which was known only to the abbot who received the confession. When the monks learn of the preparations for a funeral, they remark with surprise that no one had been sick in the Nirvana Hall or infirmary (so called because of an association of illness/death and nirvana). Nevertheless they participate in the ceremony as instructed. Pai-chang leads them to the rear of the temple and uses his staff to uncover the corpse that lies in the brush near the fox den beneath the rock. (See Figures 1–3.)

In a postmortem epilogue—a literary device apparently borrowed from folktales commenting on the elimination of an intruding spirit—during the evening sermon the abbot explains the unusual circumstances of the burial to his bewildered congregation, which continues to wonder why a fox body was allowed a Buddhist funeral. Pai-chang

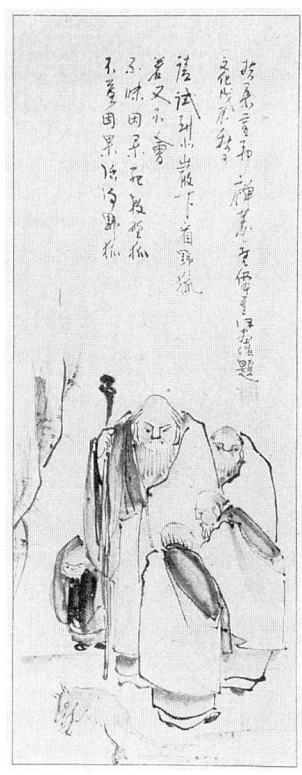

Figure 1. This print from Sengai's famous series on the *Wu-men kuan* illustrates the discovery of the fox corpse by Pai-chang carrying his mountain staff—a scene often depicted by modern Zen masters in informal drawings that accompany kōan commentaries. The poem reads (following the translation by Norman Waddell but altering the last line): "Not falling into cause and effect can bring the wild fox to life; / not obscuring cause and effect kills him stone dead. / If you still don't understand / why don't you go to the base of the rock behind the temple and see [the fox corpse] for yourself!" The print is stored in the Idemitsu Museum of Art (and is printed here with permission of the museum). The translation of the poem appears in Robert Aitken, *The Gateless Barrier: The Wu-Men Kuan (Mumonkan)* (Berkeley: North Point, 1990), p. 20.

is challenged and then slapped by his foremost disciple Huang-po. According to the biographical entry in the *Ching-te ch'uan-teng lu* (J. *Keitoku dentōroku*), Huang-po was an incredibly imposing figure standing seven feet tall with a lump like a round pearl on his forehead who became known for his own harsh treatment of his disciple Lin-chi (J. Rinzai). This slap is perhaps the first instance in Zen records of a role reversal whereby a disciple reprimands and insults the master—an insult later carried out by Lin-chi's actions toward Huang-po—and it came to define the approach of the "four houses" (C. *ssu-chia;* J. *shike*) of the Ma-tsu or Hung-chou school lineage.[4] (See Figure 4.) But Pai-chang gives his hearty approval by calling his disciple a "red-bearded barbarian"—an ironic evocation of the first Chinese patriarch, Bodhidharma (the twenty-eighth patriarch in India), who brought the transmission of Zen from "the west."[5]

Figure 2. This drawing by Sozan Genkyō shows a similar rendition of the corpse-discovery episode. (Special thanks to Stephen Addiss for drawing this work to my attention.) It contains a variant of the *Wu-men kuan* verse: "Not falling into causality, not obscuring causality / Two sides of the dice of the same color."

The Kōan's Context

The fox kōan is distinctive for several reasons involving issues in philosophy, folklore, and monastic rules. First, in the spirit of the dictum that Zen is "a special transmission outside the teachings" (C. *chiao-wai pieh-chuan;* J. *kyōge betsuden*), most kōans avoid reference to a specific doctrine. But in contrast to kōans notable for their compressed style of expression disdaining formal doctrine—by focusing on a single phrase, word, or syllable, often absurd or incongruous, as a reflection of nonconceptual, ineffable truth—the fox kōan is one of the few cases that explores a basic Buddhist concept. It focuses on the meaning of the morally determined process of cause-and-effect (Skt. *hetu-phala;* C. *yin-kuo;* J. *inga*), rewards and punishment, or benefits and retribution, as well as the question of attaining transcendence from causality that is apparently denied by Pai-chang's pivot word.[6]

At the same time, the philosophical analysis is accomplished, not in terms of an abstract, logical argument, but through a brief yet complex narrative structure derived from folktales about fox-spirit possession and

Figure 3. This informal drawing of the kōan's dramatic corpse-discovery scene by a modern Sōtō Zen thinker shows Pai-chang alone and unaccompanied by the assembly of monks. It is particularly interesting in depicting a gaunt, ascetic master seeming to emanate from the burning corpse while performing a mudra (symbolic hand gesture) over the body. From Kishizawa Ian, *Shōbōgenzō zenkō* (Tokyo: Daihorinkaku, 1974), p. 333.

exorcism that brings to the surface a supernatural and pietistic element in Zen discourse. Although numerous kōans feature animals—such as Chao-chou's "Does the dog have Buddha nature?," Nan-ch'üan's "Cutting the cat," Wu-tsu's "Pushing the buffalo through a window," and other cases containing animistic elements—the fox kōan is perhaps the only case concerning the deeds of a shape-shifting creature that makes a human appearance.[7] In accord with this thematic element, the kōan is also a rare example of Zen literature dealing with the notion of previous

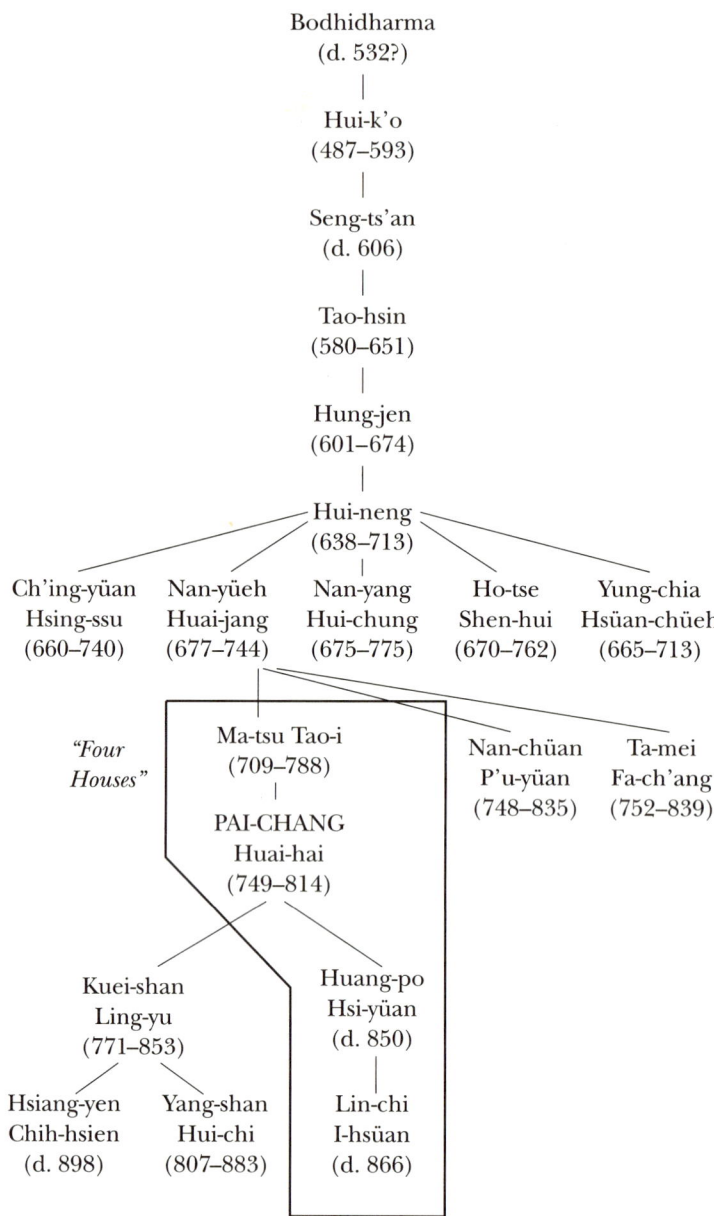

Figure 4. This Zen lineage chart locates Pai-chang by showing the lineage of the six patriarchs culminating in Hui-neng as well as Ma-tsu's Hung-chou school sublineage—particularly the four masters or "four houses" (C. *ssu-chia;* J. *shike*): Ma-tsu, Pai-chang, Huang-po, and Lin-chi.

lives. Generally, Zen writings do not consider the topic of a master explicitly remembering or claiming to be a reincarnation of a prior existence, a motif prevalent in other genres of Buddhist literature.[8]

Moreover, the kōan puts great emphasis on the role of several ritualized institutional elements of Zen monasticism: the styles of sermons delivered by Pai-chang (both in the opening scene when the fox appears and at the conclusion when the master receives the slap); the interaction between teacher and pupils who are either respectful or brash; the symbolism of the abbot's staff that uncovers the vulpine corpse; and the function of mortuary rites for Buddhist priests. The staff (C. *chang;* J. *jō;* sometimes referred to as C. *chu-chang* or J. *shujō*), a seven-foot-long, untrimmed stick that every Zen master traditionally cut for himself in the mountains, represents the structure and charisma of the master's authority. It is an important symbol of the abbot as a mountain steward—for every temple is considered a mountain and has a mountain name (such as Pai-chang and Huang-po), even if located in an urban environment, as well as a spiritual leader capable of taming wild nature.[9] In some cases the staff—along with the ceremonial fly whisk (C. *fu-tzu;* J. *hossu*) carried by masters while sitting on the "high seat" during their formal sermons and other ceremonial occasions—is given metaphysical or supernatural implications. It is referred to by Dōgen, who was fond of raising up the staff and then casting it aside during his lectures, as the "embodiment of the true nature of reality." There are also reports of staffs and fly whisks turning into dragons or being used to subdue threatening spirits, though this is no doubt intended to be taken in a symbolic or demythological sense. In a concluding remark to a sermon discussing the fox kōan, Dōgen echoes Yün-men and others in asserting: "After living on this mountain for many years, my black staff transforms into a dragon producing wind and thunder."[10]

Like nearly all accounts of the masters of the classical period of Zen in the T'ang era, the kōan case—sometimes known as "Pai-chang and the wild fox," "Pai-chang's fox kōan," the "kōan of great cultivation" (C. *ta-hsiu-hsing;* J. *daishugyō*), or the "kōan of not obscuring causality"—was published in a variety of sources in the Sung era over two hundred years after Pai-chang's death. It was subseqently discussed in several kōan collection commentaries in China, including the *Wu-men kuan* and the *Ts'ung-jung lu* (J. *Shōyōroku*, 1224, case 8), as well as by numerous Japanese masters, including Dōgen, who wrote two *Shōbōgenzō* fascicles exclusively on the case with contradictory readings in addition to a citation in the *Mana Shōbōgenzō* and comments in the *Eihei kōroku* and *Shōbōgenzō zuimonki*,[11] along with Ikkyū and Hakuin, among others. Moreover, the fox kōan has been treated extensively in the vast pedagogical materials of the late medieval and early modern Sōtō sect referred to as *shōmono* (also known as *kikigakishō*) collections of commentaries on the major kōan sources, including the *Wu-men kuan* and *Ts'ung-jung lu*, that are extant today in photo-facsimile editions.[12] In addition, the kōan is cited in the Tokugawa-era commentary on one hundred cases—the *Dōryūroku* (case 71)—and has been interpreted in numerous scholarly studies and masters' homilies on traditional kōan collections in the modern period.

The fox kōan initially appeared as a dialogical anecdote contained in the section on Pai-chang's life and teachings in the bio-hagiographic "transmission of the lamp" (C. *chuan-teng*; J. *dentō*) text, the *T'ien-sheng kuang-teng lu* (J. *Tenshō kōtōroku*, 1036), which was the second main example of the genre of genealogical historical anecdotes following the groundbreaking *Ching-te ch'uan-teng lu* of 1004.[13] Both texts were imperially commissioned and geared to an audience consisting in large part of public scholar-officials. The *T'ien-sheng kuang-teng lu* was not simply an extension of the better-known *Ching-te ch'uan-teng lu*, which stressed the role of T'ang-era masters. Rather, it developed a new approach to Zen self-identity emphasizing the continuity of the sect into the Sung era. After this edition, the kōan text underwent considerable revision until eventually two main versions emerged: the *T'ien-sheng kuang-teng lu* version (hereafter *TKL*), which appears with minor modifications in Pai-chang's recorded sayings text, the *Pai-chang yü-lu* (J. *Hyakujō goroku*), and a subsequent version with enhanced philosophical and folkloric elements appearing in the *Wu-men kuan* (hereafter *WMK*) and elsewhere, including both *Shōbōgenzō* fascicles. The *WMK* version apparently was cited from the *Tsung-men t'ung-yao chi* (J. *Shūmon Tōyōshū*), a relatively obscure but highly influential transmission of the lamp text of 1093.[14] A close look at the two versions indicates that as the standard text evolved during the course of a couple of centuries of composition and editing in the Sung era, all areas of religious significance—the philosophical issue of karmic causality, the supernatural pattern of exorcism, the rituals of Zen monastic life—were considerably strengthened by revisions and emendations.

The original version contained the basic structure of folklore imagery. Subsequent editions continued to revise the text with additional phrasing, such as referring to the monk as a *"fei-jen,"* a term used in tales of the confession of foxes and other anomalous, shape-shifting entities as being less (or, in some cases, more) than human. Another example of change is the *WMK's* inclusion of several references to the fox reincarnations lasting "five hundred lifetimes"—a mythical image that defies logical analysis in evoking a subjective, even dreamlike, nature of the perception of time.[15] Additional modifications in the *WMK* version enhance the ritual aspect of the narrative: references to the monastic institutional structure (including the rank of functionaries like the abbot and rector or the role of buildings like the Nirvana Hall), the sense of the etiquette of deference by junior disciples (as in the fox/monk's bowing to his superior, Pai-chang), and the cremation of the fox corpse taking place after the midday meal in accord with Buddhist tradition.

The references to the abbot's staff, the assembly's bewilderment that no monk has been sick, the bowing by the *fei-jen,* and the cremation do not appear in the *TKL* version. Although the *TKL* says that the fox/monk asked for a burnt offering, a typical ancestor rite, it does not refer explicitly to a request for "Buddhist rites." The *TKL* version remarks that other monks "gathered some firewood and burned the fox" without using the explicit term for "cremation" that implies a ceremonial performance. The *TKL* does, however, contain two important ritual features that were deleted in the *WMK* version. First, it begins by referring to Pai-chang's sermon as a formal *shang-t'ang* (J. *jōdō*) lecture in the Dharma Hall. Second, it says that "Pai-chang instructed the monk in charge of rules to strike the clapper and announce that the assembly would participate in the practice of communal labor (C. *p'u-ch'ing;* J. *fusei*) by burying a deceased monk after the midday meal." The reference to "communal labor" evokes a crucial requirement for monastic behavior delineated in Pai-chang's monastic rules text that is further suggested by anecdotes in his recorded sayings. Thus the *TKL* must not be overlooked but should be interpreted side-by-side with the *WMK* version.

According to conventional interpretations that view the kōan narrative as primarily emphasizing the philosophy of causality rather than ritual or folklore elements, the keys to understanding the case are the linguistic tool of Pai-chang's pivot word and the iconoclastic gesture of Huang-po's slap. The fox kōan seems like a typical Zen "encounter dialogue" (C. *chi-yüan wen-ta;* J. *kien-mondō*) in which the fox/monk admits to an impasse blocking his awakening and is liberated by Pai-chang's teaching.[16] The encounter dialogue is a style of pedagogy: a spontaneous repartee through which a master brings about the transformation of a disciple who stands on the verge of enlightenment and needs just one more insightful comment to create the breakthrough. Encounter dialogues generally rely on impenetrable, absurdist, or non sequitur language or physical demonstrations—shouting, striking, pointing one finger, cutting off a finger, leaping from a high pole—to trigger an unmediated liberation from conceptual fixation.[17] There are actually three dialogues in the case record: one between the fox/monk in his former incarnation (or the former Pai-chang) and a disciple; a second between the former and current Pai-chang; and a third between Pai-chang and Huang-po. The pivot word in the second conversation is a specialized method that fulfills the dialogical process in spontaneously transforming the roots of ignorance into the source of wisdom. In this instance, Pai-chang liberates the fox/monk's misunderstanding by a deceptively simple affirmation of cause-and-effect derived from intriguing wordplay that transmutes an erroneous view into a correct one. The argument is that an intellectual understanding alone—that is, correct thinking about the causal/noncausal ground of morality—is sufficient for release from transmigration and the attainment of enlightenment. The kōan's final dialogue offers a characteristically Zen nonlogical resolution of the philosophical dilemma—a dramatic nonverbal expression of how, from the standpoint of reason and conventional language, the basic concern remains unresolvable.

Yet the dynamics of the exchange between the fox/monk and abbot recall countless examples of folklore—many of which were integrated into the vast corpus of popular Buddhist morality tale literature known by the Japanese term *setsuwa bungaku*—based on the possession and exorcism of magical animals.[18] Unlike the conventional disciple who internalizes the lessons learned from the teacher, the fox/monk who has endured punishment for a duration calculable in mythical time cannot be released from his *fei-jen* status through his own efforts alone. Instead he relies on the master's recitation of a phrase with mysterious power; only this esoteric utterance can free him. Thus the kōan narrative reflects an altogether atypical encounter with the presence of the anomalous and the efficacy of the supernatural—an ideological exchange between Zen scholasticism and the otherness of disparity encompassing the occurrence of impurity and the possibility for reconciling the threatening through unconventional (including magical) means. At the same time, the kōan endorses monastic order through the abbot's dismissal of the intruding fox. This action evokes the image of Pai-chang as a strict moralist who lived by the (no doubt apocryphal) motto emphasizing communal labor, "A day without work is a day without food," and who is said to have created the first monastic rules code of the independent Zen sect. The kōan achieves this emphasis on monasticism by borrowing from and yet transforming—in the name of refuting—indigenous folklore beliefs about supernatural powers that represent eremitic and daimonic forces of disorder, disruption, and transgression.

Thus the fox kōan focuses not so much on the issue of causality in a speculative, metaphysical sense as on questions involving supernaturalism and ritualism: who, or what, is the anomaly that appears before Pai-chang? How is the abbot ritually effective in liberating him (or it)? Why does the prospect of the fox/monk's funeral cause consternation among the disciples? And for what reason does Pai-chang suffer from the blows of his student after delivering a successful remedy for the ancient monk? These questions lead beyond the confines of the case itself. They take us into an investigation of how a philosophical understanding of karmic causality interacts with popular religiosity in giving shape to monastic rules and rituals during the formative period of Zen as an independent Buddhist institution during late T'ang/Sung China.

Folklore Morphology

In the traditional and modern debates on causality and ethics, there is an element that is rarely addressed directly: the fox kōan expresses a topos of folklore also found in *setsuwa* literature based on the possession of a person by a demonic nonhuman spirit and the need for exorcism through ritual enactment. Indeed the kōan narrative bears a striking structural or "morphological" affinity, to borrow a term from Vladimir Propp's analysis of comparative folklore, with stories and art about the appearance and exploits of shape-shifting, trickster foxes who seduce, betray, or possess unsuspecting victims until they are eliminated by an exorcistic performance.[19] In this colloquial mythic cycle, recorded in dozens of literary and artistic forms of expression in both the high and popular cultures, foxes intrude on the spirits of vulnerable people or transfigure into human form. They appear as an irresistibly beautiful vixen or a wayward, irregular priest—either as a means of deception or punishment or mockery of sacred ceremony or, in some cases, out of compassionate motives such as providing a widower with a spouse or teaching a bodhisattva-like moral lesson. Some foxes, such as the infamous demonic "nine-tailed" fox (kyūbi-kitsune) in Japanese lore, can be vicious and in-spire terror. Others have more benign motives such as seeking out cer-tain foods—especially favored snacks such as fried sweet tofu (aburage or kitsune-dofu) or noodles (kitsune-udon)—or toys as well as romantic or play partners. Yet another category includes foxes who are truly caring and beneficent, acting either without an ulterior motive or as part of an avatar's mission of compassion. Often it is difficult to determine the trick-ster's status or intentions until the exorcism is applied. As in the kōan, possession by an intrusive, seductive fox generally affects people whose crime is self-indulgence and susceptibility to passions or delusions of grandeur rather than mean-spiritedness or downright evil—above all, then, it affects those susceptible to or the perpetrators of suffering (dukkha).

In folklore, the condition of transfiguration generally persists until the creature's true nature is exposed and expelled when an exorcism evoking an efficacious religious symbol—such as the utterance of a sutra passage or a dhāranī—releases the purified victim from the cause of possession and vanquishes the supernatural shape. The completion of the ritual co-incides with the discovery of animals scurrying underfoot or the finding of a dead fox. This reversion of the fei-jen or hinin back to its original nonhuman form at the moment of death signifies that the source of the delusion of the person whose spirit was invaded has been overcome and fully terminated. Many times the fox body is given a proper burial by survivors to conform with the wishes of the human side, which was tor-mented by being trapped in a nonhuman existence and seeks posthu-mous redemption.[20] The tales often include a reflection offered by the narrator or an epilogue, resembling the episode of Huang-po's slap, that comments on the significance of the main events.

The central dramatic element in folklore reflected in the kōan narra-tive is that the vulpine nature of the intruding anomaly remains unseen, invisible, and in many cases completely unknown to the victim who con-founds illusion and reality.[21] The existence of the fei-jen is usually imper-ceptible to anyone not directly affected—invisible, for example, to the assembly of monks at Pai-chang's temple—or in some cases the bystand-ers are so convinced of the illusion that they do not even begin to ques-tion whether or not it is human. As the verse commentary in the Ts'ung-jung lu suggests: "The other disciples must have doubted that he was really there."[22] A Tokugawa-era drawing of the opening scene of the kōan while the fox/monk is attending Pai-chang's sermons with the other

Figure 5. This illustration of the opening scene of the kōan narrative, drawing from folklore motifs, shows the fox/monk's *fei-jen* identity revealed to Master Pai-chang by the tail peeking out from under the Buddhist robe (as well as the long hair and beard). Note the homology involving the lines of the tail and those of the ceremonial fly whisk the master is holding. Although there was no tradition of scrolls or other illustrations of kōans in Sung China or medieval Japan, this Tokugawa-era print was one of several prominent series on kōan cases, including the collection by Sengai cited in Figure 1. It appears in Akizuki Ryūmin, *Zen mondo: kōan-e monogatari* (Tokyo: Chōbunsha, 1976), p. 128.

disciples illustrates this motif. (See Figure 5.) It shows the fox well disguised as an elderly monk wearing a Buddhist robe who appears to be the same as the others except for hair and beard—usually indicators of a maverick quality since monks are required to take the tonsure—and, more significantly, a bushy foxtail peeking out from under the skirt of his Buddhist robe as a giveaway of its true status.[23] This picture suggests that none of the monks are aware of the *fei-jen,* including at first the abbot, but the ancient priest is no longer able to conceal his identity, at least to himself. Overwhelmed by a sense of guilt and remorse on hearing

Pai-chang's homily, he is compelled to confess. In folklore, any party spotting the telltale foxtail (or coils bulging out of clothes in the case of a shape-shifting snake) invariably leads to the dissolution of the transfiguration or to the termination of the deception that is coterminous with spiritual release. Another clue to the folklore dimension in the kōan is that the dead fox body is found, as foretold by the ancient monk, just at the time of his liberation and attainment of nirvana. The kōan is different from certain folktales because the disclosure of the vulpine status occurs at the outset rather than near the end of the story: it is the point of narrative departure instead of the denouement. Yet it is consistent with folklore in showing the need for a penitential attitude to trigger the revelation of one's real identity.

Intersecting Perspectives

Why does this prominent record of Zen patriarchy—generally known for an antiritualistic and antisupernatural rhetoric in which the term "wild fox" consistently refers to a false claim of enlightenment by one still plagued by ignorance and attachment—couch its moral message in images borrowed from a form of popular religiosity that the tradition otherwise repudiates? Zen's demythological approach to the supernatural is primarily known through Layman P'ang's famous saying, cited by Lin-chi, that his supranormal powers (Skt. *abhijñā;* C. *shen-t'ang;* J. *jinzū*) are exemplified by the concrete, mundane activities of "carrying water and chopping wood." Master Pai-chang himself is reputed to have said: "The way of the bodhisattva is uncorrupted by supernatural practices." And he once criticized a hermit: "When it comes to supernatural powers he is excellent, all right, but for preaching the Buddha Dharma in one word, he isn't as good as me."[24] Does the discursive adaptation in the fox kōan reflect a corruption and decline or, rather, a flexibility and extension of the core Zen ideology? Or should it be acknowledged that supernatural imagery is actually quite common in Zen records? For example, strict disciplinarian Pai-chang is guided in his efforts, according to *Wu-men kuan* case 40, to open a new temple by the geomancer and *dhūtaguṇa* (C. *t'ou-t'o heng;* J. *zudagyō*) or ascetic practitioner Ssu-ma (who also figures prominently in two dialogues commenting on the fox kōan in the *TKL* version); irreverent Huang-po's traveling companion walks on water before disappearing altogether in the commentary on *Pi-yen lu* (J. *Hekiganroku*) case 8;[25] and Lin-chi enjoys a close association with a magician whose body disappears in his coffin, P'u-hua, whose name literally means "universal transfiguration," as recorded in the *Lin-chi lu.*

What is the appropriate methodology for exploring the intertwining of philosophical and popular religious elements according to which fox imagery is perceived and appropriated in divergent ways that are at once marked by inconsistency/conflict and compatibility/mutual reinforcement? Mythological elements should not be considered mere survivals of a bygone, pre-T'ang era. For in kōan collections and recorded sayings texts they are used as part of a new rhetorical strategy. In utilizing yet downplaying supernaturalism, kōan literature from the Sung period concerning earlier T'ang patriarchs like Pai-chang expresses an ambivalence due to what is perhaps a deliberate forgetting of origins that accompanies the post-T'ang "invention of tradition." But it is precisely through this ambivalence that the significance of shape-shifting fox imagery is revealed.

The Perspective of Paradoxicality

From the standpoint of philosophical investigation, the primary question is whether to interpret the kōan from a literal perspective based on the pivot word's emphasis on a strict adherence to causality—or, as the majority of commentaries maintain, from a paradoxical perspective indicating a nondual identity of the affirmation and denial of cause-and-effect. For most traditional commentators, Huang-po's slap suggests that the kōan is really intended to express the primordial inseparability and nonduality of causality/noncausality, which are paradoxically identified in accord with the Mahayana notion of the emptiness of conceptual categories. Dōgen comments on the dilemma in a discussion in the *Eihei kōroku* remarking that both responses to the question of causality, or the pivot words used by the former and the current Pai-chang, are inherently one-sided and self-limiting: "If you express the way only in terms of not falling into causality, that is invariably a denial of causality"—a heretical violation of karma, as the kōan literally asserts. "But," he adds, "if you express the way only in terms of not obscuring causality, then you have not yet given up coveting your neighbor's precious possessions."[26] Therefore, not obscuring causality, if taken as the exclusively correct response, may harbor a subtle form of desire and attachment to temptations, including a clinging to the attainment of nirvana generated from within the realm of samsara, and thus it fails to realize a genuine sense of transcendence.

The *Wu-men kuan, Ts'ung-jung lu,* and almost all other commentaries support a paradoxical reading that emphasizes the relativity and ultimate inseparability of the conflicting views of causality (or not obscuring cause-and-effect) and noncausality (or not falling into cause-and-effect). The *Wu-men kuan* verse commentary highlights an identification of opposites:

> Not falling [into causality], not obscuring [causality],
> Two sides of the same coin;
> Not obscuring [causality], not falling [into causality],
> Hundreds of thousands of transgressions!

The second line can also be rendered as "Two winning numbers, one roll of the dice." But the point remains the same: both answers are considered potentially correct depending on the situation.[27] By reversing the sequence of the images of not falling into or transcending causality, and not obscuring or remaining bound by causality, the first and third lines reinforce the sense of the equalization of standpoints. The fourth and final line drives home the idea that it is just as possible that both answers are equally incorrect if delivered in an inappropriate context.

The *Wu-men kuan* literary technique quickly became the mainstream view echoed in dozens of other verse commentaries showing the relativity and identifiability of opposites. According to a Sung-era verse, the question of the correctness of the answers, which are inherently one-sided or reflective of a single view or "tunnel vision" approach to reality, is merely a matter of perspective: "Not falling, not obscuring: / It is a question of interpretation; / If you can solve the puzzle, / Then there is no longer any hitch."[28] Following this line of interpretation, modern translator/commentator Kōun Yamada argues for the priority of the nonduality. He refers to it as an "essential nature" whereby the equalization of the realms of causality and noncausality at once undercuts and encompasses the perspective emphasizing the separation of realms: "The phenomenal changes were from man to fox and from fox to man, but there is no change in the essential nature. . . . Zen always treats things from the aspect of this essential nature. Therefore every kōan should be approached in this way."[29] Yamada sees the shape-shifting motif reinforcing philosophical paradoxicality.

For the most prominent exception to the paradoxical line of interpretation we must turn to the later writings of Dōgen. His *Shōbōgenzō* presents two nearly opposite interpretations of the fox kōan. The "Daishugyō" fascicle—written in midcareer in the early 1240s and included in the 75-fascicle *Shōbōgenzō*—strongly supports the mainstream identification of causality and noncausality:

> Because causality necessarily means full cause *(ennin)* and complete effect *(manga)*, there is no reason for a discussion concerning "falling into" or "not falling into," "obscuring" or "not obscuring" [causality]. . . . Although "not obscuring causality" released the wild fox body in the current age of Buddha Śākyamuni, it may not have been effective in the age of Buddha Kāśyapa.

But "Jinshin inga," composed near the end of his life in the 1250s and included in the 12-fascicle *Shōbōgenzō*, adamantly refutes the paradoxical standpoint in favor of a strictly literal reading reflecting the notion of "deep faith in (or profound commitment to) causality" *(jinshin inga)*.[30] Whereas "Daishugyō" refuses to criticize the old monk's view of *pu-lo yin-kuo*, or not falling into causality, "Jinshin inga" rejects the position Dōgen embraced a decade before of equating cause-and-effect and the transcendence of causality while critiquing the verse commentaries of several prominent Lin-chi school rivals and Ts'ao-t'ung (J. Sōtō) school predecessors who rationalize, though perhaps unintentionally, the deficient standpoint.[31] In the later work he asserts quite emphatically that only not obscuring causality is accurate:[32]

> The single greatest limitation of the monks of Sung China today is that they do not realize that "not falling into causality" is a false teaching. . . . The expression "not obscuring causality" of the current head monk of Mount Pai-chang shows that he never denied causality. It is clear that practice, or cause, leads to realization, or result.

The paradoxical view is seen here as a grave misunderstanding resulting in a non-Buddhist denial of causality *(hatsumu* or *hammu inga)* because of its antinomian implication that the sustained effort of religious practice to overcome samsara may be unnecessary.

In an interesting development stemming from the controversy in medieval texts, recent scholarship has considered the ethical implications of the fox kōan—which seems to stress moral responsibility as the basis of karmic punishment and release—for reckoning with social problems in modern Japan, including nationalism and discrimination perpetuated by Buddhist institutions and rituals. According to scholars in the methodological movement known as Critical Buddhism *(hihan Bukkyō)*, especially Hakamaya Noriaki, the emphasis on causality in the 12-fascicle *Shōbōgenzō* can serve as an ethical template for the reform of Buddhism that has fostered a false sense of transcendence connected with a denial of causality.[33] The consequences of inauthentic attitudes resulting from a misunderstanding of the kōan's view of karma include Buddhist support for nationalist and nativist, as well as imperialist and colonialist, hegemonic agendas during World War II and the practice of intolerance and discrimination toward the outcast or "special status" *(burakumin)* community—traditionally an untouchable group known in Japan by the perjorative term *"hinin,"* nonhumans, or sometimes referred to as foxes for their marginal status. Discrimination is particularly evident in funeral ceremonies and the bestowing of posthumous ordination names *(kaimyō)*. For Critical Buddhism, which will itself be critically examined in Chapter 4, the roots of discrimination can be traced back to Mahayana doctrines of nonduality, such as *tathāgatagarbha* (C. *ju-lai-tsang;* J. *nyoraizō*) theory or original enlightenment (C. *wen-hsüan;* J. *hongaku*) thought. These doctrines, emphasizing transcendence of cause-and-effect over ethical responsibility linked to karmic causality, preceded the development of kōan literature but flourished through paradoxical commentaries on the fox kōan, along with related notions of such as Huang-po's One Mind.

In the discourse of the philosophical debate about literal or paradoxical views of causality, the fox motif in the case narrative is stripped of animistic, supernatural overtones and functions merely as a one-dimensional rhetorical device referring to unenlightenment and attachment to self. Fox imagery as a metaphor representing delusion and self-deception is "a term critical of those who indulge in cleverness or try to claim personal liberty by repudiating cause and effect in their actions,"[34] just as the ancient monk had done in precipitating endless transmigrations as a fox. That this tendency must be eradicated is suggested in somewhat tongue-in-cheek fashion in a Dōgen sermon in the *Eihei kōroku* which asserts that a true master is able "to club to death a thousand cubs in the wild fox den located on Mount Pai-chang with a single blow of his staff."[35] This function of fox imagery is consistent with a variety of terms used by the monastic mainstream as sarcastic epithets to criticize and stigmatize rogue, counterfeit, or spurious priests who deceive or betray themselves and the Buddhist institution. The terms include "wild Zen" (C. *kuang-ch'an;* J. *kyō-zen*), "wild fox Zen" (C. *yeh-hu Ch'an;* J. *yako-Zen*), "you wild fox spirit!" (C. *yeh-hu ch'ing;* J. *yako-zei*), and the Zen of "wild fox drool (or slobber)" (*yeh-hu hsien;* J. *yako-zen*), which refers to those who slavishly follow the rules or rabidly mimic the words or gestures of their teachers without ever moving beyond a superficial understanding or attaining an authentic realization.[36] These epithets are used in a similar way in numerous non-Buddhist literary traditions that require intensive formal training or apprenticeship under the authority of a charismatic leader in order to critique those who violate codes of conduct by thinking they can achieve the heights and receive the transmission on their own without proper schooling.[37]

The Rhetoric of Ambiguity

Zen Buddhists were careful to use fox imagery to distance themselves from antistructural elements of self-indulgence, whether in hedonistic or ascetic activities, that might convey an unfavorable impression of their secluded communities to society at large. The locus classicus for the sarcastic use of the term is no doubt the *Lin-chi lu* (J. *Rinzai roku*), which mentions the term "wild fox spirit" (in the sense of sprite, ghost, goblin or fairy, or anomalous apparition) no less than five times. All these references are used in a thoroughly derisive, antisupernatural way in a text exercising a harsh judgment of any approach tending to externalize ultimate reality that should only be realized through self-effort. Lin-chi—known for his radical iconoclasm in the injunction, "Kill the Buddha!"—probably comes the closest of leading Zen masters to lacking a sense of ambivalence about popular religiosity. He denounces fox imagery and attacks supernatural beliefs in general—including an unsparing condemnation of visions and prophecies associated with worship of the bodhisattva Mañjuśri at the esoteric Mount Wu-t'ai cultic center in Shansi province. This pilgrimage site, which apparently was tremendously popular among Zen and other Buddhist itinerants, Lin-chi argues, represents an external seeking for the bodhisattva of wisdom, honored in Zen temples as a patron saint of the meditator, that distracts from realizing that the true deity is located within.[38]

In a devastating criticism that echoes Confucian scholar Hsün-tzu's sharp contrast between the common folk—who embrace rituals based on a belief in the superstitious view that rain, for instance, results from magical formulas—and the refined *chun-tzu*—who practice rituals because of their elegant ceremonial quality and understand the arbitrariness of chance—Lin-chi declares:

> And then there're a bunch of shavepates who, not knowing good from bad, point to the east and point to the west, delight in fair weather, delight in rain, and delight in lanterns and pillars. . . . Lacking understanding, students become infatuated with them. Such [shavepates] as these are all wild fox spirits and nature goblins. Good students snicker, "Te-hee!" and say, "Blind old shavepates, deluding and bewitching everyone under heaven!"[39]

Lin-chi further admonishes those who become fixated on external manifestations about awakening to the priority of their innate Buddha nature: "Followers of the Way, true Buddha has no figure, true Dharma has no form. All you are doing is fashioning models and creating patterns out of illusory transformations. Anything you may find through seeking will be only a wild fox spirit; it certainly won't be true Buddha. It will be the understanding of a heretic."[40]

A similar usage is seen in a Zen anecdote from the Tokugawa era that culminates in the recitation of a famous Sung Zen locution. In this case the term is designed to ridicule the supernatural elements and miraculous claims in other Buddhist practices misled by a false belief in supernaturalism. When a Shinshū priest boasts that the founder of his sect could write the holy name of Amida in thin air, Bankei retorts: "Perhaps your fox can perform that trick, but that is not the manner of Zen. My miracle is that when I feel hungry I eat, and when I feel thirsty I drink."[41] A modern example is found in Mishima Yukio's *Temple of the Golden Pavilion (Kinkakuji)*. Antihero Mizoguchi is disappointed on hearing the abbot's sermon marking the end of World War II and the threat of American bombing of Kyoto. When the abbot comments on the "Nan-ch'üan kills the cat kōan," Mizoguchi thinks he is resorting to antiquated polemic to avoid confronting the origins of human conflict at a time when the disciples need insightful, caring guidance. He comments: "We felt as though we had been bewitched by a fox."[42]

Even though the Zen scholastic tradition often scorns supernaturalism, for the most part these texts espouse a mixed rather than a one-sidedly critical message—in some cases, they manage to sidestep taking a decisive stand. The kōan collections, including the *Wu-men kuan* and, in particular, the *Ts'ung-jung lu* and the *Pi-yen lu,* use an ironic tone. Sometimes they employ the supernatural in order to tweak someone who supposedly has attained wisdom—as in the *Ts'ung-jung lu*'s commentary that the liberated fox/monk "still has fox drool!" or in Dōgen's comment in *Shōbōgenzō,* "Daishugyō," that although Huang-po has a steady gait he has "not yet left the realm of the wild fox." A commentary in *Ts'ung-jung lu* case 43 remarks: "Cutting off entanglements—produces more tangled vines / Cleaning out a fox den—spitting out so much fox drool."[43] The kōan commentators evoke fox terminology in a positive sense, too, as an inverted form of praise. Dōgen's approach is at times thoroughly negative, echoing Lin-chi, but in other cases he uses fox imagery in a positive way, such as referring to Śākyamuni, the patriarchs, and even himself as a wild fox. In an *Eihei kōroku* lecture, for instance, Dōgen remarks, without necessarily complaining, that despite his giving the first authentic Zen-style sermons in Japan at Eiheiji temple in the remote mountains of Echizen (present-day Fukui) province many onlookers denounce him by saying: "Just take a look at that preposterous rube on the mountain whose preaching is merely the talk of 'wild fox Zen.' "[44] In this case he transmutes a conventional indicator of stigmatization into a source of pride for those who are misunderstood by the masses.

An element of ambivalence about fox imagery is expressed in a passage in which Lin-chi contends that true masters demonstrate their worth precisely when they prove unacceptable and are driven away by narrow-minded practitioners: "A single roar of the mighty lion will split open the heads of the foxes and cause their brains to spill out. . . . But the novice monks fail to understand this and let the wild fox spirits spin their tales that tie everyone else up in knots."[45] This passage still uses the fox in a negative way consistent with other uses in the *Lin-chi lu.* But by evoking a different magical animal that defeats the fox, even if sardonic, it acknowledges the importance of a rhetorical pattern based on supernaturalism.

A similar ambivalent use of supernatural imagery occurs in a poem by Ju-ching, Dōgen's Chinese mentor. In describing a ceremonial portrait painted of him, Ju-ching displays a characteristic self-deprecating humor coupled with Lin-chi-style bravado: "I am like the empty shell of a turtle— / You bang it and there is only a hollow sound; / I raise my fist, but this just scares away the wild foxes, / If you want to draw a picture of me, / You will only capture my unsightliness, / But after thirty years [of

Zen training], / I am like a musician making magical sounds."[46] This degree of ambiguity, in which the fox remains negative but the overall effect is positive, is further conveyed in a Dōgen sermon that praises the work of the monastery rector at Eiheiji: "He is an iron hammer without any holes which rings like thunder, crushing in an instant the Zen of a wild fox."[47] And one of Dōgen's Chinese verses reads: "[Hui-neng] is an elephant-king stomping over the trails left by a fox."[48] Another example comes across in the essentially negative but nevertheless duplicitous usage in the following Dōgen verse comment on the fox kōan: "What a pity that in the era of Kāśyapa / A well-respected buddha was transfigured into a wild fox for five hundred lifetimes, / But when he hears the lion's roar [of Pai-chang], / The constant yelping from his long, drooling tongue ceases once and for all."[49]

A further example of the term "wild fox" used as a kind of disingenuous blasphemy or inverted praise—even, or especially, toward the most venerated leaders and rites as part of a strategy of using "poison to counteract poison"—is found in *Pi-yen lu* case 1.[50] Here the first patriarch Bodhidharma crosses the Yangtze River after a dialogue in which he tells the emperor in the epitome of the Zen rhetoric of iconoclasm that there is no merit in building stupas, for the dharma contains "nothing sacred," and that he "does not know his own name." In an intralinear commentary Yüan-wu suggests: "This wild fox spirit! He cannot avoid embarrassment. He crosses from west to east and back from east to west."[51] An additional example is Hakuin's fascicle titled "Licking Up Hsi-Keng's Fox Slobber," which expresses nothing but praise and admiration for one of his illustrious predecessors. Translator Norman Waddell explains that fox slobber is "a metaphor for a lethal poison; it can work miraculous cures by purging students of their mental illness and leading them to true enlightenment."[52] These examples reverse Lin-chi's imagery: the fox, rather than the conventional positive image of the lion, now functions as the hero.

Bivalent Symbolism

Thus the simple image of the wild fox comes to be used in complex, multifarious, often contradictory ways in a wide variety of Zen texts. At first the appearance of the term seems exclusively negative, but it is rarely just a one-sidedly derogatory epithet evoked as part of a demythological critique of animism. Rather, the ambivalent appropriations of the term as scorn or praise spring out of the bivalent moral implications of the wild fox in folklore and popular religiosity that manifests either as a demonic intrusion or a divine messenger: as an entity to be exorcised or an agent of purification.

Despite striking parallels with other world mythologies, as well as differences between China and Japan, there appear to be several distinctive features of the fox's role in East Asia that form a discursive background for commentaries on the fox kōan.[53] These elements—qualitative in terms of defining the nature of shape-shifting and quantitative in terms of highlighting the degree of its cultural impact—include the bivalent symbolism of metamorphosis and its relation to the Buddhist view of supernaturalism. This element is further reflected in the extensive assimilation of fox imagery into the mainstream institutional structure and practice of Zen accompanied by exorcistic trends.[54] But the most important element is the role of the fox as an indicator of moral criticism focusing on social and spiritual crises and their resolution.

The examples of polysemy I have cited—including uses of the terms "wild fox" and "fox drool" with positive intent—still function within the framework of antisupernaturalism. Yet this extreme demythologization and rejection of syncretism, which evokes the image of the fox in order to defeat a belief in spirits, must be interpreted in terms of the broader mythological background in which it is uttered, a context that presupposes the reality of supernatural folklore and the viability of syncretic beliefs. Another level of polysemy in Zen monastic life links the philosophical discourse with its apparent antithesis. Despite Lin-chi's refutation of supernatural beliefs, historical evidence suggests that Zen monks rarely rejected folklore-oriented ritual practices. On the contrary, there are numerous accounts of Zen masters in China and Japan who were said to have exorcised fox demons (or handled snakes or worsted tigers or subdued earth deities or other supernatural forces). Indeed, Zen masters are among the most prominent exorcists of demonic foxes. Again and again one finds them competing for popularity and patronage with rival priests, wizards, and shamans precisely by demonstrating their effectiveness in this capacity.

Dōgen's texts tend to move back and forth on the general issue of supernaturalism. In some passages he forcefully disdains superstition, magic, and animism. Yet the 75-fascicle *Shōbōgenzō* "Raihaitokuzui" fascicle seems to endorse fox worship in asserting that "we revere the dharma, whether manifested in a round pillar, a garden lantern, a buddha, a fox, a demon or a deity, a man or a woman," although it is not clear that this refers specifically to Inari beliefs.[55] The later, 12-fascicle *Shōbōgenzō* text has been singled out by Critical Buddhism for its uncompromising resistance to the supernatural, but a careful reading suggests that the viewpoint of the text, which frequently cites *jātaka* tales and *setsuwa* sources, requires a more complex analysis.

The process of bivalence is dramatically played out in the Japanese Sōtō Zen institutional structure. Sōtō Zen not only supports the greatest degree of Buddhist intimacy and syncretism with the fox cult but also highlights the most famous case of fox exorcism reported in a multitude of Zen records as well as secular folk tales and Noh plays involving the Muromachi-era priest Gennō Shinshō (1329–1400). This juxtaposition of assimilation and repulsion provides further evidence of an ambivalence in Sōtō Zen that is expressed on yet another level in Dōgen's contradictory readings of the fox kōan.

Folklore vixens may be mischievous and malicious or faithful and affectionate. And in a broader spiritual sense the bivalent fox image can appear as protective and redemptive as well as deceptive and cunning. On the positive side, divine fox images representing the messenger of the Shinto rice deity, Inari, are constructively assimilated in Japan with Buddhist and especially Zen deities and shrines to the point where the sects are nearly indistinguishable—thereby contributing to the tradition of *shinbutsu shūgō:* the oneness of buddhas and local gods *(kami).*[56] The fox cult that was apparently quite powerful in pre-T'ang and T'ang China never developed a full-fledged institutional structure.[57] In Japan, however, the fox known as *kitsune* has since the eighth century been enshrined and worshiped in a pervasive network of sacred associations in connection with Inari. The widespread cult—it claims more than thirty thousand shrines nationwide—portrays *kitsune* as a divine messenger of the rice god who promotes agrarian fertility as well as productivity and prosperity in a much broader sense.[58] The Inari/*kitsune* pantheon has been associated with Buddhist deities and often syncretized or conflated with a Buddhist fox deity known as Dakini-shinten. This syncretism has been incorporated directly into the Sōtō sect's institutional structure, which also produced some of the most celebrated fox exorcists in another reflection of twofoldness.

The Inari cult, in which the fox is valorized and sacralized as the messenger of the rice deity that has the power to protect against and exorcise demonic spirits, including the fox spirit which possesses souls, is generally considered a Shinto movement although it is not one of the officially recognized sects. Yet its icons, symbols, and ceremonies are present in dozens of Zen temples, especially those affiliated with the subnetwork of the Sōtō Zen Myōgonji temple in Toyokawa City in Aichi prefecture and subsidiary temples located throughout Japan, including Tokyo Akasaka, Osaka, Yokosuka, Fukuoka, and Sapporo.[59] Also known as Toyokawa Inari, the fox shrine occupies the same compound as the Zen temple where *zazen* training takes place. (See Figures 6–8.) These shrine-temple complexes under the jurisdiction of the main Sōtō temple at Eiheiji worship the fox on several levels of a pervasive network of sacred associations. The compound venerates the Shinto *kami* Inari as well as the esoteric Buddhist deity Dakini-shinten (*"shinten"* suggests a "true heavenly being" to distinguish this image of Dakini from the often better known sorcerous one), and the fox icons of the two gods are often mixed or used interchangeably. A Buddhist image of Dakini-shinten borrowed from tantric mandala expressions portrays a goddess riding atop a flying white fox as an image of good fortune and a protector of the dharma. At Myōgonji the fox carrying the goddess, protected by Inari fox icons, is enshrined in the Shrine Hall (*daihonden*) adjacent to the Dharma Hall

Figure 6. An image of the goddess Dakini-shinten riding on a flying white fox that is enshrined at Toyokawa Inari/Myōgonji in Toyokawa City, Aichi prefecture, Japan.

Figure 7. This photograph of the memorial spirit-fox mound at Toyokawa Inari/Myōgonji in Toyokawa, a recent addition to the compound, shows an inscribed stone at the gateway.

(hattō) where the Buddhist goddess Kannon is venerated. In addition, Dakini-shinten is also assigned as the main deity *(honzon)* of Inari conceived as a localized manifestation or avatar *(gongen)* or guardian spirit *(chinjū)* of the universal Buddha nature—though in some cases this relation is reversed and either one can be assigned the role of *chinjū* or proctector of the monastery. Thus the subsect, in venerating and enshrining several forms of the fox deity as the primary *honzon,* is a rare case in which the indigenous god is given a status superior to the imported, universal buddhas. Such syncretism raises the question of the degree to which folk religion infiltrates and influences the great tradition. Hence it seriously challenges the conventional two-tiered notion of the relation between Zen's philosophical and popular dimensions.

But alongside these examples of theological symbiosis stands a large body of literature expressing a contradictory view. There are hagiographies of a number of Zen masters in China and Japan, especially the Sōtō sect, who were known precisely for their ability to subdue and exorcise demonic foxes and other magical animals.[60] Thus the process of assimila-

Figure 8. This photograph of the memorial spirit-fox mound at Toyokawa Inari/Myōgonji shows fox statues that are now used as dedications instead of traditional stupas.

tion is inseparable from—can even be considered to necessitate—the practice of its apparent opposite: exorcism. Perhaps the most famous of all legends of fox exorcism performed by Buddhists involves Gennō Shinshō, a fourteenth-century disciple of Gasan Jōseki, the main descendant of Keizan Jōkin and abbot of Sōjiji temple whose followers are credited with the tremendous regional expansion of medieval Sōtō achieved by the conquest and conversion of local spirits including Inari. According to legends recorded in Sōtō texts and countless versions of popular literature, folklore, and Noh theater, in 1389 Gennō exorcised one of the most demonic of foxes: the notorious, malevolent nine-tailed fox that had been banished from the capital in Kyoto by a sorcerer. After its ejection the fox then took possession of a "killing stone" *(sesshō seki)* in the provinces where it was murdering people and other living things, as also recorded in the *Oku no hosomichi* by Bashō who visited the site during his poetic pilgrimage to the north country. The demonic stone was subdued by Gennō's use of a purification stick and his chant based on one of the best-known phrases of Dōgen: "*Genjōkōan* (spontaneous realization) is the great matter."[61]

In general, a prominent theme in East Asian fox legends is the opposition set up between universal Buddhist institutions, which have the capacity to perform an exorcism, versus the colloquial cult that utilizes the spirit's ability of transfiguration in order to bewitch and betray its victims. Buddhist exorcism generally uses a ritual gesture (mudra) or utterance (mantra, *dhāranī,* or sutra passage) or the administering of the precepts as performed by a variety of cult figures. These figures include Vinaya masters and devotees of Kuan-yin (J. Kannon) or another bodhisattva. In Japan they are represented by Nichiren priests, in addition to Zen masters, who have frequently been in competition with non-Buddhist practitioners—local shamans, Taoist and yin/yang wizards, *yamabushi* ascetics and, in modern times, with Japanese New Religion movements such as the *okiyome* rite in the Mahikari (True Light) cult.[62] The general rule in Buddhist/folk religious syncretism is that whichever method of exorcism is efficacious in the particular context prevails. In many instances victims and their associates are willing to try several approaches, or even combine them, until the desired results are attained.

The Fox as Symbol of Moral Criticism

In folklore, the wild fox as a shape-shifting trickster is a multivalent, polysemic image that suggests either bewitchment, falsity, seduction, and illusion or the compassionate and edifying manifestation of an otherworldly entity, perhaps a bodhisattva or divine messenger. Actual foxes make their mysterious appearances and disappearances from transitory dens located just beyond the reach of human traffic—the far side of cultivated fields, around the unkempt parts of graveyards, behind temple compounds—a fact that lends itself to an association with the productive and fertile or the ominous and fateful.[63] In other words, the comings and goings of foxes come to be interpreted as a sign of a disruption or a harbinger of change for the better.

In either negative/demonic or positive/beatific senses, the fox is an image reflecting a state of liminality as one undergoes a moral crisis requiring reflection and repentance. The connection between the levels tending toward a stigmatization of the rogue and an idealization of the outsider, whether summoned to endorse animism or to refute it, is that the wild fox, as an undomesticated loner existing on the fringes of human society, represents a realm of marginality or peripherality: challenging and undermining yet being chastised and governed by the conceptual center or mainstream. In East Asia, anomalous *fei-jen* phenomena "provide a lever for intellectual, ideological, and social change . . . [including] those places where a community's cognitive systems or social structures palpably bump up against a recalcitrant, external reality, giving exponents of internal reform or revolution an opportunity to make their case."[64] The symbolic fox indicates the crossing of boundaries—which highlights not only the importance of limits but also the moral quandaries generated by being lost or confused during times of sudden or dramatic transition.

From its opening passage on the confession of the monk's identity as a *fei-jen*, therefore, the fox kōan creates an atmosphere hospitable to the major supernatural elements in folktales that evoke phenomena known as the *kuai* (J. *kai*)— the anomalous and unknowable associated with Six Dynasties literature—and the *chi* (J. *ki*)— the exotic and extraordinary associated with T'ang literature. The term *"fei-jen"* (Skt. *amanuṣya*) is commonly used in Buddhist cosmology to refer to other-than-human beings ranging from gods to beasts and demons or *nāga*—a multivalent term for snakes, reptiles, or dragons that disguise themselves as humans in order to attack or, once they have been converted, to protect faithfully and selflessly the Buddhist dharma.[65] In Sanskrit literature nonhumans include *yakṣa*, *preta*, and *deva;* in East Asia the category encompasses foxes and other magical animals as well as indigenous demons, ghosts, spirits, and sprites referred to as anomalous or *kuai* phenomena. The early Vinaya considers offenses (such as illicit sex or murder) committed against nonhumans to be as serious as those against human victims—or at least to be assessed in a parallel way, which means that the reality of these entities, as well as the borderline between the human and nonhuman, and illusion and reality, was highly problematic and constantly tested. Stories about *nāga* are reported not as parables or legends but as a concern for the institution in a vein that takes seriously the supernatural implications.[66] At the same time, as a reflection of bivalence, novice monks are referred to as *nāga* and arhats are sometimes called *mahānāga*.[67]

An interesting example of shape-shifting in early Buddhism that may have served as a background influence on the fox kōan is the Vinaya story of a *nāga* who manages to disguise itself sufficiently to join the monastic order and live as a monk until its nonhuman identity is discovered.[68] In the days of the early *saṃgha*, certain prerequisites for ordination were established emphasizing proper birth, upbringing, occupation, and prior behavior, but the question of human status—the inclusion and acceptance or exclusion and expulsion of nonhumans—had not yet been addressed. This particular *nāga* is ashamed of its state of existence and thinks that participation in the order would be an effective means of regaining human status—implying perhaps that its nonhuman state is a temporary and potentially redeemable karmic punishment. Taking on the form of a young *brahmin*, the *nāga* is initiated, granted full ordination, and comes to live with another monk in a cell at the edge of the monastery. One day, thinking his roommate is away for a long period and complacent about the way he has been passing himself off, he falls asleep and reverts to his snake's body—which fills the entire room with coils jutting out through the windows. Now that the disguise is exposed and the identity revealed, the monks in the assembly ask the Buddha for advice and he counsels that a nonhuman cannot attain the dharma through meditative discipline. The *nāga* feels sadness and anguish and decides to leave the community. The Buddha, however, suggests that observing the Uposatha (C. *pu-sa;* J. *fusatsu*) ceremony of repentance through reciting the precepts twice fortnightly would result in the *nāga's* quick reclamation of humanity. The Buddha's advice suggests that from the Buddhist standpoint nonhuman or *kuai* phenomena require an act of ceremonial confession through which they can cross over the boundary into human existence.

The main Chinese sources of fox folklore are the *Sou-shen chi* (335–349), one of the earliest texts, and the *T'ai-p'ing kuang-chi* (completed 978), an immense encyclopedic collection of tales of the anomalous. The *T'ai-p'ing kuang-chi* was published just at the time the Zen transmission histories—which borrowed from the monk biographies in recounting the teachings of the early masters including Pai-chang—were beginning to appear. This was half a century before the record of the fox kōan in the *TKL* version. The main Japanese folklore sources include the *Nihon ryōiki* (ca. 821), *Konjaku monogatari* (ca. 1100), *Uji shūi monogatari* (early thirteenth century), and *Kokonchomonjū* (1254), among many others, which contain numerous stories translated into Japanese or refashioned in the new cultural setting.[69] While many of these collections in China and Japan contain non-Buddhist and secular materials, they also incorporate a genre of popular morality tales known as *setsuwa bungaku:* brief didactic narratives that articulate supernatural themes about the moral effects of karmic retribution (C. *yeh-pao;* J. *gōhō*) occurring throughout the three times of this life, the next life, and future lives. The karmic effects are often referred to as *ming-pao* (J. *myōhō*), "mysterious or unseen retribution," because they can pervade almost imperceptibly across boundaries of time until their significance is clarified. But many of the tales are primarily concerned with the impact of *hsien-pao* (J. *genpō*), "here-and-now retribution" and release, in which the effects are immediately felt.

The category of nonhumans who appear as people or resemble people includes spirits, sprites, or fairies (C. *ching,* J. *sei,* including various sorts of foxes), as well as ghosts *(kuei),* goblins, demons, genii, nymphs, ogres, and evil spirits of forests and waters. In Japan *oni* (horned demons), *tengu* (mountain goblins with long beaks, often syncretized with Buddhism, including Sōtō Zen Master Ryōan Emmyō in addition to *yamabushi* practitioners), and *tanuki* (badgers) with excessive phalluses are among the mischievous *fei-jen* creatures populating *setsuwa* and other *kuai* folklore and also assimilated into Buddhism, sometimes as demons and in other cases as gods.[70] Shape-shifters like the *nāga* or the fox continually struggle with a sense of bondage due to the ever present though permeable boundaries separating natural and supernatural (or human and nonhuman) realms. Beings who were human before their punishment began and could regain their humanity after repentance—but are prevented from doing so by some fatal moral flaw or karmic impediment—are eager to cross the boundary and regain human status in a legitimate and final fashion. Their identity is given away by a foxtail or snake coils protruding out of their garments at just the wrong moment, however, resolving the tension about crossing between realms or being trapped in a nonhuman existence that appears as human and yet cannot attain humanity.

Setsuwa literature actually stems from numerous Chinese folklore texts that have an explicitly Buddhist orientation. These include the *Ming-pao chi* (J. *Myōhōkī*) by Hsi Ch'ao in the fourth century on mysterious retribution and the *San-pao kan-ying yao-lü lu* in the following century by Hui-yüan on retribution in "three tenses of past, present, and future" (C. *san-pao;* J. *sanbō*)—both of which were to a large extent absorbed into the *T'ai-p'ing kuang-chi* and other comprehensive collections in China or translated/transmitted into Japanese beginning with the *Nihon ryōiki.*[71] The continuing influence of these texts on the psychological, social, and moral outlook in East Asian literature is evident in late medieval and early modern works like the Ch'ing-era *Liao-chai chih-i,* which the compiler originally planned to title "Devil and Fox Stories,"

and Ueda Akinari's Tokugawa-era *Ugetsu monogatari,* which was influenced by a variety of early *setsuwa* sources.[72] The impact continues in
modern times in a remarkably wide variety of cultural expressions. These
range from the cinema version of *Ugetsu* directed by Mizoguchi Kenji,
and many other films such as Kurosawa Akira's *Dreams,* to the fantastic
literature *(gensō bungaku)* of Izumi Kyōka, Akutagawa Ryūnosuke,
Nagai Kafū, and Enchi Fumiko—the latter two have important stories
dealing with magical foxes—which embodies many features akin to the
"magical realism" of contemporary Latin American literature.[73] The influence also encompasses innumerable examples of popular culture including detective stories, animation, comics, and children's books.
Indeed, the widespread, multilevel cultural influence was commented on
by Lafcadio Hearn: "There are legends of foxes discussed by great scholars, and legends of foxes known to every child."[74]

The main meaning that emerges from folklore constructions is that the
fox—as a creature poised seductively in the twilight—represents a doorway into a liminal realm or constitutes a "thin veil between worlds" of sacred and secular: between an animistic realm populated by otherworldly
beings, such as spirits and ghosts, and the materialistic realm of
objectified entities.[75] As portrayed in the opening sequence of
Kurosawa's *Dreams,* in Japanese lore the mysterious and threatening "fox
wedding" *(kitsune-yomeiri,* sometimes accompanied by foxfire,
kitsune-bi) is said to take place when the sun shines in the midst of rain
(or when yin meets yang or clarity intermingles with obscurity). It is a forbidden, macabre sight suggesting a kind of oedipal nuptial rite. *Jen-shih
chuan*—in which a vixen begins as a femme fatale but proves more faithful than her human lover and dies in anguish when her *fei-jen* identity is
discovered—is perhaps the first and most complex T'ang tale of fox
anthropomorphosis that seems to have became paradigmatic for countless subsequent versions in East Asian literature and art, especially morality tales. Here the fox is portrayed as possessing an elusive allure that
appeals to lonely people who are craving love or companionship or are
dimly aware yet deeply disturbed by their vulnerabilities. But because of
the vixen's doomed efforts to live in the phenomenal world—like Miss
Jen, who may really want to be a good wife or mother—the relationship
cannot be fulfilled.

In the realm between worlds, the conventional distinctions between
reality and illusion, Buddha and Māra, freedom and bondage, life and
death, purity and defilement, are mixed and merged in confounding ways

that must be confronted as a "gateless gate" (C. *wu-men kuan;* J. *mumonkan*) to attain salvation. Fox folklore often has an inherently subversive quality in that it acknowledges and represents the forces of confusion, disorder, injustice, and pain—thereby emerging from the marginal, antistructural elements of society and personal psychology. It explains what is problematic in society at large or in the specific contexts of Buddhist morality or Zen monastic life. It can explain the cause of evil as a disturbance that requires the mainstream community to embark on a program of domestication and regulation. But the bivalent quality is noticeable in the sense that any change or entrance into a new realm, even for the sake of fertility and good fortune, is disruptive and challenging.

Thus a key pedagogical factor, as explained by the narrator of *Jen-shih chuan,* is that unlike the hapless hero Cheng who only admired the vixen's beauty but was too insensitive to appreciate her character, "one should investigate the principle of transformation and *examine the boundary separating spirits and humans." Jen-shi chuan* was no doubt a tremendous influence on *setsuwa* tales, and *Dreams* borrows extensively from their imagery, but neither story has a Buddhist element. This means they lack an encounter between the power of Buddhist spirituality and the power of shape-shifting: the dynamic of Buddhist saints, scriptures, or amulets transforming the forces of contamination and pollution, not only by defeating and neutralizing them, but by converting them into representations of purification or salvation.[76] A typical pattern in Buddhist morality tales is that people deluded or possessed by shape-shifters (which visit those who are particularly susceptible) or by *fei-jen* (disguised as humans to gain entrance into a world denied them) experience a dramatic renewal. They come to repent of past karma through their experience of peril and rescue, and thereafter they become devout followers of Buddha. Their salvation is coterminous with the overcoming of self-deception and the arising of faith in their hearts. In this pattern, "repentance of past karma leads to the confession of sins in the present as well as to the making of a vow for the future."[77] What is required to complete this process is the intercession of the appropriate efficacious religious symbol: Pai-chang's turning word, for example.

Despite important differences in distinct historical periods and cultural constructions there are certain enduring themes and common morphologies that represent a continual refashioning of *setsuwa* tales in the portrayal of the nature, perception, and overcoming of illusion. The approach to exposing illusion in fox lore, despite the seeming simplicity of certain narratives, reflects a sophisticated theoretical base that draws from Yogācāra idealist thought in the Buddhist tradition, which stresses the link between perception and levels of reality (and unreality). It also recalls recent literary movements such as expressionism and magical realism in the West and fantastic literature in East Asia in which figments of the imagination or supernatural images are portrayed with a sense of utter realism. All of these ideologies emphasize an underlying convergence between the state-of-mind being analyzed and the reality that is depicted. There is, strictly speaking, no objective reality: the external world is no more or less than a mirror reflection of internal mentality, whether deluded or enlightened. But these ideologies also emphasize that portraying subjectivity as externalized in supernatural imagery is not necessarily intended to suggest the inverse—that is, the reduction of the otherwordly to an inner, psychological state. Rather, they highlight the inseparability of the seemingly polarized realms of interiority and exteriority.

Fox lore evokes the innate connection between the natural and supernatural. It involves both the more-than-human—gods and immortals that transcend but may descend back into the realm of humanity—and the less-than-human—demons and vixens that reflect the weaknesses of their all-too-human victims. In the realm of liminality both parties, vixen and victim, possessor and possessed, are struggling to reconcile with feelings of being trapped by their identities and attempting to overcome their flaws by crossing over restrictive borders. The reality the participants perceive is nothing other than a manifestation of the level of their awareness and the degree of their success in understanding their own basic moral nature or the karmic impact of their words, thoughts, and deeds. That the victims of bewitchment cannot resist and lose themselves in delusion is not, however, the cause of irremediable damage. Rather, it dramatically confirms the spiritual debilitation that has already transpired and comes to the surface demanding resolution. That the presence of the *fei-jen* in the fox kōan is known to Pai-chang but not to his assembly of monks, for example, may be a sign of his superior wisdom or ability to perceive the invisible. Or perhaps it suggests that the lesson the fox teaches applies only to him as the victim—or the simultaneously intrusive source/victim/liberator—of the bewitching apparition.

Throughout *setsuwa* literature the distinctive feature is that the shape-shifter is not just a being that performs tricks, however challenging. Rather, the presence of an apparition triggers a struggle with moral self-criticism and the need for a spiritual resolution through repentance. Rania Huntington notes that in "the Chinese tradition a change of form, whether from human to animal or, far more commonly, animal to human, is not an external circumstance. It is the result of internal causes: flaws of character or behavior in the case of transformations of human into beast, and determination and self-cultivation in the case of beast into human."[78] Shape-shifting signals the onset of a moral crisis and the emotion of shame that drives the participants toward its resolution; its elimination is just as clearly linked to moral rectification through the removal of delusion and the practice of repentance. Similarly, in the European Reynard cycle, the "possibility [for moral edification] has been exploited from ancient times by treating the beasts as if they were humans in animal disguise indulging in escapades from which some lesson or other may be drawn."[79] Even Chu Hsi, the leading Sung-era Neo-Confucian philosopher who was known for a strong interest in Buddhist thought despite his critique of superstition, acknowledged the importance of supernatural entities in relation to human morality. According to an anecdote, "The [disciples] were speaking of spirits and monsters and [Chu] said: When a man's mind is arranged in balance things are fine; if it dallies around ghosts and monsters appear."[80] These examples suggest that the philosophical approach of the fox kōan is grounded on the pietistic implications of fox folklore whereby "a human's transmogrification into beast form is clearly linked with moral lapses."[81]

The kōan seems to borrow structural elements, in the literary sense discussed by Propp, that are found in *Jen-shih chuan* and other fox tales in crafting a narrative that uses mythical time (such as the five hundred lifetimes stemming from a mythical era prior to Śākyamuni, whether counted as human or vulpine) and dramatic shifts in geography or landscape (as from the lecture platform to the rock behind the temple and back to the Dharma Hall) to reflect the psychological movement from ignorance/attachment to wisdom/release. As the narrator of *Jen-shih chuan* comments after the vixen heroine who has been existing with her human lover in conventional reality is identified: "Ah, the emotions of supernatural beings reflect the meaning of human existence!" The main folkloric morphological element in the kōan, which will be analyzed more fully in Chapter 5, is the way the appearance of the fox is associated with the onset of a moral crisis and its disappearance represents the removal of delusion. In folklore and in Buddhism, shame or revulsion about one's failings is the driving force generating the dynamic of displacement and projection that operates in fox mythology. The rhythm of the appearance and disappearance of the *fei-jen* entity is a sign of disruption. In other words: the apparition dramatizes the inner dynamics of the arising and overcoming of delusion, creating a unity in the kōan of narrative form and content: a unity of medium and meaning. This is a process of exposing and overcoming illusion by means of the illusory phenomenon of the fox—whether one considers it more or less than real or more or less viable than human existence. No longer mysterious or possessive of supernatural power, the anomaly turns out to be some kind of animal or human being that is known to be of inferior moral status.[82]

These themes are beautifully illustrated in two Edo-period floating world prints *(ukiyo-e)*. A painting by Utagawa Kuniyoshi shows a transfiguration into a vixen while the vulpine source remains hidden from the view of the bewitched victim.[83] A fox appears to the left side as the apparition of a seductive woman emerges from it and looms over her possessed lover. Surely the man in the midst of his excitement and passion is unaware of the source of the transfiguration, although the spectator is tipped off. This suggests an innate affinity between the type of delusion the person suffers and the bewitchment he receives, which is in turn perfectly suited to the victim's psychic needs. This form of expression recalls the situation of Joseph K. in Kafka's *The Trial:* while wandering in a dizzying labyrinth of dead-end halls and endless spiraling stairways, K. suddenly realizes that "an attraction existed between the Law and guilt, from which it should really follow that the Court of Inquiry must abut on the particular flight of stairs which K. happened to choose."[84] Whereas the Kuniyoshi print portrays the initial manifestation of the fox spirit, another print by Tsukioka Yoshitoshi shows the reversion back to its true identity once it is recognized. Its bushy tail has been seen as the daughter tugs on the skirt of her fox/mother's kimono.[85] The shadowy vulpine visage emerges behind a shoji screen as the fox/mother tries to escape the situation. This represents an important concluding stage in the overall pattern of bewitchment: the moment when the *fei-jen* is spotted and the apparition immediately dissolves or disappears, often accompanied by foxes scurrying in the vicinity or a fox corpse mysteriously found. As with Miss Jen, the remains of the *kuai* being are left behind in the tangible, visible world.

Because of its emphasis on inner awareness as reflected by the shifting dimensions of outer appearance, fox lore highlights abrupt alterations in conventional space and time. A prime example of the approach to spatiality is the way a glorious mansion is depicted in thoroughly realistic terms at the peak of one's bewitchment until it is exposed as "only some broken-down walls" (in *Jen-shih chuan*, one of the earliest tales) or as a burned-out hovel in a pile of weeds (in *Ugetsu*, a contemporary cinematic rendering of the mythic cycle). A similar sense of the shock of revelation occurs in a tale involving Buddhist clerics from the *Otogizōshi* collection as an old priest succumbs to fox bewitchment: he thinks he has lived with a beautiful woman for seven years in a large mansion with a big gate. When the bodhisattva Jizō manifests in the form of a young priest carrying a long staff *(shakujō)*, the old priest, now liberated, feels that he has awoken from a long dream. A fox appears as the old priest realizes, "The mansion, the splendid large dwelling house with a big gate was gone! The fine bamboo-blinds and mats were now changed into scraps of straw-mats!"[86] Radical shifts in temporality also reflect the nature of illusion and its overcoming. Whether the actual self-deception is long-lasting or fleeting, the perception of time is distorted as in a dream so that "thirteen days seems like thirteen years" in a *Konjaku* tale of obsessive love for a fox apparition. This distortion conveys a sense of the apparent appropriateness and immediacy of the bewitchment: it monopolizes the victim for a long time that seems to pass like a moment, or for a moment that seems to last forever, but in either instance has an overwhelming and irreversible effect that utterly devastates.[87]

The fox kōan bears a formal resemblance to anomaly stories, "which often stress the disjunction between mundane reality and the other world."[88] The kōan narrative consists of several stages akin to the pattern of folktales that generally begin with an apparition manifesting due to karmic retribution and continue with an expression of shame about prior wrongdoing: the appearance of the fox disguised as a human form; a ritualized act of confession of true identity followed by an identification and purgation of the *fei-jen* status through an exorcism of the invading spirit; a reversion of the body to animal form and a burial of the corpse in funeral ceremony that saves the human spirit; and finally an expression of contrition or illuminating commentary by the narrator as a postmortem repentance and transformation. The sequence reveals how the kōan selectively and perhaps purposefully incorporates the pattern of fox possession legends in expressing a philosophy of repentance and monastic order.

As in fox folklore, the need for a stunning existential turnaround in the kōan is generated by the cognitive gap between what seems to be real and what is really real behind this illusion—as well as by the emotional gap grounded in repentance between the attitudes preceding and following the encounter with the source of illusion. Yet, folklore narrators, at least until the Ch'ing era, generally did not try to articulate a theory of illusion. And kōan commentators resisted discussing whether or not they disbelieved in illusory phenomena at least until the modern period when the supernatural was denied from a rational standpoint. In both cases, the silence is probably due to the fact that the authors already participated in what Aron Gurevich calls an ideological "force field" that remained beyond disputation.[89] To the extent that the kōan collection commentators recognized this situation, they may have been concerned that their philosophical approach would be seen not as the primary level of discourse but as a secondary structure—a reversal of the hierarchical discursive order they were trying to present. To counter this problem in a preventive strike, Huang-po's slap, and the line of paradoxical interpretation it engenders, seem to mark an effort to challenge the force field by reprimanding Pai-chang for believing in the supernatural event—a reaction that in some ways, ironically, ends by reinforcing the importance of the folklore context.

2 · The Kōan's Multivalent Discursive Structure

Behind the thin animal disguise, it is universal human frailty and folly that is displayed before us.
—D. D. R. Owen, on *Roman de Renart*

Since its initial publication in the early eleventh century, the fox kōan has inspired diverse and competing interpretations about its ambiguous message concerning the meaning of causality—a message expressed in the highly suggestive symbolism of a folklore narrative. A leading commentator from the Yüan era, Chung-feng Ming-pen (J. Chūhō Myōhon)—known for providing the classic definition of kōans as "magistrate or public (C. *kung;* J. *kō*) records (C. *an;* J. *an*)" emulating legal cases argued before a bench—has said that after twenty years of study the fox kōan remained for him an impenetrable mystery.[1] He considered it one of the most disturbing yet potentially rewarding cases for Zen disciples and thought it should be utilized as a pedagogical tool with utmost care and respect. Furthermore, the fox kōan, discussed in numerous commentaries in China and Japan, was ranked in Hakuin's Tokugawa-era system as a *nantō* kōan: a case that is "difficult to pass through" but has the potential to enhance "postenlightenment cultivation" or "realization beyond realization" *(shōtaichōyō).*[2]

Chung-feng's comment stressing the sense of conundrum created by contemplating the fox kōan from an experiential standpoint shows that the case has been seen as especially perplexing within the orthodox tradition that employs it as a method for seeking or expressing enlightenment.

41

This view is supported by the *Wu-men kuan* paradoxical commentary that defies a literal reading, by Dōgen's conflicting interpretations, one endorsing the *Wu-men kuan* view and the other rejecting it, and by Hakuin's ranking the case in the highest category of difficulty. But the kōan is also an extremely challenging text to interpret from the standpoint of contemporary contextual studies that approach it by combining a hermeneutics of traditional sources with an interdisciplinary approach to humanistic and social scientific methodologies, including philosophy, literary criticism, social history, and folklore studies. The kōan, including the source narrative and voluminous commentaries, is difficult to decipher because it weaves together two seemingly diametrically opposed viewpoints: demythology and mythology.

Overcoming the Two-Tiered Model

How is the appearance of the wild fox and the supernaturalism it evokes related to the philosophical commentaries on causality that distance themselves from, if not altogether scorn, the supernatural? To quote Aron Gurevich's study of the relation between elite/scholastic and popular/syncretic religiosity in medieval Christianity: "How can these levels combine and penetrate each other within a single mind? What transformations do they suffer in this confluence?"[3] Are the philosophical and supernatural implications complementary or contradictory modes of discourse? Or must we abandon the opposition between a philosophical reading and a folklore reading? Perhaps we must, as Pierre Bourdieu suggests in a somewhat parallel context, "undertake a simultaneously . . . *dual reading* of writings which are defined by their fundamental *ambiguity,* that is, by their reference to two social spaces, which correspond to two mental spaces."[4]

In dealing with this issue we need to consider, as Judith Zeitlin suggests, that in East Asia ghosts and spirits "can be accepted as both psychologically induced *and* materially present," so that what is anomalous or strange is "paradoxically affirmed and denied at the same time."[5] This comment recalls Gurevich's argument that medieval European religion is "both-wordly" in encompassing otherworldly phenomena operating in a this-worldly environment.[6] Because of the multidimensional symbolism of the fox, it is possible to develop interpretations of the kōan narrative along several lines. The kōan may express the positive side of a bodhisattva's choice to make a theriomorphic appearance as a pedagogical means, for example, or it can symbolize the negative image of an exorcism of the old monk's spirit possession as applied by the current Pai-chang. Another reading is that the narrative depicts an interior dialogue between the attached and awakened sides of one person, Pai-chang, who in struggling to understand the relation between karma and transcendence projects his inner turmoil, as in a dream or fantasy, onto the envisioned *fei-jen.*

The basic hermeneutic dilemma is whether the fox should be understood as an otherworldly entity with a distinct reality or as representing the illusory fabrications of a confused mind, such as the deluded side of Pai-chang coming to terms with his own sense of shame about his self-indulgent attitude. If the fox is considered real, this view tends to discredit Zen philosophy because supernaturalism seems to incorporate an extreme form of externalization that is antithetical to meditative practice and must be repudiated. But if the fox is purely symbolic, this view suggests a domestication of otherness which refuses to acknowledge that supernatural elements may exist in their uniqueness and separateness. It also raises certain issues: Why would Pai-chang need to reprimand himself? But why is there no special intellectual standpoint or ritual structure available for self-correction in the context of Zen monasticism other than the traditional Vinaya mechanism of the confessional Uposatha ceremony? A purely demythologized interpretation evoking a monochromatic view of fox imagery overlooks the crucial role of the folklore narrative: to convey a paradigm of psychic pollution and ritual purification that amplifies the notions of karmic causality and transmigration. Given the pervasive influence of supernaturalism in hagiographic accounts of the early patriarchs, including Pai-chang, a denial of the mythical dimension probably results from a tendency to evade Zen's origins and their close association with wizardry and exorcism. This attitude is noted in Bernard Faure's analysis of the encounter between great and little traditions in Zen discourse: "The opaque, ambivalent, at times dangerous world of folk religion has been dispelled by the clear, haughty vision of the enlightened mind."[7]

To paraphrase by inversion the title of Paul Veyne's book on classical philosophy and folklore, "Did the Greeks Believe in Their Myths?",[8] the central question is: Did Zen masters really disbelieve in the supernatural imagery they used so handily? And if they exercised a suspension of disbelief combined with a skeptical suspension of belief, what does this attitude reveal about the interface of elite Zen with local traditions? The ironic Zen philosophical approach is epitomized by the commentary in

Pi-yen lu case 22 on Hsüeh-feng taming the "turtle-nosed snake": "If you regard the strange *(kuai)* as not being strange, its strangeness dissolves on its own. How very strange!" And how very ambivalent this passage reads! It could be interpreted as a masterful strategy for disarming supernaturalism. But it may also represent an eloquent description of shape-shifting powers as well as the skills of Zen patriarchs who transcend categorization. The passage carefully conceals its ambivalence within ambivalence.

An alternative to the impasse is to see that the kōan functions on several levels in order to address the concerns of disparate social and intellectual trends. Thus it encompasses the intersection of two main discursive structures that are at times overlapping and at other times conflicting: one is the main, prominent, or overt structure based on a philosophical debate about causality from a theoretical standpoint in which supernaturalism is thoroughly demythologized and disdained; the other is the hidden, secondary, or "muted" structure deriving from folklore and popular religiosity based on a supernatural belief in ritual efficacy underlying and driving the encounter dialogue.[9] The covert or muted structure concerning divine intervention required for the banishing of demonic powers is deeply embedded between the lines of the main structure. The kōan depends for its rhetorical force and flavor on Buddhist and lay folktales concerning fox-spirit possession as well as fox-cult veneration—especially in drawing from bivalent images of foxes as demonic and possessive or beneficent and protective and evoking a moral universe guided by magical efficacy and supernatural powers. The kōan's muted structure is for the most part an inarticulated level of meaning that is vital for the viability of the text because it appeals to a specific audience or to a dimension of experience of the main audience. Yet it tends to be overlooked or even suppressed by interpreters who wish to present the more rational side of Zen discourse. John Wu dismisses the supernatural dimension by arguing that "the story of the wild fox can hardly be taken literally," for example, and Shibayama Zenkei suggests that "the superficial ghost story is just a means to illustrate the point [of emancipation]."[10]

The paradoxical/philosophical and folkloric/supernatural paradigms are not necessarily mutually exclusive but are deliberately played off of one another to generate a creative tension between discursive levels. The convergence derives from the way the kōan reflects the profound interaction of Zen's "high" mystical religion and the popular religious traditions of East Asia: a long-term process of Zen thought transforming and being transformed by indigenous animism. Both paradigms explore the meaning of karma and its relation to noncausality, as well as the dynamics of the experience of repentance that is required to attain the goal of spiritual freedom. The two sets of discourse—demythology/mythology or Buddhist/indigenous religiosity—developed in intersecting yet competing ways. They reflect a profound intertextual interaction between sources of distinct genres—kōan records and morality tale collections—about the meaning of karma and release. Although referring to a twofold structure indicates a plurality that lies beyond a single level based strictly on philosophy, I do not mean to limit the discussion to these levels or exclude other perspectives or the delineation of additional structures, especially the level of discourse about the monastic institution.

In dealing with anomalous imagery the main structure—which involves a philosophical debate concerning the paradoxical identification of opposites from the standpoint of nonduality—uses the fox as a scapegoat in order to brand misunderstandings and scorn renegade monks and their misbehavior.[11] This paradigm highlights the fox as an indicator of the self-deception of unenlightenment that must be overcome by a philosophical understanding of karma grounded on the identity of causality and noncausality. The muted structure revolves around a bivalent view in that the fox, like many indigenous *fei-jen* folklore entities, is a two-sided symbol: a double-edged sword moving back and forth between the poles of good and evil, beneficence and demonism. Whereas paradoxicality tends to collapse or bypass the distinction between opposites, bivalence tends to hold the polarity as polarity while also allowing for the interplay between contradictory tendencies. Furthermore, the interaction between discursive levels is characterized by a fundamental ambivalence that seems to reflect the bivalent approach of popular religiosity. Although the traditional kōan commentaries do not support supernatural elements, they also generally do not reject them directly but comment only in a detached, indirect, or ironical fashion. The author of the *Ts'ung-jung lu* commentary, for example, remarks sardonically that "my tailbone is showing more and more."[12] Thus the text uses the fox image not only to defeat a reliance on supernaturalism but also to challenge false claims by those who think they have overcome such a conceptual dependency.

Attempting to put the "fox" back in the "wild fox kōan" by sorting through complex textual congruences, practical syncretisms, and cultural resonances that are often concealed or camouflaged recalls an intriguing anecdote by Maxine Hong Kingston concerning the perplexity and purposefully disturbing elusiveness of East Asian mystery traditions. According to Kingston, "Long ago in China, knot-makers tied string into buttons and frogs, and rope into bell pulls. There was one knot so complicated that it blinded the knot-maker. Finally an emperor outlawed this cruel knot, and the nobles could not order it anymore. If I had lived in China," Kingston remarks, "I would have been an outlaw knot-maker."[13]

The knottiness of whether the demythological/paradoxical and the supernatural/bivalent implications of fox imagery represent complementary or contradictory modes of discourse must be considered in light of a broader issue: the relation between elite and popular religions, as well as the tension between ritual and iconoclasm, other-power and self-power, or prayer and meditation. This topic has been at the forefront of recent studies of both Eastern and Western religion concerning the connection between magic (based on colloquial spirits of the little tradition) and scholasticism (based on a universal theology of the great tradition that rejects supernaturalism). For too long the philosophical/philological analysis of texts was segregated from ritual studies of popular religious practices. As scholars almost never dealt with both areas at the same time, the role of popular religion in Zen discourse was long neglected. There prevailed an image of Zen as a privileged ideology characterized by pristine purity and timeless idealism free of any taint by compromise with ritual activity aside from meditative discipline. In the case of the fox kōan it was assumed that the Zen philosophical use of folklore about the fox was successful in disentangling what it wanted to say from the indigenous, animist, magical matrix of the original, pre-Buddhist beliefs about foxes.

The case of Buddhism is somewhat similar to the engagement between great and little traditions in medieval Europe. According to Gurevich, two worldviews confront one another: an anthropomorphic Christian view that humanizes the world by personifying the divine versus a pagan, pre-Christian magical view that naturalizes humans by embedding them in an all-embracing, living cosmos permeated with otherworldly forces. The encounter between worldviews becomes apparent in a variety of religious expressions and symbols—such as cults of relics and saints, appeals to the power of sorcery and amulets, or the texts of penitential or grotesque writers—which generate two competing interpretations: one emphasizing the interior, intellectual meaning and the other the efficacy of exterior ritualism. In these expressions, Gurevich maintains, Christian doctrine represents not a breach but the culmination of indigenous beliefs: "Ancient, pre-Christian magical practices did not vanish. However, they existed now in an entirely new mental context. Their practitioners and participants had to become aware of the limits of magic and had to develop a critical attitude towards it."[14] At the same time, he points out, it is necessary to recognize that even the beliefs and ideas in elite church writings that denounce and vilify paganism reflect "a deeper, 'primary,' layer of popular consciousness . . . which were much less vestiges or 'survivals' of pre-Christian practices than integral elements of daily life."[15]

There are important differences between the role of Christianity in Europe, which tends to be intolerant and exclusive, and of Buddhism in East Asia, which tends to be open and assimilative. Take, for example, the cult of the sacred dog or "holy greyhound," St. Guinefort, which worships and enshrines an animal known for saving a child from being eaten by a snake and also venerates a doe that was the first to recognize the saint—a cult that spread throughout countryside chapels in medieval France but was condemned as a wicked heresy by official church policy. Jean-Claude Schmitt notes that from the standpoint of the church: "With superstition, then, God is the victim and the devil the beneficiary . . . its only purpose being to seduce *(seductio)* and to mislead *(ludificatio)*."[16] In the case of Buddhism, by contrast, indigenous deities including the fox were enshrined and elevated in a variety of sects and rites into the foremost position of veneration. And although they were also the object of exorcism, it was often the case that it took the deified fox to eliminate the demonic one. Nevertheless, as Gurevich and Schmitt suggest, while the dog cult and other examples of paganism were attacked as superstition by the elite and eliminated through exorcism on another level, many of the elements of folk religiosity including sacred symbols and sites were at the same time preserved through conversion into Christian rites. Practitioners were admonished, for example, to accept and believe in the supernatural appearance and performance of miracles by saints. In a similar way, the fox kōan is an example of medieval Buddhism creating a new context for understanding supernatural beliefs or for decoding and reencoding local gods. The indigenous beliefs did not simply disappear but were transmuted by virtue of a critical, transcendental attitude at once exploiting and surpassing their original literal meaning.

My analysis of the relation between philosophy and folk beliefs builds upon several excellent studies of the role of popular religions in the practices, rhetoric, and institutions of Buddhism in medieval China and Japan. These works demonstrate that Zen is not a unitary, pure, discrete, and unchanging essence but consists of complex, diverse phenomena continually interacting and interpenetrating with other theories and practices.[17] Contrary to its reputation as an iconoclastic, monistic, demythological, philosophical approach, Zen is after all a religious movement that has depended on extensive syncretism with indigenous deities and esoteric Buddhist rites for its popularity and institutional survival. Zen religion was created not in armchair isolation but as part of a pervasive socioreligious context involving revelatory dreams, oracles, divination, pilgrimage, miracles, saints, healings, exorcisms, and funerals, as well as bids to establish legitimacy and lines of authority in order to attract patronage and power. For the most part, however, these studies have not dealt directly with the popular religious aspect of kōan literature—which thus remains stereotyped as epitomizing the philosophical dimension—although there have been several important works on the role of post-Dōgen Sōtō Zen dealing with esoteric commentaries on kōans known as *kirigami*.[18]

A thoroughgoing reevaluation of Zen raises the specter of decline—an implicit question about whether an essentially incorruptible tradition has been contaminated by popular religiosity. The process of syncretism in the history of religions is usually portrayed in terms of a two-tiered model in which the great tradition remains ever aloof from and yet filters down to a marginal, inferior little tradition representing a degenerate form of belief that threatens to pollute and infect the great tradition. To overcome bias in assuming a hierarchical evaluation, it is relevant to ask the reverse question: To what extent does folk religion infiltrate and influence the great tradition? How is the mental context of philosophy affected and changed—that is, what are the benefits to the architects of scholasticism, including the possibilities for enhancing a metaphysical understanding of morality, in addition to the concessions made to accommodate supernaturalism? Or, without presupposing a hierarchical ranking, how does the little tradition function as an element of difference, disruption, and subversion that may lead to multifunctional effects in its encounter with the great tradition? Gurevich asks: how does each side suffer (and gain) in the relationship? In other words, the reciprocity of influences operating in the assimilative process must be emphasized to show an underlying connection yet fundamental difference between elite and popular religions.

Reckoning with these questions requires looking at popular religion neither as a shadow or partial reflection of elite religion, nor as a burden or hindrance, but as a level of discourse that has its own autonomy and integrity. One approach to overcoming the two-tiered model perhaps goes too far in suggesting that the very category of popular religiosity must be abandoned because it originates in and can never extricate itself from a hierarchical bias. According to this approach, the notion of a popular or little tradition has been imposed on East Asia by the West with its "tendency to regard philosophy as elite reflection while relegating magic to the base level of folk superstitions, conveniently dividing thereby the intellectual few from the vulgar many. However, this two-tiered model of society, first employed by David Hume in his essay *Natural History of Religion* and followed by many modern scholars of religion, more often distorts reality than clarifies it." In East Asia, on the contrary, "it is not uncommon that we find both aspects together in one text revered by social elites and common folk alike."[19] Although the main example cited is the *I Ching*, the comment could also apply with certain qualifications to the fox kōan. While these remarks are quite perceptive in uncovering the roots of methodological bias in Humean empiricism, they fail to point out that the two-tiered model is deeply rooted in the very origins of religions in both the East and the West. Peter Brown shows, for example, that the elitist sense of contrast with popular religions long precedes Hume. In early medieval Christianity paganism or boorishness, parallel to *rusticitas*, was defined as vulgarity, crudeness, lack of polish, illiteracy, or the idiotic—such as resorting to the use of tangible symbols like amulets instead of the worship of invisible saints—in contrast to *urbanitas*, which was a refined, cosmopolitan, sophisticated, and literary approach.[20]

The existence of two levels of discourse is not just a Western invention, modern or otherwise, for it is found throughout the history of East Asian religion. The Confucian philosopher Hsün Tzu, for example, makes a fundamental distinction between how the educated elite and the common folk understand rituals *(li):* "You consult the arts of divination before making a decision on some important matter. But it is not as though you could hope to accomplish anything by such ceremonies. They are done merely for ornament. Hence the gentleman regards [rituals] as ornaments *(wen-tse),* but the common people regard them as supernatural *(shen-tse).* He who considers them ornaments is fortunate; he who considers them supernatural is unfortunate."[21] Furthermore, Buddhism has distinguished between true teachings or the right dharma (C. *cheng-fa;* J.

shōbō)—based on the diligent practice of meditation, the reading of sutras, or the practice of repentance—and false teachings (mixed with noncanonical, extracanonical, or non-Buddhist customs), commonly or officially labeled vulgar or superstitious beliefs (C. *mi-hsin,* J. *meishin;* or C. *su-shin-yang,* J. *zatsu shinkō*).[22] These practices are frequently based on the misuse of supranormal powers—a misuse that engenders the rhetoric of "wild fox" criticism.

Sung kōan texts make it clear that the native gods and demons remain inferior to the spiritual powers attained through meditation of realized Zen masters. The following commentary in the *Ts'ung-jung lu* kōan collection on case 10 (concerning Chao-chou's investigation of an old woman at the foot of Mount Wu-t'ai who has been outsmarting monks, also included in *Wu-men kuan* case 31) follows a passage that cites ironic, quasi-apocryphal comments by Chuang Tzu and Confucius about a spirit turtle's powers of divination: "Demons and ghosts become spirits through the power of bewitchment; spells and medicines become spirits through the power of causing effects; heavenly beings and dragons become spirits through the power of retribution; the wise and sagely become spirits through supranormal powers *(shen-t'ang);* buddhas and patriarchs become spirits through the power of the Way."[23] All of these categories possess spiritual power. But the indigenous gods, which surpass the category of ghosts and demons who have an ability to affect rewards and punishments for humans, remain on the third of five levels and cannot be compared to the power of buddhas and patriarchs who are enlightened by virtue of a realization of the Tao. An important difference with the West is that in Buddhism folk religions are generally not considered heretical in the sense of an evil element that must be scorned, so that while the Zen philosophical mainstream asserts the priority of meditation the marginal or counter elements are still incorporated into its overall worldview. Yet the existence of a hierarchical ranking is clear—as is the need for an exorcism of demons, according to other sources in the tradition, as well as the effort to convert their powers into a force protecting the Buddhist law.

Therefore, overcoming the two-tiered model should not involve efforts to eliminate the double structure: such an approach would actually violate the tradition and ironically recreate the Humean presupposition of right versus wrong beliefs in the name of refuting it. Rather, it is preferable to examine popular religion not as an accident or embarrassment but on its own terms and in light of the dynamics of its engagement with its discursive partner—that is, in a way that is fair to both parties.[24] This process involves: (1) transforming the methodological outlook from a stance that is evaluative with an implicit prescription (and covert proscription) to one that is nonjudgmental and descriptive; (2) regarding Zen discourse not as a filtering down from an active top layer to a passive bottom one but as a dynamic, horizontal, competitive model with multiple tiers interacting along various lines of discourse; and (3) assessing the positive contributions of popular religiosity to the meditative tradition particularly in regard to the practice of repentance.

One method for achieving a horizontal outlook is the nexus approach suggested by social historians who stress that behind the diversified meanings of a metaphor operating within a common framework of shared ideas there stands the presence of an unspoken level of understanding framing the spoken—a primary layer of consciousness that Gurevich calls the force field. Bourdieu argues that the discursive context underlying the polemic generated by the conflict between orthodoxy and heterodoxy derives from a more general universe or "doxa" where there is no need for disputation about commonly accepted assumptions. Therefore, the main structure and the muted structure of the kōan are two storehouses: each contains the full range of meanings of the opposite side with which it is often conflated (or as which it may even be camouflaged).

Part of the reason for the ambiguity and disingenuous blasphemy lies in the reliance on the discursive nexus connecting philosophy and folklore. According to Roland Barthes, the metaphorical nature of symbols has a polysemous quality because of the interaction between overlapping or conflicting discourses. Thus an image such as the wild fox may be appropriated in diverse (and frequently reverse) fashion by competing discursive elements—including thinkers or texts in interlocking traditional and countertraditional perspectives. Extending Barthes' observations, Emiko Ohnuki-Tierney stresses that within a single polysemous sign the overt structure and the inverted structure (which harbors latent meanings) are simultaneously present and mutually dependent, causing an entire text or a ritual performance to be multivocal and ambivalent. "Symbols, including linguistic ones," Ohnuki-Tierney writes, "are rarely univocal. As a signifier, a polysemic symbol can take on additional meanings; in fact, it always has more than one meaning. Polysemic symbols therefore embody an inherent mechanism to overcome the basic contradiction between the signifier (form) and the signified (meaning)."[25] Thus a negative side of the sign continually breaks out in forms of inversion, subversion, or reversion of the positive meaning (or vice versa).

Furthermore, Bourdieu and Gurevich focus on the unity underlying two main social groups—the mainstream or overt structure and the covert or muted structure—competing for the use of an idea or term. They show that the structures are neither inherently separate and different nor identical and undifferentiated; rather, they are part of a nexus or doxa standing behind the exchange between orthodoxy and heterodoxy. Bourdieu refers to the doxa as a homological *"field of opinion, the locus of the confrontation of competing discourses,"* the sum total of the theses tacitly posited on both sides of an inquiry that is simply taken for granted by all parties and thus often not articulated.[26] This sense of interconnectedness is depicted by Gurevich as an "ongoing hidden dialogue between official doctrine and folkloric consciousness, leading to their convergence but not to their fusion."[27] He argues: "Only in the force-field created by both poles—the consciousness of the elite and the consciousness of the *idiotae*—did medieval culture, with all its alogisms, 'oddities' and paradoxes, acquire its social meaning."[28]

But it is not sufficient simply to see Zen functioning within the nexus. Now the question becomes: What is accomplished through the interaction between structures?[29] The divergent discursive perspectives converge in shaping Zen's view of social order reflecting moral authority and spiritual power represented by contradictory images of the wild fox as a focal point for criticism and refutation as well as for praise and admiration. The image of Pai-chang, standing in competition with rival viewpoints including the pietistic awakening expressed in *setsuwa* sources, seeks to combat its rivals through establishing his charisma and authority by at once demonstrating skepticism about supernaturalism and showing that his abilities are equal to those who operate primarily in the realm of exorcism. More than playing a game of one-upmanship, the kōan makes a statement about the morality of repentance, dovetailing with Pai-chang's monastic rules, that could not be made so effectively without recourse to fox imagery.

Pai-chang's Monastic Rules

The dialogues on causality in the fox kōan are presented in the context of Zen's need to establish an ethical principle of fidelity to the law of karmic retribution. Such a principle helps sustain the orderliness of the monastic institution in the face of several interconnected challenges: not only the Confucian critique of Buddhism as an antisocial practice reflecting an antinomian ideology and the dissipation of pure dedication to training in meditation through the absorption of local animism, but also the government's suppression of Buddhism during the Wu-tsung proscription lasting from 842 to 845 and the Huang-ch'ao rebellion that raged for nine years in the 870s and 880s and devastated many aspects of Chinese society including Buddhist institutions. The kōan text composed in 1036 during the Northern Sung dynasty to recount the exploits of T'ang masters reveals key features in the development of the Zen monastic system that responded to these challenges. Zen monasticism relied on the role of the charismatic abbot who maintained spiritual authority and authenticity by combining a daily round of formal and informal sermons and other innovative pedagogical techniques, including encounter dialogues, with detailed rules for various functionaries, funerals, and other ceremonies as well as strict regulations requiring banishment for transgressors. The Zen monastic rules were either taken over from early Vinaya rules or borrowed from the practices of other Chinese Buddhist sects that were, in turn, influenced by secular laws. The elimination and burial of the "negative charisma" of the wild fox as a symbol of indigenous animistic beliefs that infiltrated and polluted Buddhism conveys a sense of order, stability, and the domestication of the subversive elements of popular religiosity.[30]

Furthermore, the narrative in which Pai-chang emerges as a savior of the ancient monk because of his assertion of the inviolability of karma has a resonance with his reputation in Zen historical records as a stern moralist and no-nonsense disciplinarian who initiated Zen institutional life as a training process distinct from other sects. Pai-chang is said to have composed the original set of monastic codes—known as the *Ch'an-men kuei-shih* (J. *Zenmon kishiki*) or the *Pai-chang ch'ing-kuei* (*Hyakujō shingi*)—that appeared as a supplement to his biography in the first transmission of the lamp text: the *Ching-te ch'uan-teng lu* (*chüan* 6), released in 1004 just three decades before the publication of the kōan in the *TKL*, although the authorship and dating have been challenged in recent studies.[31] The fact that both the kōan and rules texts attributed to Pai-chang originated nearly two centuries after his death suggests that they were not designed as factual, historiographic accounts but were crafted as hagiographies. The aim of these texts was to create a moral message in the period of Sung Zen's rapid growth after a period of state suppression and decline in the late T'ang. (See Figure 9.)

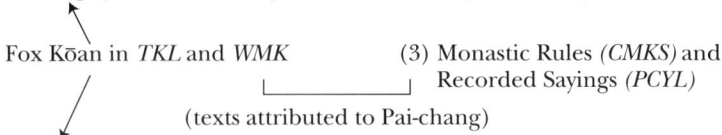

(1) Philosophy (debate about paradoxical identity of causality and noncausality)

Fox Kōan in *TKL* and *WMK*   (3) Monastic Rules *(CMKS)* and
                                         Recorded Sayings *(PCYL)*
                (texts attributed to Pai-chang)

   (2) Folklore narrative of retribution and repentance in light of popular
       religious syncretisms of veneration/exorcism

Figure 9. This diagram illustrates the interaction between philosophy, folklore or popular religiosity, and monastic codes as expressed in the fox kōan and rules texts attributed to Pai-chang—thereby indicating the importance of a third level of the kōan's discursive structure.

Pai-chang's rules stress the requirement, evoked in the *TKL* version of the kōan, of full and equal participation in communal labor, regardless of rank, based on the admonition that "a day without work is a day without eating" (C. *i-jih-pu-tso, i-jih-pu-shih;* J. *ichinichi fusaku, ichinichi fushoku*), as well as a refusal to accept tax-exempt status for monasteries or to beg from poor laypersons.[32] This attitude is symbolized by an anecdote at the end of Pai-chang's recorded sayings that as an old man he took no food on the day his disciples stole his tools to spare him work in the fields, as they knew he would not relent otherwise, an episode that inspired a famous ode by Ikkyū.[33] Pai-chang's response to his followers was the self-effacing, "I have no virtue; how can I make others toil?", and he fasted.[34] The rules also make repeated threats to expel corrupt, insincere, or irresponsible members of the *saṃgha* as a "warning of the disgrace and humiliation" that will haunt all possible offenders. The abbot is to flog the renegade with the staff and burn all his belongings before banishing him through the side gate of the compound. This severe punishment is exercised not just for breaking one of the major precepts or committing severe offenses (Skt. *pārājika*) condemned by the traditional Vinaya and requiring permanent banishment, but for displaying any sign of disrespect or inauthenticity.

In the early Vinaya, the four examples of *pārājika*—which implies defeat or spiritual downfall in the struggle against the temptations of Māra or evil in the general sense—specifically involve sexual misconduct, killing, taking what is not given, and falsely claiming the attainment of supranormal powers beyond what is prescribed in the meditation instructions. Although Pai-chang's rules are in some ways harsher than Vinaya discipline, covering a much broader area of offenses leading to ostracism, we can only speculate as to the extent to which they were actually enforced. One reason for this attitude was the way the Vinaya had been applied, or misapplied, for several centuries prior to Pai-chang's rule. In China, where a knowledge of the social context behind the original Vinaya rules was for the most part lost, there was a tendency for monks' transgressions to be treated either with nonchalant acceptance or, swinging to the other extreme, quick and decisive banishment.[35]

In Zen the term "wild fox" can imply irregular or inauthentic priests who violate the fourth *pārājika* by making false claims about their supranormal or intuitive powers based on an egotism that supersedes the rigors of discipline (Skt. *abhijñā;* C. *shen-t'ang;* J. *jinzū*—literally "spiritual or divine penetrations" in Sino-Japanese rendering, which implies there are no obstructions). As described in *Nikāya* literature, including the *Majjhima Nikāya,* the six supranormal powers reflect a mastery over karma through the power of prediction as well as a transcendence of the boundaries of cause-and-effect. This mastery is attained by passing through the four *rūpa dhyāna* (meditations in the realm of form) and entering into the four *arūpa dhyāna* (meditations in the realm of the formless).[36] There are six supranormal powers: miraculous powers, such as taming wild animals and transforming oneself at will, like shape-shifting into other, including nonhuman, forms—the body does whatever one wants; clairvoyance, or the divine eye that sees all the sights of the universe, including the death and rebirth of all beings through an analysis of cause-and-effect; clairaudience, or the divine ear that hears all the sounds of the universe; the ability to read others' minds or to mirror their thoughts; the memory of the past lives of self and others through a retrogressive analysis from effect to cause; and the knowledge of the destruction of all defilements and thus the ability to predict the attainment of nirvana.[37] These powers can be legitimately attained as a by-product of enlightenment realized either through meditation in the realms of form and formlessness or alternative spiritual techniques such as ascetic practices *(dhūtaguṇa),* including forest meditation during prolonged periods of solitude in mountain huts or hermitages.[38]

The *Digha Nikāya* divides supranormal powers into two categories: the noble and the ignoble. The ignoble includes invisibility, levitation, passing through walls, bilocation, flying like a bird based on mental intoxication, and the pursuit of material benefits (*genze riyaku* in Japanese); the noble includes many of the same powers, but they are deployed in a way that is free from desire and reflects the attainment of self-mastery as well as the compassionate assistance of those who suffer.[39] The sole legitimate use of the spiritual penetrations is soteriological—that is, to guide suffering sentient beings to nirvana. A power must never be used as an end in itself or for personal show or gain, let alone for sorcery, or evil intentions, or combined with other occult abilities such as divination, providing protective charms, casting out malevolent spirits (exorcism), psychic healing, performing as a medium, and the like.[40] Practitioners found guilty are ridiculed in a society that rejects marginal elements as a threat to the carefully regimented system for being no better than protean, demonic foxes. Any laypersons believing in the magical powers of mere tricksters or false ascetics (boasting itself is a punishable offense in the Vinaya) are condemned for a heresy deriving from being deceived and deluded by a bewitching fox.[41] According to the version of Pai-chang's rules in the monk biography text of 988, the *Sung kao-seng chuan* by Tsan-ning, known as the "Tiger of Regulations" for his strict adherence to Vinaya rules:

> When Pai-chang entered the scene, he established an independent set of monastic regulations with the idea of using them as expedient devices *(upāya)*. The underlying aim was to entice practitioners specifically devoted to austerities *(dhūtaguṇa)* to follow the correct way and abandon erroneous practices."[42]

The maverick may correspond to what Mahayana Buddhism has labeled the *pratyekabuddha:* the practitioner who is self-enlightened through a mixture of Buddhist and non-Buddhist practices and lives in seclusion without the need for either teacher or disciple in the chain of transmission. At its worst, the maverick becomes a reckless and at times harmful priest with unharnessed powers.[43] Although the great Zen masters like Pai-chang spent time in retreats or hermitages to perfect their spiritual realization, as leaders of monastic communities they warned their followers against wayward independence and threatened to expel the unworthy who could intrude on the legitimate community. Yet they needed to remain open to test and in some cases acknowledge the merits of irregular practitioners. Numerous kōans, especially two cases in the *Wu-men kuan* involving Chao-chou (J. Jōshū), deal with the encounter and testing of mavericks by institutionally approved leaders—often with characteristically enigmatic results in that the kōans leave it unclear who has won the exchange or what the standards are for judging it.[44] In case 11, for example, Chao-chou, known for offering tea to disciples regardless of how they reply to his queries, receives identical responses from two hermits—both silently hold up a fist—but he declares one genuine and the other inauthentic.[45] And in case 31, a Zen granny gives him the same rude treatment accorded junior monks yet he proclaims himself the victor.

In the *Shōbōgenzō* "Tajintsū" fascicle on the power of reading the minds of others, Dōgen cites a kōan that uses fox imagery as a form of criticism. The kōan narrative concerns the meeting at the behest of the emperor between an early T'ang master, National Teacher Hui-chung, and a maverick practitioner from India known as Ta-erh. This tale is particularly interesting because Hui-chung, prior to attaining his status as an imperial priest, was famous for becoming enlightened by himself through a remarkable manner of ascetic training. Then, once established, he was called on by the emperor to test the abilities of a foreign priest who claimed to have mastered the *abhijñā* of reading others' minds. After failing to answer Hui-chung's probing question correctly the first two times, Ta-erh remained silent the third time and finally was scolded by the national teacher for being no better than a "wild fox spirit."[46]

The prevalence of such epithets must be considered in the context of the highly competitive religious environment of the Northern Sung. Zen theory and practice stood in competition with rival Buddhist and Taoist meditative schools and a wide variety of popular cults in an atmosphere generally dominated by Neo-Confucian ethical concerns and criticism of Buddhism as a wasteful, idle, elitist pursuit stemming from foreign, "barbarian" influences. Furthermore, all sects in the stratified, compartmentalized, authoritarian society were carefully and sometimes repressively regulated by government legislation. Indeed, Buddhism was proscribed more than once. The most severe instance was the Wu-tsung persecution during the Hui-ch'ang era (841–846), a generation after Pai-chang's death, when thousands of Buddhist temples were shuttered and hundreds of thousands of monks and nuns were returned to lay life. Yet this was by no means the only period in which Buddhism suffered political persecution, for the problem persisted throughout the T'ang and Sung eras. Although Confucianism tended to criticize Buddhism as life-negating, this attitude was not altogether one-sided, for Confucian scholar-officials also depended upon Buddhist evangelism in the effort to overcome local folk religions. Buddhist priests, who served as soothsayers and healers with "their magical tricks and store of edifying tales" and "their rituals and charms, their promise of salvation cast in simple terms, perhaps driven home by one of the stories which dramatized the working of karmic law"—a strategy designed to assimilate local tutelary deities abiding in the countryside or on mountains—were useful to Confucianism in the task of disseminating Chinese culture.[47] Since Buddhism adhered to strict rules of discipline and monastic conduct as exemplified by the Pai-chang rules, its evangelists were "seen [by Confucians] as a 'civilizing' competitor against native shamanistic rites [and magical Taoism]—a field of competition in which Confucianism was ill-equipped."[48]

The accusations against Zen by its rivals were at first repudiated with references to anomalous imagery in some of the same kōan collection and hagiographical texts that included the fox kōan in which a haunting vulpine presence is symbolically laid to rest and buried. By evoking the image of the wild fox—which literally means a "(roaming) field fox"—the kōan suggests that the *fei-jen* suffers from a presumptive or disruptive attitude that must be called into question and brought into line by the current abbot known from his rules text for his willingness to expel and excommunicate uncooperative monks. Field foxes are among the most unruly vulpine creatures according to East Asian folklore, and the term implies a state of false enlightenment whereby one fools himself and others into thinking it is genuine.[49] As the fox is associated with a femme fatale, the metaphorical use of the term suggests someone who is bewitching and seductive or thrives on pretense and deceit. Yet the rhetoric of wild fox criticism may also stem from conventional clerics' jealousy or misunderstanding of hermits and other irregular practitioners who demonstrate a superior or at least a different kind of spiritual attainment or skill in exploiting supranormal powers gained by the perfection of ascetic practices.

One of the features of early Vinaya that is missing from Pai-chang's rules—as well as from more comprehensive Zen monastic codes that derive from this early, sketchy text—is an emphasis on repentance. Moreover, the Vinaya offers a stipulated procedure for acknowledging and confessing evil acts during the fortnightly Uposatha ceremony: either to another cleric or before the entire assembly depending on the degree of the offense and its impact on individuals or community. The Vinaya sets various levels of penance and probationary periods adjusted to the severity of the transgression—analyzed in terms of intention, action, and result—as well as the effectiveness of the repentance already carried out for previous offenses. Additional penalties are meted out for those who do not confess promptly or for repeat offenders.[50] Vinaya codes also mention the possibility of a monk accusing another who has not yet confessed during the Uposatha (still followed in Zen temples today, though often in a mechanical fashion); the judgment of the case is determined by means of a hearing and democratic vote. The fox kōan introduces the notion of redemption from sin by means of the supernatural practice of exorcism—"a deeply reassuring drama for men anxious about themselves and their society"—rather than the public self-criticism of Vinaya repentance.[51] But this process still requires the fox/monk's willingness to admit the error of his ways before the abbot and, posthumously, through the process of the burial, to the full assembly of monks. Although the fox is eliminated in the kōan as a symbol of disorder, the use of fox imagery, which can symbolize sacrality in a positive sense, points beyond the discourse of supernaturalism set up in contrast to rationality. It suggests the onset of a moral crisis and the possibility of attaining genuine understanding unbound by artificial conceptual dichotomies—including a division between elite/popular and between great/little traditions.

A Tale of Two Rocks

The diverse but interrelated discursive dimensions of the fox kōan seen in the context of the development of the Zen institution are vividly represented in a diagram/map of the main features of the monastery in its setting on Mount Pai-chang in Kiangsi province.[52] (See Figure 10.) In the foreground lies the temple compound with its gate and main buildings, including a Dharma Hall and abbot's quarters. This was presumably one of the first structures based on the "seven-hall monastic model" found in Sung Chinese and Kamakura Japanese Zen temples. But the real story of Mount Pai-chang is told by the symbols lying outside the compound gates, especially two inscribed stones and a mountain peak.[53] According to the diagram, there is a stone inscribed as the "wild fox rock" (C. *yeh-hu yen;* J. *yako-gan*) located behind the gates of the temple, up a hill, in densely forested terrain that is difficult and forbidding to climb. (See Figure 11.) This is supposedly the rock under which the fox corpse was found in the kōan narrative. The rock can still be seen today standing above what appears to be an active fox den (although it is likely that the temple was moved, perhaps several times, from its original location). To the left of the temple, in a more accessible

Figure 10. This 1624 drawing of the temple in the setting of Mount Pai-chang shows four main elements: the monastic compound (1); two inscribed stones, including the "wild fox" stone (2) behind the temple compound and the "monastic rules" stone (3) to the left; and Ta-hsiung Peak (4) looming over the compound. The drawing also depicts the presence of many hermitages—some simple and isolated, others more elaborate and sophisticated—throughout the mountain area. Ta-hsiung Peak, where Pai-chang was said to meditate in isolation, was also well known as a site for solitary hermits, some of whom were "tamed" and converted by Lin-chi.

site about thirty meters away from the first stone, there lies another inscribed rock: a memorial stone celebrating the master's regulations by proclaiming that "Vinaya prevails throughout the world (or covers everywhere under heaven)" (C. *t'ien-hsia ch'ing-kuei;* J. *tenka shingi*). (See Figure 12.) The term "Vinaya" is used here in the broad sense to encompass Zen monastic codes (C. *ch'ing kuei;* J. *shingi*) reflecting the assimilation of the Buddhist institution in China that, according to Pai-chang's commentary, are to be distinguished from the Vinaya records of early Buddhist practice. Pai-chang suggests that his codes are not identical to the Mahayana precepts, either, but represent a "third

Figure 11. A close-up of the inscribed "wild fox" stone on Mount Pai-chang. Although the inscription is concealed by the overgrown brush, there still appears to be a fox den under the rock.

Figure 12. A close-up of the inscribed "monastic rules" stone on the mountain.

way" that synthesizes and transcends the best features of the early (or Hinayana) and Mahayana approaches.

The images of the overall diagram and the rocks reflect a conceptual polarity between discipline and disorder. Yet the presence of the wild fox rock reinforces a sense of establishing order by suppressing the transgressive. Also standing outside the compound gates are small hermitages: some of them may have been supported by wealthy patrons and were rather sophisticated in their construction; others were sparse huts for the practice of rigorous austerities. At the same time, a third main image looms over the rocks and hermitages: Ta-hsiung (J. Daiyū), or Great Sublime Peak, the elevation within the Mount Pai-chang range that is located fairly close to the temple yet far above the Vinaya (or monastic codes) rock. This peak is where Pai-chang, known for his gaunt body and ascetic bent, was said to have practiced a strenuous form of meditation while isolated in retreat from the assembly. A number of other hermits were known to have practiced at the site. The presence of Ta-hsiung Peak discloses the Zen aspiration for a spiritual transcendence that goes beyond a blind obedience to rules and evokes the image of the wild fox transformed in a positive, Taoist sense indicating freedom from all constraint.[54] The symbolism associated with Ta-hsiung Peak—which is drawn not to scale but to exaggerate its steepness and height in accord with a conventional topos in art of the Ch'ing dynasty—represents a mixture of supernatural and antisupernatural beliefs.[55]

In an anecdote cited in Pai-chang's recorded sayings just before the fox kōan, in which Huang-po also slaps his teacher, the disciple tells Pai-chang that he has been picking wild mushrooms on the mountain peak. The master, who is famous in another anecdote for having had a premonition as a child that he would become a buddha when he was walking by an icon with his mother,[56] asks the disciple if he saw the tiger who lives up on Ta-hsiung Peak. This comment may refer to an actual beast or to a shape-shifting animal like the wild fox, only more terrifying. After Huang-po defuses the issue of supernaturalism by making a tiger's roar and slapping Pai-chang, the abbot warns the monks about his disciple: "There is a tiger on the mountain. You people should all watch out for him coming and going. This morning I myself got bit by him!" The verse commentary in *Pi-yen lu* case 85, which refers to four prominent hermits dwelling on the peak who later became masters while training under Lin-chi, alludes to the Pai-chang/Huang-po dialogue as the "remarkable encounter on Ta-hsiung Peak of which the vast sound and light shook the earth."[57]

The spiritual significance of the peak is further evidenced in another *Pai-chang yü-lu* anecdote that also appears in a kōan, recorded in case 26 of the *Pi-yen lu* collection, which is commented on extensively by Dōgen and his mentor, Ju-ching (J. Nyojō).[58] Here Pai-chang is asked by a disciple: "What is the most extraordinary (C. *chi;* J. *ki*) thing?" The disciple is using a term that generally refers to anomalous supernatural beings. Pai-chang responds: "It is sitting alone on Ta-hsiung Peak." This response may imply the need to go off from the monastery for a period of intensive meditation secluded in a hermitage. Or since the master takes his name from the precipitous mountain location of the temple (Pai-chang literally means "a hundred fathoms high"), the master's answer may indicate an indirect first-person reference in the sense that "I sit alone in meditation" (regardless of whether this indicates inside or beyond the temple gates). The verse commentary likens the "extraordinary" achievements of Pai-chang to the feats of a heavenly horse or tiger: "In the realm of the patriarchs, there gallops a heavenly horse, / Within the gate of skillful means, revealing and concealing are different paths, / But he adapts his methods in a flash of lightning or the igniting of a spark; / Someone once tried to tweak the tiger's whiskers—what a joke!" This tongue-in-cheek identification of magical animals with the Zen master, expressed in an admiring yet sardonic fashion, is a key element of the rhetorical strategy used in the fox kōan.

The interaction of the symbols in the diagram suggests that the Zen message expressed by the representations and associations of Pai-chang was not a simple endorsement of monastic discipline as an avenue to enlightenment: it was multifaceted. While Zen repudiated certain abuses represented by the image of the bewitching fox, its commentaries also allowed room for a spiritual transcendence of the rules of conduct if properly understood. Thus the question becomes: Where do the self-indulgent tendencies of inauthentic practice leave off and the genuine, eccentric antics displaying a transcendental outlook rising above petty concerns begin? Or perhaps the kōan commentaries hope to navigate a balance between two aspects of Zen symbolized by dual images of the fox: one negative and the other positive. On the one side we have a ritual, precept-oriented Zen supported by Pai-chang's rules as symbolized by the *t'ien-hsia ch'ing-kuei yen* or Vinaya stone and expressed in the kōan's eradication of the intrusive anomalous spirit symbolized by the *yeh-hu yen* or exorcism stone. On the other side we have the wild, transcendental Zen that lies outside of conventional boundaries as reflected in positive uses of fox imagery as well as the kōan about the sacred site of Ta-hsiung Peak. The first reading, more conservative and less threatening to mainstream society, is available to mollify Zen's rivals and official critics. The second reading, the paradoxical view, may represent an esoteric level of interpretation that remains hidden from wide dissemination beyond the intellectual elite, including Sung Neo-Confucians, who were initiated into an intensive study of kōan commentaries. In any case, the debate suggests a fundamental uncertainty—or perhaps a deliberately crafted ambiguity derived from the polysemy of wild fox imagery—about the moral message Zen seeks to convey.

Part Two

Text-Shaping

3 · Philosophical Paradigm of Paradoxicality

This being, that arises;
This not being, that does not arise.
                        —*Majjhima Nikāya*

The main philosophical debate is whether the fox kōan should be interpreted literally for its affirmation of causality and denial of noncausality or interpreted paradoxically from the standpoint of the unity of causality and noncausality based on the deeper significance of the relation between opposites. The extent of the debate may seem rather surprising given the apparent clarity and simplicity of Pai-chang's pivot word—*pu-mei yin-kuo*—but it is generated by the complexity of the case narrative, which falls into two divisions. First is the tale of spirit possession containing the exchange between the fox/monk and the abbot—or between the former and the current Pai-chang—which culminates in the release from transfiguration and burial. The second division is the demonstrative encounter in which Huang-po challenges Pai-chang's pronouncement of the meaning of causality and gains the master's approval.[1]

Furthermore, the kōan narrative harbors several interconnected levels of paradoxicality. These levels can be categorized as the *textual* level—what is explicitly stated in the case record, especially in the first division—and the *contextual* level that is primarily reflected in commentaries explicating concealed yet more comprehensive meanings implicit in the second division, including the paradoxical relation between divisions. The *textual* paradox is that in verbally denying causality the old monk is victimized by karma and must endlessly suffer its effects—yet in

67

hearing Pai-chang affirm the impact of causality he finally becomes free. Thus the conceptual negation of bondage to cause-and-effect results in its perpetuation whereas the affirmation results in liberation. The *contextual* paradox is based on the notion that falling into causality results not from denying karma, as in the literal view derived from the textual paradox, but from negating the inseparability of karma and transcendence—that is, by doing exactly what the literal view insists is incorrect. As Shibayama argues in his modern commentary on the *Wu-men kuan:* "An infinitesimal discrepancy is at once a vital difference, poles apart, and you are turned into a fox and fall into hell."[2]

Contours of the Philosophical Debate

The debate between literal and paradoxical readings revolves around two distinct hermeneutic maneuvers, each of which can be understood as an outgrowth of a compelling stream of Buddhist thought. One maneuver is that, in diametrical opposition to what the first division of the kōan says about the need for a strict adherence to causality, most commentaries argue that causality and noncausality are one and the same. The paradoxical view based on the contextual level emphasizing the nondual relation between the first and second divisions tends to see enlightenment as transcendent and unbound by karma. This view aligns the fox kōan with the stance of many other kōan cases that derive their significance from the basic Mahayana doctrine of the emptiness of conceptual categories. But a consistency with *śūnyavāda* thought leaves the commentaries open to the charge of fostering a morally ambiguous or even antinomian ideology that seems to contradict Pai-chang's motto—"no work, no food"—as well as his monastic rules dealing with the requirement of vigilantly maintaining an ethical outlook based on an uncompromising commitment to a communal work ethic.

The second hermeneutic maneuver is Dōgen's apparent reversal from his enthusiastic support of the mainstream paradoxical line of interpretation to his renewal of a literal reading. This shift is hailed in some quarters, particularly by Hakamaya Noriaki's Critical Buddhism, as a reawakening of the spirit of early Buddhist thought. But it also leaves Dōgen open to the charges of inconsistency and a betrayal of Mahayana philosophical ideals. Although the literal reading seems to negate paradoxicality by upholding a strict, incontestable denial of noncausality and assertion of causality as the only principle holding sway before, during, and after enlightenment, it is actually driven by the textual paradox in the kōan's first division. This view seems consistent with the early Buddhist doctrine of the universality of cause-and-effect and also helps eliminate an unintended sanctification of defilement that may result from the equalization of transcendence and delusion in the contextual paradoxical reading. Nevertheless, supporters of the literal interpretation must deal with the central question: in the context of a thoroughgoing affirmation of causality, what happens to the status of noncausality, which is traditionally associated with the attainment of enlightenment?

The literal view argues that both causality and noncausality are invariably bound by the causal process. The paradoxical view maintains that both causality and noncausality are inherently liberated from cause-and-effect. To some extent, the shifting between polarized perspectives among the commentaries results from the topsy-turvy, upside-down, duplicitous world of Zen rhetoric in which insults are praise and slaps are acts of kindness—a world in which masters deliberately revise source dialogues and commentaries with creative, critical comments about what the participants could, should, or would have said. An important aim of the fox kōan is to dramatize this impasse. And while both the literal and paradoxical interpretations strive for a comprehensive view of conditioned, impermanent reality, each side contributes to a heightening of the conceptual dilemma, thereby generating an additional sense of twofoldness.

Yet the significance of the philosophical debate is not just that it reflects a rhetorical game of one-upmanship in order to defeat arbitrary viewpoints. Rather, it reveals how the kōan draws on the force field of bivalent fox imagery to construct a multilevel message about the Zen approach to morality and society. One level of the message associated with the literal reading emphasizes the role of monastic order in a universe where religion was strictly regulated by government and Buddhism was severely criticized by Confucian moralism. The other level associated with the paradoxical reading evokes the authentic transcendental Zen maverick who moves freely in and out of a legalist system. The dominance of the paradoxical reading indicates that Zen was eager to stress freedom; but the forcefulness of Dōgen's rebuttal suggests the complementary concern to emphasize restraint. Traditional commentators do not deliberate on how an indebtedness to the force field of fox imagery shapes their arguments and discloses Zen's attempt to construct an ethical standpoint in light of the morality expressed in popular Buddhist religiosity. But by borrowing the exorcism motif from fox folklore, Zen seems to acknowledge a lacuna in its approach to overcoming evil karma—that is, a deficiency in defining the processes of repentance, absolution, and restitution for transgressions and sins committed. This chapter and the next examine the antisupernatural philosophical debate in relation to the Zen institutional structure and its place in traditional and modern society. Chapter 5 highlights the issue of repentance in connection to the folklore force field.

One side of the problem raised by the fox kōan is that if enlightenment is considered to transcend karma through a denial of causality or an emphasis on noncausality, as the paradoxical view implies, this can lead to a diminishing of the ethical imperative or even a disdain for social responsibility—that is, a state of moral laxity often referred to in Zen Buddhism as acting like a "wild fox spirit." But if enlightenment is never free from karma, as the literal view suggests, then a so-called buddha or realized master might appear no more elevated than the unenlightened person who is likewise considered to possess the innate, universal Buddha nature. This can result in a state characterized as "wild fox drool or slobber," that is, blind obedience to a leader without ever actualizing genuine freedom or creativity. In both cases the effect is a sense that ethical regulations do not need to be followed—either because one has falsely transcended and left behind the necessity for rules or because they are considered mere behavioral constraints which, even if strictly enforced, cannot hope to result in the anticipated goal that is conceived as an emancipation from such mundane requirements. On the dilemma in interpreting the significance of adhering to the Buddhist precepts in the training program, the postscript to the *Wu-men kuan* cautions:

> To observe the rules and regulations is to tie yourself up without a rope. To act with carefree abandon regardless of consequences is to behave like the heretics and demons. To illumine the mind in solitude is the specious path of Zen quietism. To let your will prevail and ignore the effects of karma is to plunge headlong into the [wild fox] den. To be vigilant and never obscure [causality] is to walk in chains with an iron yoke. To discriminate good and evil is to wander between heaven and hell. To have a Buddha view and a Dharma view is to be enclosed by two iron mountains. . . . Now, tell me, what will you do? Strive ceaselessly to attain realization here-and-now or your regrets will continue eternally![3]

Thus on both sides of the dilemma there may appear the irregular, self-indulgent implications of the wild fox—even as authentic masters break out of conceptual constraints or moral restrictions to become foxes in the positive sense attributed to patriarchs ranging from Śākyamuni to Bodhidharma and Dōgen.

What, then, is the correct or—if it is misleading to speak of correctness versus incorrectness—the appropriate Zen view of causality in relation to noncausality? The Zen standpoint, as a "special transmission outside the scriptures," is at once parasitic on and uncommitted to several prior interpretations of a cluster of doctrines expressing the basic Buddhist view of the multiplicity of causal and conditioning factors that determine all aspects of phenomenal reality. These doctrines—including the twelve links of dependent origination (Skt. *pratītya samutpāda;* C. *yüan-ch'i;* J. *engi*), the five *skandhas* or aggregates of human existence, impermanence, and karma—derive from the principle expressed in the *Majjhima Nikāya:* "This being, that arises; / This not being, that does not arise." Or in a longer rendition: "When this is, that is / This arising, that arises / When this is not, that is not / This ceasing, that ceases."[4] Yet the fundamental question throughout the history of Buddhist thought concerns how enlightenment—that is, the realm of the nonarising of causality or noncausality—comes to bear within the all-pervasiveness of causality. If enlightenment is conditioned by unenlightened practices stemming from the realm of causality that prepare for its attainment, then it never escapes from bondage to causality. But if enlightenment is supposed to be understood as unconditioned, then the universality of the causal process is vitiated by the central doctrine for which the analysis of causality has been undertaken. In a dialogue in *Siddhartha* between the the hero and Gotama, Herman Hesse encapsulates the dilemma: "You show the world as a complete, unbroken chain, an eternal chain, linked together by cause and effect," Siddhartha says before leaving the teacher. "But according to your teachings, this unity and logical consequence of all things is broken in one place. Through a small gap there streams into the world of unity something strange, something new, something that was not there before and that cannot be demonstrated and proved: this is your doctrine of rising above the world, of salvation. With this small gap, through this small break, however, the eternal and single world law breaks down again."[5]

Each of the subsequent standpoints in the development of Buddhist thought strives in its own way to express a middle path or compromise vantage point that accounts for the arising of "something strange, something new" or for the nonarising of causality in the "single world law" of

causality. The Sarvāstivādan Abdhidharma analysis of the factors of phenomenal existence (dharma), for example, emphasizes a basic bifurcation
between various causal factors operating in the realm of conditioned reality *(saṃskṛta)* and the transcendence of conditioning or the realm of
the unconditioned *(asaṃskṛta)*, which is based on the attainment of nirvana associated with space *(ākāśa)* and the extinction *(nirodha)* of desire.[6] This view suggests a binary opposition—a firm line of demarcation
between causality and noncausality—implying that if one realm prevails,
the other cannot apply. Thus even though the Abhidharma view is associated with the rejection of noncausality, in a sense it too supports the *pu-lo
yin-kuo* standpoint for understanding enlightenment, which indicates
that the charge of antinomianism haunts this perspective as well. The
hermeneutic situation is more complex than this however, because the
attainment of the unconditioned state implies a recognition that the duality of causality and noncausality results from an epistemological act of
discrimination—based on one's ability (or inability) to perceive reality
correctly, not on an ontological distinction. The attainment of
noncausality in this transcendental, epistemological sense suggests that
the opposition of causality (which rules in the realm of samsara) and
noncausality (understood as the inverse of causality which rules in the
realm of nirvana) is overcome. Strictly speaking, neither answer, causality
or noncausality, is either wrong or right.

The Mahayana *śūnyavada* philosophy—expressed in the paradoxical
formulas of the *Heart Sutra* in the *Prajñāpāramitā Sutra* collection,
"form is emptiness, emptiness is form," and those of the
Mulamādhyamakakārikā, "the limits of nirvana are no different than the
limits of samsara"—starts with a recognition of a pervasive ontological
nonduality.[7] This view breaks down any sense of bifurcation, not merely
by equalizing causality and noncausality, or conditioned and unconditioned dharmas, but by exposing both realms as conceptual constructs
empty of autonomous own-being *(svabhāva)*. According to the *śūnyavada* view, causality is from the start really noncausality—which is not
the opposite or absence of causality but the perpetual overcoming of the
dichotomy based on a realization that whatever is governed by causal
laws reveals itself to be innately insubstantial. According to Nāgārjuna
(*Mulamādhyamakakārikā* 24:16–18): "If you perceive the existence of
the existents in terms of self-nature, then you will also perceive these existents as noncausal conditions. . . . You will also contradict [the notions
of] effect, cause, agent, performance of action, activity, arising, ceasing,

as well as fruit. . . . We state that whatever is dependent arising, that is emptiness."⁸ To think otherwise—to remain committed to a belief in the substantive reality of causal existents—is a delusion that perpetuates an attachment to a false sense of causality. The aim of early Mahayana *śūnyavāda* thought (Mādhyamika and the *Prajñāpāramitā Sutras*) is to refute this distinction by demonstrating its illogicality. For Mādhyamika neither/nor thinking, the cause-and-effect nature of so-called conditioned reality cannot be shown: if the effect is part of the cause, then these are not two separate phenomena; and if the effect is separate from the cause, then there is no clear connection between them. At the same time, nirvana cannot be understood as lying beyond causality—in that on some level it is an effect stemming from conditioning (the meditative path)—and yet it is not simply a part of causality because it represents freedom from the conditioning process.

Later developments of Mahayana thought in East Asia, such as the Hua-yen (J. Kegon) doctrine of the harmonious interpenetration of forms with forms (C. *shih-shih wu-ai;* J. *jiji-muge*), suggest a paradoxical affirmation of phenomenal reality, or the realm of causality, as the manifestation of noncausality or emptiness. This standpoint discloses a realm in which "the real [is] harmonized, or the world in which actuality attains harmony in itself." Harmony arises "because of [the] mutual reflection of all activities—as in a room surrounded by mirrors, the movement of one image causes the movement of the thousand reflections."⁹ The Hua-yen standpoint is in accord with the *śūnyavāda* view of the identification of polarities based on an ontology that surpasses the distinction of causality remaining separate from noncausality. But instead of stressing that causality is from the start really noncausality, it stresses the reverse view: noncausality is really causality that functions as the locus for the manifestation of the noncausal.

Thus Abhidharma thought has a dualistic implication about the relation between causality and noncausality but culminates in a philosophy of nonduality. Mahayana thought (both *śūnyavāda* and Hua-yen), by contrast, stresses nonduality but without sacrificing altogether an awareness of duality, which continues to be a viable perspective on a lower level of understanding or in dealing with the realm of samsara. The underlying connection between the higher and lower standpoints is the conviction that the enlightened person—who according to the *Wu-men kuan's* fox kōan verse commentary sees causality and noncausality with a "single eye," or from a vantage point that unifies opposites in terms of nonduality—has a middle-way perspective that views causality for what it is: at once a form of bondage and of liberation. The main Mahayana rationale for the conjunction of nonduality operative in the realm of nirvana and of duality operative in the realm of samsara is the theory of the coexistence of Two Truths: the absolute or ultimate truth *(paramārtha)* of nonduality and the relative or conventional truth *(samvṛiti)*, which ideally functions in the world of duality as an expedient means (Skt. *upāya;* C. *fang-pien;* J. *hōben*) or heuristic device to disclose the transcendental. The two truths represent a provisional but, in the final analysis, collapsible distinction between alternative perspectives that depend upon one another and become intertwined. According to Nāgārjuna (*Mulamād-hyamakakārikā* 24.10): "Without relying upon convention, the ultimate fruit is not taught. Without understanding the ultimate fruit, freedom is not attained."[10]

From the Mahayana perspective, causality is noncausality because cause-and-effect cannot be proved and noncausality is causality because even nirvana is subject to conditions. But in collapsing the distinction between causality and noncausality, it is necessary to create another distinction in terms of two levels of noncausality: one level is the logical opposite of causality, which is denied independent status by virtue of a paradoxical epistemological identification of thesis and antithesis; the other is the realm ontologically prior to and beyond the distinction of causality and noncausality, a liberation from all categories, a state of transcausality based on awakening to emptiness *(śūnyatā)* or suchness *(tathatā)*. Yet the freedom from categorization is inevitably considered to function in terms of one of the categories that are paradoxically identified. Mādhyamika thought tends to identify the opposite categories by emphasizing the side of noncausality in refuting causation as a logical category. In the next stage of Mahayana thought—the Hua-yen and T'ien-t'ai (J. Tendai) sects in China and Japan, which are associated with the doctrines of *tathāgatagarbha* and original enlightenment thought—the tendency is to equalize opposites by emphasizing the side of causality in that all causal phenomena, just as they are by virtue of their original Buddha nature, are already characterized by the transcendence or nonarising of causality.

Yet when the inseparability of the realms of the conditioned/causality and the unconditioned/noncausality is asserted, a subtle but crucial question remains: If causality and noncausality are identified, to which side of the nondualistic equation is the distinction collapsed when the nonduality of the two truths is realized and spiritual freedom attained? Is it to the side of causality as the locus of noncausality, as in Hua-yen, or to the side of noncausality, as in the *śūnyavada* view of the emptiness of the conceptual constructs of causality and noncausality? In other words, does the equalization suggest what Dōgen calls the naturalist heresy—that causality is considered from the standpoint of fundamental reality to be part of noncausality? This might be taken to imply that one is already free from the effects of causality and thus does not have to make an effort to attain purification by overcoming deficiencies through sustained effort and acts of repentance. Or does it suggest the equally problematic deterministic position that noncausality is equalized on the side of causality? This implies that one may never be able to attain freedom from causality no matter how much effort is exerted and thus there is no imperative by which one feels compelled to reverse the tendency toward irresponsible behavior. In either case, the moral implications of the inevitability of karmic retribution and the need for repentance in the genuine sense are lost. So that while the fox as a target for vilification is very much present, the other side of vulpine imagery as a bivalent symbol for redemption is absent. The basic question of whether either viewpoint fosters a slippery slope to antinomianism has not been solved, therefore, but arises again and again in various structures and restructures.

The traditional paradoxical commentaries on the fox kōan seek to heighten the impasse and then to collapse or bypass the dilemma, though these are very different modes of establishing nonduality. "Collapse" suggests an active synthesis of opposites; "bypass" suggests dispensing with the dilemma itself by negating or dismissing its significance. But in either case, the rhetorical strategy typical of the kōan tradition is to bring the conceptual impasse to its breaking point in order to inspire an experiential breakthrough that "smashes all barriers," according to the *Wu-men kuan* preface, and leads intuitively and instantaneously to the paradoxical reconciliation of polarities. There are numerous kōan cases that follow a pattern in forcing a double bind whereby one can neither utilize nor reject—neither support nor refute—the use of language. In the *Wu-men kuan* collection of forty-eight kōans, nearly one-fourth of the cases repeat a double-bind pattern in which the impasse is carried to an extreme breaking point.[11] In case 32, for example, an outsider or non-Buddhist questions the Buddha: "I do not ask about the spoken, I do not ask about the unspoken." And when the Buddha just sits there, impassive and silent, the outsider declares his own enlightenment inspired by the Buddha's comportment.[12] In case 43, Master Shou-shan holds up a bamboo stick before the assembly of monks and says: "If you call it a bamboo stick, you will be clinging to names; if you do not call it a bamboo stick, you will be ignoring the facts. So tell me, what do you call it?"[13] In case 19, Nan-ch'üan responds to Chao-chou's question of whether one should try or not try to seek knowledge of the Tao by saying: "Tao does not belong to knowing or not-knowing. Knowing is illusion, not-knowing is blankness."[14] Moreover, Te-shan is known for the saying (apparently a locution borrowed from the legal system in which a magistrate hearing a case can dish out punishment on the spot): "If you answer correctly, I will give you thirty blows of the stick; if you do not answer correctly, I will also give you thirty blows of the stick!"[15]

The double bind is further evoked in three consecutive kōans in the *Pi-yen lu* collection (cases 70, 71, and 72) in which Pai-chang demands of his disciples: "Keeping your throat, mouth, and lips shut, how will you speak!"[16] Pai-chang is apparently satisfied with the first two answers, by Kuei-shan and Wu-feng respectively, even though they give opposite responses: the former tells him, "Please, Teacher, why don't you speak!"; the latter says, "In that case, why don't you shut up!" The commentary on the first case praises Kuei-shan in ironic, demythological fashion as a tiger who is "sprouting horns as he emerges from the wild weeds (without doubt, he is extraordinary *[chi]*) / In the realm of the wizards, spring ends and the flowers fade and wither." But of the third, unsatisfactory response to the basic challenge the commentary says: "On Ta-hsiung Peak Pai-chang snapped his fingers in vain."

These cases show that for many kōans paradoxicality is not the source of, but the answer to, the conceptual dilemma concerning binary oppositions between speech and silence, or meaning and meaninglessness, whereby the polarity of problem / resolution is itself dissolved by the act of heightening the degree of the impasse. The double-bind pattern is applied not only to the question of how to use language but also to a variety of issues in which the need to confront a desperate deadlock concerning conceptualizations that are blocking enlightenment is considered a pivotal liberating experience. For example, the *Wu-men kuan* prose commentary on case 6 in which the silent Śākyamuni, holding a flower, transmits the dharma to the smiling Mahākāśyapa reads: "If you say that the true dharma can be transmitted, then the yellow-faced old man with the loud voice deceived simple villagers. But if you say that the true dharma cannot be transmitted, then why was the transmission to Mahākāśyapa approved?"[17]

Were the typical double-bind pattern applied to the dilemma in the fox kōan, a likely scenario would involve a master admonishing a disciple who claims an awakening experience: If your enlightenment is beyond causality, then you are nothing but a wild fox. And if your enlightenment is bound by causality, then you still have wild fox drool around your lips. Now tell me, what is your enlightenment? An appropriate response in this hypothetical dialogue might range from silence to a demonstrative gesture or even to a wild fox utterance in a positive, authentic sense of outwitting the master's question—such as "How much fox drool can you swallow (or spit out)?" or "Go back to hiding in your fox den before I club you with my staff!" In other words, it is to be expected that a Zen kōan dealing with the issue of causality would exaggerate the impasse concerning causality and noncausality to the breaking point and deliberately leave us without a single, simple, straightforward solution.

The *Ts'ung-jung lu*, for example, reports a dialogue overheard by Tao-yüan who is disturbed because two monks misunderstand the meaning of causality. According to this account, one monk says of the ancient fox/monk or former Pai-chang: "Since there is no obscuring causality, why is he not yet released from the fox body?" The other monk responds: "As this itself is not falling into causality, when was he ever transfigured into a wild fox body?"[18] Tao-yüan becomes alarmed—apparently because both sides of the discussion are rooted in an inappropriate understanding of noncausality: the first question stresses ironically that since causality always prevails, there was no need for transfiguration; the second question reaches the same conclusion based on the opposite contention that ultimate reality is noncausal. Tao-yüan then travels to a hermitage in the bamboo forest on Mount Huang-po, but while crossing a valley stream he is suddenly enlightened. After informing his master with tears falling down his cheeks, he writes the following verse: "Not falling, not obscuring, / For monks or laypersons there are no taboos; / The behavior of a commoner is the same as a king's, / There is no enclosure or covering; / A staff can be either horizontal or vertical, / The wild fox enters the lair of the golden lion."

Despite his misgivings about the monks' dialogue, according to the interpretation of the dilemma in Tao-yüan's verse paradoxicality means that the opposites are collapsed or fully reconciled to form a harmonious union: we note here the images of the identical behavior of commoner and king, the staff that is horizontal or vertical, and the merging of the wild fox and golden lion. In the same vein, a modern Japanese commentator suggests that Pai-chang's two-sided exclamation about Huang-po—"the barbarian has a red-beard" and "the red-bearded barbarian"—reflects a complete paradoxical synthesis of opposites: the former phrase indicates the realm of causality, conditioned reality *(engi)*, and practice *(shū)*; the latter phrase indicates the realm of noncausality, emptiness *(kūkan)*, and realization *(shō)*.[19] Another recent commentator compares the paradoxical reading to the modern logical formulation of Nishida Kitarō's notion of *zettai mujunteki jiko dōitsu* (absolute contradictory self-identity), which equates all opposites based on a philosophical dialogue with Kantian epistemology and Husserlian phenomenology on the relation between subjectivity and objectivity.[20]

But in many traditional commentaries the impasse is not dissolved altogether but is bypassed—purposefully taken to a new level of complexity in order to further confound—as commentators try to outfox one another as well as the participants in the source dialogues. According to the *Ts'ung-jung lu,* for instance, "Those who understand the teaching of the vehicles even slightly can see this [answer to the kōan] clearly. But even though they have shed their hairy [fox] hide, they still have fishy skin." Another verse commentary in this text suggests: " 'Not falling,' 'not obscuring,' they haggle, / Too stubborn to stop their drooling." On the question of the phrase "red-bearded barbarian," it is important to note *Wu-men kuan* case 4, in which Huo-an surprisingly asks, not why Bodhidharma's beard is red but, "Why is it that the barbarian from the west has no beard?" To this the *Wu-men kuan* comments: "Do not try to discuss your dreams / In front of a fool; / [He says,] The barbarian has no beard: / How this just obscures the clarity!"[21]

Yet for the fox kōan—referring now just to the kōan record taken literally in itself and not to the prose and verse commentaries that take the debate in a different direction—the emphatic affirmation of causality and denial of noncausality in the first division may at first glance appear to be anything but an ambiguous, open-ended, deliberately inconclusive dialogue between a master and disciple, thus departing from the double-bind pattern exemplified in the hypothetical scenario discussed here. Rather, the kōan seems altogether clear in presenting a straightforward affirmation of the inexorability of karmic causality in a way that is vastly different from other kōans that valorize paradoxicality. The literal reading does not merely construct an antithetical standpoint in the sense of representing a duality in opposition to nonduality. It expresses a simple, unambiguous philosophy that eliminates any concern with the debate about duality versus nonduality. In its denial of noncausality, the kōan is to be distinguished from the Hua-yen view of causality as the locus of the noncausal—as well as the Abhidharma distinction between conditioned and unconditioned realms—because here there is no reference to the validity of the standpoint of noncausality from any perspective.

Why does the kōan in the literal reading reverse centuries of Mahayana argument in seeking accord with basic Buddhist doctrines concerning universal causal laws? The key to understanding this issue is that the narrative in which Pai-chang emerges as the hero/savior has a profound resonance with the master's role as a strict, no-nonsense moralist and disciplinarian who refutes self-indulgent tendencies that may derive from the equalization of causality and noncausality in the various Mahayana standpoints. The construction of the image of Pai-chang, the moralist, helped Zen complete a transition of values pertinent to an intellectual environment strongly influenced by Confucian ethics in which all religions were regulated by government supervision through legislation including times of proscription. This view of the meaning of the kōan is further supported by the fact that in Japan thinkers as diverse as Dōgen, the puritanical monastic, and Ikkyū, the licentious poet, stress that denying the effects of causality *(hatsumu inga)* is one of the greatest problems facing the Zen practitioner.

The Monastic Institution: The Context

The moral issue underlying the debate between literal and paradoxical interpretations indicates that the kōan narrative expresses a much more complex and multilayered message than is suggested by a purely abstract discussion about karma and causality—however compelling and persuasive, even in their perplexity, the arguments may prove to be. The debate about causality reflects the concern of the Zen sect near the beginning of the Northern Sung era with crafting a moral message which strikes a balance between, on the one hand, strict legalism that adheres to rules of monastic purity and, on the other, spiritual transcendence that is unrestricted by any regulations. The polysemic, multifunctional image of the wild fox, demythologized in a way that is inextricably linked to popular mythology, enabled Zen to walk a fine line between orthodoxy and subversion that had an effective appeal to—while at the same time seeking to go beyond—some of the concerns of Confucian ethics that came to be ritually integrated into Buddhist monasticism based on the charismatic authority of patriarchal abbacy.

Part of the message about monastic morality is conveyed by the fact that packed into the brief anecdotal kōan passage are numerous indicators of key factors of the Zen institutional system probably established in the Sung but attributed retrospectively to the works of T'ang patriarchs, especially Pai-chang's rules. The main ritual factors indicated in both the kōan narrative and monastic rules are liturgical, ecclesiastical, and pedagogical elements: the role of sermons in the daily routine; the process of lineal transmission; the function of monastic leaders like the rector of the Monks' Hall; the prominence of ceremonies including clerical funerals; and the need for the expulsion of monks who commit offenses against the *saṃgha*. These features show Pai-chang—not necessarily in the sense of a historical personage, as this cannot be verified, but as an icon standing for Zen monastic order—to be both revolutionary and conservative. Some of the features reinforce the image of Pai-chang upholding the mantle of the Ma-tsu style of pedagogy based on spontaneity and incongruity in manner and speech. The use of pivot words as a key to lineal transmission in encounter situations—deriving their effect from wordplay, paradox, and irony—as well as the role reversal in Huang-po's slap reveal Pai-chang as a charismatic, antiauthoritarian figure who sets a paradigm of "wild Zen" in the positive sense. Although the kōan commentaries generally endorse the standpoint of nonduality and paradoxicality—and although he was the leading disciple of Ma-tsu, known for his affirmation of everyday activity in the saying "this very mind is buddha" (C. *chi-hsin shih-fa;* J. *sokushin zebutsu*)—a literal reading of the narrative enhances the image of Pai-chang as a specialist in monastic discipline who tamed the antistructural activities known as "wild fox Zen."

Furthermore, according to traditional sources (whose historiographic accuracy is now being challenged because they date from at least two centuries after the time of the events), Pai-chang was responsible for developing the innovations that molded the Zen monastic system. He is said to have composed the first set of Zen rules, the *Ch'an-men kuei-shih*, advocating rituals that revolve around the deeds and words of "a spiritually perceptive and morally superior" abbot who guides his disciples by exemplary behavior and a variety of instructional methods. These methods include not only formal sermons and open debates with the entire assembly in the Dharma Hall but personalized pedagogy in the abbot's quarters referred to as a Vimalakīrti-like "ten-foot-square" room (C. *fang-chang;* J. *hōjō*).²² The *Ch'an-men kuei-shih* first appeared as a passage appended to the hagiography of Pai-chang in the *Ching-te ch'uan-teng lu,* although nearly all the material in this version is included in different sequence in the section on Pai-chang in the monk biography text, the *Sung kao-seng-chuan, chüan* 10, published sixteen years earlier in 988.²³ The *Ch'an-men kuei-shih,* sometimes referred to by Dōgen and other commentators as the *Hyakujō shingi* (C. *Pai-chang ch'ing-kuei*) or *Hyakujō koshingi* (C. *Pai-chang ku-ch'ing-kuei*), apparently became the inspiration for the much lengthier sets of monastic codes: the *Ch'an-yüan ch'ing-kuei* (J. *Zen'en shingi*) of 1103 and the Yüan-dynasty rules text completed by Te-hui and others of Mount Pai-chang in 1338 (variously dated 1333), the *Ch'ih-hsiu Pai-chang ch'ing-kuei* (*Chokushū Hyakujō shingi*).²⁴ ("Pai-chang" in this case, five centuries after the patriarch, refers to the mountain temple.) Although these texts, especially the latter, claim to have been modeled on the *Ch'an-men kuei-shih,* both contain much more detail meticulously defining and regulating the duties of the abbot and the daily functions of monks. Moreover, both texts reflect the absorption of elements of popular religiosity, including rules for the enshrinement of local earth gods in the *Ch'an-yüan ch'ing-kuei* and tantric prayer formulas and explanations of cultic buildings in the *Ch'ih-hsiu Pai-chang ch'ing-kuei.* (For the sequence of Pai-chang texts see Table 1.)

Table 1. Sequence of Major Text Containing Either Pai-chang's Rules or the Fox Kōan

988: *Sung kao-seng chaun*	portions of rules text
1004: *Ching-te ch'uan-teng lu*	*Ch'an-men kuei-shih* plus anecdotes on communal labor [kōan not included]
1036: *TKL*	fox kōan" [rules text not included]
1100: *Tsung-men tung-yao chi*	fox kōan [basis of WMK version]
1144?: *Pai-chang yü-lu*	fox kōan [no rules text, but anecdotes on communal labor]
1147: *Cheng-fa yen-tsang*	fox kōan cited
1166: *Hung-chih sung-ku pai-tse*	fox kōan commentary
1224: *Ts'ung-jung lu*	fox kōan commentary
1228: *WMK*	fox kōan commentary
1244: *Shōbōgenzō,* "Daishugyō"	fox kōan commentary
1252: *Shōbōgenzō,* "Jinshin inga"	fox kōan commentary

The *Ch'an-men kuei-shih* text may well be apocryphal. Certainly the picture of Pai-chang as the founder of the first pure Zen monastic system does not emerge in his biography in the *Tsu-t'ang chi* of 952, over a hundred years after his death, or even in the main section on his life in the *Ching-te ch'uan-teng lu.* The roots of the work can be traced to a couple of short texts produced at the Mount Pai-chang temple in the 880s that were integrated into the *Sung kao-seng chuan* and then the *Ching-te ch'uan-teng lu* a century later. These late-ninth-century bridge texts seem to reflect a series of dramatic political upheavals affecting the temple: its devastation during the severe suppression of the Hui-ch'ang era (841–846) at the hands of imperial authorities under Wu-tsung; the subsequent Huang-ch'ao rebellion; the rebuilding of the temple; and the establishment of new, productive associations with the government administration.[25] As the detailed instructions provided in the later rules texts are not present, it appears that significant parts of the text attributed to Pai-chang were either lost or anachronistically ascribed to his inventive hand.

All of the Zen hagiographies of the period have been increasingly challenged from a historiographic standpoint due to the gap between the patriarch's life and the publication of his recorded sayings. As John McRae points out: "We simply do not have any texts relevant to the earliest period of classical [T'ang era] Ch'an that did not pass through the hands of Sung dynasty editors, who either knowingly or unknowingly homogenized the editions they produced."[26] Their pseudohistorical materials, however, remain important for their symbolic meaning. The voluminous records that started to appear in the postsuppression Sung era sought to establish the sect's credentials on several levels: Zen's role as a scholastic tradition that generated its own body of literary classics revolving around kōan studies and patriarchal hagiographies in competition with Neo-Confucianism; a monastic meditative tradition centered on the sermons and lectures of a charismatic abbot guiding disciples in sustained *zazen* practice in competition with T'ien-t'ai Buddhism; and a vigorously expanding sect that was able to assimilate indigenous shamanistic/animistic folk religions in competition with popular schools of Buddhism (especially those based on bodhisattva worship) and Taoist cults while maintaining a rational, antisupernatural attitude that actively dispelled this influence.

At the time of the composition of the kōan and rules text in the early eleventh century, Buddhism was still in the process of rebounding from the period of the Hui-ch'ang-era persecution when 4,600 monasteries were closed, 260,000 priests and nuns were returned to lay life along with 150,000 dependents of monasteries (including slaves) who had escaped taxation and forced labor for the state, and 40,000 small temples and shrines were demolished or converted to other uses.[27] Thus an overriding concern amid the various goals sought, influences absorbed, and audiences targeted was the need to react to criticism from Neo-Confucian scholar-officials as well as from regulatory government edicts and legislation purporting that, from the standpoint of society's well-being, Buddhist monastic training could result in an antinomian form of behavior further exacerbated by the irreverent, sometimes scatological, tone of Zen rhetoric. The Zen ambiguity about issues such as supernaturalism, when applied to ethics, might appear to overlook the need for moral restraint.

The main reason for the suppression, according to a passage from the edict of 845, was that the monasteries were parasitic on society—which requires collective economic cooperation—while offering little or no social benefit in return: "Now, when one man does not farm, others suffer hunger, and, when one woman does not weave, others suffer from the cold. At present the monks and nuns of the empire are numberless. . . . The monasteries and temples are beyond count, but they all are lofty and beautifully decorated, daring to rival palaces in grandeur. None other than this was the reason for the decline in material strength and the weakening of the morals."[28] In addition to being isolated in lofty and lavish mountain retreats, the Buddhists were also vulnerable to charges of moral laxity and a general sense of degeneration involving, for example, real estate holdings and the sales of transmission certificates and robes. Arthur Wright notes: "These misgivings [about growing strength] were deepened by widespread abuses of clerical privilege, by mass retreat into holy orders to escape the corvée and taxation, and by the wholesale and often fraudulent transfer of land-titles to the tax-exempt monasteries and temples."[29] The corruption in Buddhism at this time was directly linked to several interrelated factors. One was the decline of the Vinaya—which was due, in turn, to the haphazard way that monastic guidelines were applied in China where "monks did not regard the Buddhist rules as categorical prescriptions. Holiness, for them, was a matter of degree and faithfulness to the precepts that depended on an individual's capacity."[30] Another factor was the flourishing of an entire class of irregular, intinerant monks, tricksters, wonder-workers, soothsayers, magicians, exorcists, and healers who, living on the performance of magical arts among the people, "benefitted from the fiscal advantages granted to regular monks and enriched themselves by displaying their magical talents . . . [for] economic motives."[31] In response to many of these factors, a broad socioethical criticism is expressed in the Sung era by the leading Neo-Confucian philosopher Chu Hsi. Despite personal friendships and the borrowing of ideas from leading Zen thinkers, Chu Hsi was a severe critic of Buddhism as a nihilist philosophy that failed to see "the specific distinction between right and wrong in each and every human situation."[32]

The observations of Dōgen during his journey to China—an outsider with the idealistic intent of finding true Buddhism—confirm that nearly four centuries after the suppression the general state of corruption persisted. Dōgen reports in the *Shōbōgenzō* "Shisho" fascicle that his mentor Ju-ching, considered beyond reproach because of his commitment to an uncompromising approach to training, was able to criticize convincingly the misdeeds of others: "My late master and old buddha admonished [the abbots of] all corners of the world: 'In recent times, there are many who are called patriarchs indiscriminately, wear the dharma robe, let their hair grow long, sign their monastic title, and consider this the symbol of success. What a pity! Who can save them?' "[33] With characteristic hyperbole Dōgen further comments on the corrupt sale of transmission certificates: "It is rare to see any one among [the Sung practitioners], not even one among a hundred thousand, who knows the document of succession and the transmission of the dharma. This is the sign of the gradual demise of the way of the patriarchy under heaven."[34]

Pai-chang's Rules: The Text

The implication of the external and internal criticisms is that Buddhist detachment was directly linked to a moral decline originating inside the monastery gates and then spreading outside the temple compound to infiltrate society at large. Terms such as "wild fox Zen" were coined by the compilers of Zen records in order to dissociate the sect from deficient moral implications. With the use of these terms as sarcastic epithets for self-criticism—or at least for criticism of a deficient sector within the religious community—Zen was eager to demonstrate that it was an institution governed by rituals that provided order and civil decorum in addition to a reverence for ancestors through funerals and memorial worship of deceased patriarchs. A century and a half after the suppression, Zen emerged as the dominant sect—apparently by enabling the rulers to feel that they had succeeded in getting Buddhism to govern itself. Although a contemplative tradition, Pai-chang's rules proclaimed that Zen was not escapist or otherwordly but a strictly ritualized discipline in a carefully self-regulated monastic community that used training in meditation to contribute to society by maintaining a self-sufficient economy through communal manual labor rather than by begging or accepting tax-exempt status. An anecdote in *Pi-yen lu* case 35 makes an interesting contrast between monks who spend their time in encounter dialogues and those who adhere to Pai-chang's work ethic by carrying out their chores with dedication and determination: Have you not heard about how Chi-tsang of Cheng-chou asked a monk, "Where have you just come from?", and the monk said, "The South." Chi-tsang asked: "How is the Buddha Dharma upheld there?" The monk replied: "They are constantly engaged in dialogues (C. *wen-ta;* J. *mondō*)." Chi-tsang said: "How does that compare with the way we sow paddy fields and reap in rice?"[35]

As expressed in the succinct rules text (see Appendix II for a complete translation)—which is probably a pastiche made from fragments of earlier texts that are also included in the *Sung kao-seng chuan*—Pai-chang's approach marked a dramatic shift in Buddhist monasticism from an institution supported by mendicant monks who were prohibited from engaging in labor as an "unhealthy" method of gaining livelihood. The original prohibition was undertaken partly because labor might lead unwittingly to the taking of life and partly because it would become a source of distraction in an otherwise isolated world of contemplation. Pai-chang made the transition to a form of Buddhist monasticism that was praiseworthy from society's standpoint because it was sustained by laboring monks who would never give up working lest they risk the extreme form of punishment: banishment.[36] The view of Zen as a self-reliant and self-contained system was further enhanced by the image of the master tilling soil in his old age—even to the point of fasting when his disciples hid his tools one day in jest. Pai-chang saw practical activity as an expression of enlightenment and apparently insisted, according to his rules text and stupa inscription, that labor requirements must be the same for all members of the religious community regardless of rank. Pai-chang's approach was not, however, a Vinaya revival: he did not attempt to resurrect or purify early Vinaya rules as a key to restoring discipline; nor did he abandon them in pursuit of Mahayana ideals. In the opening passage, Pai-chang remarks that the Zen sect is not confined by Hinayana (Lesser Vehicle) rules. And when asked about the Mahayana (Greater Vehicle) precepts his response is to "seek a middle ground that synthesizes the spirit of these teachings without being limited to either approach." The Zen approach at once synthesizes and remains independent from the major vehicle traditions.

The fact that the *Ch'an-men kuei-shih,* like the fox kōan, was published for the first time in the early eleventh century has raised critical questions about whether Pai-chang's role as a legalist was exaggerated or even fabricated. There have been two main theories concerning the function of the rules text in the development of Zen monasticism. According to Martin Collcutt, Pai-chang was probably not the first Ch'an legislator and his was not the original written Ch'an code. "It seems likely, however," Collcutt argues, "that some of the Ch'an regulations had been drawn up before Pai-chang's time. He probably did little more than lend his name to a developing corpus."[37] Collcutt also points out the "remarkable silence" concerning support for Pai-chang's role as the premier legislator in other relevant sources—including the writings of his contemporaries and disciples as well as his memorial inscription—a silence that calls into question his position in the development of the Zen system.[38] Griffith Foulk takes the remarks about the absence of sources a step further. But he reaches the opposite conclusion by arguing that the idea of Pai-chang forming an "original" or "pure" form of Zen based on communal labor is false because pure Zen training never really happened. Foulk considers this picture of the sect to be one of several examples of Zen inventing its own tradition retrospectively, based on the model of other Buddhist sects, for "the very features deemed most characteristic of Ch'an monastic practice were neither unique to nor invented by the Ch'an school."[39] According to Foulk, Zen monasticism was very similar to the T'ien-t'ai school. And the ideal image of monks refusing contributions while working the fields for their survival flies in the face of voluminous reports of sumptuous monastic compounds supported by elite patronage. Thus Collcutt maintains that Pai-chang did not create Zen monasticism, which he believes was in practice long before, while Foulk argues that the Zen of communal labor as characterized in the *Ch'an-men kuei-shih* was a fabrication.

Although both the rules and kōan texts published thirty-two years apart may well be apocryphal and historiographically misleading, their significance lies mainly in showing that the need to establish procedures

Figure 13. An icon of Pai-chang holding the ceremonial fly whisk used by Zen masters on ritual occasions—a throwback to shamanistic purification devices. This statue is located at Saijōji temple in Odawara, Kanagawa prefecture, Japan. Its mountain location is known as Daiyūzan (or Ta-hsiung Peak in Chinese) after the original Chinese site of Pai-chang's temple.

for identifying and eliminating moral deficiencies—represented by the symbolism of the fox—was associated with Pai-chang, whose ceremonial portraiture was venerated as one of the three central figures in the Sung patriarchal pantheon alongside Bodhidharma and Hui-neng. Thus the term " 'Pai-chang' came to mean either the man, the mountain, the book, or the rules therein," although numerous books of rules were generated by the mountain long after the patriarch's demise.[40] Though in many ways he was a less prominent figure than the first and sixth patri-

archs—even less prominent than his teacher Ma-tsu who devised the en-
counter-style dialogues as well as his "grandson" Lin-chi known for his
tough-minded approach to training—Pai-chang-as-icon may have played
the most important role in constructing an image of Zen that was effective for purposes of legitimation and evangelism in the Sung (whether or
not the Pai-chang monastic order depicted in Zen records took place in
the early ninth century prior to the period of suppression).

A passage in the *Sung kao-seng chuan* states: "Throughout the empire,
the Ch'an school is like a wind making the grass bend. The independent
cultivation of Ch'an methods owes its origins to Pai-chang Huai-hai."[41]
According to the *Ch'an-men kuei-shih*, Zen monks did not abide in independent monasteries prior to Pai-chang but banded together in small
cloisters that were governed by larger temple compounds of the Lü (J.
Ritsu) school. The term "Lü" technically means Vinaya. But while the
"Lü school" undoubtedly refers in some cases to monasteries that specialized in precept training as the main path to enlightenment, the desig-
nation was somewhat of a misnomer.[42] In the T'ang/Sung periods it
mainly referred not to a specific kind of practice but to a monastic social
structure—that is, to private temples with a transmission system based
on heredity. The separation of Zen, as a "lineal school" (C. *tsung-men;* J.
shūmon), from the Lü school environment attributed to Pai-chang indicated, therefore, that Zen had come to be supported as the leading public
sect with a transmission process based on the transfer of the abbot's charisma and spiritual cultivation to the most worthy disciple, whether he
was from inside or outside the temple.[43] Pai-chang's rules and related
texts borrowed heavily from the transmission methods of other Buddhist
behavioral models—including early Vinaya rules on the seniority of
monks and the need for constant vigilance during meals and other occasions as well as Lü school (public temple) ceremonial practices. The Zen
rules also relied on non-Buddhist models—including Confucian patriarchy, imperial court practices concerning the geography of sacred compounds and the layout of the buildings therein, and the *Book of Rites*
codes of ritual etiquette.

For Buddhism in India, Brahmanist behavioral purity associated with
spiritual authenticity and authority often became a standard for Buddhist
saints trying to establish their credentials. In China, however, Confucian
family morality centering on the role of the patriarch was a primary
model for constructing the image of the Zen abbot.[44] According to
Pai-chang's rules, the abbot is considered a "living embodiment of spiri-

tual transformation" and the key to the efficacy of rituals (rather than traditional Buddhist precepts, prayers, sutra readings, or repentance ceremonies). Thus he is to be "revered as the Honored One" (C. *tsun;* J. *son*), a term usually reserved for the icon of a buddha or bodhisattva in other sects. This renders altogether unnecessary the Buddha Hall, the central building in other sects' compounds, as a place for the worship of idols—although it is unlikely that the call for the deletion of this structure, so crucial for public occasions including fund-raising, was ever actually put into practice. Instead the rules give priority to the role of the Dharma Hall as the site of convocations led by the abbot. The rules further assert that the abbot's room is not merely a bedroom but a place to indoctrinate special students who are invited to "enter the room [the abbot's personal quarters]" (C. *ju-shih;* J. *nyushitsu*) for private, intensive instruction—often, but by no means exclusively, personal meetings. Another important building in the Zen compound is the Monks' Hall. It is here that the disciples, considered to have equal responsibilities with rank based purely on the length of residence, as in the early Vinaya, dwell together, keep their meager possessions, eat two frugal meals while contemplating the dharma, practice meditation for undetermined lengths of time, head off for communal manual labor that sustains the monastery, and take short periods of sleep lying in the position of the Buddha's final repose that are referred to not as slumber but as "reclining meditation." In Pai-chang's text, as well as in some of the later codes, the length and rigor of *zazen* practice is not strictly regulated by the abbot but is left up to the discretion of the monks themselves.

The main features of Zen life depicted in Pai-chang's rules and vividly dramatized in the fox kōan are several kinds of lectures and instructions, delivered during the daily routine, which give the abbot the opportunity to demonstrate that his charisma is based not merely on office but on a finely crafted, routinized sense of spontaneity and intuitive insight in a Weberian sense. The rules call for the abbot to present two lectures a day: one in the morning and one in the evening (or after the midday meal). Both are accompanied by debate with the rank-and-file who line up for the lecture in the Dharma Hall in a manner influenced by court procedures as well as Confucian learning and Taoist discussion groups. In the later codes, especially the *Ch'an-yüan ch'ing-kuei,* both kinds of lectures are carefully scheduled for a list of half a dozen days each on a monthly schedule and are also sometimes regulated by topic, though memorials and other special services could also be slated. Although

Pai-chang's rules require lectures twice a day, it seems likely that this policy was never carried out. At least the records of Zen sermons are far sparser, although it is possible that some sermons were delivered but not recorded or that the twice-a-day model was executed in the presuppression period but not in the Sung. And although the *Ch'an-men kuei-shih* does not make a distinction between the styles of the morning and evening lectures—both are referred to as *shang-t'ang* (J. *jōdō;* "entering the hall [and ascending the high seat]")—by the time of the *Ch'an-yüan kuei-shih* there were two different kinds of sermons. One kind, the lecture that the assembly is attending when the fox/monk first appears in the kōan, is a formal sermon delivered during the daytime in the Dharma Hall—this is known as *shang-t'ang* and is also referred to as *ta-ts'an* (J. *daisan,* literally "major convocation").[45] Although the *shang-t'ang* was a very controlled setting for the delivery of brief sermons about the inner meaning of dialogues, the masters were also free to make jokes that defamed the patriarchs in order to shock and stir the minds of their listeners. In the fox kōan there is no indication of the content of the sermon, but apparently it was sufficiently moving to attract the attention of the penitent *fei-jen.* One imagines that it had something to do with the topic of karmic retribution and repentance.

A second kind of presentation is an informal sermon given in the evening either in the Dharma Hall or the abbot's quarters during which, in the kōan, Pai-chang explains the reason behind the events leading up to the cremation. This is known as an "evening convocation" (C. *wan-ts'an;* J. *bansan*) or "minor convocation" (C. *hsiao-ts'an;* J. *shōsan*), although in some cases there are technical differences between these terms.[46] Huang-po's confrontation and slap of Pai-chang—appropriate in this informal setting—would no doubt be unthinkable during the formal sermon when the master's word and will rule. Finally, the kōan alludes to another style of instruction cited in the rules text: private instruction (*ju-shih*) that takes place on an unscheduled basis after or between the main sermons in the abbot's room or in an impromptu setting, such as another room or a hallway outside one of the main chambers, as when the fox/monk stays behind to make his confession and ask for a turning word.[47]

Another important aspect of the monastic ritual dimension of the kōan narrative is the issue of the cremation and funeral desired by and provided for the fox/monk, the propriety of which became a major bone of contention in several prominent commentaries. Like other features of the Zen institution, the procedures for funerals involving the placement of the body, libations, and invocations became standardized in the monastic codes of the Sung, particularly the *Ch'an-yüan ch'ing-kuei*.[48] Although funerals are not mentioned in the *Ch'an-men kuei-shih*, their association with the monk credited with forming the first monastery code is a significant feature of the kōan record. When Buddhism first came east it was severely criticized by Confucianism for failing to acknowledge the value of ancestor worship by advocating the use of cremation, a practice imported from India that was considered a sacrilege in China. Eventually Buddhist cremation gained acceptance—in part because much of the ritualism surrounding it was reoriented in terms of Confucian practice, first for priests only and then for laypersons as performed by temples.[49] The practice of lay funerals became very popular in China and then in Japan, where there was no precedent (or competition) for a ceremony burying and honoring the dead.[50] In time the religion has come to be labeled derisively as "funeral Buddhism" (*sōshiki Bukkyō*) because in many ways performing burial ceremonies is the major—or for some lay believers the only—social function it serves today. Funerals are sometimes ritually performed for donations in a way that has at least a trace of corruption and discrimination, especially against the outcast community or dispossessed sectors of society.

During the transformation of the role of Buddhism vis-à-vis funerals, the Sung Zen rules texts, ever mindful of encroaching government regulations, tried to standardize the performance of burial rites with unsparingly detailed instructions. In the fox kōan, the reaction of concern and dismay expressed by the assembly of monks to the announcement of the funeral by the senior monk in charge of rules—which occurs even before the vulpine corpse is discovered by Pai-chang—suggests the careful procedures for the deployment of these ceremonies a century before the *Ch'an-yüan ch'ing-kuei*. Thus it is not surprising that the cremation and burial of the fox has been challenged by several commentators including Dōgen and, centuries later, Hakuin. Dōgen's objection recognizes in a way that legitimates—even in the act of criticizing and suppressing—the role of shape-shifting powers. From the standpoint of the kōan's folklore structure, the fox/monk's wish to be buried shows the desire of *fei-jen* entities to gain recognition from the realm they are barred by their status from entering. Dōgen and Hakuin would probably not care to object if they did not believe in the presence of *fei-jen*. That they take the *fei-jen* status of the ancient monk seriously shows that the kōan expresses an encounter and domestication of the marginal, subversive elements of folklore imagery through the symbolism of the funeral. This stands in contrast to William LaFleur's comment: "Invisible bodies, no doubt by definition, can be done away with much more easily than visible ones. The liquidation of them involves no bloodletting, leaves no corpses, and calls for no official inquiry."[51]

The main point of convergence between the kōan and rules texts is that Pai-chang's treatment of the spurious priest in eradicating the vulpine shape very closely resembles the *Ch'an-men kuei-shih*'s call for the swift, severe punishment of unruly troublemakers and deceivers through public humiliation and in some cases expulsion and excommunication:

> But anyone who makes a false claim of membership or is insincere or deceitful in his practice and abuses his office, or anyone who breaks the rules or otherwise stirs up trouble among the dedicated members of the monastic community, will be punished by the rector, who is to remove the imposter's possessions from the Monks' Hall and to expel and excommunicate him from the compound. This severe discipline serves as a warning to the other monks of the humiliation and disgrace that will ensue should a similar offense be committed.[52]

According to the rules text, there are four main reasons for the severity of the punishment that goes beyond the traditional Vinaya in what is considered a banishable offense: it leaves the rank-and-file uncompromised; it keeps Zen's reputation for purity in practice from being besmirched; it avoids public litigation; and it prevents news of the affair from spreading to other temples. In short, this approach makes clear that Zen is not a subversive "wild fox" cult that succumbs to a violation of morality based on ignoring or not falling into causality. Indeed Zen is grounded on a rigorous ethic—of not neglecting or not obscuring causality—that could be effective in taming deficient moral tendencies for the sake of the greater social good. Of course, the main factor underlying the last three rules is a concern with the way the sect appears to outsiders.

But there is an important difference between the texts: in the kōan, the fox/monk beseeches Pai-chang for assistance in liberating him from karmic retribution and the master responds with understanding and compassion; in the *Ch'an-men kuei-shih*, however, there is little room for caring about the offender's transformation. This indifferent attitude as evidence of the behavior of Zen abbots is supported by an incident referred to as the "Gemmyō Ostracism" that occurred at the time of Dōgen's trip to Kamakura—a crucial period for the Critical Buddhist interpretation of his approach to moral issues in the 12-fascicle *Shōbōgenzō*.[53] According to the traditional biographical sources, particularly the *Kenzeiki*, which no doubt contain exaggerations and fabrications in relying in large part on a confession from the offending priest's ghost, Dōgen tried to persuade the shogun, Hōjō Tokiyori, to restore the throne's rule rather than create a military regime.[54] Denied this request, he retired to Eiheiji—considered an act of great integrity that earned him the ruler's respect and a generous land grant. Although Dōgen declined the grant, one of his disciples, Gemmyō, who had been a member of the Daruma-shū sect that was discredited due to its antipreceptual approach, decided he would receive it anyway. Apparently Gemmyō felt that there really was no such thing as a corrupt act based on the doctrine of the purity of original enlightenment. Enraged, Dōgen drove the pupil (and one of his companions) away and ordered his seat on the meditation platform torn out and destroyed, the ground under the chair dug seven feet deep, and the earth discarded. Reports of Dōgen's demonstration of fierce independence apparently caused the master to gain greater popularity.

While the legalist approach of the rules text and Dōgen's dismissal of his impetuous student has the merit of preserving a sense of purity by firmly avoiding reprehensible behavior, it expresses little concern for the dynamics of repentance and redemption: the process of transforming transgressions into meritorious or praiseworthy behavior. The kōan does raise the existential issue of repentance. But in doing so it turns to the standpoint of supernatural, exorcistic, other-power religiosity in which the *fei-jen* cannot accomplish a moral/spiritual transformation without reliance on the master's powers. Thus there appears to be a shortcoming in both the *Ch'an-men kuei-shih* stressing expulsion and the fox kōan stressing exorcism in coming to terms with the issue of making amends and redeeming transgressions. And as we shall see, this issue is not treated effectively in the paradoxical line of interpretation either.

The Mainstream Paradoxical Reading

From the paradoxical standpoint, there are several limitations in a literal reading of the kōan's view of causality—a reading that focuses on the ritual, institutional dimension associated with Pai-chang's rules text. First, an emphasis on requirements for external work and administrative chores, while typically used in utopian communities as a means of preventing misdeeds and providing moral uplift, can all too easily lead to a state of spiritual lassitude—the problem that is the opposite of antinomianism—if it is lacking in a sense of inspiration or spiritual transcendence. Second, this emphasis must be seen in the context of the overall intent of Zen discourse—as expressed in hagiographic literature about the exploits of the eminent T'ang patriarchs—on maintaining creativity and ingenuity precisely by cultivating a "crazy" approach to Zen (C. *kuang-ch'an;* J. *kyōzen*) manifested in "strange words and extraordinary deeds" (C. *ch'i-yü ch'i-hsing;* J. *kigen kikō*). Zen masters, celebrated for their "divine madness," know when to follow rules and when to break them in order to enhance rather than violate the spirit that generated them.

The fine line of ambiguity separating authentic from inauthentic wildness is expressed in *Wu-men kuan* case 12.[55] Like other kōans such as *Pi-yen lu* 93, this case uses antisupernatural rhetoric against the background of bivalent fox imagery to show that problematic behavior lies not so much in acting in an eccentric or crazy way, which is often to be applauded, as in blindly following those who do so, which is nothing other than a state of salivating fox drool. According to the case record—known as "Jui-yen calls out, 'Master' "—Master Jui-yen (J. Zuigan), a disciple of Yen-t'ou (J. Gantō), has what seems like a disturbing habit. Every day he calls out to himself, "Oh, Master!" and then calls back an answer. "Are you awake?", he asks. And he responds, "Yes!" "Always be on guard, never be deceived by others," he cries. "No!", he answers. In an example of deliberate ambivalence, the kōan leaves us to wonder whether Jui-yen (who was known to have sat for long periods of meditation on a certain stone) is a fool who has perhaps lost his composure from too much isolation or a worthy successor to Pai-chang (who was known for sitting alone on Ta-hsiung Peak), as well as numerous other hermits and eccentric practitioners. The prose commentary makes two references to supernatural imagery that reveal the importance of the folklore force field for understanding this issue:

> The old master Jui-yen buys from and sells to himself. He dons the masks of many different ghosts and goblins. Why? Think about it (C. *chien;* J. *nii*)! There is the one who calls out, the one who responds, the one who is awake, and the one who is never deceived. But if you be-

come attached to any of these [as being real], that is an error. And if you try to imitate Jui-yen, your understanding will be that of a wild fox.

The last line uses typical antisupernatural supernaturalism to criticize the imitators of Jui-yen and is reinforced by the verse commentary: "Seekers of the way do not find the truth, / When they are entangled in discriminating consciousness, / Which is the cause of the endless cycle of birth and death, / Yet fools mistake this for the original person." But the final sentence of the prose commentary could also be interpreted to mean: "If you follow Jui-yen, you would realize that his understanding is that of a wild fox." Another interesting supernatural feature of the commentary is the use of the term *"chien,"* which is rendered here in a nonsupernatural way: "Think about it!"[56] The term is used in other Zen dialogues, such as *Wu-men kuan* case 40, as an injunctive to remind disciples to look at or listen to a situation carefully—so that other possible renderings include "Hark!" or "Listen!" A Zen master will frequently utter this term for emphasis or dramatic effect. But the term as it appears in the kōan commentary harbors an ambiguity in evoking the original folkloric meaning of the word, which refers to what a ghost becomes at death. In popular religious practice, the character for *"chien"* is written on a piece of paper that is then fastened to a doorway or gate as a charm to ward away ghosts and goblins (that is, *fei-jen*) from intruding on a dwelling. In this sense, the commentary mocks Jui-yen's dubious accomplishments even as it chides those who would inauthentically imitate his actions. It suggests that one should not follow Jui-yen: not only because that would be slavish imitation (fox drool) of a great master (a wild fox in the positive sense) but because he is not worthy of admiration (a fox in the negative sense).

Looking at the fox kōan in light of the paradoxical implications of supernatural imagery in *Wu-men kuan* case 12, the main problem with the literal, institutional reading is that the clear-cut conclusion emphasizing an either/or style of thinking at the textual level does not convey the real significance of the kōan or its complete view of causality. The literal reading overlooks the paradox played out in the first division of the case narrative in which the false view is punished according to the law of karma by perpetual fox transfiguration and the correct view is rewarded by release from retribution and the attainment of enlightenment symbolized by the priestly mortuary rites. Even so, the textual level of paradox seems—paradoxically—rather unparadoxical because one standpoint is asserted to the exclusion of the opposite standpoint. To avoid a reductio ad absurdum on this issue, the vast majority of traditional commentaries focus on accentuating the elusive quality of the case by reversing the strict assertion of cause-and-effect and highlighting the provisionality and ultimately the indistinguishability or nonduality of the not-falling and not-obscuring responses.

In addition to the passages from the *Wu-men kuan* and "Daishugyō" already cited, the commentary in the *Ts'ung-jung lu* maintains: " 'Not falling,' 'not obscuring,' it is just a matter of words, / Too stubborn to stop drooling."[57] The text also suggests that haggling over "not falling" and "not obscuring" is like "entering a nest of complications."[58] Furthermore, a natural image in Ling-yüan's verse commentary on the kōan—"Pai-chang lifted the autumn moon all the way up over the peak"—seems to show "how the ultimate freedom and enlightenment of Zen transcends rigidly divisive either/or thinking in terms of yes and no."[59] According to one of several dozen Sung verses on the fox kōan (cited in Chapter 1) that follow the *Wu-men kuan* pattern of relativizing the two key terms, *pu-lo yin-kuo* and *pu-mei yin-kuo,* the difference between causality and noncausality is a matter of juggling equally delusory interpretive perspectives: "Not falling, not obscuring, / It is just a matter of interpretation; / If you know the clue to solve the puzzle, / Then there is no longer any hitch." Another verse approaches the issue of relativity from the holistic standpoint of causality embracing noncausality: "Ask about coming, and answer about going— / Both exhaust the process of causality; / He fell into a fox incarnation five hundred years ago, / But we are still transmitting the story from one to another to another."[60]

The link between the textual and contextual levels of paradoxicality is based on Pai-chang's liberating pivot word—*pu-mei yin-kuo*—at the climax of the first division and on Huang-po's irreverent slap as the key to the second division. (See Figure 14.) The pivot word is a linguistic device that navigates the border between the use of words and no-words—the boundary between what Tung-shan Shou-ch'u calls "dead words," which are discriminative and thus ineffective, and "live words," which are nondiscriminative and have the power to affect the listener profoundly.[61] The pivot word, "which reveals the speaker's degree of insight or which transforms the listener's mind at a crucial psychological moment," is mentioned in numerous recorded sayings texts, most notably the *Lin-chi lu* and Hung-chih's writings.[62] It functions as a transformative trigger

Figure 14. This calligraphy of *"pu-mei"* or *"fumai"* by Jiun illustrates the process of abbreviation in Zen discourse by which the kōan is reduced to a single phrase—"not obscuring"—which captures the full meaning of the case in contrast to elaborate discussions about metaphysical implications. From Stephen Addiss, *The Art of Zen: Paintings and Calligraphy by Japanese Monks, 1600–1925* (New York: Abrams, 1989), p. 155 (The Kinami Collection); permission courtesy of Stephen Addiss.

mechanism deriving from the Ma-tsu-style encounter dialogue—which can also be called "satori dialogue" because it captures the moment of spiritual transformation and lineal transmission—that brings about a spontaneous awakening of the participants by virtue of being intensely subjective (suited to the individual's needs) and eminently situational (reflective of a particular spatial-temporal context). First words are live words expressing a genuine understanding by plumbing the depth of the dead words expressing a deficient opinion and making a necessary alteration that transmutes their meaning in a way that is uniquely suited to the person involved.

When extracted from the context of the fox kōan narrative, the pivot word can function as an abbreviated, nonconceptual headword or "main phrase" (C. *hua-t'ou*; J. *watō*) device as proposed by Ta-hui as an object of contemplation. It also resembles Yün-men's notion of the one-word barrier. The phrase from the final dialogue, "red-bearded barbarian," also functions as a main phrase. These approaches emphasize the transformative capacity of even a simple syllable, word, or phrase—such as Chao-chou's "*Wu* (J. *Mu*)" in *Wu-men kuan* case 1. The pivot word understood in this way reinforces the literal, unambiguous reading of the kōan case. In this sense the phrase appears able to stand on its own and need not refer to the narrative background for its impact. (See Figure 15.)

But the pivot word, designed to prompt sudden awakening in a way that fits an individual's needs in a particular context, is not limited to one meaning: it has a polysemic implication.[63] As the personal psychology or the context changes, so too does the utility of the specific pivot-word phrasing. Pai-chang's pivot word affirming the role of karma captures the correct view of enlightenment and refutes the incorrect view. But even though not-obscuring causality appears to be the incontestable conclusion of the kōan's first division, that is not necessarily the intention of the linguistic device. In changing one of the characters in the four-character source phrase from *lo* (J. *raku*) to *mei* (J. *mai*), the phrase does not express an absolute truth but functions as a provisional, pedagogical tool apropos to the moment and subject to multiple, often contradictory, interpretations that are ultimately reconcilable in that each discloses an aspect—with integrity in and of itself but still only an aspect—of a Zen holistic realization. The pivot word used in this way reflects the rhetorical function of bivalence in allowing opposite interpretations to coexist and interact in a single phrase. Furthermore, Dōgen offers a metaphysical

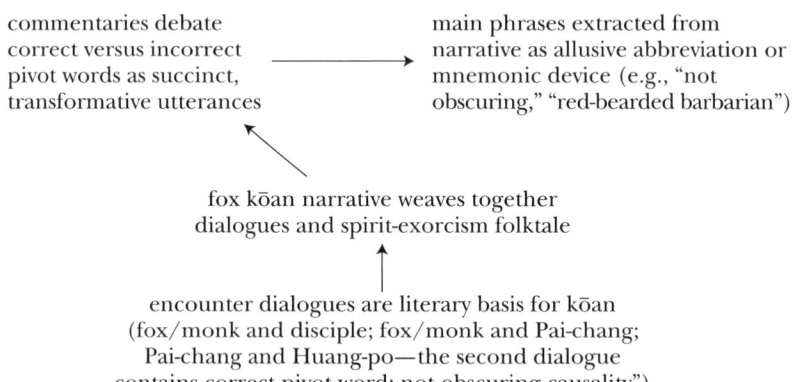

Figure 15. Flow chart of the main phrase technique. This diagram shows the connection between the fox kōan and the encounter dialogues, pivot words, and main phrases that it contains.

view of the pivot word in the following verse commentary on the kōan. This commentary suggests that at the appropriate moment the entire natural world is manifested as a reflection of the fox/monk's release due to the effects of Pai-chang's utterance:[64]

> For saying, "A person of great cultivation does not fall into causality,"
> He was transfigured into an anomalous spirit, but he was not just another old fox.[65]
> On receiving a pivot word that released him from being an apparition,
> The mountains and rivers were instantly transformed as confirmation of his liberated state.[66]

Moreover, the concluding dialogue between Pai-chang and Huang-po suggests a contextual approach to the paradoxical nature of causality. Huang-po's challenging question and exaggerated gesture—a demonstrative style also associated with his disciple Lin-chi (known for his use of "shouts") as well as Te-shan ("thirty blows of the stick!")—imply that there is no accurate or even relevant understanding or expression of the issue. Since all answers are arbitrary and empty of conclusive meaning, causality is ineffable. In "Daishugyō" in the early, 75-fascicle *Shōbōgenzō* text, Dōgen takes the contextual paradoxical approach a step further by asking why Huang-po even referred to not falling as "incorrect," since not falling and not obscuring are neither correct nor incorrect. Both answers, Dōgen argues, must be understood in terms of their fittingness for the eras—the primordial era of Kāśyapa and the historical era of the T'ang, respectively—in which they were uttered. (He does not comment that one era is mythical and the other historical.) Thus the early Dōgen joins the commentaries by Sung/Kamakura masters Hung-chih, Yüan-wu, and Ta-hui, as well as by numerous modern Zen thinkers and scholars, which in varying ways consistently express the relativistic, nondualistic standpoint shown here. According to "Daishuygō": "Due to a fundamental misunderstanding, [the old man] was first transfigured into a wild fox body and then released from being a wild fox. And although 'not falling into causality' was incorrect in the age of Buddha Kāśyapa, it may not be incorrect in the age of Buddha Śākyamuni. Although 'not obscuring causality' released the wild fox body in the current age of Buddha Śākyamuni, it may not have been effective in the age of Buddha Kāśyapa."[67]

Huang-po's act of slapping his mentor in the midst of an eye-ball-to-eyeball confrontation is at once in accord with and a significant departure from the encounter dialogue tradition. In this approach an irreverent demonstrative gesture or utterance—a slap, kick, shout, or other rebuke, such as cutting off a finger, putting shoes on one's head, responding in tautologies or absurdities—can be used by the master to test, to taunt, or to elevate and inspire an unproductive or inflexible disciple. It is reported that during one of their first encounters Ma-tsu tweaked the nose of Pai-chang—one of the few disciples with the privilege of "entering the abbot's room"—so hard that it hurt.[68] Ultimately Pai-chang attained enlightenment when Ma-tsu, disgusted with his student's inability to answer a question, "drew himself up and shouted so loud that [Pai-chang's] ears were deafened for three days"—apparently a symbol for overcoming one-sided views (Skt. *dṛṣṭi*).[69] But Huang-po in the Hung-chou school's third generation sets the precedent for a gesture demonstrating the disciple's insight in a way that challenges and even surpasses the master, who is eager to acknowledge his own comeuppance and to applaud the student's newly established independence. Huang-po also mistreated his own disciple, Lin-chi, the school's third patriarch, whose enlightenment, in turn, was marked by striking his teacher.

Based on the ambiguity of the pivot word and the duplicity of the slap, the kōan commentaries' aim is to equalize opposites fully and flexibly by maneuvering through each side of the equation without attachment or bias from the standpoint of transcausality beyond dichotomization. According to Shibayama: "When 'not falling' and 'not ignoring' [or 'not obscuring'] are both transcended and wiped away, you can for the first time yourself . . . get hold of the real significance of this kōan. . . . What I want you to know is that Zen is alive and active in quite another sphere where it makes free use of both 'not falling' and 'not ignoring.' "[70] The commentaries avoid endorsing a naive or reductionist sense of oneness. Thus multiplicity is eclipsed not by a monistic stance but by the freedom to shift perspectives in a provisional fashion that continually overcomes limitations caused by fixed habits of mind. Since the pattern seems to be more a matter of bypassing the conceptual impasse than synthesizing or collapsing polarities, it may be misleading to compare the traditional commentaries to Nishida's *zettai mujunteki jiko dōitsu* formulation. For example, an attachment to the not-obscuring view of causality is challenged by the first part of the *Wu-men kuan* verse—"Not falling, not obscuring: / Odd and even are on one die"—and an attachment to the not-falling view of noncausality is overcome by the second half of the verse: "Not obscuring, not falling: / A thousand entanglements, ten thousand entanglements!"[71] Similarly, the introductory section of the *Ts'ung-jung lu* eliminates a fixation on the correctness of not-obscuring as a panacea by asserting: "If you swallow just one drop of fox drool, it cannot be spit out for thirty years."[72] The point about transcending any commitment whatsoever is taken even further in the Tokugawa era by Bankei. When asked by a disciple how to solve the difficult fox kōan, he responds: "I don't make people here waste their time on worthless old documents like that."[73]

An example of Sung doxology highlights the paradoxical relativity of opposite views left polarized in the two divisions of the kōan by reversing their sequence in the first and third lines—a feature seen in numerous verse commentaries—and suggesting a transcendence of the debate in the last two lines: "Not obscuring and not falling, / Did the old man make a great mistake? / Not falling and not obscuring, / This is obviously correct. / I explain this again to all of you, / Do you understand it now, or not? / A green mountain rising above the field, / A pilgrim traveling even beyond the mountain."[74] Several other verses stress: "There is no rope / So how can you tie yourself up?"

Why do these commentaries differ so drastically from the literal meaning? And what are the implications of understanding Zen's view of morality and the charges of self-indulgence in relation to fox imagery? One reason for the change probably has to do with a revival of the Hinayana versus Mahayana philosophical debates. The literal meaning at once seems to echo and negate by pointing out the contradiction in the Abhidharma separation of samsara, which is the realm of cause-and-effect, and nirvana, which is "not the result of anything. If [nirvana] would be a result, then it would be an effect produced by a cause. It would be [*saṃskṛta*] 'produced' and 'conditioned.' Nirvana is neither cause nor effect. It is beyond cause and effect. Truth is not a result nor an effect. It is not produced like a mystic, spiritual, mental state, such as *dhyāna* or *samādhi*."[75] By reversing and perhaps violating the literal meaning of the kōan, the Sung commentaries invariably argue for a self-contradictory identity of bondage and freedom, or causality and noncausality, and reinforce the Mahayana doctrine of the nonduality of emptiness. The distinction between opposites is seen as empty and transcendent of dichotomization. This recalls Nāgārjuna's dismantling of the logical categories of causality and identification of dependent origination and emptiness in terms of the middle way (*Mulamādhyamakakārikā* 24.17–18, cited earlier). Similarly, Hung-chih writes: "To debate 'not falling' and 'not obscuring' / Is to get lost in entanglements, / And remain captive to the discriminating mind / How absurd this is; / If you liberate yourself from this / You will be unobstructed and harmonious."[76] Moreover, in the *Wu-men kuan* the affirmation and denial of causality as well as the fox and human existences are ultimately equalized, for the monk is said to have experienced his fox incarnations as a joyful blessing: "If you can see this with a single eye [of insight] you will understand how the former head of Pai-chang monastery cultivated his five hundred incarnations."[77] The point seems to be that not falling into causality is itself a complete realization of causality and that not obscuring causality is itself a complete realization of causality.[78]

But the issue of why Pai-chang could be considered to "cultivate" (or, in some renderings, "enjoy") his fox lives raises an important question about the ethical implications of karma—a question that is not directly addressed or resolved in the commentaries emphasizing paradoxicality. One possibility is that the former Pai-chang transfigured as a bodhisattva-like mission. This reading, however, conflicts with the statement that he has been punished and also appears to represent an overt endorsement of supernaturalism that the kōan commentaries otherwise dismiss or sidestep. The suggestion that he valued his fox lives, even if expressed tongue-in-cheek, may be effective in highlighting nonduality not as a state of noncausality transcending causality but as rooted in the side of causality as a realm already encompassing noncausality. Yet this approach is problematic and inconsistent with regard to its lack of a moral injunction. If causality contains its own transcendence by embracing noncausality, as the majority of commentaries suggest, then wherein lies the imperative to follow the Buddhist precepts as a path of moral purification?

And is there not a problematic implication, leading to misbehavior, in that the equality of causality and noncausality eventually results in a privileging of the not-falling standpoint that may be oblivious to ethical restraints—a view that was originally denied by the kōan narrative and then refuted for various reasons by both the early and later *Shōbōgenzō* texts? Once the standpoint of noncausality takes priority, one could be led either to the path of Buddha or to its opposite, the path of Māra, which is paradoxically identified with Buddha, as suggested in the *Vimalakīrti Sutra* passage, "If the bodhisattva treads the wrong ways (C. *fei-tao;* J. *hidō*) he enters the Buddha path," or in Ikkyū's famous saying that "it is more difficult to enter the realm of Māra than the realm of Buddha."[79] An aphorism from the *Lin-chi lu,* a recorded sayings text that rejects animism and positive uses of supernatural imagery, asserts the priority of the not-obscuring view in a way that accords with the literal reading of the fox kōan: "If [a seeker] cannot distinguish Māra from Buddha, then he has only left one home to enter another. He may be dubbed a karma-creating sentient being, but he cannot be called a true renouncer of home."[80] This admonition warns of the danger in the Zen paradoxical view that "unconsciously lapses into Māra in the name of Buddha and yet believes itself to be practicing Buddha."[81]

4 · Deep Faith in Causality

"Delusion," "enlightenment"—just fox-words fooling Zen monks everywhere.

— Daitō

The multilevel ambivalence in Dōgen's writings, which embrace contradictory philosophical interpretations of the fox kōan as well as a flirtation with and repudiation of animistic beliefs in fox veneration, reveals the powerful effects of the folklore force field affecting the unfolding of the kōan tradition in the formative Sung Chinese/Kamakura Japanese period. In the commentary on the kōan in the early, 75-fascicle *Shōbōgenzō* "Daishugyō" fascicle, which supports an equalization of karmic causality and the transcendence of karma in accord with standard Sung commentaries, Dōgen makes two interpretive maneuvers that are characteristic of his style of reading kōans. First, he argues for the enlightened status of all parties involved at every stage of their interaction. Dōgen asserts that the fox/monk spoke the truth in his original denial of causality and that these words, which in the narrative he regrets and repents, are of equal value to Pai-chang's maintaining the importance of not obscuring causality. Second, Dōgen recommends that the participants in the dialogue, including Master Pai-chang and disciple Huang-po, should ideally be able to continue their discussion beyond what is recorded in the case record. The combined effect is at once to cast doubt on as well as to praise Huang-po, the uncontested hero in most interpretations, for making the point that the fox/monk's understanding of *pu-lo yin-kuo* may not have been mistaken. By taking the mainstream view of the paradoxical identity of opposite responses to its logical conclusion in dismissing Huang-po as nothing more than a "wild fox spirit" for even doubting the ancient monk, Dōgen devises a novel way of bypassing—rather than collapsing—the basic hermeneutic dilemma of choosing between causality and noncausality. Yet his ironic tone leaves open the possibility that he is dissatisfied with the moral implications of the paradoxical view he seems to support for unconventional reasons.

The Literal Reading and Dōgen's Contradictory Interpretations

To combat the antinomian tendency in the mainstream standpoint, the "Jinshin inga" fascicle seeks to clarify the meaning of *pu-mei yin-kuo*, not as a logical opposite to noncausality, but as an all-encompassing principle—at once embracing yet distanced from phenomenal reality—with a distinct moral imperative based on a commitment to the principle of karmic conditioning and retribution. "Daishugyō" and "Jinshin inga" actually have much in common. Both are critical, for different reasons, of the "Senika" or naturalist heresy, which advocates the spirit's "return" to an original nature or primordial source and sees the release from the fox body as a symbol of the monk resuming his true nature. Both fascicles criticize the elements of superstition and supernaturalism in the kōan that may distract one from pursuing the dharma. Yet they also wonder why the case does not deal directly with the issue of the status of the fox/monk's rebirth after the time of his release, thereby questioning the veracity of Pai-chang's account of the death and burial. Although "Daishugyō" refrains from criticizing the ancient monk's view of causality that earned him punishment, the literal reading in the 12-fascicle *Shōbōgenzō* rejects the earlier position that "both transfiguration and release constitute the causality of the wild fox."[1] "Jinshin inga," composed near the end of his life when Dōgen apparently rewrote several fascicles from the 75-fascicle *Shōbōgenzō*,[2] remarks that seeing the states of not falling into and not obscuring causality as "one and the same" is a heretical (or non-Buddhist) view of naturalism that will inevitably result in "great misfortune."[3] "It is a pity," Dōgen writes, "that even though [Zen practitioners] encounter the true dharma of the Tathāgata correctly transmitted from patriarch to patriarch, they accept the views of those who would deny causality."[4] By negating causality in the name of transcending the opposition of causality and noncausality, this view violates basic Buddhist moral precepts and reverts to a dualistic contrast between the pure and impure, flux and serenity, and freedom from and subjection to causation.

Dōgen apparently felt that the paradoxical view had infected the practices of Buddhism in China. He was also concerned that the same deficient approach had infiltrated into some of the forms of Zen that were being introduced into Japan—particularly the Daruma-shū sect, which many of Dōgen's disciples at Eiheiji temple in Echizen province had first practiced. The Daruma-shū, denounced by Eisai in the *Kōzen gokokuron,* was proscribed in the 1190s (and its last temple in Yamato was burned down by rival monks from Kōfukuji in 1228) precisely because the Tendai church accused its leaders of not adhering to the precepts as a requirement for ordination. Although Japan did not experience a situation like the suppression of Buddhism during the T'ang, the government did regulate religion closely, especially regarding the use and abuse of supranormal powers. Dōgen's move to Echizen probably reflected a conflict with Tendai over the status of his Daruma-shū followers.

In "Jinshin inga," Dōgen criticizes the verse commentaries supporting the paradoxical view of several prominent Lin-chi (J. Rinzai) school rivals and Ts'ao-t'ung (J. Sōtō) school predecessors who had all been eminent abbots at T'ien-t'ung monastery where he studied in China. These figures include: Hung-chih, the compiler of the kōan collection that inspired the *Ts'ung-jung lu* and an ancestor of Ju-ching; Yüan-wu, the compiler of the *Pi-yen lu* based on an earlier collection by Hsüeh-tou; and Ta-hui, the main disciple of Yüan-wu and critic of Hung-chih whose kōan collection, the *Cheng-fa yen-tsang* (J. *Shōbōgenzō*), was a model for the 75-fascicle *Shōbōgenzō*—although Dōgen was very critical of this leading thinker from the Lin-chi sect who had been a major influence on the Daruma-shū.[5] Thus Dōgen refutes the three towering figures in Sung-era Zen for their lack of a genuinely dynamic approach to causality by affirming the transcendence of cause-and-effect.

The verse by Hung-chih, which is included in the *Ts'ung-jung lu* along with Wan-sung's interlinear comments, reads:

> A foot of water, a fathom of wave,
> For five hundred lifetimes of transfiguration, what could he do?
> "Not falling," "not obscuring," they haggle,
> Like poking their heads into tangled vines;
> Ah, ha, ha!

Get it?
If you are fully released,
You won't mind my babble;
The divine songs and sacred dances spontaneously create a har-
mony,
Let's clap our hands in the intervals and sing, "La de da."[6]

According to Dōgen, this approach overemphasizes the relativity of causality and noncausality, which are seen as inseparable conceptual entanglements. In the last few lines Hung-chih lapses into an annihilationist
position by disregarding cause-and-effect in favor of a spontaneous harmony—thus avoiding the issue of what happens to the *fei-jen* entity once
it experiences release.

Yüan-wu's verse, however, has the reverse problem in expressing a
standpoint that is eternalistic and yet is imbued with fatalist implications:

When fish swim, the water becomes murky;
When birds fly, their feathers fall off.
Everything is reflected in the polished mirror of causality,
Which is vast and universal as the empty sky.
For five hundred lifetimes he lived as a wild fox,
A victim of the law of causality affecting even a person of great cul-
tivation,
Striking like a bolt of lightning and raging like a fierce typhoon,
As unchanging as a brick of gold that has been purified hundreds of
times.[7]

Yüan-wu's approach seems more appropriate than Hung-chih's in emphasizing that the fox/monk was a "victim" who could not escape karma.
But even this reading has traces of denying cause-and-effect in identifying causality with the "empty sky." At the same time, it comes too close to
an eternalist position in viewing causality as an unchanging force that is
not affected by free will.

Ta-hui's verse epitomizes the naturalist heresy:

Not falling into and not obscuring causality,
Fit together like a stone resting on the ground;
On encountering an anomalous creature,
Pai-chang smashes an iron mountain to pieces;
Later he claps his hands and laughs approvingly,
Just like P'u-tai [J. Hotei] of Ming-chou.[8]

In Dōgen's interpretation, this approach remains trapped by the duality it claims to have surpassed. Ta-hui denies causality in asserting Pai-chang's ability to create a transcendence associated with the mirth of the "laughing buddha," P'u-tai. In a sermon for a bereaved lay follower and in other writings Ta-hui—often the object of Dōgen's sometimes scornful criticisms aimed in part at the defunct Daruma-shū sect—ponders the relation between two views of death: one based on karmic causation and retribution, for which merit accrued during this lifetime may lead to a Pure Land rebirth; and the other, its seeming philosophical opposite, in which there is a genuine Zen realization that "since there is no birth and extinction, and no cycle of rebirth, / There is neither changing nor destroying of the diamond body."[9] Ta-hui did not attempt to reconcile the two perspectives or explain the sequence of merit and emptiness. He left the issue of their relation open for further meditative questioning—an attitude that Dōgen would find problematic because in emphasizing the priority of an original state of enlightenment it recreates the equalization of causality and noncausality from the side of the former.

Critical Buddhist Methodology: A Critical View

What does Dōgen accomplish by reconstructing the debate about causality from the perspective of the priority of the otherwise discredited literal reading of the kōan? And what are the implications for understanding the role of supernatural fox imagery in relation to morality? It is not likely that Dōgen's interpretation of the kōan was merely an attempt to rehabilitate an early Buddhist standpoint that never existed in pure form in Japan. After all, he was probably not familiar with Pali literature (*Agonkyō*) or aware of the classical Hinayana versus Mahayana philosophical controversy as it is understood in historical studies today.[10] But he may have been receptive to the idea of a pure Buddhist ideology uninfected by the forces that dissipated Sung-era practice and similarly affected Kamakura Japan. There are two main interpretations of Dōgen's later standpoint. According to the majority of Dōgen scholars, the "Jinshin inga" and other fascicles in the 12-fascicle *Shōbōgenzō* were written, or in some cases rewritten, for novices who could not appreciate the subtlety of the paradoxical view expressed in the 75-fascicle text.[11] As a variation on this theme, some scholars suggest that Dōgen's later interpretation of the fox kōan was designed as a limited critique of the Lin-chi school, or of certain features in Chinese Zen, or of particular masters such as Ta-hui, although he also criticizes Sōtō ancestor Hung-chih. But they nevertheless find a basic continuity between the early and later standpoints based on the theory of the two levels of truth. According to Critical Buddhism, however, the 12-fascicle *Shōbōgenzō*, which mentions the doctrine of deep faith more than two dozen times, expresses a bold about-face on the doctrine of causality and a sweeping refutation of any trace of animism or antinomianism. And for Critical Buddhism these tendencies are very much related because they are rooted in original enlightenment thought *(hongaku shisō)*, which the paradoxical view still allows because of its preoccupation with maintaining an aloof, noncommittal, ambivalent outlook.

Critical Buddhism is concerned with two interrelated issues, one specific and the other broad. The specific issue pertains to the status of Dōgen's later writings: the existence of a separate, 12-fascicle edition of the *Shōbōgenzō* was long suspected but not confirmed until the discovery in 1930 of an important colophon in a manuscript of the last of the fascicles.[12] The general issue involves a far-ranging examination of the implications of traditional views of karmic causality for dealing with social problems in contemporary Japan. Critical Buddhism attempts to evaluate from a socially critical theological standpoint the philosophy of East Asian Buddhism as a whole in light of the question of its fidelity, or apparent infidelity, to a cluster of basic Buddhist doctrines concerning causality: doctrines including dependent origination, nonself, karmic retribution, an analysis of the causal and conditioning factors of all phenomena, and impermanence. For Hakamaya Noriaki the connection between these issues is that the interpretation of the fox kōan in the later fascicle represents a devastating criticism of metaphysically substantialist and morally deficient trends in original enlightenment thought that pervaded medieval East Asian Buddhism—including the kōan tradition. *Hongaku shisō*, which advocates a paradoxical unity underlying the diametrically opposed aspects of reality, including causality and noncausality, or conditioned and unconditioned realms, was particularly influential in Sung China and late-Heian/Kamakura Japanese religion, especially the Tendai church. The use of this ideology allowed aspects of naturalism, syncretism, and assimilation to distort Buddhist doctrines and social applications through contact and amalgamations with the indigenous traditions of Taoism, Confucianism, Shinto, shamanistic/animistic folk religiosity, and nativist ideologies. In this regard, Critical Buddhism admires the later Dōgen for criticizing folklore. But its approach totally overlooks or even suppresses the indebtedness of the 12-fascicle text to the force field of popular morality tale literature.

Thus the overall aim of Critical Buddhism stems from—but ultimately involves more than—studies of the *Shōbōgenzō* and leads to a debate about classical Buddhist doctrine and textuality. The movement began in the mid-1980s with a series of lectures and publications by scholars who were interested in the contemporary implications of Dōgen's view of karma. Their intent was to interpret the relevance of Buddhist thought for a variety of social discrimination *(sabetsu shisō)* issues affecting Komazawa University and its affiliation with the Sōtō sect as well as Japanese society as a whole.[13] Among these issues was the granting of Buddhist initiation names to the deceased based on the person's social rank—a practice that resulted in the unjust treatment of the outcast community and other minority groups.[14] Buddhism in Japan, particularly Sōtō Zen, had evolved over the course of history into a religious institution primarily concerned with funeral ceremonies—known as *sōshiki Bukkyō*—and it began to realize that it had been performing this social function in a reprehensible fashion, especially for the dispossessed classes.[15] Critical Buddhism was part of a widespread response to a sense of frustration and disappointment in Buddhism. As a modern religion Buddhism appears to be an anachronistic, authoritarian, dogmatic, and socially rigid institution by fostering discrimination in the name of resisting it, rather than a genuinely contemporary, progressive, and flexible advocate for justice and reform.

Critical Buddhism has tried to take discussions primarily concerned with the theoretical meaning of causality and reorient them in terms of the concrete question of how karmic theory is applied to the contemporary issue of discrimination against outcasts who have been defined traditionally by Buddhism as *sendara* (Skt. *caṇḍāla*): those too contaminated by deficient karma to ever attain enlightenment.[16] Critical Buddhism is probably best known for its bold claims that "*tathāgatagarbha (nyoraizō)* thought is not Buddhism" or that "Zen is not Buddhism."[17] But the real significance of such hyperbole lies in using Dōgen's change of heart *(henka)*—expressed in the later writings, especially his reading of the fox kōan—as a starting point to challenge *hongaku* orthodoxy that has perpetuated intolerance and tacit support for the status quo disguised by claims of epistemological nondiscrimination and ontological non-differentiation and dynamism. Hakamaya argues that Dōgen's critique in "Jinshin inga" reflects ethical principles in accord with early, pre-*hongaku* thought—whether or not Dōgen actually studied those texts—which serves as a model for Buddhist reform movements in post-war Japanese society plagued by nationalism and bias.[18]

Hakamaya contends that *hongaku* ideology—by denying causality based on a nondualistic doctrine, the real aim of which was to assimilate local animistic/naturalistic cults for hegemonic purposes—promotes a false sense of equality that mitigates the need for moral responsibility. Original enlightenment and related doctrines such as *tathāgatagarbha* and Buddha nature *(busshō)* espouse an uncritical syncretism that fosters in the name of universal, nondiscriminating compassion such problematic viewpoints as the notion of demanding social harmony *(wa)* at the expense of individuality and a tacit compliance with militarism. These attitudes are in turn supported politically by totalitarian and nationalist ideologies as well as intellectually by *nihonjinron* ("Japanese-ism") rhetoric that ends up abetting ethnic injustice.[19]

The basic weakness of *hongaku* thought is that because ontologically it does not allow for the existence of the Other—since all things are considered to arise on the basis of the single, undifferentiated, primordial *dhātu,* or topos or locus *(ātman)*—epistemologically and ethically it is incapable of dealing with the inevitably complex manifestations of Otherness that force concrete ethical choices. As Sallie King points out in discussing Buddha-nature doctrine: "The texts prized in East Asian Buddhist traditions have tended to emphasize such things as nondiscrimination (in the epistemological rather than social sense) and nonconceptual wisdom, which are difficult to reconcile with the complexities of resolving competing claims, for example, or balancing needs against resources, which require that one be very precise in distinguishing particulars, that one make informed judgments, and that one regard such activities as important and valuable."[20] That is, the *hongaku* and Buddha-nature doctrines lack a mechanism for making situationally specific, ethical judgments—and the result is an unreflective endorsement of inauthentic conditions. According to Hakamaya: "Although some interpret the doctrine of original enlightenment as a theory of equality because it claims to recognize the fundamental universal enlightenment of all people, in reality, this is a gross misunderstanding. In fact, the doctrine of original enlightenment, which in a facile way requires seeking out the fundamental unified ground of enlightenment, must be considered the primary source of [social] discrimination."[21] In Japan this means an acceptance, even support, for the "myth of Japanese uniqueness" and related nationalist/nativist/Nihonist rhetoric that has pervaded post-Tokugawa, especially prewar, intellectual life.[22] Zen, in particular, has often hidden its support for the status quo behind an elitist aestheticism based on the notion that everything reflects the Buddha Dharma *(zen'ichi-buppō)*.

As for the specific issue of Dōgen's text, most scholars agree that Dōgen initially exposed the limitations underlying *hongaku* thought in his famous "doubt" recorded in the *Kenzeiki* and other medieval sectarian biographies: why has every buddha throughout history been required to practice if, from the standpoint of original enlightenment, all beings are already enlightened by virtue of possessing Buddha nature?[23] This doubt, experienced at the outset of his career, is traditionally considered to have been resolved by Dōgen in terms of his critique—beginning with "Bendōwa," one of his first writings—of substantialist tendencies referred to as the Senika Heresy, which maintains the primacy and endurance of a soul despite the life and death of the body. Moreover, Dōgen's doctrines of the oneness of practice and realization *(shushō-ittō)* and the impermanence of Buddha nature *(mujō-busshō)*, especially according to the earliest Kamakura-era *Shōbōgenzō* commentaries by Senne and Kyōgō, stress the dynamic, here-and-now *(genjō)* dimension of *hongaku* thought. Dōgen rarely mentions let alone criticizes *hongaku* in his writings, although he often criticizes this ideology indirectly.[24] In fact, in the 75-fascicle text, particularly "Bendōwa," he occasionally uses other *"hon-"* compound terms favorably—such as *honshō-myōshū*, or original realization and marvelous practice. ("Daishugyō" is an exception.) He is said to have constructed a creative compromise throughout his career by indirectly refuting problematic aspects of original enlightenment while reorienting its basic implications in terms of the continuing process of realization. In the traditional view, these doctrines are expressed in fascicles such as "Genjōkōan" and "Busshō," which form the core of the 75-fascicle text. (These are two of the first three fascicles in the standard editions.) They were developed by Dōgen in the middle part of his career—especially from the mid-1230s to the early 1240s when he lived outside Kyoto and then left to settle in Eiheiji temple in the Echizen mountains. The 12-fascicle version of the *Shōbōgenzō*, compiled posthumously by first disciple Ejō in 1255 largely from texts written in the 1250s once Dōgen was ensconced in the Echizen mountains, was primarily directed toward monks at an entry level of training. It is regarded as an extension that does not change or add significantly to the message of the 75-fascicle text.

The main issue in the debate between traditional and Critical Buddhist scholars concerns the intent underlying the two versions of the *Shōbōgenzō* text known respectively as the "old" or "early" *(kyūsō)* 75-fascicle and the "new" or "later" *(shinsō)* 12-fascicle versions. In comparing the fascicles dealing with the fox kōan, the question is whether the later fascicle was actually a rewritten version of the earlier one—perhaps in order to correct a mistaken view—or whether the two fascicles offer different perspectives pertinent to divergent audiences. The conventional interpretation, which relies on the theory of two levels of truth, is that the message reflecting a nondual religious vision is the same but the earlier version is appropriate for a philosophically advanced monk who could appreciate the subtleties of nonduality whereas the former is appropriate for a novice only able to grasp the literal meaning of karma. For Critical Buddhism the 12-fascicle *Shōbōgenzō*—traditionally perceived as a secondary text or an addendum or appendage of the better-known 75-fascicle text that targeted an audience of laypersons and new initiates rather than advanced monks—is crucial to the entire enterprise of overcoming various *hongaku* positions. Hakamaya maintains that the new text is the product of a decisive change of heart based on Dōgen's heightened awareness of karmic causality that expresses a highly critical view of original enlightenment thought as a misguided absolutization and affirmation of natural existence.[25] In his later writings, Dōgen refines an emphasis on the meaning of impermanence—still left rather vague because it is haunted by *hongaku* ideology in the 75-fascicle text—in accord with the early Buddhist doctrine of the inescapability of cause-and-effect as the key to a realization of nonsubstantiality.

Thus Critical Buddhism reverses the conventional textual hierarchy by asserting that the 12-fascicle text exemplifies Dōgen's essential teaching based on dependent origination, which Matsumoto Shirō insists was developed by Buddha as "antithetical" to substantialist, *dhātu-vada* ideology. And the 75-fascicle text, which embraces a holistic, naturalist perspective still ambivalent toward *hongaku* thought, is now seen as a preliminary, incomplete, and therefore secondary and even dubious body of writing.[26] Like Indian and Tibetan Mādhyamika Buddhism, which Critical Buddhism greatly admires as exponents of true (critical, not topical) Buddhism, Dōgen was now thoroughly clear and penetratingly critical about what he negated. The fundamental change in Dōgen's attitude occurred around 1248 when he returned from a disillusioning visit of preaching at the invitation of Hōjō Tokiyori at the Rinzai Five Mountains center in

Kamakura, where he found Buddhism dominated by the emerging military culture.[27] This radical reversal *(gyakuten)* is different—though by no means unrelated historically and spiritually—from an earlier transition that occurred around 1243 when Dōgen was first leaving Kyoto.[28] The change of the Kyoto-to-Echizen period, a number of non-Sōtō sources suggest, was apparently marked by a dissipation and decline in Dōgen's writing output accompanied by an aggressively sectarian, dogmatic, and argumentative outlook in which he all too eagerly abandoned previously advocated liberal social views—such as supporting women and laypersons in the quest for enlightenment—perhaps in pursuit of aristocratic patronage. According to some traditional scholars (primarily of Rinzai orientation, such as Yanagida Seizan and Furuta Shōkin), the puritanical monastic outlook of the 12-fascicle text can be seen as a product of Dōgen's extended decline. Yet other traditionalists (primarily of Sōtō orientation, such as Kagamishima Genryū and Kawamura Kōdō) view this text as part of a renewed effort at strengthening discipline in Zen training.

But according to the Critical Buddhist view, even the latter position does not go nearly far enough in highlighting the significance of the change that generated the 12-fascicle text. This change even supersedes Dōgen's sense of determination when he came back "empty-handed" *(kūshū-genkyō)*, according to an early passage of the *Eihei kōroku*, after attaining enlightenment in China twenty years earlier.[29] Hakamaya maintains that the shift does not simply represent a puritanical stance (either condemned as inflexible or applauded as rigorous). It is, rather, a fulfillment of Dōgen's spiritual quest inspired by his initial doubt about *hongaku* thought in terms of a deeply moral view of the cause-and-effect of rewards and punishments. Dōgen's fulfillment is based on his understanding the need for instructing disciples in the inviolability of karmic retribution: a process often referred to as "the karma produced is the karma received" *(jigō-jitoku,* or "you get what you deserve," in contemporary idiom). This approach undermines the original enlightenment view of Buddha nature as a primordial endowment transcendent of bondage to karma—in large part by emphasizing the act of repentance (probably influenced by *setsuwa* sources that are not discussed and hence implicitly denied by Critical Buddhism), which must be carried out in a genuine way rather than as a mechanical routine that would only compound the problematics of *hongaku* ideology.

The *hongaku/tathāgatagarbha* view that infects the commentaries on the fox kōan in Sung Zen records and the 75-fascicle *Shōbōgenzō*—as well as the modern comments of Yamada Kōun cited in Chapter 1 about an "essential nature" underlying fox and monk transfigurations—represents a naive affirmation of phenomenal reality that actually aggravates the conceptual and spiritual dilemmas implicit in the naturalist heresy. By identifying ultimate reality with concrete phenomena, *hongaku* asserts nonduality from the standpoint of causality swallowing up noncausality and yet—because it accepts things as they are and does not require an act of purification—it is swallowed up by noncausality. Hence there is no genuine freedom or nondiscrimination as claimed under the banner of universal freedom and equality. This view is conveyed in the verse by the Tokugawa-era Sōtō poet, Ryōkan, who alludes to earlier doxologies on the fox kōan: "Delusion and enlightenment / two sides of a coin / Universal and particular / just parts of one whole."[30] The real problem for the later Dōgen is not simply a matter of identifying polarities or shifting the conclusion from one side to the other: the real problem is equalizing them so that the moral component of karmic causality is highlighted rather than concealed. If the morality of cause-and-effect is obscured because it is influenced by an emphasis on noncausality, then genuine noncausality cannot be attained.

For Critical Buddhism, Dōgen resolves this dilemma by asserting in "Jinshin inga" that although "the law of causality *(inga)* is clear and impersonal [or selfless] *(watakushi nashi),*" it is based on the subjective experience of deep faith *(jinshin).* That is, the freedom of noncausality can be attained only in and through the continuing process of moral purification perfected within the realm of causality.[31] From this perspective, causality functions continuously and relentlessly in an impersonal, impartial, and irreversible manner regardless of whether it is accepted or rejected, affirmed or denied, by particular persons. From the standpoint of not obscuring causality, Shibayama's argument about the "free use" of subjection to and independence from causality misrepresents enlightenment, which must be based on a wholehearted acceptance of selfless causality. The correct view recalls Nāgājuna's view *(Mulamādhyamakārikā* 25:9–10) that nirvana is found in terms of causality: nirvana occurs in the midst rather than as an escape from samsara, yet it is attained only through a fundamental change of perspective rather than the mere acceptance of causal relations. By contrast Dōgen's approach is based, not on a nonrelational freedom from karma, but on an eminently flexible and polymorphous process in which the stages of practice and realization, while often simultaneous and overlapping, occur in irreversible sequence.[32]

The Critical Buddhist methodology is effective in highlighting the role of the 12-fascicle *Shōbōgenzō,* long overlooked or relegated to secondary status, and in raising the question of inconsistency between the two fascicles concentrating on the fox kōan. But this approach is problematic. Hakamaya examines the 12-fascicle text in one-sided isolation from Dōgen's other writings, which must be properly understood in order to gain a full picture of his intellectual development. For example, Dōgen cites the fox kōan in all stages of his career—including another early, 75-fascicle *Shōbōgenzō* fascicle, "Ikka myōjū," which mentions the importance of *fumai inga* (C. *pu-mei yin-kuo*), as well as early and later sermons in the *Eihei kōroku* collection, which offer varied interpretations that do not necessarily coincide with the image of the late period created by Critical Buddhism.[33] Another example of *fumai inga* maintained in the early period is found in *Hōkyōki,* the record of his experiences in China while training under Ju-ching. Dōgen notes that when asked if it was necessary to adhere vigilantly to cause-and-effect, his mentor asserted: "Do not deny the law of causality." For those who do so from a nihilist standpoint cannot claim to be descendants of the buddhas and patriarchs.[34]

Yet the Critical Buddhist conclusion, which overwhelmingly supports the merit of Dōgen's thought vis-à-vis other Zen thinkers who partake of *hongaku* ideology, is in some ways not so different from the outlook of traditional Dōgen scholars. Both parties can be accused of being uncritically sympathetic to the Sōtō patriarch. But the main problem is that the Critical Buddhist view of the late Dōgen mirrors traditional scholarship in failing to acknowledge the influence of popular religiosity and the role of ambivalence about supernaturalism throughout Dōgen's work, including his later thought. Although Hakamaya does an effective job of linking the question of the moral viewpoint of the fox kōan to the issue of the dynamics of repentance, he neglects (or suppresses) the influence of supernatural *setsuwa* sources on the Kamakura-era thinker's understanding of causality.

Dōgen's Ambivalence about Supernaturalism and Precepts

In examining the fox kōan strictly in terms of the philosophical level of discourse, one encounters a major problem: the debate between literal and paradoxical readings does not grapple with the crucial issue of what exactly transpires in the dialogical exchange that releases the fox/monk and on whom does it have an impact—a human *(jen)* or a nonhuman *(fei-jen)* being? These questions touching the realm of the supernatural are not dealt with directly by traditional commentaries, which seem to interpret the case for its metaphysical significance and generally decline to take a stand on belief or disbelief or persuading other monks on the topic of the anomalous. Kōan commentaries are primarily concerned with a rhetorical use of the fox image in order to steer clear of any attachment to one or another aspect of the conceptual polarity of causality and noncausality. Yet the role of fox imagery is consistently ironic, as suggested by Daitō's view that even the words delusion and enlightenment are innately deceptive—"just fox-words fooling / Zen monks everywhere."

Nor are the questions treated effectively by Critical Buddhism. Whereas traditional interpretations of Dōgen stress the consistency between his early paradoxical and later literal standpoints—an approach that ultimately supports the priority of the paradoxical view—the Critical Buddhist view emphasizes Dōgen's decisive change that eliminated ambivalence on two levels: there was, first, a reversal from *hongaku*-like paradoxicality to a literal view or a commitment to causality, which was accompanied by, second, a change from incorporating animistic trends to a strict antisupernaturalism. For Critical Buddhism, the special feature of the later Dōgen is that he refutes both paradoxicality and supernaturalism—as opposed to Lin-chi, for example, who rejects the latter but accepts paradoxicality, which indicates an inability to escape the influence of *hongaku* thought.[35] The Critical Buddhist evaluation seems to be supported by several factors during the period after Dōgen's return from Kamakura: not only his disciplinarian behavior during the Gemmyō Ostracism, recalling the stress on the banishment of miscreants in Pai-chang's rules, but also the emphasis on adhering to the precepts in the 12-fascicle *Shōbōgenzō* "Jukai" and other fascicles based on the notion of *jinshin inga*.[36]

Despite its insightful arguments about the intent of Dōgen's authorship, Critical Buddhism obscures many of the ambiguities in his thought due to its preoccupation with identifying a "correct (or true) form of Buddhism" *(tadashii bukkyō)* in contrast to an incorrect topos-bound *(dhātu-vāda)* or *hongaku*-oriented ideology. The Critical Buddhist approach does not take into account the full range of Dōgen's later writings in which various degrees of ambivalence are clearly evident. The ambiguity about the role of supernaturalism in the fox kōan occurs in a context of contradictions noticeable throughout Dōgen's writings. In the 75-fascicle

Shōbōgenzō "Raihaitokuzui" fascicle, Dōgen goes so far as to affirm the status of fox-cult worship. But at the other end of the spectrum, in the 12-fascicle *Shōbōgenzō* "Kie-buppōsōbō" fascicle, Dōgen, like Lin-chi, refutes an assortment of local folk religions and supernatural beliefs frequently assimilated by East Asian Buddhist sects, including Zen.[37] His critique, which recalls the refutation of Vedic ritualism and magic from the standpoint of causal logic as expressed in the *Tevijja Sutta* of the *Digha Nikāya*, has been cited by Critical Buddhism as a template for criticizing the antiquated, goal-oriented, animistic tendencies that continue to infect modern Japanese chauvinism and consumerism:

> We should not act like those who, awe-struck, vainly take refuge in mountain deities and spirits or worship at non-Buddhist shrines, for it is impossible to gain release from suffering in this way. There are those who, following other non-Buddhist religions, think they can gain release from suffering and gain merit by imitating the actions of a cow, deer, demon, hungry ghost, deaf and dumb person, dog, chicken, or pheasant. . . . Such actions are completely false and without benefit. The wise person does not engage in such practices, for they only increase suffering and obstruct beneficial rewards. You must not take refuge in erroneous ways but clearly repudiate them.[38]

Dōgen's ambivalence about supernaturalism reflects in part the distinctive hermeneutic situation in Japan where Tendai Buddhism had pervasively assimilated indigenous gods through the theology of *honji-suijaku* (buddhas as source and local *kami* as manifestations). Further complicating the picture of Dōgen's approach after his return from Kamakura in 1249 are a couple of short sermons preached at Eiheiji to official and noble ladies: the *Jūroku rakan genzuiki* and *Rakan kuyō shikibun*. These texts celebrate the miraculous appearance of supernatural arhats *(rakan)* that protect Buddhism while according to Dōgen's first disciple, Ejō, celestial blossoms rain down on the beholders of the visions, gongs from an unearthly bell echo through the valley, the fragrance of unknown incense gently wafts by, and clouds roll past in beautiful and mysterious colors.[39] Dōgen states that such visions had been known previously only at Mount T'ien-t'ai in China. But the popular religious element expressed here has affinities with local beliefs in the numinosity of Mount Hakusan, the sacred mountain that encompasses the peak where Eiheiji is located as part of its geomantic network.

Although the supernatural implications of the fox kōan narrative are rarely mentioned directly, there are several fascinating controversies discussed extensively in "Daishugyō" that reflect the impact of the force field on Dōgen's thought. Dōgen begins by stressing that the true pivot word is not Pai-chang's utterance, *"pu-mei yin-kuo,"* but the narrative's suggestion that Mount Pai-chang existed as a Zen temple in the primordial age of Buddha Kāśyapa. He follows up this remark by contending that the past and present temples are not different—thereby affirming mythical time. He goes on to discuss whether or not the fox/monk, if a *fei-jen* as reported, could have had sufficient self-awareness to tally its five hundred lifetimes, since an animal does not know even a single lifetime outside its current one. Either way, and whether or not the count is reliable, the controversy tends to support the reality of the *fei-jen* status of the ancient monk. Dōgen questions the basic evidence of the transfiguration, however, since it occurred thousands of years before it was recorded in the kōan and is based on the claims of a wild fox that can hardly be trusted. He asserts: "We should not belittle the principles of the buddhas and patriarchs by foolishly believing that the apparition of a fox spirit is real."[40] One implication of the absurdity of the claim for the animal's memory is that beyond illusory appearances there really was not a fox present in the assembly—and thus no elimination ceremony was actually performed—although Dōgen does not explicitly argue the demythological view that the kōan narrative is purely imaginary.

A related controversy concerns a central question: what happens to the fox/monk after its liberation? As Dōgen points out, its fate apparently was not mentioned by Pai-chang in his sermon that evening. Upon being released by the pivot word, is the former Pai-chang still subject to cause-and-effect—or does he attain full nirvana? Looking at the issue from another angle: what is the fate of the fox once the transfiguration is terminated? And, from the standpoint of Zen monastic ritual, is there not a profound indiscretion in that the funeral rite was bestowed on the vulpine corpse? Several commentaries criticize Pai-chang for sanctioning this ceremony on behalf of an entity whose human (let alone Buddhist) status is highly questionable. A large portion of "Daishugyō" delves into the issue of burial rites, and Dōgen severely protests Pai-chang's instructions. Dōgen suggests that since a fox spirit might have deceived Pai-chang into believing it was really a monk, the fox corpse should not have received a Buddhist burial. "But why," Dōgen asks, "according to the teachings, was a dead wild fox treated as if it were a deceased monk?

It had not received the precepts, engaged in practice, demonstrated dignity, or studied with a master."[41] Futhermore, he maintains, "Even if kings, ministers, Mahābrahmin-rāja, or Shakra Devānām Indra should ask for a burial accorded deceased monks, we should not give permission so long as they are not full-fledged monks."[42]

Dōgen's remarks challenge the burial because—despite the *fei-jen's* claims about being a former head of the temple—it has not been convincingly proved that the fox/monk had taken the precepts. The logic of this argument, in contrast to the discussion of the fox's lack of self-awareness and memory, is that by denouncing the *fei-jen's* right to a burial Dōgen affirms the existence of an entity that is not human. Even in the act of calling for its suppression, the text recognizes and legitimates shape-shifting power—which is a different conclusion than Dōgen reached in the other controversy. And there is another implication: since Pai-chang must have known that he should not bury a fox, the fact that he did so shows that the entity really was not a *fei-jen* after all. In a bit of ironic polemic, Dōgen warns against an acceptance of mythical elements: he suggests that if the former Pai-chang "was transfigured into a wild fox body [five hundred times] by virtue of karmic causality based on his incorrect answer to the disciple's question, then in more recent times Lin-chi, Te-shan, and many other Zen masters [Dōgen is wont to criticize from a sectarian standpoint] would have suffered through hundreds of thousands of wild fox rebirths."[43]

Dōgen's comments about the assembly of monks being surprised and disturbed by the ceremony for a fox were echoed centuries later by Hakuin[44]. They show the importance of the propriety of funeral ritualism based on strict regulations about cremation and burial in Sung monastic life influenced by Confucian propriety and ancestor worship.[45] The Zen rules for ritual burial of monks and abbots were recorded in the *Ch'an-yüan ch'ing-kuei* monastic code of 1103.[46] Dōgen's remarks recall debates in the early Vinaya about the status and treatment of *nāga* (reptilian or dragonlike creatures) and other nonhumans who transfigure into or otherwise disguise themselves as people. Indeed there were even discussions concerning punishments for killing or harming nonhumans as well as rules for allowing their entrance into the *saṃgha*. The very existence of these rules, conceding the reality of the *fei-jen's* presence, represents a recognition of supernatural beliefs even while repudiating them.

Moreover, Critical Buddhism overlooks two important passages in the *Eihei kōroku*—a crucial though generally neglected later text that collects *jōdō*-style sermons spanning the last ten years of Dōgen's life, including the entire Eiheiji period both before and after the journey to Kamakura. The first passage is *Eihei kōroku* 3.251: the sermon Dōgen delivered in 1248 on the morning of his return from Kamakura. According to the *Kenzeiki* and other medieval biographies, Dōgen traveled to the new, temporary capital at the request of Hōjō Tokiyori to minister to the ruler. Recent revisionist studies, however, suggest that he really went at the behest of his patron, Hatano Yoshishige, who had been called to Kamakura for political reasons.[47] In any case, the brief but significant sermon, which is the lone autobiographical reference to the journey, states that Dōgen had been preaching to donors and laypersons. (It turns out to be rather vague about the reasons for the trip and its results.)

In the sermon Dōgen seeks to allay the concerns of the Eiheiji monks who may have been wondering if he had presented some new, secret doctrine while away for seven months. His response sounds at first as if it supports Critical Buddhism: he tells the monks that they will be surprised to hear that he taught the law of karma. He had admonished his Kamakura disciples, many of whom were undoubtedly samurai who had violated the Buddhist precepts: "Those who do good for others and renounce all evil action will reap the rewards of cause-and-effect. So cast away tiles and pick up jewels. This is the one matter I, Eihei abbot, clarify, explain, believe, and practice. Followers, you must learn this truth!"[48] Here Dōgen seems to be explaining that he had experienced a turn—perhaps a fundamental change of heart—toward the philosophy that Critical Buddhism considers the trademark of the 12-fascicle *Shōbōgenzō*.[49] After a pause, however, Dōgen says to the Echizen monks: "You may laugh to hear my tongue speaking of cause-and-effect so casually." And he goes on to make it clear that the injunction about causality was a provisional teaching designed for lay disciples. This sermon actually undermines the Critical Buddhist theory, therefore, and supports the way the 12-fascicle edition has been interpreted by most scholars: as an introductory text for novices not yet ready to tackle the more sophisticated philosophy of the 75-fascicle *Shōbōgenzō*.

Furthermore, if Dōgen's attitude in the later period were entirely consistent with the literal reading of the fox kōan in "Jinshin inga," his views could be easily associated with Pai-chang's rules text. But once again the *Eihei kōroku* indicates that this is not so clear-cut—especially concerning the relation between the precepts and meditation. In an early passage in the *Shōbōgenzō zuimonki* collection from the mid-1230s, Dōgen indicates that *zazen* practice forms the basis of all other aspects of religion, including the precepts: "When you are doing *zazen*," Dōgen rhetorically asks, "what precepts are not upheld and what merits are not produced?"[50] In *Eihei kōroku* 6.437 from the post-Kamakura period, Dōgen makes it clear that sustained *zazen* practice takes priority over the accumulation of merits and demerits through good and evil actions.[51] And in a passage celebrating the isolation of Eiheiji (*Eihei kōroku* 7.498), he continues to maintain that all people can practice *zazen* regardless of qualifications or prior training: "Whether they are bright or dull, wise or foolish, [Zen trainees] should dwell in steep mountains and deep valleys."[52] Furthermore, even in the 12-fascicle *Shōbōgenzō*, Dōgen argues that monastics will be able to attain enlightenment even if they violate the precepts.

Perhaps the key passage for understanding how ambivalence about the precepts remains crucial for understanding the late Dōgen is *Eihei kōroku* 5.390 (dated 1251), which evokes fox imagery to explain his relation to Pai-chang's rules.[53] The sermon opens with a lengthy discussion of meditation techniques involving awareness and regulation of breathing. Dōgen says that the Hinayana (Lesser Vehicle) approach to counting breaths is not authentic and results in "leprous foxes," but the Mahayana technique of being aware of long and short breaths while exhaling and inhaling is also not satisfactory. This discussion concludes by rejecting both Hinayana and Mahayana views on meditation and segues into a consideration of the passage in the *Ch'an-men kuei-shih* which asserts that neither of the two vehicles alone is appropriate to the rules of the Zen sect. When asked if Zen is to follow the precepts according to the Hinayana teachings or the sutras that express the Mahayana precepts, Pai-chang replies: " 'For our sect the guiding principles should not be constrained to follow strictly the rules according to either the Hinayana or Mahayana teachings; nor should they totally disregard them. Rather, we must seek a middle ground that synthesizes the spirit of these teachings without being limited to either approach in establishing regulations that are most appropriate to our style of practice."

Dōgen comments that this view does not reflect his own approach: he strives not for a synthesis but a transcendence of the distinction between the vehicles. With the use of double negatives and characteristic wordplay, Dōgen rewrites Pai-chang's reponse to his disciple:

I do not not follow the Hinayana teachings, nor do I not disregard them. What is the Lesser Vehicle? It means that the donkey has not yet taken

off. What is the Greater Vehicle? It means that the horse has not yet ar-
rived. Having nothing to increase means that the greatest vehicle is the
same as the least vehicle; having nothing to decrease means that the
least vehicle is the same as the greatest vehicle. My approach does not
seek to synthesize, but to cast off the very distinction between Lesser
and Greater Vehicles. This I have already done. What more can I say?

The sermon record indicates that a lengthy pause ensued—leaving time
for discussion or debate with the assembly of monks which was not recorded—after which Dōgen makes a pithy final comment: "When
healthy I do *zazen* without rest; when hungry I eat till I am full." Thus the
bottom line for Dōgen is an emphasis on meditation and a relative disregard for precepts and rules. This new policy represents the inverse of the
attitude expressed in the *Ch'an-men kuei-shih* and thus vitiates the Critical Buddhist emphasis on the later Dōgen's single-minded change.

Noncausality and Repentance

Critical Buddhism makes an important point: the 12-fascicle *Shōbōgenzō*
(along with *Eihei kōroku* 3.251) stresses the doctrine of karmic causality
in relation to repentance. But in regarding the later Dōgen as an
antisupernaturalist and antianimist, Critical Buddhism fails to see how
his views on causality, especially concerning the issue of repentance and
redemption, are shaped by folklore religiosity that influenced *setsuwa* literature. Hakamaya shows that in some passages in the 12-fascicle text
Dōgen emphasizes the role of repentance or confession (J. *zange*; C.
ch'an-hui) in reversing negative karma and attaining transformation—a
notion that is also featured, somewhat surprisingly, at the conclusion of
the "Keisei-sanshoku" fascicle in the 75-fascicle *Shōbōgenzō*.[54]
Hakamaya also argues that Dōgen's emphasis on genuine repentance is
coupled with a strong criticism of the ritualization of *zange* that is prevalent in a variety of East Asian *hongaku*-based practices. These practices
invite the misconception that evil karma can be facilely absolved through
zange metsuzai or the extinction of sin through a purification ceremony—a false sense of noncausality. There are many such rites: a mechanical recitation of the precepts without necessarily incorporating
them spiritually; a penance that seeks to wash away bad karma and annul
disasters by transferring enough merit from a past, present, or future
buddha to gain a worldly benefit (such as causing an end of drought, ill-

ness, or war) or an exotic display of supranormal powers as still seen to-day in *yamabushi* practices such as hanging upside-down from a tree limb or precipice for prolonged periods.[55] The problem with *zange metsuzai*—the title of one of five sections in "Shushōgi," an essay for lay Sōtō followers culled in modern times from the *Shōbōgenzō* (though the term is not used by Dōgen himself)—is that it regards all manner of de-filement and evil behavior as extraneous to the basic purity of an essen-tially undefilable Buddha nature.[56]

Hakamaya's comments call attention to the fact that despite the impor-tant role of repentance in the early Vinaya and other forms of Buddhism in China and Japan, in Zen its meaning is generally suppressed if not alto-gether lost because of the *Platform Sutra*'s emphasis on "formless repen-tance." This refers to repentance based on principle or noumenon (C. *li;* J. *ri*) rather than fact or phenomenon (C. *shih;* J. *ji*)—that is, on an aware-ness of the nonproduction of evil based on the purity of original enlight-enment (though this term as such is not used in the text). From the *Platform Sutra* it follows that once one recognizes that transgressions, as well as the overall distinction between good and evil, are at the root empty conceptual constructs grounded in an original purity, there is no need to be concerned with instances of wrongdoing or misbehavior. Al-though Zen monasticism does employ traditional Buddhist repentance rituals daily, monthly, and yearly, these are barely mentioned in the *Ch'an-yüan ch'ing-kuei,* which deals extensively with other forms of ceremonialism. Nor is the topic dealt with in recorded sayings texts or kōan collections. The apparent disinterest in repentance is further high-lighted, if somewhat ironically, by the absence of a sustained refutation of the practice that was so popular in many other kinds of medieval Bud-dhism, including T'ien-t'ai meditation and Pure Land devotionalism.[57] Although the *Platform Sutra* as well as certain passages by Dōgen could be seen as providing a justification for the deemphasis of repentance, there is no systematic critique in Zen comparable, for example, to Lu-theran criticism of the sacrament of penitence that accompanies a refuta-tion of magic.

The failure to view repentance as a sustained process of self-reproach, self-criticism, and self-correction—not that it always functions in such a positive way—may have hindered the development of a cogent Zen moral philosophy (as opposed to the proliferation of monastic rules stressing ritual etiquette and propriety) subsequent to Pai-chang's rather harsh call for banishment. Hakamaya further contends that the devaluation of repentance—deriving from the same outlook that promotes the equalization of causality and noncausality which is refuted in "Jinshin inga"—has helped foster antinomian attitudes that are nonethical in the sense that they reflect a turning away from a direct confrontation with ethical responsibility and decision making. Perhaps Zen has cultivated this attitude deliberately, on a rhetorical level, in the name of a transethical, "wild fox" perspective that goes beyond conventional standards of good and evil in a Nietzschean sense. But this rationale has a hollow ring in light of the sect's acknowledged participation in discrimination, nationalism, imperialism, and corporatism that Hakamaya links to a lack of emphasis on confession.[58]

Yet in dealing with the issue of whether Zen puts too little emphasis on repentance or too much on a mechanical, spiritually bankrupt form of repentance—with both trends fostering self-indulgence—Critical Buddhism like most Buddhist scholarship in Japan overlooks the interface of Zen texts and popular Buddhist literary genres and thus reaches a conclusion that seems too clear-cut and one-sided. Dōgen frequently criticizes shamanistic and animistic practices in the 12-fascicle *Shōbōgenzō* in favor of a literal reading of karma that seems to derive from demythological Pali sources concerning a philosophy of impermanence and causality. Yet he often appeals to another early Buddhist source—the mythological, supernatural *jātaka* tales that were integrated into *setsuwa* literature, such as the tale of Indra's prostration before a bodhisattva in the form of a fox—to illustrate his view of the inviolability of karmic retribution and the possibilities for transforming karma through the act of repentance. Dōgen cites anecdotes concerning numinous bodhisattva-like magical animals, for example, including foxes and bears whose presence leads to the redemption of fools or sinners, as well as a eunuch who regains his potency and a prostitute who is redeemed by a single moment of touching a Buddhist robe as a joke (which may derive from the *Abhidharma Mahāvibhāṣā*).[59] The "Sanjigo" fascicle tells the story of how a man responsible for betraying kindnesses and killing a bear, which appeared as an incarnation of a bodhisattva, is punished by having his arms fall off more quickly than if they were struck with a sword.

Indeed, the view of karma expressed in the 12-fascicle *Shōbōgenzō* is quite similar to the view expressed in the early-ninth-century *Nihon ryōiki* collection, which cites the *Ming-pao chi* ("Record of the Imperceptible Workings of Karmic Retribution") as its primary influence: "Manifest retribution comes immediately. We must believe in karmic causality."[60] According to the preface of the *Nihon ryōiki*—the full title is *Nihonkoku genpō zen'aku ryōiki,* or "Miraculous Events in Japan Connected with the Immediate Retribution for Good and Punishment for Evil"—fools deceive themselves into "ignoring the consequences of good and evil deeds. But the wise . . . stand in awe and believe in the law of karmic causation *(inga)*."[61] Furthermore, the 12-fascicle *Shōbōgenzō* from Dōgen's later period seems to accord with the *Nihon ryōiki* moral injunction: "Good and evil deeds cause karmic retribution as a figure causes a shadow. . . . Were the fact of karmic retribution not known, how could we rectify wickedness and establish righteousness? And how would it be possible to make men mend their wicked minds and practice the path of virtue without demonstrating the law of karmic causation?"[62]

One of the main features of *setsuwa* literature is an emphasis on the redemptive or exorcistic quality of a key Buddhist symbol such as a sutra or icon. Many of the fascicles in the later *Shōbōgenzō* text are likewise concerned primarily with the ritual efficacy of symbols, especially the robe, bowl, and stupas. In the longest of the fascicles, "Kesa kudoku" ("Merits of the Robe"), Dōgen cites the words of the Buddha in arguing for the remarkable moral power of the robe that can cause an instantaneous spiritual turnabout even in nonhumans or supernatural beings, regardless of prior fears, hostilities, or transgressions: "Suppose that there are those who become antagonistic, feel mutual resentment, and continuously fight among themselves. Whether they are celestial beings, dragons, demons, deities . . . whether they are human or nonhuman beings, if they happen to come in contact with a robe, or bear it in their mind, its virtue will cause them to have a compassionate, tender, unresentful, enlightened, and disciplined mind. In that way they will be purified."[63] Dōgen concludes the fascicle by asserting the superiority of the robe's power over indigenous or secular forces: "We [the followers of the Buddha] should stop worshiping heaven, deities, kings, or ministers in pursuit of fame and fortune, for nothing can offer greater satisfaction than venerating the Buddha's robe."[64] Yet the negation of native gods does not support Hakamaya's view of Dōgen's antisupernaturalism.

The ambivalence in Dōgen—an ambivalence neglected by Critical Buddhism—is that a strict affirmation of causality is ironically based on an acceptance of supernaturalism in a text that also rejects it. Critical Buddhism is correct that the 12-fascicle *Shōbōgenzō* is a work about the power of karma. But this theme is carried out not so much in terms of a logical analysis of causality—although the "Hotsubodaishin" fascicle examines the doctrine of momentariness—as in terms of the way ritual functions such that a single instant of wearing or viewing the robe results in enlightenment. The main point is that neither the 12-fascicle *Shōbōgenzō* nor the late period as a whole is exclusively concerned with the doctrine of causality as opposed to noncausality in the sense of the supernatural. While the 12-fascicle *Shōbōgenzō* may have been based on a refutation of *hongaku* thought, therefore, it is also plausible that Dōgen's later, revised interpretation of the fox kōan was reacting to the conception of karma presented in the genre of *setsuwa* texts—a genre that was becoming increasingly popular and influential in the thirteenth century and perhaps influenced his early ambiguity in "Daishugyō" about the propriety of the *fei-jen*'s funeral ceremony. Dōgen was not so much interested in a literal reading of the kōan, or a rejection of supernatural beliefs, but in overcoming the antinomian view and restoring the moral implications of karma. This he achieved by touching base with the undiscussed background or force field of fox imagery as a symbol of illusion, neither explicitly endorsed nor refuted, underlying the ambivalence in his early and later interpretations.

For both the literal and paradoxical approaches—and for "Daishugyō" and "Jinshin inga," which tend to negate the viability of supernaturalism and use animistic symbolism to refute any involvement in popular religiosity—the fox suggesting Otherness represents elements that are problematic or unconventional from a rigorously antisupernatural standpoint that dismisses them. The vulpine presence is a force that must be eliminated, although different reasons are offered for doing so. A literal reading of the kōan associates the image of the fox with the misconception of not falling into causality and supports an emphasis on rules (or on not obscuring causality). In the paradoxical view, by contrast, the fox reflects an attachment to either not falling or not obscuring in a way that opens the door to the possibility of going beyond rules—which after all are nothing but "fox words" according to Daitō's verse.[65]

But underlying the view shared by the philosophical perspectives is the fundamentally bivalent image of the fox—an image that encompasses its function as a one-dimensional metaphor for ignorance and attachment or for those who stubbornly cling to their passions while claiming to have transcended them. The attachments include the conflating of supranormal powers legitimately attained through meditation with the apparent but misguided powers of supernatural and superstitious practices. Once the dimension of bivalence is regarded not only as a muted, secondary structure but as the force field of the discourse that claims to reject it, fox imagery can be seen to have a transitional function as a doorway between realms—a function that is often evoked indirectly or hesitantly by philosophical commentaries, including Dōgen's. The main factor that links the rhetorical ambiguity about supernaturalism found in these commentaries and the bivalence of *setsuwa* constructions of shape-shifting foxes is the theme of morality and repentance. This issue provides the key to resolving the exegetical question of the status of the being who experiences release, whether *jen* or *fei-jen,* as well as the methodological question of why Zen discourse turns to supernatural imagery in order to express an antisupernatural moral message.

5 · Folklore Morphology and the Issue of Repentance

Fox or woman, woman or fox,
That figure in the misty moonlight standing?
         —Natsume Sōseki, *The Three Cornered World*
         (*Kusa makura*)

Kōan commentaries generally try to distance themselves from the mythological roots of Zen discourse by defusing, reorienting, or suppressing any focus on the reality or unreality of folk beliefs in favor of the rhetoric of abbreviation and iconoclasm. Yet in many kōans supernatural themes share a discursive arena with morality tale literature—providing a narrative framework and force field that may rise to the surface of expression. The fox kōan is one of numerous examples in the *Wu-men kuan* and other collections in which key aspects of popular religiosity are evident: pilgrimages to cultic sites and shrine worship; iconography and demonology; esoteric symbols; ascetic self-mutilation; shamanistic trance and bilocation; and the banishing of demons and converting of indigenous gods through the use of miraculous symbols and icons. The example of Chü-chih (J. Gūtei) cutting off a disciple's finger with a knife (case 3), which recalls the famous anecdote of Hui-k'o dismembering his arm as proof of his dedication, along with the case that enjoins jumping off a hundred-foot pole (case 46), must be seen in light of the accounts of self-mutilation as a process of purification in monk biography texts.[1] Although the context is alluded to or evoked, it is often critiqued and scorned as well, a reflection of the bivalence of folklore imagery.[2]

131

Contrasting Kōan and *Setsuwa* Literature

For most interpreters, kōans based on self-emancipation and *fei-jen*-oriented literature based on divine intercession cannot be juxtaposed as interacting discourses, for there is simply an epistemological (though not necessarily historical) gap that divides them. While the major kōan commentaries deal to a large extent with philosophical arguments, often in competition with Taoist metaphysics and Neo-Confucian ethics—although doctrine per se is not placed at the forefront of their discussions—*setsuwa* literature represents a style of preaching that refashions popular religiosity in terms of the doctrine of the immediate retribution of good and evil (C. *hsien-pao shan-ê;* J. *genpō zen'aku*), as in the *Nihon ryōiki.*[3] The concrete, inescapable effects of causality are played out in narratives expressing themes of temptation, lust, greed, ambition, betrayal, delusion, and revenge, as well as the release of karmic turmoil by means of repentance, forgiveness, redemption, transformation, protection, and compassion.

Setsuwa literature, which literally means "stories expressing or disclosing [the dharma]," refers to a genre of short anecdotes and vignettes that use supernatural images of ghosts, spirits, and an assortment of anomalous creatures to construct moral messages about the vanquishing of demons through the use of potent Buddhist symbols, amulets, prayers, or relics. These tales, which were by no means intended for the lower classes alone but were often read by the intellectual elite, are sometimes merely entertaining or moral in a limited, proverbial sense in issuing a warning or reprimand, occasionally from a "blame the victim" standpoint. (A woman molested by a magical snake should know better than to flirt.) The more profoundly religious tales deal with the meaning of karma as an impersonal process of rewards and punishments significantly affected by divine intervention that is played out with dramatic effect in the lives of ordinary people ranging from aristocrats who experience a comeuppance to peasants who become heroes. The tales teach lessons that drive home the need to avoid succumbing to the foibles of deceit, arrogance, and false pretense by cultivating an attitude of acceptance and gratitude for one's lot in life. People are urged not to give in to the temptation to overstep the bounds of fate and circumstance symbolized by the fox's transfiguration; instead they are to identify sympathetically with the plight of family and friends and to heed their pleas.[4] In *setsuwa* tales, the consequences of rewards for good behavior and punishments for evil are understood literally as an inexorable, unmitigated law.

William LaFleur's chapter "In and Out of the Rokudō" in *The Karma of Words* is one of the few studies to discuss the fox kōan directly in the context of morality tales, particularly the *Nihon ryōiki*. LaFleur examines the basic medieval Japanese belief in karmic causality involving transmigration through the "six realms" (C. *liu-tao;* J. *rokudō*) encompassing humans, divinities, titans, hungry ghosts, creatures of hell, and animals. He argues that there were four modes of accepting and applying this doctrine to a theory of escape or relief from suffering *(rokudō-baku)*: infiltration of a bodhisattva such as Kannon or Jizō into the world of turmoil where the deity is greeted with piety and devotion; transcendence to a utopian realm of the Western Paradise, beyond the other six realms, that could be attained through a kind of deathbed conversion in which the final thoughts of purity are decisive; a process of copenetration that represents a combination of the first two possibilities by realizing that samsara and nirvana, and suffering and salvation, are ceaselessly intertwined here-and-now; and ludization, the most subtle approach, whereby "the entire *rokudō* system is conceived of as an arena of play . . . [that] produced much humor, spoof, the pleasures of a 'floating world,' the lyrics of an Ikkyū or a Ryōkan, and the comedy of *kyōgen.*"[5]

The main examples of ludic discourse are the *Vimalakīrtī Sutra,* which suggests that a bodhisattva who preaches the dharma by skillful means ought to enjoy what he is doing, the *Hua-yen Sutra,* which stresses the playfulness of spiritual activities, the *Lin-chi lu,* according to which karma should be accepted for what it is by one who has the freedom to "kill the Buddha," and, in the example he considers the most striking and effective form of expression, the fox kōan. LaFleur concludes that popular morality operates through the paradigms of the infiltration of deities into the world and the transcendence (or rebirth) of believers in the Pure Land. Although it deals with the theme of transmigration, which is portrayed in allegorical fashion in *setsuwa* literature, the fox kōan exemplifies the copenetration of ultimate and phenomenal realms or, further, a ludization in which everything, including moral judgments, is conditioned, relative, and nonhierarchical.[6] The equalization of causality and noncausality—as well as the comment that the wild fox enjoyed his five hundred lives as a blessing—reflect the enlightened master's true freedom. Therefore the genres of *setsuwa* and kōans represent separate, parallel, but incompatible paradigms.

LaFleur's argument fails to see, however, that kōans and morality tales are part of the "move to assimilate shamanic symbols . . . in which the threat of defilement is domesticated and assimilated into the structure of the sacred."[7] *Setsuwa* literature, much of which was compiled coterminously with Zen records, is distinct from and yet in some cases interfaces with the narrative context of encounter dialogues. Furthermore: "Some of the kōans . . . retain the flavor of the popular literature . . . a narrative genre in which Buddhism and folk religion, entertainment and moral instruction, were richly intertwined . . . [such that in some kōans] pilgrims have visionary dreams, supernatural beings appear and disappear, and animals assemble to hear sermons on the Dharma, their 'eyes glistening with tears.' "[8] But the genres portray encounters with the supernatural from opposite though complementary standpoints reflecting inverted manifestations of the twofold discursive structure. Kōans store supernaturalism in a muted structure while the main structure forefronts a paradoxical perspective of critical transcendence collapsing all dualities from an ironic standpoint. Morality tales are the inversion of this: they forefront supernaturalism and mystery as the main structure while harboring a demythological, allegorical level of symbolism based on the bivalence of fox imagery beyond literal claims of divine intervention.

The two genres are primarily didactic. Often they refashion themes and syntax from a pre-Buddhist oral tradition in which the extraordinary is not implausible but is understood as a driving force for moral truth. Both argue that Buddhism offers a salvation that is superior to the religiosity of indigenous shamans and wizards. In some cases, the aim of kōans is to make a sectarian argument by showing how a Zen master tests and proves himself in relation to the powers gained through non-Zen, irregular, or unorthodox methods of spiritual practice. *Setsuwa* tales, however, generally take a pan-Buddhist, assimilative perspective by accepting and adapting the efficacy of many sorts of practice.

LaFleur is correct in arguing that the main difference between genres "is not just a matter of rusticity versus sophistication."[9] Kōans, which often contain vernacular forms of expression, have an affinity with *setsuwa* literature in advising that one must jump off a hundred-foot pole or in recording a Zen master cutting off a disciple's finger, cutting a cat in half, or putting his shoes on his head. Other kōans record the spiritual encounter of a master with the symbols, centers, icons, and personalities of popular religiosity: magical snakes, field or land deities, hermits, shamans and wise "grannies," the Mount Wu-t'ai pilgrimage site for those seeking visions of Mañjuśrī, staffs that can turn into dragons, or dreams and visions of bodhisattvas and gods. Kōans—which are sometimes referred to as the "folk stories of Zen"—have often lent themselves to a *monogatari*-zation in sermons and commentaries geared to laypersons in which the moral lesson taught by the dialogue is the main factor highlighted.[10] The association of kōans and folk religiosity is further reflected by the fact that one of the main folklore genres of the medieval period in China, bearing the same name *(kung-an),* was a collection of detective stories often based on legal investigations that have an ethical component.[11]

A main area of convergence is the way many kōans and *setsuwa* tales stress a confrontation with the need for self-responsibility. A terrible fate befalls those who do not follow the dharma. And the punished, including those reborn in animal form, must have transgressed severely. The means of reversing negative karma is to understand illusion for what it is by successfully negotiating a spiritual dilemma with a spontaneous and sincere sense of resolve. For *setsuwa* the impasse usually requires an ethical decision leading to clear, straightforward trust in the salvific power of a temple, icon, or sutra. In Zen the impasse is conceptual and is reconciled in terms of the master's charismatic embodiment of the virtues of self-denial. Kōans point in deliberately ambivalent, indirect fashion to the innate Buddha nature, suggesting a process of internalization but without necessarily refuting the efficacy of external symbols.

Folklore Elements in the Kōan Tradition

How does folklore enter into kōans and kōan collection commentaries, which are generally understood as the peak accomplishments of the literate, scholastic approach in the Zen tradition? Kōans—paradigmatic cases based on the traditional records (C. *ku-t'se kung-an;* J. *kosoku-kōan*) of Zen patriarchs—are noteworthy for their extensive and highly refined use of allusion, wordplay, irony, and humor. And the commentaries, which often take the form of paradoxical poetry, are celebrated for their metaphysical musings on emptiness and lyrical reflections on the psychology of attaining enlightenment. The verse and prose commentaries in the major kōan collections of Sung China, the *Pi-yen lu, Ts'ung-jung lu,* and *Wu-men kuan,* among many others, represent from a "literary point of view . . . a pinnacle in the history of [Zen] literature."[12] Indeed, a "more complex genre of literature can hardly be imagined, rivaling any of the exegetical commentaries of the doctrinal [Buddhist] schools."[13] The

Pi-yen lu and *Ts'ung-jung lu* have an especially intricate structure. In both texts there are prose and verse commentaries on one hundred kōan cases composed by the original compilers, Hsüeh-tou and Hung-chih respectively, which were further interpreted through prose and verse comments on the commentaries decades later by the second editors, Yüan-wu and Wan-sung, thereby creating a multilayered "wraparound" commentary that evokes through direct and indirect allusion countless other texts and doctrines of the classical period in the formation of the sect. For the way they absorb and reflect in their interlinear commentarial form the historical fabric of the full development of Zen thought in the late T'ang and Sung, these collections are cited by Heinrich Dumoulin as the "epitome of poetic composition in Zen literature . . . [and] one of the foremost examples of religious world literature."[14]

From a philosophical standpoint kōans, though quite diverse in style and meaning, can be analyzed in terms of a shared literary form and intellectual message deriving from the basic literary unit of the encounter dialogue in which the master functions as spiritual midwife. He is able to evaluate and emancipate the aspiring student with just the right sense of what to say—or, more importantly, how to refrain from speech in order to elicit an inner realization without imposing his own instructions or will. Often his responses involve an intimidating or humiliating command or the use of body language or a nonverbal gesture such as shouting, holding up a staff, or hitting with a stick. Yet the master invariably finds that his own level of enlightenment is refined as well through participating in the dialogue. In some cases there is a role reversal—as when Huang-po strikes or reprimands his teacher—which is then acknowledged as a sign that the student has successfully completed his training. Or the dialogue may culminate in an apparent impasse suggesting a realization beyond words or one about to issue forth after further prompting or an additional dialogue, perhaps by engaging another master who has a special insight into the student's blockage. In any case, the encounter represents the opportune moment for an existential breakthrough that is seized upon by both parties whose respective degrees of spiritual attainment are enhanced by the exchange.

In expressing a philosophical message, kōans almost always avoid explication of a specific theory or doctrine (although traditional Buddhist concepts such as impermanence, dependent origination, emptiness, Buddha nature, or causality are often assumed as a backdrop for understanding the case). Rather than offering a straightforwardly rational exposition of a teaching, which is included in certain Zen texts, especially the *Platform Sutra* and some recorded sermons, the main theme of many kōans involves pushing the limits of language to the logical conclusion in order to test and overcome any reliance on rationality. The kōans thereby suggest a position of ontological nonduality and epistemological noncommitment and nondiscrimination in accord with the Mahayana doctrine of *śūnyatā*. In kōans such as Chao-chou's *"Mu"* (in response to the question of whether a dog has Buddha nature) or his saying "oak tree in the garden" (in response to the question of why the first patriarch came to China from the west), the concerns of plot and character development appear to be irrelevant or are disdained—although the latter example relies on hagiographies of Bodhidharma and both cases evoke the personality of Chao-chou expressed in other hagiographic narratives. The tendency in approaches such as Yün-men's one-word barrier, Ta-hui's main phrase, and Lin-chi's pivot word is toward further abbreviation by isolating and extracting from out of the kōan record the essential linguistic ingredient. Thus for many interpreters the fox kōan is associated simply with the single phrase "not obscuring causality."

Despite such expressions of protest against the viability of language and conceptualization, the antidiscursive message of kōan records is not merely an endorsement of the ineffability of the enlightenment experience. Rather, the message must be seen as part of a wide-ranging effort to explore all possible vantage points in a provisional, pedagogical way without attachment to any particular view. To challenge a one-sided viewpoint, therefore, some kōans project an impasse that is designed to create an excruciating sense of futility that helps deconstruct the obstacle to enlightenment. But if the deadlock so projected becomes an object of fixation itself or becomes the source of attachment to the experience of frustration and silence, then it too must be deconstructed. The strategy of many of the commentaries on the fox kōan is to alternate the *pu-lo yin-kuo* and *pu-mei yin-kuo* responses. Thus the antidiscursive meaning is conveyed through a sophisticated literary vehicle that utilizes the tools of Zen discourse, especially paradoxical, ironic wordplay, as well as nonverbal devices that cannot be included in the written account, such as gesturing, posturing, body language, and eye contact. The result is not a blanket rejection but an iconoclastic, irreverent, demythologizing use of language that serves as an instructional tool which can be discarded when its utility has been exhausted.

The creative wordplays and gestures couched in the surprises and drama of dialogues are set against a background of legends about the lives of the participants. Because the demythological rhetoric—whether designed to support or refute any particular standpoint concerning the role of speech and silence—unfolds as part of an overarching, multidimensional narrative structure, the philosophical significance should not be seen as the exclusive meaning of kōans or isolated from other aspects of Zen discourse encompassing mythology and demythology, textuality and nontextuality. The kōan collections compiled in Sung China and subsequently interpreted by Kamakura and post-Kamakura Japanese commentators supposedly deal with the dialogues of T'ang masters who lived several centuries prior to the records. An examination of the historical and textual evidence suggests that much of the demythological intent is associated with mythological portraits of a retrospectively constructed golden age of generation-to-generation transmission between masters. Demythology is part of a highly stylized use of language that also employs mythology in an effort to invent tradition or to craft an ideology retrospectively. The aim is to establish sectarian legitimacy and dominance in an intellectual climate in which Zen competed with the rationalism of Neo-Confucianism and T'ien-t'ai scholasticism as well as the supernaturalism of Taoism and folk religions in addition to other Buddhist sects.

In the Sung Zen texts, observes Griffith Foulk, "the realism that characterizes the records of the patriarchs' words and deeds is often so finely detailed that it betrays the works as fiction." Furthermore: "In many cases the use of realistic, concrete settings is a purely literary device [in] that the descriptions of the monastic environment of the T'ang masters often contain anachronistic details" concerning temple compounds and institutional structures that are characteristic of the Sung.[15] The gap between the alleged time of the occurrence of the events in the T'ang and the recorded versions in the Sung does not necessarily mean that the dialogues are entirely apocryphal or invented and devoid of legitimate historical foundation. They may represent an exaggeration or the taking of poetic license. The precise nature and degree of accuracy will probably remain indeterminable. Yet Zen chronicles seem to disavow factual historiography because their ideology dictates that the main characters—the attained masters who preach and the aspiring disciples who receive instruction—are not substantive entities but represent interchangeable and transpositional possibilities for spiritual self-discovery as well as sectarian identity and authority. The fictional quality suggests that kōans ought to be examined, not only in terms of what they express on a philosophical level, but also from the contextual perspective of evaluating their purpose and function—that is, how and why they reflect pseudohistorical strategies for crafting tradition in a competitive ideological environment.

Thus the privileging of a philosophical examination that focuses exclusively on the role of linguistic methods used to surpass language may overlook other important aspects of the overall discursive strategy of the kōan tradition—some of which complement or enhance while others may appear to conflict with or even undermine the philosophical level. Some of these aspects are metatextual and involve the social function of kōans in Zen institutional life. For example, kōans are records of a highly conventionalized, almost stereotypical form of what in the original context is supposed to be spontaneous behavior expressing collective representations about the suddenness of satori and the intuitive nature of the transmission process. But when interpreted, studied, and deployed as an instructional device, kōans play a ritual performative role in supporting monastic hierarchy and authority. The social function of kōans contributes to the legitimation of patriarchal hierarchy and to specific genealogical affiliations and occasions of lineal transmission. It contributes, as well, to endorsements of marginal standpoints—as in the feminist message of several *Wu-men kuan* cases, such as cases 31 and 42, in which a female religious figure either outwits or outpractices her male counterparts including bodhisattvas.

Moreover, the rhetorical flavor of many examples of the kōan—a term borrowed from secular society that literally refers to the magistrate's bench where the "public records" of juridical decisions were deliberated, debated, and announced—tends to adhere to a legalistic paradigm of rewards and punishment. The abbot's role as the final arbiter of paradigmatic kōans used as test cases for monks in training appears to be modeled on that of a judge hearing a case and determining his judgment in a court of law. Numerous dialogues culminate in the use of the stick or the striking of blows, as in Te-shan's "thirty blows" admonition, which echoes the function of the civil authority. Kōans are precedents, so to speak, in the Court of Dharma. The encounter dialogue supersedes, but does not necessarily replace, the traditional robe and begging bowl as a marker of fulfillment of the transmission process. The *Wu-men kuan* postscript borrowing from the legalese of the day compares its commentary to judging the confessions of criminals: "This completes my judgment of the legal case files of the instructional dialogical encounters of the buddhas and patriarchs without resorting to any superfluous rhetoric."[16]

Other discursive aspects of kōans are sometimes overlooked in examinations focusing on the demythological role of language. These aspects, involving the inseparability of kōan records and various literary forms or genres of the Sung, are intertextual. Intertextuality has two dimensions: intrasectarian and intersectarian. The intrasectarian dimension encompasses the interconnectedness of kōan collections and other Zen texts—especially mythological, hagiographic writings about the life and teachings of eminent masters. Although these writings contain many of the same dialogues, they are used in different contexts and for different purposes, primarily serving as biographical anecdotes rather than as philosophical exercises. One of the reasons why the dimension of popular religiosity exists as a muted structure stems from the multiple roles that encounter dialogues play in the diverse but intertextually connected Zen texts compiled in the eleventh through thirteenth centuries. The dialogues cited as kōans were also contained in the voluminous texts of two other genres of the early Sung—a period marked by a veritable explosion of the creativity of Zen records documenting the development and thought of the sect then emerging as the dominant Buddhist denomination in postsuppression China. One genre was the pseudohistorical transmission of the lamp texts, which present Zen's patriarchal genealogy through hagiographic anecdotes about a series of eminent masters often borrowed from monk biography texts that stress the role of thaumaturgical divination, spells, and exorcisms. The other genre was the recorded sayings texts, which collect the sermons and biographical materials of seminal masters who exhibited distinctive styles of instruction. The recorded sayings texts are in an intermediate position: for the most part they are similar to kōan collections in emphasizing philosophy, but they also contain mythological narratives about their heroic subjects. The three genres—kōan collections, transmission texts, and recorded sayings records—often include nearly identical material, but the kōan collections and some parts of the recorded sayings stress a demythological, philosophical message and the transmission texts stress mythology and hagiography. Thus when kōan collections are seen as an independent genre isolated from other kinds of texts, the philosophical structure seems to prevail in a way that obscures the foklore dimension. But the reverse is true for hagiographies. So that when kōans are viewed from the standpoint of intrasectarian intertextuality, it is possible to recover the narrative context underlying the encounter dialogues.

The other dimension of intertextuality is intersectarian. This dimension encompasses an interplay with the literature of other religious or literary traditions—from classics such as the *I ching* and the *Chuang tzu* to contemporary texts and oral literatures generated by Confucian scholar-officials, Taoist shamans, and Buddhist Vinaya and meditation masters, including *setsuwa* texts. Intertextuality has an important impact in shaping the narrative content of the hagiographic texts from which the dialogues that form the basis of kōans cited in commentaries are extracted. It also reveals the extent to which Zen borrows from—yet contests and conflicts with—rival ideologies. This borrowing is an attempt to decode and reencode competing viewpoints and symbols in order to assert dominance by putting its distinctive ideological stamp on indigenous belief systems. Yet because of the pervasiveness of intertextuality the lines separating what lies between and within a sect are often blurred, so that cause and effect, origination and imitation, may be difficult to determine. The proliferation of highly charged polemical rhetoric—Lin-chi (Rinzai) versus Ts'ao-t'ung (Sōtō), Zen versus T'ien-t'ai, or Buddhism versus Confucianism—has often been retrospectively created and functions as a filter obscuring an appropriate access to the source materials.

An important feature of intersectarian intertextuality is the interface of kōans with popular or folk religiosity mediated by the incorporation of this imagery and symbolism into Zen hagiographies. In many instances a supernatural, mythological narrative context of the dialogues used in hagiographies informs the antisupernatural, demythological orientation of the same material used as kōans. The narratives underlying the kōan dialogues reflect Zen's interaction with elements of popular religions: masters performing miracles, supernatural feats in fending off local spirits, empowering Buddhist amulets. The elements of popular religious practice evident in Zen narratives are often assimilated from pre-Buddhist or non-Buddhist indigenous cults—especially the methods of shamans or wizards—or from other Buddhist sects, movements, or texts, especially motifs in bodhisattva worship or in the parables of sutras that may have already absorbed native practices. Or they may stem from amorphous folklore traditions—recorded in literary and fine arts collections but rarely officially organized or institutionalized—of highly localized animistic spirits, including both demons and benefactors, from which the major religions draw symbolism, imagery, or literary techniques. Thus the kōan genre is part of an intra- and intersectarian intertextual range of texts without strict borders in which philosophical paradoxicality is shaped by bivalence.

An Analysis of Folklore Themes in Several Kōans

Many kōan cases represent dialogues that are extracted from their source context or narrative structure in the other Zen genres. Generally kōans do not include the supernatural background or mention it only in a compressed or encoded fashion. Yet the truncated form of the kōan no doubt was designed to depend for maximum effect on the fact that the monastic audience knew how the context was being used in other texts. The fox kōan is somewhat of an exception. In this case the encounter dialogue is fully woven into the folktale, whereas the "Ch'ien's two souls kōan" (*Wu-men kuan* case 35) epitomizes the rule of abbreviation because an elaborate romance narrative is not cited at all in the one-line kōan case. This kōan—which reads simply: "Master Wu-tsu said, 'Ch'ien (J. Senjō) and her soul are separated. Which one is the true soul?' "—is reliant upon images and symbols absorbed directly from lay folk beliefs in supernatural powers.[17] Although the case is usually interpreted in terms of the issue of nonduality by asking which manifestation is the true Ch'ien, this philosophical query is inseparable from the folklore motif of trance and bilocation. The philosophical topic is: How can a person or object be divided into component parts such as body and soul—or causality and noncausality—when they all constitute an indivisible collective unity? Yet universality is not one-sidedly asserted, since that might conceal the distinctiveness of particular manifestations. The *Wu-men kuan* verse commentary establishes identity and difference in the first two lines and concludes with an ironic, rhetorical question that scrupulously avoids a commitment to either view as an exclusive side of the polarity: "The moon amid the clouds is ever the same, / The mountains and the valley are different from one another; / Myriad blessings! Myriad blessings! / Is this one, or two?"

While the "Ch'ien's two souls kōan" functions on an abstract philosophical level when understood as a scholastic exercise, the case is clearly based on a famous T'ang ghost tale, recorded in the *Li-hun chi* (J. *Rikonki*), expressing the theme of duty versus passion (or *giri* versus *ninjō*, which later became such an important influence on Tokugawa-era Japanese literature).[18] The folktale uses supernatural elements such as a spirit journey in the story of a young woman who appears to her parents, who have resisted her wedding plans, to be sick and lifeless when she is separated for five years from the man she loves. The spirit of Ch'ien manifests in another physical form when she is saddened by her parents' proposal for an arranged marriage and her alienated soul runs off with her lover while her former self spends five years in a sickbed unable to move. Early in the story Ch'ien's father promises her hand in an arranged marriage that distresses her childhood sweetheart, her cousin, whom the father once jokingly suggested should marry his daughter. On hearing the news the young man decides to flee the village, and as he is leaving in his boat he makes out a shadowy figure on the shore chasing after him. He and Ch'ien go off to a remote area and are married, but five years later they decide to return home out of a sense of duty to her family. At first the father is incredulous because his daughter has been terribly ill, but he realizes that the "other Ch'ien" has run off with her lover and spent the time in a secret marriage. Ch'ien is reunited with her tormented soul that was present in a body lying motionless in bed the entire time of her flight. Everyone, now purged of feelings of guilt and deception, is able to experience a sense of harmony and fulfilled responsibilities. Yet, as in the case of Chuang Tzu's "butterfly dream," Ch'ien admits that she herself cannot tell which is her real identity: the person sick in bed or the one who has been married.

A connection between the philosophical issues and folklore elements is indicated in a verse commentary dealing with the imagery of death that is suggested by the narrative's reference to Ch'ien's double identity:

> Peach branches and reeds in front,
> Paper money after the funeral cart,
> O disciples of the old foreigner,
> You will not enter into the realm of the dead.[19]

The first two lines refer to customs for keeping away demons in traditional funeral processions—indicating that the mythical issue of where the dead soul resides and how it returns to life is intertwined with the demythical issue of how to attain nirvana. The third line is a frequently used ironic self-criticism of Zen monks, disciples of the foxlike first patriarch Bodhidharma who brought the transmission to China from India. The final line suggests that the central philosophical question about the permeability of boundaries separating pairs of opposites such as life and death has a paradoxical conclusion. The boundaries are at once navigable and impenetrable: life is inseparable from death; yet life is distinctively life and death is distinctively death; universality and particularity, oneness and manyness, are ever intertwined. The conclusion in the form of a challenge moves the kōan beyond mere intellectual abstraction and dares the Zen disciple to attain the degree of insight of folk heroine Ch'ien who in a sense rode in the funeral cart—or escaped this fate—to and from the land of the dead (or enlightenment).

Wu-men kuan case 40, "Kicking Over a Water Pitcher," demonstrates how important it is to recover a deleted or suppressed narrative structure in order to understand a kōan's meaning.[20] In this case, Pai-chang intends to award his chief cook, Kuei-shan, the abbacy of a new monastery to be built on Mount Ta-kuei, a nearby but heretofore remote mountain area. Nevertheless he interviews both the cook and the head of the assembly of disciples, Hua-lin, apparently to create at least a pretext of democracy after Hua-lin complains about being treated unfairly. Pai-chang announces that whoever excels in the contest will win the appointment. To test his two followers, the master holds up a water pitcher and demands: "You cannot call this a water pitcher. What, then, do you call it?" The head disciple responds by saying: "It cannot be called a stump." When his turn comes, Kuei-shan proceeds to kick over the pitcher and spill out its contents and then walk off—one of the most compelling of the manifold irreverent Zen actions. Just as he had approved of Huang-po's slap, Pai-chang laughingly approves of this dramatic gesture. He declares the head disciple "the loser" of the contest, and Kuei-shan goes on to establish the new monastery.

A key to understanding the case is the narrative structure in the *Ching-te ch'uan-teng lu, chüan* 9, and the *Wu-teng hui-yüan, chüan* 9, which depends for effect on a number of supernatural factors that occur prior and subsequent to the encounter dialogue.[21] The tipoff is in the *Wu-men kuan* prose commentary, which says that "after careful consideration, Pai-chang selected the 'heavy' and turned down the 'light.'" The main figure in this episode is neither Pai-chang nor Kuei-shan but Ssu-ma, an irregular monk also involved in a dialogue with Kuei-shan about the fox kōan, who was an expert in *dhūtaguṇa* or ascetic practices and also skilled in indigenous occult arts such as geomancy, divination, and physiognimy. Before Pai-chang tests and evaluates the two disciples, Ssu-ma, using his powers of divination and geomancy, has already selected Kuei-shan for stewardship of Mount Ta-kuei. As Ssu-ma felt that Mount Ta-kuei was ideally suited to the formation of a formidable monastery with a large assembly of over a thousand monks, he rejected Pai-chang, a gaunt man with ascetic habits, as too withdrawn and retiring for such a post. He had also tested the head disciple, Hua-lin, by asking him to cough deeply and walk three paces and found him wanting. But he approved of Kuei-shan, "a mountain of flesh" with a vigorous personality, on first sight, even without putting him through an ordeal. Thus the encounter dialogue between Pai-chang and Kuei-shan was a staged affair: its result had already been predetermined in large part by supernatural powers rather than philosophical insight. This situation is hinted at in the *Wu-men kuan* prose and verse commentaries. The prose commentary suggests that Kuei-shan "could not escape Pai-chang's trap, but after careful examination he was able to make use of what was heavy while dispensing with what was light. How? Think about it *(chien)!*"—using the same term, suggesting the practice of providing protection from ghosts, that is evoked in the *Wu-men kuan* case 12 prose commentary. Moreover, the poetic commentary refers to "the tip of [Kuei-shan's] foot kicking out myriad buddhas."

What transpires in the *Ching-te ch'uan-teng lu* narrative subsequent to the dialogue preserved in the kōan record is equally important for its use of supernatural imagery that is usually interpreted in a strictly demythological vein. Kuei-shan lives for several years like a hermit on the peak of Mount Ta-kuei—heretofore an inaccessible region far from any sign of human habitation—and subsists on wild nuts and berries with only animals, monkeys, and birds as his companions. Nevertheless, his reputation for genuine spirituality spreads and eventually the villagers in the valley below gain support from government officials in their efforts to construct for him a monastery on the mountain. Once established, Kuei-shan receives numerous visitors seeking instruction in the dharma, including the prime minister as well as Zen monks such as Yang-shan, who became his main disciple. In one lecture recalling the literal reading of the fox kōan, but perhaps going against the grain of Hui-neng's famous verse in the *Platform Sutra,* Kuei-shan cautions his followers to reject the teaching of an originally pure Buddha nature that can never be contaminated by karmic defilements and to strive constantly to remove evil thoughts and deeds.

In a version of the hagiography not included in the *Ching-te ch'uan-teng lu,* prior to his successes in the monastery Kuei-shan gets discouraged after eight years of solitude and decides to leave the mountain. On the pathway down, he meets a friendly tiger who appears to beckon him to return to the peak. Kuei-shan follows this omen and shortly thereafter his fortunes improve. Meanwhile his rival, Hua-lin, the former head disciple, becomes involved with sacred tigers as well. He is living as a hermit on another mountain when a visitor asks if he is not disheartened by the absence of disciples. The monk replies that he is not alone but has two attendants—and then calls out for Tai-k'ung (J. Daikū) and Hsiao-k'ung (J. Shōkū), literally "Great Emptiness" and "Small Emptiness." In reply to the call, two fierce tigers come roaring out from the back of the hermitage. The visitor is terribly frightened but the tigers, instructed by the monk to be kind and courteous to his guest, crouch at his feet like two gentle kittens.

Perhaps the central theme in hagiographies that comes through in a number of encounter dialogues is the contest between the supranormal powers of Buddhist masters derived from meditation and the supernatural powers of animistic spirits that derive from their *fei-jen* status. This is part of a long-standing assimilative pattern expressed in early *jātaka* and *avādana* literature whereby buddhas and bodhisattvas are skillful in subduing and converting local gods—often referred to as *nāga* (serpents, dragons, reptiles)—by demonstrating superior power based on compassionate activity, sustained ascetic discipline, or the performance of miracles and wonders. In China the role of the *nāga* is taken up by *kuai* phenomena including foxes, tigers, and snakes. In a number of kōans the strategy is the transmutation (from the standpoint of critical transcendence) of the theme of "the veneration of the accomplished meditator—the great ascetic, sunk in profound *samādhi* or wielding the psychic powers of *dhyāna*,"[22] which was also a standard morality tale topos. An example of this is a kōan known as "Nan-chüan Meets the Earth Deity."[23] The background is the notion, found throughout Buddhist hagiographic literature, of the encounter between a master and local spirits, celestial beings, or demons who have jurisdiction over a particular geographical or spatial domain such as a mountain, valley, village, or field. Before attaining full realization, the master-to-be both makes and receives offerings from the gods. But once perfected he escapes from ever being seen or known by the otherworldly entities because his powers surpass theirs. If the attained master is subsequently spotted by a field god, however, it is taken as a sign of failure—highlighting the need to continue his training and appease the deity. According to the kōan, Nan-chüan is surprised as he enters a vegetable patch, where he usually goes unnoticed, when he is greeted by a novice who says that the field god had notified him of the master's imminent arrival. Nan-chüan must now make an offering to the deity before resuming his discipline.[24]

An understanding of the discursive function of the case, whether mythological or demythological, is based on the context in which it is cited and interpreted. When used in transmission-of-the-lamp texts such as the *Ching-te ch'uan-teng lu,* the original source of the anecdote, for example, the kōan contributes to the genealogy of the master by establishing his credentials. The case is also mentioned in Dōgen's "Gyōji" fascicle (part I), the closest his *Shōbōgenzō* writings come to the transmission text genre, as he retells his lineal history in light of the doctrine of "sustained [*zazen*] practice" (*gyōji*) which has the spiritual power to support buddhas and sentient beings, heaven and earth, self and other. Early in the fascicle Dōgen refers to masters Ching-ching and I-chang as being notable because they cannot be perceived by the native gods. Then he contrasts Nan-chüan, who has been spotted, with Hung-chih, before whom a local deity is literally stopped in its tracks as its feet will not budge (recalling the "immovable robe" in the legend of Hui-neng's escape as discussed below). Here Dōgen seems to be scoring a sectarian point on behalf of Hung-chih, a predecessor of his mentor Ju-ching, while denigrating a master from a rival Rinzai lineage. Up to this stage Dōgen is operating within, though at the same time refashioning, the standard mythological framework. But he then moves on to demythology by commenting that the real meaning of being seen or not seen lies not in supernatural power in the literal sense but in the perpetuation of authentic discipline. This requires an ongoing process of casting off conventional pursuits. Yet Dōgen's demythological turn reveals an assumption of the efficacy of the indigenous spirit world.

A number of prominent examples in the *Wu-men kuan* demonstrate the pattern of a narrative with supernatural elements taken from lay or Buddhist folk religion framing the kōan's philosophical message. The text contains several cases that borrow their symbolism from pre-Zen popular Buddhism expressing the power of bodhisattva worship and the viability of Buddhist symbols over other forms of sacrality—although they are usually interpreted in terms of the issues of language or the debunking of supernatural powers rather than for their visionary imagery. These examples include case 25, in which a young disciple dreams that he is called to give a spontaneous sermon before the future buddha, Maitreya; case 42, which is based on a traditional Buddhist folktale in which a woman in the presence of the Buddha can only be brought out of profound absorption by a lowly bodhisattva after hundreds of thousands of Mañjuśrīs fail to rouse her;[25] and case 48, in which a magical fan ascends to the upper worlds and brushes against celestial rulers. Several *Wu-men kuan* cases come straight out of the Zen hagiographic tradition: in case 6, the Buddha gives a sermon before an assembly on a sacred, primordial mountain by holding a flower which he then transmits to the smiling Mahakaśyāpa, who became the second patriarch in India; in case 12, a master calls out and answers his own questions; in cases 11 and 31, Chao-chou tests his extrasensory mental faculties when checking out two hermits living independent of the monastery with whom he enters into dharma combat (case 11) as well as an elderly laywoman (case 31), perhaps a witch or shamaness or at least a symbol of indigenous religious practice. The "Zen granny" has been outsmarting monks struggling on their way at the foot of the Mount Wu-t'ai cultic center, considered the earthly abode of the bodhisattva of wisdom, Mañjuśrī, and his celestial attendants. She has been giving monks a difficult time when, after a long and arduous journey to the mountain in the far north, they ask for directions to the pilgrimage site. She tells them, "Go straight ahead," and then remarks sardonically "Watch him go off" when they follow her directions. Although Chao-chou receives the same treatment as the others, he returns to the assembly and apparently declares it a "win": "I've gone to the foot of Mount Wu-t'ai and checked out the old woman for you."

Moreover, there are numerous examples in other kōan collections. Such kōans often evoke land deities, pilgrimages to sacred sites, supernatural events, and the magical efficacy of Buddhist symbols. There is a cluster of kōans on spirit turtles and snakes in *Ts'ung-jung lu* cases 24 and 59, for example, the former of which is also cited in *Pi-yen lu* case 22, as well as a dialogue between Mañjuśrī and a pilgrim referring to visionary experiences at Mount Wu-t'ai in *Pi-yen lu* case 35, which touches base with *Wu-men kuan* case 31 and *Ts'ung-jung lu* case 10.[26] Mount Wu-t'ai is part of the network of sacred mountain centers in China that were considered the abode of bodhisattvas and became the pilgrimage spots for seekers of visions and oracles.[27] The dwelling place of Mañjuśrī, the mountain was one of the main destinations of Zen pilgrims, although the practice was explicitly rejected by the *Lin-chi lu* as mere superstition. In *Pi-yen-lu* case 35, Mañjuśrī engages in a dialogue in which he answers a question with a tautological non sequitur typical of a Zen master.[28] The commentary makes an ironical interpretation of the deity's role: supporting it insofar as it reflects Zen wisdom but not necessarily refuting its supernatural status. One notes that Mañjuśrī, whether or not he is considered of stature equal or superior to the enlightened Zen practitioner, is a traditional Buddhist deity often enshrined as a patron saint of meditators in the monastery, whereas the elevation to *honzon* status of Dakini-shinten or Toyokawa Inari in Japan reflects a greater degree of veneration of what is in all likelihood a folk (or autochthonous) deity.

Wu-men kuan case 23 combines philosophical and supernatural elements revolving around moral issues and monastic order. Although this case relates the story of Hui-neng's miraculous, immovable robe, it is best known for generating the famous, deeply challenging rhetorical question: "What is your original face?"[29] Like the fox kōan, the case features a fairly complex and highly symbolic narrative structure. But it is also distinctive in that the narrative is clearly a snippet extracted from the traditional hagiography of the sixth patriarch which is no doubt exaggerated if not altogether fabricated. According to this account, the young, illiterate Hui-neng was fleeing the monastery where jealous monks resented the fact that he won the all-important poetry contest to determine lineal succession, defeating Shen-hsiu, with the following verse: "Bodhi is not originally a tree, / Nor has the bright mirror a stand, / From the start there is nothing, / Where can the dust alight?" Hui-neng was given the sacred robe and bowl of the fifth patriarch in secret on a dark night as proof that he had received the transmission. Chasing him for days along with several other monks who were outraged by the upstart, Ming finally catches up to Hui-neng at the ridge of a mountain. In some versions Ming demands: "We cannot afford to see an illiterate like you carry off the robe and bowl. I have come to take them back. Hand them over at once without making a fuss."

Hui-neng responds with great courage and integrity by throwing down the robe and bowl on a rock and declaring: "This robe and bowl are symbols of faith in the virtue of the dharma transmission. They cannot be fought for out of self-interest or taken by force. If you dare to take them by violence, do as you like." When Ming bends to lift them, the robe proves "immovable as a mountain" to the stunned pursuer who is stopped in his tracks in fear and trepidation. "I have come for the dharma, not for the robe," he beseeches Hui-neng, who responds: "Not thinking of good, not thinking of evil, show me right at this very moment your original face." Ming experiences a great satori. With his whole body dripping with sweat and tears flowing he makes a bow and asks: "Besides these esoteric words and their esoteric meaning, is there anything further you can instruct me?" Hui-neng asserts: "What I have just disclosed to you are not esoteric words. Their aim is to turn you around to see the light of your inner self, for the real secret exists within you." Ming admits that in his previous studies he was unable to awaken his original face, and he now thanks Hui-neng for his enlightenment experience: "I am like one who drinks water and knows for himself whether it is cold or warm."

Shibayama's commentary stresses that the key to understanding the kōan is the role of repentance and transformation experienced by Ming. "Even though [Ming] touched the robe and the bowl as they lay there on the stone," Shibayama argues, "in his emotional agitation he could not lift them up. Hesitating and trembling, he simply stood there, petrified. This unexpected spiritual impulse must have thrown the sincere and forthright [Ming] into the bottomless abyss of Great Doubt. His ego-centered and enraged self was at once completely smashed. This inner conversion, which fundamentally changed [his] personality, was the most important moment in his whole life. Yet there are scarcely any commentators who make mention of it."[30] Although Shibayama emphasizes repentance from a demythologized psychological standpoint, he seems to overlook that this dimension of Ming's experience revolves around two supernatural elements: the magical robe and the reference to esoteric words. The magical powers deriving from Chinese folklore ascribed to the Buddhist robe is an important influence in the hagiographic anecdote used in the kōan and in Zen ceremonialism in general. In Indian Buddhism there was a concern with the robe's style and substance—what materials it was made of and how it was worn—with the penalty of forfeiture threatening those who disobeyed the rules by, for example, accepting forbidden materials from lay supporters. But the notion of the robe possessing salvific powers emerged in East Asia. Dōgen's 75-fascicle *Shōbōgenzō* "Den'e" and 12-fascicle *Shōbōgenzō* "Kesa kudoku" fascicles (both composed in midcareer in 1240) probably derived from accounts of celestial figures who, for example, lose their supernatural powers when their robe is stolen or hidden, sometimes forcing them to do good deeds on earth to recover it. While Shibayama's argument that Ming could not lift the robe due to his inner fears is persuasive, we note that none of the traditional commentaries refute—or support—the notion that the robe is immovable because it is an empowered talisman. Similarly, even though Hui-neng denies that his pithy demand for Ming to reveal his original face is an esoteric formula, the fact that his partner in dialogue jumped to such a conclusion conjures the importance of supernatural uses of language functioning as part of the force field of Zen discourse.

The Illusionary Realism of *Setsuwa* Literature

Kōans transmute supernaturalism from a transcendental standpoint culminating in paradoxicality. Morality tales, however, generate a "polarity pattern" based on the creative tension between delusion and redemption—encompassing repentance—as a continual back-and-forth movement between the opposite possibilities for transition of transgression and transformation.[31] The ingenuity of the fox kōan and other cases lies in the way they integrate and utilize the themes and syntax of the polarity pattern. It appears that in the pre-Buddhist view of supernatural beings representing a combination of nearly indistinguishable angelic/benevolent/self-sacrificing and demonic/chaotic/destructive elements, there is no clear moral judgment but a tacit acceptance of their bivalence without an interpretive commentary.[32] In indigenous religiosity, the supernatural beings tend to exact revenge rather than retribution and foster gratification instead of spiritual fulfillment. Buddhist morality literature draws on the bivalent imagery of foxes and snakes as deities or demons, protectors or cunning opponents, to create a shift from a horizontal, nonevaluative, or amoral twofoldness of guardianship and demonism to a vertical, evaluative, or moral contrast of the forces of compassion (Buddha) and deception (Māra). Whatever is threatening, disorderly, disruptive, and chaotic gets translated into bad karma or the lower end of the vertical pole. Buddhism claims that its deities are effective in performing exorcisms—or exist at the upper end of the pole—because they have a universal power that overcomes the fragmentized abilities of unassimilated spirits.

Yet the appropriation of supernaturalism is more complex than that: animals that are demons in one context can function as compassionate Buddhist gods once their power has been confronted, tamed, and transformed. While opposite forces are generally held apart in a folktale, they shift roles and reverse positions when the literature is surveyed as a whole. In some morality tales involving clerics, Māra-like foxes seduce virtuous priests (or priests who are too virtuous are suspected of being foxes in disguise). In other tales, bodhisattvas take the form of foxes that function as catalysts leading people to the verge of a breakthrough. The wild fox is assimilated and stigmatized—a bivalent view captured from a different angle in Zen's antisupernatural rhetoric and its inversion. Foxes in Japan associated with Inari shrines that are often amalgamated with Buddhist and Zen deities can be used to exorcise demons, for example, but foxes associated with the area near the Izumo shrine on the west coast are excluded from this category and their sorcery must be exorcized by other foxes charged with sacred powers.[33] Thus there are two levels of bivalence: the level of the fox image—representing the dual possibilities of protection and deception, redemption and betrayal, good and evil—and the level of the Buddhist approach, which is both for and against, assimilative and purificatory, of and by the fox.

How does supernaturalism become a symbol of an interior struggle requiring repentance within the structure of the polarity pattern? For an illustration consider the film *Ugetsu* (1953), a postwar refashioning by renowned director Kenji Mizoguchi of Tokugawa-era didactic tales by Ueda Akinari, *Ugetsu monogatari* (Tales of Rain and Moon), that were influenced in turn by a variety of medieval Chinese and Japanese folklore collections, including *setsuwa* literature.[34] At the beginning of the narrative, Genjuro, a potter, and his brother-in-law Tobei decide to pursue their fortune in the city during a civil war—despite the warnings of their wives and the village headman that they stick to their trade and not overstep their talents or fate. The village headman cautions that "gains made in wartime have a way of vanishing into thin air." While they heedlessly venture off in pursuit of fame and fortune and bask in the glow of their illusory successes, their wives suffer miserably without their love and protection. It is the encounter with the depths of their spouses' downfall that leads Genjuro and Tobei on the path to repentance and, eventually, to some degree of redemption when they are fully reconciled to the karma they have produced.

The hopeless Tobei's dream of becoming a powerful samurai with a sword and shield and a retinue of soldiers is granted by a warlord as a bonus for stealing the severed head of an enemy chieftain. Although the warlord suspects that some deception is involved in the feat, he decides to reward Tobei anyway. But in his absence Tobei's wife, Ohama, is brutally raped at an abandoned temple by renegade soldiers who compound the violence by tossing down a few coins in payment out of the money they steal from her. Just when Tobei is at the peak of his bravado, celebrating and bragging about his bogus successes as he is traveling to show off at home to his wife, he learns that Ohama has had to become a prostitute at a roadside inn to support herself. "Here I am," she scornfully announces, "the great man's fallen wife. I know what! You can join the ranks of my customers tonight." Tobei pleads that his success means nothing without her and promises to make amends for her defilement. Realizing that although he had been on his way home, it was only to impress her with his prestige, at first she resists his advances. But the scene ends in their embrace, and they go on to rebuild a life together.

Whereas Tobei confronts the shock of harsh reality when he discovers his wife at the inn, Genjuro undergoes several incidents of emotional trauma and comeuppance shrouded in a mystique of supernaturalism that vacillates between the bewitching and the horrifying. Early on, the potter and his wife, Miyagi, trying to escape looting in their village, travel with their son, Genichi, by boat on Lake Biwa in a cloudy mist. There they think they have come upon a ghost—actually a man whose ship has been ransacked by pirates—but this ominous event does not discourage the potter's ambition. Genjuro then goes to the city by himself and becomes wealthy or so it seems. But he later discovers—after accepting the truth about his supernatural fantasies—that his wife has been attacked and killed while he was away.

Coterminous to the tragedy—since his bewitchment has already begun—Genjuro fantasizes about buying his wife an expensive kimono with his new fortune, although she has already told him that she loves the clothes he has given her not for their fineness but for the love they reflect. She says she is content simply to have her family together and kept out of harm's way. Just as Genjuro enters a kind of trance while standing at a stall envisioning his wife wearing the new garment, he becomes bewitched by a beautiful ghost—according to one of the stories in *Ugetsu monogatari* it is a trickster fox—whose identity is fully concealed and who demands his devotion, which is similar to the *kuai* phenomenon in a famous Kuniyoshi woodblock print discussed in Chapter 2. The film seems to be based on two, or perhaps three, stories in the original collection by Ueda Akinari of nine tales in five volumes dealing with supernatural foxes, serpents, ghosts, and spells in a highly moralistic context. One main influence is "The Cauldron of Kibitsu" ("Kibitsu no kama"). In this story a man who is haunted by the ghost of the wife he deserted for a beautiful mistress is at one point shocked back to his senses by the barking of a dog—according to early Chinese fox lore, dogs are the one natural enemy of fox spirits. The wife/ghost later transfigures into the form of a serpent. The husband is taken to a Buddhist soothsayer/diviner who performs an exorcism by writing spells in ancient characters over his entire body while warning him to stay pure, which is quite similar to the exorcism rite that Genjuro receives. (See Figure 16.) In the film the Buddhist spells are written in special esoteric Sanskrit script known as Siddham, supposedly devised by Kūkai, but the point is that the symbols have an antidotal quality because they are foreign and antithetical to the local demonic spirit. In the Ueda tale, however, the man does not offer a full confession of his sin and he is eventually tortured and devoured by the ghost.

Another important influence on Mizoguchi's film is "The House Amid the Thickets" ("Asaji ga yado"). In this story a man leaves home to seek his fortune and returns after seven years pass "as in a dream" to find that his wife has died. Yet, "bewitched by a fox," he thinks at first that he has found her and the house intact—which is just what happens to Genjuro when he returns home thinking he has conquered all his illusions after the exorcism. When the man in "Thickets" recognizes that his wife is a ghost and sees the desolation that has overtaken his former home, foxes

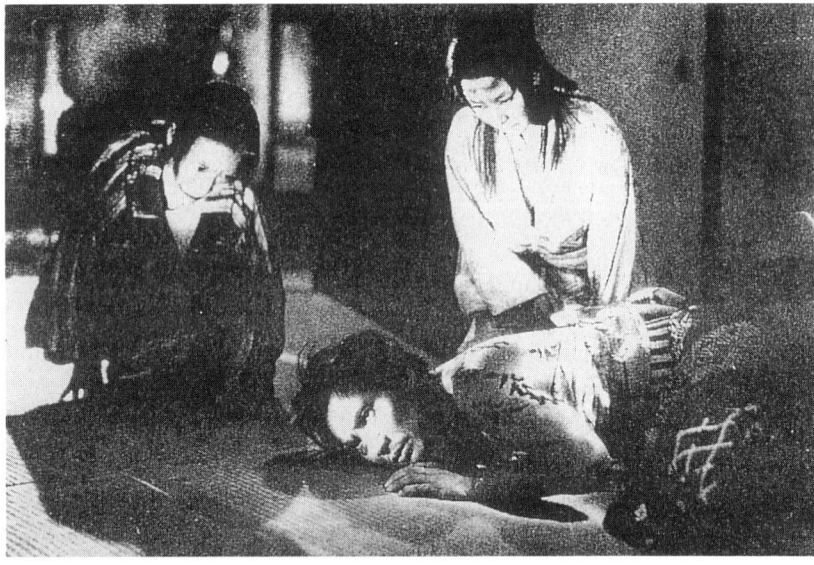

Figure 16. The exorcism scene in *Ugetsu* when Genjuro, whose body has been painted with special ritual Sanskrit characters (Siddham) by a Buddhist priest, returns to the mansion of Lady Wakasa—who recoils in horror at the sight of the symbol that she realizes is antithetical and destructive of her *fei-jen* existence.

and badgers appear in the area. In this story the husband, like the potter in the film, is filled with contrition and confesses his guilt to his grandfather. A third story cited by some critics as an influence on *Ugetsu* is "The Lust of the White Serpent" ("Jasei no in") in which a man who "sat amid the broken-down and dilapidated ruins—the sort of lair one would expect a goblin to inhabit," is tormented by a serpent that, due to his "lack of courage and spirit," causes him to do vile things. In this case, after several unsuccessful attempts at exorcism based on various prayers, chants, gods, and symbols, there is a successful elimination of the shape-shifting form of the demon that is exposed and destroyed by a Buddhist robe soaked in mustard-seed incense—often used in esoteric rites because the seed's hardness and bitter taste are considered effective in destroying illusions.

The tale of Genjuro has elements of bewitchment and deception borrowed from the three stories and culminates in a redemption that combines the exorcistic rite of "The Cauldron of Kibitsu" with the confession of "The House Amid the Thickets." The supernatural events begin when he is ensnared by a *kuai* phenomenon who expresses admiration for his supposedly wonderful pottery, which Genjuro calls his "real children," having forgotten about his family during the bewitchment that appears to be tailored to appeal to his pride and greed. The apparition known as Lady Wakasa is actually the ghost of a princess whose clan was destroyed by Nobunaga and is now living in a mansion on a mountain near the outskirts of town. She and her attendants hope that marriage to the young and vigorous Genjuro will restore her to normal existence—probably at the expense of the dissipation of his life force for the sake of her fulfillment. Though the potter remains oblivious, the audience is tipped off to the princess' *fei-jen*, sirenlike status by the expression on her face—alternately melancholic and joyful, resembling a Noh mask—and by her ghostly veil and unnaturally light gait. She serenades him with an eerie, telltale song suggesting a demonic view of Buddhist impermanence and karmic inevitability: "The finest silk, of rarest shade, may fade away, and quickly, too / So may the love I offer you if your heart proves false to me." Her deceased father's voice, accompanied by Buddhist drums and chants, intones in the background.

Genjuro is seduced by Lady Wakasa in a hot spring bath, and at a picnic in a meadow, while the camera pans very briefly between these scenes over a Zen-like barren, raked rock garden evoking emptiness and impermanence as well as the passage of time. "I wouldn't care if you were a demon!" he declares in the midst of his passion while living in her luxurious home and gardens, thus betraying the fact that on some level he sees through the illusion and understands the reality of the situation. "I will not let you go! I never imagined such pleasures existed! This is divine! It is paradise!" At one point when he chases after her, as she frolics in the grass, her body appears ungraspable, as if she were not really there, although Genjuro, still oblivious, at least on a conscious level, is only more enchanted. But when Genjuro goes to town to buy a gift for his ghost bride, the fearful shopkeeper lets him have the goods for free on learning that he resides in the haunted mansion. Then a Buddhist priest (the sect is not identifed) observes him walking down the street and immediately recognizes his ailment. Reminding him of his familial obligations, the priest counsels him to return to his home and give up the forbidden love that will surely lead to his death. When Genjuro insists on going back to the mansion, the priest paints esoteric Sanskrit letters on his body for protection while sutras are chanted in the background. For the last time the potter sees Lady Wakasa, who recoils in horror when she touches his inscribed back and accuses him of betraying their love. After struggling against the ghost, which starts to dissolve now that its true identity is recognized, thereby starting a fire, Genjuro falls into a deep sleep. He is awakened by a Shinto priest and local official only to find the mansion revealed in its true form—as in many early Chinese stories beginning with *Jen-shih chuan*—as nothing but a burnt-out hovel. In his first moment of genuine repentance, following the exorcism that was externally induced by the priest, Genjuro surveys the damage reflecting his dilapidated state of mind. Apparently he is thinking of returning to Miyagi while the princess' demonic song in the background reminds him eerily yet ironically of the law of causality.

But the full significance of Genjuro's repentance is about to come. He journeys home to seek out his wife and succumbs to one last delusion that she is still alive and waiting for him. Late at night, he sees her tending the hearth and summons an apology: "I've come to my senses. . . . I was so mixed up, so lacking in judgment." After thinking he has spent the night with his wife, as in the Ueda tale, he is told by the village headman the next morning that she had been killed—and when he realizes that this occurred during his illusory dalliance, he suffers an intolerable grief. His sorrow is mollified only by the supernatural yet calming voice of his wife's spirit that encourages his everyday labors while he cares for his son, who places his food before the mother's grave alongside the similarly chastened Tobei and his wife. Genjuro has undergone several levels of repentance marked by supernatural imagery: beginning with the external exorcism administered by the knowing priest, continuing with the realization that Lady Wakasa was an apparition, and culminating in the encounter with his wife's ghost, which heightens his remorse as does the consoling communication with her spirit. The progression is a matter of internalizing and actualizing the meaning of self-reflection and self-criticism brought about by adjusting his perception to the reality of cause-and-effect in order to vanquish the fundamental illusion that the moral causality of actions is inconsequential. The shape-shifting entity (*bakemono*) has been temporarily experienced as real. But the repentance shows that it must never be elevated in one's mind to the status of reality. The ghost's appearance is a projection of the process of testing Genjuro's moral being and provides the opportunity of bringing him to his senses. The multiple stages of repentance, which continue after he sees the hovel of the mansion and realizes the death of his wife, provide a key to interpreting the second division of the fox kōan—especially for explaining Huang-po's slap of Pai-chang, since the master/exorcist would appear to be beyond reproach.

When morality tales are interpreted for their multifaceted literary symbolism rather than taken literally or seen as truncated theological tracts that merely assert the efficacy of magic, they have a distinct communicative power. This power derives from a sophisticated theoretical base on the nature of frailty and possibilities for overcoming human folly that converges with the metaphysical understanding of karma. The *setsuwa* philosophy can be called an "illusionary realism" because the chimerical is more real than what is apprehended with the senses.[35] The conceptual structure revolves around a fundamental tension: an "apparent conflict . . . between the narrative realism in which the demons are portrayed . . . and the frequent explicit statements that demons are nothing more than illusory fabrications of a confused mind."[36] There is a Kafkaesque quality here: although the ultimate aim is to eliminate illusion, the hallucinatory events are necessarily portrayed at a crucial point in the narratives in realistic language, even while accompanied by supernatural occurrences. As in the case of Kafka, the depictions are at once so realistic they cannot possibly be a dream and so dreamlike they cannot possibly be real. This establishes a convergence of perception and external reality, akin to the Yogācāra philosophy of idealism, so that when the hero is in the depths of illusion, such as the potter's ghostly mansion, that is just what is depicted. The reality of illusion (the literal depiction of chimera) equals the illusion of reality (the character's inability to resist the temptation of his or her fantasies). In a way that is parallel to paradoxical Zen verse commentary, *setsuwa* literature shows the instability and emptiness of the conceptual constructs staged by the various perceivers: victim and ghost, narrator and audience.

The power of animals to transfigure and bewitch functions as a symbol of attachments and misdeeds—for it never affects people who are not currently suffering from these problems or karmically deserving of trials and tribulations. The fox promises people something they desire, only to deliver another unwanted item, or it foils their arrangements (such as spoiling wedding plans by shape-shifting into a bride in disguise in order to lead away the unsuspecting groom) that were in fact ill-founded or never meant to be. In *Ugetsu* the ghost is a mirror image of how the potter's all-too-human wartime opportunism has resulted in lust, greed, and betrayal of his family. In *Konjaku* tales, "transformation into a snake was that which happened to individuals who valued [things of this world] too highly. But it posed no threat to innocent bystanders. It merely lurked behind the scenes as the symbol of the evil inside us all. Interestingly, it was mostly Buddhist monks and women who needed to fear the snake within themselves."[37] Thus an exorcism of the interior snake or fox is not merely an external ritual but operates as a thorn to remove a thorn or a poison to counteract poison—a characterization often applied to the function of kōans, especially pivot words that transmute a phrase that expresses ignorance to one that expresses wisdom. The exorcism is based on the power that exists within people to recognize and come to terms with their shame. It symbolizes a consequent sense of revulsion and profound change of heart.

The main moral implication is that being enraptured by illusion must be taken to its logical extreme or "bottoming out" stage—as in the potter's delirious passion—as an emotional turning point before attaining transformation. In one traditional tale, for example, a vixen begs to ride on the backs of men's horses, then jumps off and laughs at their folly.[38] Deciding to put an end to this trickery, a conscientious palace guard offers her a ride and then captures and ties her down. Back to the capital he rides to show off his prize, but she transfigures into a small, agile fox shape and escapes. The guard realizes that he has been the victim of "an elaborate illusion: what he thought was the capital and the lights of the city have been created by the fox, and in reality he is in the forest without his horse." But after recovering from an illness caused by the failed first attempt, the guard returns to the area and this time succeeds in scaring off the fox/woman. In contrast to some kōan commentaries in which correct understanding alone is sufficient for attaining liberation, morality tales require a full cycle of karmic suffering and emancipation encompassing the nonhuman dimensions of the six realms of samsara, such as transmigration into animal, godlike, and ghostly forms.[39] Undergoing bewitchment eventually results in the drama of self-realization that philosophy alone cannot express. The *setsuwa* approach resembles practices in esoteric Buddhism in which the experiences of suffering, hell, and even symbolic death are necessary for spiritual rebirth.[40]

There are many examples of Chinese literature in addition to kōans that interact with elements from accounts of anomalies. One of the primary early instances of this kind of intertextuality is fifth-century poet Tao Ch'ien's utopian poetic essay, "Peach Blossom Spring." According to Tao's work, a stray fisherman accidentally discovers a society that has been kept hidden for five hundred years, a place where the vegetation is lush and beautiful and the people are peaceful and harmonious because they live in accord with the principles of nature (thereby revealing a union of Confucian and Taoist influences). The society does not use calendars or clocks, for instance, because people judge time based on natural cycles. But when the fisherman leaves the ideal village, it returns to its hermetic state and he is unable to find it again. It seems clear that Tao Ch'ien was greatly influenced by folktales recorded in the *Sou-shen chi* and *Sou-shen hou-chi* collections. In these tales a standard topos is that "a man loses his way in some grove or grotto, stumbles upon an immortal realm (or at least arrives at its threshold), encounters immortals before reverting to the mundane world, and subsequently tries in vain to return again."[41]

Looking at the fox kōan in terms of force-field elements contained in *setsuwa* literature sheds new light therefore, on some of the philosophical commentaries. For example, the denial of polysemous perspectives expressed in the following verse can be understood not merely as reinforcing the paradoxical equalization of opposites but as a surrender of conceptuality to an existential experience of repentance leading to tranquility: "Not obscuring, not falling, / Mistake, mistake, mistake, mistake number one. / Not falling, not obscuring, / No, no, no, no again. / Sitting in great serenity, / It is all a puzzle to me."[42] Another verse commentary stresses a spiritual turnabout that is attained through a realization that the puzzling disarray of conceptual constructs is all a mistake. As in the case of Genjuro, there is an acceptance of ephemeral reality and the fateful inevitability of karmic consequences: "Not falling, not obscuring, / Both are wrong, / Giving and receiving, / Are not yet forgotten; / Recognize your emotions and attachments, / Words are incomplete; / There is no rope, / So how can you tie yourself up? / When it is spring, flowers blossom, / When autumn arrives, leaves fall, / Who knows how many mistakes have been made, / But everyone is saved with the ringing of the bell."[43]

Supernatural Cycle of Appearance and Disappearance

The intersection of philosophical paradoxicality and folk religious bivalence in the fox kōan is reflected in the rhythm of the appearance/disappearance of the *fei-jen,* which coincides with the stages in the former Pai-chang's spiritual progression from the deluded to the liberated side of the polarity pattern. A tale from the *Konjaku monogatari* collection (no. 16.17) pointedly illustrates the rhythmic structure that is evident in fox lore from *Jen-shih chuan* to *Ugetsu*.[44] Yoshifuji, whose wife has gone for a trip to the capital, is seduced by a beautiful woman under the approving eye of her father who says that he "was always meant to come here." The couple pledge their eternal love, have a child together, live in her mansion, and Yoshifuji feels that he has not a care in the world. His brothers, worried at home while he is missing, call upon Kannon for help in finding him. Suddenly a man with a stick, a messenger of the Buddhist deity, arrives at his new home, scares everyone in the household away, and Yoshifuji crawls out from the storehouse under his old house. Still under the sway of the bewitchment, he starts to show off his new son to his older boy, declaring the youngster to be his true heir, but there is in reality no one with him. After a servant finds lots of foxes under the storehouse, it turns out that Yoshifuji had been tricked into marrying a vixen. A yin/yang diviner—the second form of ritual purification that is required—is called upon to perform an exorcism and eventually Yoshifuji comes to his senses.

In a classic expression of the theme of illusionary realism—especially the moment of comprehension and thus the reversal of the negative effects of karma—the narrator writes: "The thirteen days he had spent under the storehouse had seemed to him like thirteen years, and the few inches of clearance between the ground and the floor of the building had looked to him like a stately home. The foxes had done all this." This recalls the *Otogizōshi* tale cited in Chapter 3 in which an old priest realizes: "The mansion, the splendid large dwelling house with a big gate was gone!"—just as a fox comes into view. Several important aspects of exorcism are evident in these tales: syncretism, in that Yoshifuji is released by a combination of Kannon and yin/yang divination; homeopathy, because Buddhist symbols, including bodhisattvas and sutras, are effective tools in the case of a priest's possession/delusion; and, most significantly, repentance, since the rituals coincide with the victims of possession shamefully coming to terms with the error of their ways.

The main principle underlying the cycle is that foxes at first remain invisible by hiding themselves behind their transfigured pose. It is only "when a supernatural creature has conceded defeat, [that] it will show its true form" and thereby allow the dilapidated mansion to come into view for victim and companions.[45] In a *Konjaku monogatari* tale (27.5), for example, when a creature that had been frightening people was caught it confessed, "I am a water spirit," and then it disappeared, never to be heard from again.[46] In the case of Yoshifuji, foxes are at first nowhere in evidence, but they appear as soon as his illusory world starts dissolving due to the exorcism. In the fox kōan, the monk says that he is a fox but he appears as a man who is seen only by Pai-chang. The other monks are told a funeral will be taking place but they are surprised because they do not know of the *fei-jen*'s existence and no one else has been sick in the infirmary. This cognitive gap is recognized in Dōgen's "Daishugyō" commentary in that he questions the propriety of granting a ceremony to a being whose human, let alone Buddhist, status has not been verified. When the current Pai-chang uncovers the fox corpse behind the temple, its death and burial represent the demise of the former Pai-chang's illusion. Unlike the case of the *nāga* who wanted to participate in the *saṃgha* by disguising himself as an acolyte, the ancient monk in the kōan concedes defeat and begs for an exorcism. In contrast to *setsuwa* tales, the fox/monk comes forward willingly at the beginning of the story (although Miss Jen does reveal her identity right away). This seems to indicate one of two possibilities: the fox/monk may represent the manifestation of a bodhisattva who has chosen to reveal himself in a fallen form for pedagogical purposes; or the narrative may actually be focused more on the moral challenge presented to the exorcist receiving the confession and expiating wrongdoing—the current Pai-chang, whose feats are tracked throughout the kōan's tale—than on the concerns of the confessor, who is actually a reflection of the exorcist's repentance.

Based on the morphology of fox folklore, it is possible to reconstruct five stages of the cycle of appearance/disappearance that symbolize the sequence of repentance and self-realization taking place in the kōan:

1. Possession: the daily appearance of the *fei-jen*
2. Confession: the former Pai-chang's acknowledgment of his error
3. Exorcism: the current Pai-chang's pivot word
4. Renunciation: the reversion of the ancient monk to his vulpine shape
5. Postmortem reflection: the incident of Huang-po's slap

This analysis helps answer a number of the questions previously raised about the *fei-jen* status of the confessor, Huang-po's slapping his teacher, and the general role of supernaturalism in relation to Zen's anti-supernatural discourse.

The first stage is the transfiguration—the appearance of the fox that represents an experience of liminality or a crossing over into the realm of bivalence. This state can take place in one of two directions: either a fox anthropomorphizes in order to deceive and seduce; or a person is changed into a fox as punishment or as a bodhisattva's compassionate choice (far less common though not improbable in East Asian lore). In the kōan, the first stage applies to the old monk who as a *fei-jen* due to karmic retribution attends the sermons each day with the congregation, disguised as his former self. The kōan seems to be an intriguing combination of three possibilities for transfiguration: (1) the ancient monk claims to be a human being punished as a fox, although (2) this might be part of a bodhisattva-like strategy to teach a lesson, yet (3) he is also a fox taking human form who reverts to a vulpine shape at the time of death, which is the typical folklore pattern. Regardless of the direction of the shape-shifting, the meaning of the *fei-jen*'s presence is the coming to the surface of a karmically determined illusion that follows the rules of two corollary principles of transfiguration. One rule is that the more deep-seated the delusion, the more convincing or frightening is the status of the apparition. Thus the beauty of the lovers of Genjuro or Yoshifuji and the glory yet devastation of the mansions they behold reflect the heights of their arrogance as well as the depths of their self-deception. The other rule pertains to the duration of illusion: "Time is taken as a correlative measure of the prowess attained by the fox spirit: the longer an object or animate being exists, the higher its spiritual attainment will be."[47] Or as an inversion of this: the longer the deception, the greater the degree of punishment. The duration corollary has a resonance with the rule in the early Vinaya that the time of penance or banishment is increased for those who do not confess promptly; in some cases, the exact number of days since the time of the transgression is added to the period of punishment. Both corollaries apply in the kōan. The apparition is so convincing that Pai-chang himself does not realize at first that the fox/monk is not a member of the assembly when he attends the daily sermons; at the same time, the other monks are not at all aware of his presence until the burial. Moreover the five hundred lifetimes of transmigration—whether counted, as Dōgen wonders, as human or fox lives—is a formidable sum. In Chinese folklore, one thousand years is considered a threshold point indicating the attainment of supernatural powers, a figure surpassed at least by severalfold in this case. At the same time, according to Zen thought, especially in the *Ts'ung-jung lu* commentary, a single moment of ignorance or deception if sufficiently severe can cause an inestimable period of karmic retribution. In folklore, a single moment of touching a robe or some other efficacious instantaneous act can redeem a thousand lifetimes of transgression.

The next two stages—confession and exorcism—refer to the way delusions are exposed and brought to a level of self-awareness leading to their elimination through ritual purification. In *setsuwa* tales, the *kuai* being "appears only *after* the man has acknowledged his past evil and begged for compassion in the life to come. . . . It is only when he has taken the two steps of confession and repudiation of past evils that he can be saved."[48] Thus the *fei-jen* or *kuai* phenomenon has already recognized, or has been recognized in, its true identity and it either desires to repent or can no longer resist the forces compelling repentance. Although an early Chinese folktale depicts the case of a fox resisting repentance, the encounter still inspires a contrite attitude in those who had been suffering but are released from bewitchment. Here a demon fox disguised as a father beats up on two boys who end up killing their real father, who had been trying to protect them, by mistaking his identity for the demon's. The demon then takes up residence in the house, once again passing himself off as the father, this time for many years, while the sons have no idea of what they have done. Some years later a priest walking by the house realizes that the demon has a malevolent aura and, despite the fox's

protest, enters the home chanting incantations. The bogus father immediately reverts to his fox shape and scurries under the bed where he is
cornered and killed. Realizing that they have slain their own father, the
sons rebury him with a proper funeral, but one son commits suicide and
the other dies of remorse shortly thereafter.[49] Another early example of
fox lore expresses the case of a *fei-jen* who wishes to repent. One day a
holy monk who is proficient in reciting the *Lotus Sutra* is approached on
his way to the lavatory by a demon who has been fated through several incarnations to a life of eating excrement in latrines. When the demon tells
the monk where he has hidden money stolen in a previous lifetime, the
monk uses the money to have the sutra copied. Later the demon reports
to the monk in a dream that he has been reborn in a better life due to the
redemptive power of the scripture.[50] In the fox kōan, the old monk gives
no outward sign of being a fox; but in explaining his true identity he is
forthright in recognizing the wrongdoing that caused his retribution. He
asks for and receives assistance from the current Pai-chang—all before
the fox body becomes perceptible as a corpse once he has been released
from his punishment. This requires two steps.

The first step is confession: the former Pai-chang's contrite explanation
of the attachments and misdeeds that caused his downfall. The next step
in eliminating the possesion—the third stage overall—is the exorcism:
the use of an appropriate gesture or utterance to complete the eradication of the invading spirit and the purification of defilement. Buddhist
exorcisms can be homeopathic—setting up a symbol, whether an icon or
scripture, as morally superior and purificatory of another symbol derived
from a common discursive pattern—or nonhomeopathic in using a symbol to overcome a symbol from an antithetical discourse. Both common
and antithetical symbols are embraced by the bivalent force field. The exorcisms may also be categorized as ecstatic—compelling the victim to
stand beyond his normal frame of mind or become subject to a positive
possession by a bodhisattva in order to eliminate an intrusion—or
enstatic in causing the victim to undergo a greater degree of introspec-
tion or self-reflection to attain freedom. *Ugetsu* is an example of
nonhomeopathic exorcism because the use of Sanskrit letters evokes the
foreign, universal Buddhist doctrine and creates an antipathy with the indigenous spirit world. Although the result of the purification is a state of
enstasis, reflected in Genjuro's new, contemplative lifestyle, ecstasis still
applies to some extent because the potter remains influenced by the
voice of his wife's ghost. Nonhomeopathic exorcism is also the case in the

record of the Muromachi-era Sōtō priest Gennō, who exorcised the notorious killing-stone fox by reciting a passage from Dōgen's writings. The
okiyome rite as an expulsion of spirit foxes in the New Religion known as
Mahikari (True Light) is ecstatic because it results in hysteria, convul-
sions, and glossolalia when the believers are liberated from their bondage
that caused sickness, poverty, conflict, and misfortune.[51] Yet many Buddhist exorcisms are homeopathic and enstatic (though these factors are
not necessarily associated)—as in the use of dialogue to communicate
with the intruding power and discover its needs or demands. Enstasis applies to Genjuro and others who internalize and reflect on the moral implications of the process of appearance and disappearance once they
realize the extent of the damage caused by the illusion generated by the
fei-jen.[52]

Homeopathic/enstatic exorcism is the pattern that is most appropriate
when the source of defilement emerges from within the realm of Buddhist discourse, or comes to be so defined, because the rite is generated
by internal forces and leads to self-reflection, self-criticism, and
self-correction. The pivot word in the fox kōan is an example of this category because the liberating power is based simply on the substitution of a
single character in a four-character phrase: from *pu-lo yin-kuo* to *pu-mei
yin-kuo*. The term *"lo"* (J. *raku*) generally has positive connotations in a
Buddhist context because it implies the casting or falling off of attachments—as in Dōgen's notion of "casting off body/mind" (C. *shen-hsin
t'o-lo*; J. *shinjin datsuraku*)—and the term *"mei"* generally has negative
connotations because it implies the blindness or foolishness of delusions
that obscure genuine insight into the true nature of reality. When the
negational prefix *"pu"* is added to both terms, however, the connotations
are reversed and *"pu-mei"* becomes positive as a double negation, which
suggests that the exorcistic quality of the pivot word touches base with
paradoxical wordplay leading to sudden release as emphasized in philosophical interpretations. In a way that is both like and unlike the
nonhomeopathic use of an incantation or sutra recitation, the simple utterance has a powerful, magical quality precisely because it delves into
the depths of the fox/monk's illusions, which he is forced to encounter
and overcome.

The ritual function of the pivot word helps answer the question: Why
could not the former Pai-chang, who must on some level have understood his error and been capable of correcting it intellectually, liberate
himself without the need to consult the current Pai-chang after endless

transmigrations? An aspect of the polarity pattern is that, as an icon of delusion, fox imagery allows for a metaphorical distance or psychological displacement by the deluded person who can thereby avoid direct blame or at least have a sense of shared responsibility while working toward a resolution of the crisis. Exorcism in Buddhist literature and practice does not deny the role of individuality or interiority altogether—especially in examples of homeopathic enstasis—but it tends to create a neutral focal point based on the integration of external and internal, or objective and subjective, factors. According to Winston Davis, the psychology of exorcism "distributes guilt and responsibility in a way that is quite foreign to Western notions. One's misfortunes and failures need not be borne alone, since those in the spirit world share the responsibility. In other words, responsibility is partially shifted to an external cause, reducing individual guilt."[53] Carmen Blacker observes that because of the deemphasis of individuality, "cases of fox possession only rarely find their way into mental hospitals in Japan. The patients will prefer the drama of the therapy to be conducted in religious terms, the malady caused by a being from another plane and the cure effected by a priest initiated into the sacred life."[54] The external ritualism the former Pai-chang requires can be understood as subduing rather than increasing "bad faith" in the Sartrean sense of avoiding self-responsibility to overcome one's delusions.[55]

The Dynamics of Repentance

Even granting the projectional function of the exorcism, the question still remains: why does self-power ideology need to engage in such discourse? This question goes to the heart of the larger issue of understanding the role of supernaturalism as a matter of compromise or consistency with Zen's essentially iconoclastic rhetorical standpoint. The answer to the question is twofold: on the one hand, Zen claims not to refrain from performing exorcism but to do it in superior fashion by directing it inwardly toward enstasis; on the other hand, the reliance on supernaturalism to articulate a philosophy of repentance indicates the need to fill a crucial lacuna in Zen monastic life by borrowing from popular religiosity. As noted earlier, Zen monasteries generally observe the basic Buddhist repentance rites on a monthly cycle (the Uposatha ceremony) and annual cycle (the Pravāraṇa ceremony that follows the post-rainy-season retreat), and they also include remorseful reflection as part of daily sutra reading or meditative walking exercises *(kinhin)*. According to the early Vinaya, the main rite of the Uposatha ceremony in which all monks or nuns were requested to participate was the recitation of the disciplinary code *(pratimokṣa)*. This rite brought the members of the community together to reaffirm their unity and provided them with an opportunity to discover and confess any offense that might have been committed. Mohan Wijayarata observes: "In fact, the ceremony was not a simple recitation. Monks and nuns were actually requested to undertake a thorough self-examination. We can say that the ceremony was a kind of 'quality control' for the Community."[56] Yet there was no guarantee that the ritual was always genuine and effective. Perhaps the "ceremony was more a ritual recitation of the *pratimokṣa* rules, a reaffirmation of community, than an actual public confession."[57]

Except for some famous exceptions, Sung Chinese and Kamakura Japanese Zen texts—including transmission of the lamp histories of lineal succession, recorded sayings of individual masters' sermons and lectures, and kōan collection prose and verse commentaries—do not speak extensively of the need for repentance or its benefits (or lack of same) in depicting Zen hagiography, practice, or philosophy. Even the main monastic code, the *Ch'an-yüan ch'ing-kuei*, contains only brief references, and the plans of the typical monastic compound did not contain a special chamber or repentance hall. Among the exceptions are Northern School texts such as the *Ta-sheng wu-sheng fang-p'ien men* and *Leng-ch'ieh shih-tzū chi;* two *Shōbōgenzō* fascicles, the 75-fascicle text "Keisei-sanshoku" and the 12-fascicle text "Sanjigo"; Ming-dynasty monastic revival texts by Chu-hung; the modern Sōtō essay, the "Shushōgi," constructed by culling from the *Shōbōgenzō;* and anecdotal, *monogatari*-like testimonies of social leaders, such as samurai in Tokugawa Japan, who saw the error of their ways and repented before converting to Buddhism.[58] Zen stands in contrast with several other medieval Buddhist traditions that did emphasize repentance rites: T'ien-t'ai, which integrated repentance involving ritual ablutions in sacred chambers into the practice of the Four Samādhi based on Chih-i's distinction in the *Fa-hua san-mei ch'an-i* between formless repentance in the realm of principle (C. *li;* J. *ri*) and form repentance in the realm of phenomena (C. *shih;* J. *ji*);[59] repentance practices based on a variety of mythological sutras dedicated to the supernatural powers of bodhisattvas who have the capacity to grant mercy, as followed in devotional and esoteric Buddhism;[60] and, of course, popular *setsuwa* tales of pious awakening, which employ many of these mythic themes.

What is the reason for the deemphasis in Zen that seems to lead the fox kōan to compensate by means of a supernatural explanation of repentance? Two of the basic Zen texts put an emphasis on repentance while providing a rationale to turn away from the need for confession—particularly in the sense of repentance or confession of specific misdeeds: the *Platform Sutra* and the *Shushōgi*. This is the case in the *Platform Sutra*'s focus on formless repentance. At first this text's view, which stresses that evil karma must be seen as originally empty and thus part of the purity of self-nature (C. *tzu-hsing;* J. *jishō*), seems to coincide with the T'ien-t'ai distinction between *shih-ch'an-hui* (J. *ji-zange*), or repentance for misdeeds committed in the realm of phenomenal reality, and *li-ch'an-hui* (J. *ri-zange*), or recognition of the absolute nature of reality, which is that all things are empty of own-being, including sin. The main difference is that whereas T'ien-t'ai acknowledges the role of *shih-ch'an-hui* while advocating its transcendence, the *Platform Sutra* denies *shih-ch'an-hui* as part of delusion that prohibits a realization of transcendence.[61]

The main sections dealing with the theme of formless repentance in the *Platform Sutra* are sections 22 and 33. Section 22 "explains the formless repentance that eradicates the sins of the triple world." According to this passage:

> If your past, present, or future thoughts as well as moment-to-moment thoughts are not stained by delusion, and if in a single instant you cast aside previous evil actions by virtue of self-nature, this itself is confession (C. *ch'an,* J. *zan,* seeking forgiveness). . . . What is repentance [made up of two characters, C. *ch'an,* J. zan, and C. *hui,* J. *ge,* regret]? Confession *(ch'an, zan)* is the nonproduction [of evil] throughout your life. Regret *(hui, ge)* is to realize your previous evil karma and never let this slip from your mind. *There is no reason to make a verbal confession before buddhas. In my teachings, forever to engage in nonproduction is the meaning of repentance.*[62]

This passage stresses the need to discard any trace of form repentance as so much distraction and delusion. In other words: verbal confession is counterproductive because the aim is to realize the nonproduction of evil based on the original purity of self-nature. The view that self-nature is inherently free from defilement is further highlighted in Lewis Lancaster's translation of several important lines in the preceding passage: "Remorse [*hui*] is being free of purposeful action (Skt. *apranihita*) for the whole of your life. Repentance is *knowing that with regard to the past there is no evil action* and never let this slip from your mind."[63] Section 33, "a verse of formlessness that will eradicate the sins of deluded people," continues this theme:

> Though [the ignorant person] hopes that making offerings and at-
> tending memorial services will bring boundless happiness,
> This only perpetuates the three karmas (of past, present, and fu-
> ture) in his mind.
> If you seek to eradicate sins by practices based on the pursuit of
> happiness,
> Then even if happiness is attained in the future the sins will not be
> eliminated.
> *If the mind is liberated from the very causes of sin,*
> *This is the true meaning of repentance within each self-nature.*
> If you awaken to the great vehicle and truly repent,
> Then you will surely attain a state of sinlessness.
> Contemplation of the self by those who are studying the Way
> Is the same as the awakening of those already enlightened.[64]

Here the *Platform Sutra* argues that true repentance is to awaken to a state of sinlessness, resembling the notion of original enlightenment, prior to the production of evil karma. According to David Chappell's insightful analysis of five types of repentance, the *Platform Sutra* creates a reversal from earlier notions of external, ceremonial confession by stressing the priority of the internal, mental world (enstasis): from this vantage point testimonies, offerings, and memorials (ecstasis) appear trapped in the pursuit of worldly benefits, which only perpetuates karma in the name of terminating it.[65] Moreover, Chappell sums up the differences between the Uposatha/Pravāraṇa ceremonies and the *Platform Sutra*: the ceremonies are based on rectifying wrongs in the sense of incorrect external behavior with regard to the Buddhist precepts in the immediate present through penance, exclusion, probation, restitution, or confession; the *Platform Sutra* is based on casting aside wrong thoughts and attitudes throughout the past, present, and future by realizing the purity of self-nature in that the true precepts stem from the threefold buddha body (Skt. *trikāya*) within each person.[66] Furthermore, the *Platform Sutra* points to the identification and equalization of those still practicing and the already enlightened: the unity of practice/attainment *(shushō ittō)* in Dōgen's terminology.

Dōgen similarly stresses that authentic spiritual attainment requires going beyond the ritualization of repentance when he cites his mentor Ju-ching's aphorism: "To study Zen is to cast off body-mind. It is not burning incense, worship, recitation of Amida's name, repentant practice *(shū-zan)*, or reading sutras, but the single-minded practice of *zazen*-only."[67] The message of "Shushōgi," however, a short text compiled from the *Shōbōgenzō* by Meiji-era Sōtō leaders, is somewhat different. The aim of this text is to provide an accessible theological framework used in Sōtō liturgy in modern times for monastics and laypersons alike. Although the content of "Shushōgi" does not necessarily correspond to the intent of the medieval source materials, it is especially important for understanding contemporary Sōtō thought and the roots of the problem of discrimination raised by Critical Buddhism. Section 2, titled *"zange metsuzai,"* or the elimination of evil karma through repentence, seems to stand in contrast to the *Platform Sutra* in that it supports repentance in the conventional ritualistic sense. Yet its message can also be seen as converging with the T'ang text in providing a rationale that vitiates the need for a systematic approach to *ji-zange* confession:

> Although karmic retribution for evil actions must come in the past, present, or future, to make repentance transforms things and accrues merit, and it results in the destruction of wrongdoing (or sin, *metsuzai*) and the realization of purity. . . . If you repent in the manner described, you will invariably receive the invisible assistance of the buddhas and patriarchs. Keeping this in your mind and following the rules for your bodily behavior, you must repent before the buddhas whose power will lead to the elimination of the causes of wrongdoing at their roots.[68]

This passage emphasizes the virtue of repentance in transforming evil deeds based on the power of forgiveness and the compassion of buddhas. It appears close to a mythological, supernatural perspective yet still requires self-discipline and meditative training. Like the *Platform Sutra*, "Shushōgi" suggests that wrongdoing can be fully eliminated and a state of sinlessness attained. In other words: both the *Platform Sutra*'s notion of the nonproduction of karma and "Shushōgi" 's notion of the destruction of karma *(metsuzai)* imply that ultimate human nature (or Buddha nature or *hongaku*) remains untainted by the effects of evil actions. But there is an underlying ethical problem: by giving priority to transcendence, these approaches may overlook some of the unintended consequences that arise from a deemphasis of feeling remorse and repentance for actual wrongdoings in the phenomenal realm of karmic causality.

This view is also expressed in a kōan recorded in *Eihei kōroku juko* case 9.5. This case is a direct takeoff on another, more famous case—*Wu-men kuan* case 41, in which Bodhidharma pacifies second patriarch Hui-k'o's "unobtainable mind" (C. *hsin-pu-hua-te;* J. *shin-fukatoku*) —combined with the syntax of Taoist faith healings (rather than that of Buddhist Uposatha).[69] In this version a lay disciple tells Hui-k'o—who has learned the lesson his master taught—that he is ill and would like to repent for his sins, which apparently were responsible for causing the illness in a literal view of karmic determination.[70] Hui-k'o tries to defeat the literal view, or to reorient it in terms of the doctrine of original purity, by saying: "Bring me your sins, and I will repent for them for you." After a while, the lay disciple says: "I cannot find my sins [or my sins are unobtainable]." And Hui-k'o proclaims: "I have repented for your sins for you. Now, you must take refuge in the Buddha, the Dharma, and the Saṃgha."[71] In this kōan, a sleight-of-hand piece of wordplay can cure all for the penitent whose affliction could not be attributed to a specific wrongdoing. The affliction is expiated by a full disclosure and renunciation of all sins, which are empty at their source by virtue of the purity of original enlightenment.[72] Although the approach seems to resemble Taoist or folk religious faith healing more than the Uposatha ceremony, it is based on the philosophical paradigm of the equalization of opposites: guilt and innocence, sin and sinlessness, illness and well-being. The fox kōan resembles the Hui-k'o repentance kōan in drawing from popular religious beliefs. But at least in the literal reading it seems designed to provide the antidote to the paradoxical approach, which negates form repentance, by stressing a belief in the inexorability of causality. Yet it also expresses the notion that repentance requires externalization and projection in a supernatural setting. It thereby swings Chappell's pendulum back in the direction of ceremony— though not to the Uposatha rite, which had been rendered more or less inapplicable by developments in Zen monasticism founded on the ideological legacy of the *Platform Sutra*. The pendulum is swinging, rather, to the more extreme standpoint of the efficacy of ritual exorcistic purification.

Five Hundred Lifetimes?

The final two stages of the cycle of appearance/disappearance—renunciation and postmortem reflection—have the capacity to reverse negative karma and lead to equanimity and release. In the tale about Yoshifuji the foxes flee from the storehouse as he comes to his senses. Similarly, in a *Konjaku monogatari* tale (13.17) a monk during a pilgrimage takes refuge in a cave where he is frightened and recites the *Lotus Sutra* for protection.[73] A large snake about to devour him consequently disappears. Then, "after a pounding rain, a man comes to the cave and thanks the monk, telling him that the rain drops were really tears of repentance, and that he has now been released from his evil existence as a snake."[74] In the kōan the de-transfiguration of the fox, which turns up dead and is buried by Pai-chang, represents the old monk's renunciation. But as in fox folklore, the telling moment is not so much the disappearance of the apparition as the unearthing of the vulpine shape—an event that causes all involved to recoil in horror and shame. Thus this stage also points out that the kōan is primarily focused on the current Pai-chang, the creator of Zen monastic rules for the taming of irregular ascetics and the banishment of miscreants, who uses his staff to uncover the fox corpse and furthermore reestablishes and reinforces monastic stability and order through the cremation and burial. As in *setsuwa* tales, this marks "the riddance of the supernatural intruder and the reestablishment of the natural (i.e., human) order which has been temporarily disrupted by the 'defeat' of the human representative."[75]

The concluding stage requires an act of contrition to demonstrate that one regrets prior wrongdoing and has learned from the experience of overcoming illusion—as when the potter in *Ugetsu* returns with his son to daily chores while maintaining a spiritual communication with his deceased wife. In the fox kōan, Huang-po's slap is a public display of the chastising and humiliation of his mentor Pai-chang: an intriguing role reversal that becomes paradigmatic in Zen lineal transmission narratives of disciples gaining approval by challenging or surpassing their masters. But the question remains: why is the current Pai-chang chastised when he was successful in administering the exorcism? From a demythological standpoint, Huang-po is awakening Pai-chang from a kind of intellectual slumber. For Pai-chang may have lulled himself into thinking the *kuai* apparition was real and thus may have created a self-deception in the midst of the attempt to break free from bondage to illusion.

From a mythological standpoint, Huang-po is performing an identification of vulpine or human existence—a common theme in fox folklore—knowing better than simply to trust that his master is no different than the former Pai-chang.[76] This interpretation sees the slap as "the exorcism of the exorcist." Since fox mythology has created a state of mystification, equivalent to a dream-within-a-dream, two acts of awakening are required from the Zen standpoint. As Pai-chang explains why the fox is receiving a monk's burial, all the other monks look on with disbelief. They are amazed that he has been deceived by a *fei-jen*—a sure sign of having lost a power basic to all Zen masters since the early days of the wizardry of "meditation masters." Huang-po's slap demonstrates the fact of nondeception to the other monks. And at the same time Pai-chang, who was preoccupied with his exploits in the realm of the supernatural, gratefully praises his disciple for bringing him back to his senses by pointing out the interior dimension of his encounter with the fox spirit.

In both the demythological and mythological interpretations, Huang-po's slap drives home the point made repeatedly in *setsuwa* tales that multiple acts of repentance, as in the cases of Genjuro and Yoshifuji, are required to deepen one's existential realization of the moral implications of releasing from illusion. We note that even the irreverent Ikkyū—especially Ikkyū—stressed the paramount significance of repentance. In the *Kyōunshū* (Crazy Cloud Anthology), Ikkyū admits that after ten days of his abbacy, he escaped the confines of the monastery for the "fish shop, tavern, or else a brothel." Yet he also repeatedly stresses the necessity of not ignoring the inviolability of cause-and-effect and the impact of karmic retribution.[77] Commenting specifically on the fox kōan, he writes self-reflectively about the inescapable moral dilemma caused by a life of licentious behavior:

> A monk who has broken the precepts for eighty years,
> Repenting a Zen that has ignored cause and effect
>   (*jisan-inga-hatsumu-zen*).
> When ill, one suffers the effects of past deeds;
> Now how to act in order to atone for eons of bad karma.[78]

From the standpoint of the morphology of the narrative structure, the slap only makes sense if the former Pai-chang is identified (though not as a formulaic equalization) with the current Pai-chang, who has throughout the narrative been facing himself. In other words, he has been confronting an image of himself, bearded and irregular, standing in the liminal realm where the fox in the positive sense (of a genuine outsider) and the fox in the negative sense (of a rogue) intersect and manifest an appearance that is applicable to one undergoing a continuing process of repentance.[79] In encountering himself, he is confronting the realm of otherness in self and sect: a reprehensible yet necessary element that must at once be tamed for its disruptiveness by monastic rules but, because of its creativity, not altogether eliminated. Pai-chang has been enduring a profound sense of shame—either because he thought the apparition was real or because he refused to acknowledge its presence—and does not know what to repent for. But either way he deserves the slap. His shame, whether lasting for five minutes or five hundred moments, had seemed unendurable for

the five hundred moments felt like five hundred lifetimes . . .

and Pai-chang realized that the image lurking in the fox den beneath the boulder behind the temple compound gates that he beheld and expiated was none other than—and at the same time completely different from—his sense of himself. As we find in the commentary on "A Fox Dream": "So he wasn't dreaming, and yet it was a dream; he was dreaming, and yet it wasn't a dream. How was it not a dream? How was it *not* not a dream? How was it *not* not not a dream?"

The actions of the fox/monk and Pai-chang (or those of the former/current Pai-chang) can be provisionally distinguished in terms of two factors: cause and effect. If the action itself is considered a link between them, the process can be analyzed in terms of a tripartite structure. As illustrated in Figure 17, the cause is the intent of the actor, which can be based either on ignorance and defilement or on wisdom and illumination. If the cause is based on samsaric impulses stemming from ignorance in the realm of conditioned dharmas, then the act expresses an attachment *(pu-lo yin-kuo)* and the consequence results in transgression, sin, or evil leading to a further consequence of retribution (the demonic possession or transfiguration). But the experience of retribution becomes a turning point when the victim/perpetrator real-

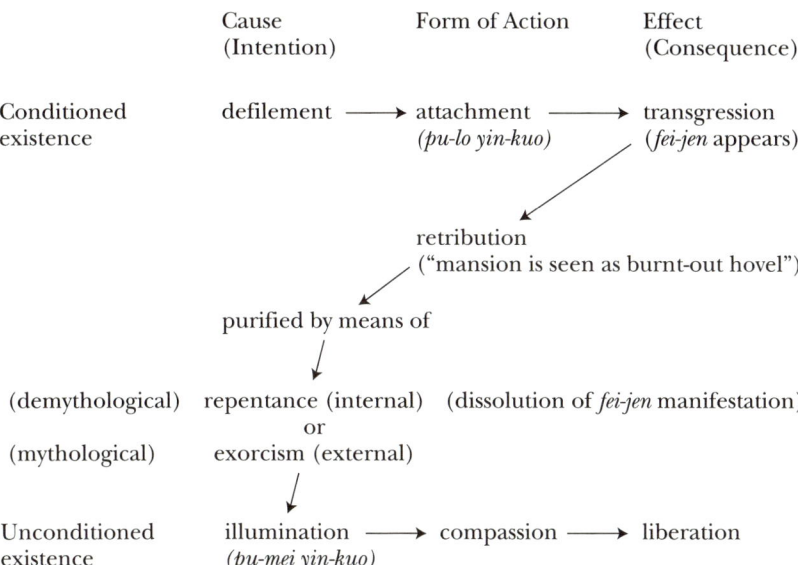

Figure 17. This diagram shows the dynamics of the repentance experience stemming from the encounter with retribution, which is both a result of and yet free from cause-and-effect: hence the "unity" of the *pu-lo yin-kuo* and *pu-mei yin-kuo* perspectives.

izes that the once glorious mansion is nothing but a burnt-out hovel in a pile of weeds and is compelled to confront the source of his illusions. When the contrition (for those who take self-responsibility in a demythological sense) or exorcism (for those who rely on the efficacy of other-power supernaturalism) is acted upon as a new intention or cause (*pu-mei yin-kuo*)—in a manner that is both bound by and free from causality—then the consequence is experienced and cultivated as a liberation and blessing.

6 · Unconcluding Methodological Reflections

—Master: Soup first, or noodles first?
—First, observe the whole bowl.
—Yes, sir.
—Appreciate its gestalt, savor the aromas. Jewels of fat glittering on
    the surface. Shinachiku roots shining. Seaweed slowly
    sinking. Spring onions floating. Concentrate on the three
    pork slices. . . . They play the key role, but stay modestly
    hidden. First caress the surface . . . with the chopstick tips.
—What for?
—To express affection.
—I see.
—Then poke the pork.
—Eat the pork first?
—No, just touch it. Caress it with the chopstick tips, gently pick it up,
    and dip it into the soup on the right of the bowl. What's
    important here . . . is to apologize to the pork by saying,
    "See you soon."
(pause)

    Finally start eating, the noodles first. Oh, at this time . . .
    while slurping the noodles, look at the pork.
—Yes.
—Eye it affectionately.
—From Itami Jūzō's 1987 film, Tampopo

    This chapter reconsiders the methodological implications of interpreting the relation between the paradigms of philosophy/demythology and folklore/mythology in attempting to overcome the hierarchical, two-tiered model of great and little traditions. Our main goal here is not to dispense altogether with the notion of distinct structures as a view that has somehow been superimposed on the kōan tradition by extraneous forces such as modern Western ideologies. Such a move would likely end in distorting rather than appropriating the development of the tradition. Like Buddhism in general, this tradition has consistently demonstrated a discrimination of correct or authentic versus incorrect or inauthentic beliefs in notions—such as the distinction between conditioned and unconditioned reality, the theory of Two Truths, and the assimilative doctrine of *honji-suijaku*. Our aim, rather, is to recognize the influence of the mythological perspective and to evaluate the connection between structures in terms of a nonjudgmental and nonhierarchical (or horizontal rather than vertical) framework. This approach avoids privileging the mainstream line of interpretation based on paradox by highlighting the elements of bivalence that, as part of the force field of the kōan narrative, drive the paradoxical viewpoint. The bivalent elements are further reflected in the *am*-bivalent attitude of philosophical commentators toward the issue of supernaturalism.

But we must be careful not simply to reverse priorities by accentuating the muted structure as being somehow primary since that would perpetuate an imbalanced, one-sided standpoint. The goal is to preserve and yet bracket the perspective of tiers from a standpoint that embraces polarized discursive structures: to identify how the two paradigms complement and enhance while remaining distant and critical of one another in stemming from a force field that uses the fox as a symbol of moral crisis. The convergence between paradigms is based on a call for overcoming illusion that must occur within the bounds of the causal process, which is constantly tested and redefined in light of an encounter with some aspect of noncausality.

A demythological approach regards the fox not as a being that literally possesses people but as a transpersonal icon: an open-ended, polysemous sign that allows for the complex crossing over and mediation between otherwise severed or facilely identified conceptual realms, including conditioned and unconditioned reality. But this representation of the fox turns out to be quite similar to the mythological perspective since, for example, the narrator of *Jen-shih chuan* has scolded Jen's lover, Cheng, for failing to take his tragic affair with the vixen Miss Jen as an opportunity to investigate the boundary—the discrepancies as well as similarities—between spirits and humans. The narrator refers to a boundary—in this in-stance, the boundary separating the noble actions of the *fei-jen* from her petty, narrow-minded human companions—that must be questioned in order to clarify the shape of the discursive arenas that exist on either side of the flexible, ever shifting borderline encompassed by the force field. In the case of the fox kōan, the boundary between the ancient nonhuman master and the current human master of Mount Pai-chang must be ac-knowledged and clarified before it can be erased.

Methodological Overtones and Undertones

Coming to terms with the relation between paradigms—and different manifestations of Pai-chang—depends on forming a methodology for ex-amining the dynamic movement between realms separated by the *Jen-shih*-like boundary. The movement operates on three interlocking levels in which the influence of bivalence is apparent: the interior level, or the inner turmoil of the victim/exorcist (in this case, Pai-chang repre-sents both parties); the intra- and intersectarian level, or the relation be-tween Zen and other Buddhist and non-Buddhist sects in establishing legitimacy and authority in a competitive environment; and the intertextual level, or the profound mutuality of influences and borrowing of ideas, imagery, and icons deriving from the force field and crossing over sectarian lines. After discussing the first two levels, including a criti-cal examination of how various scholars have dealt with these issues, I will explain an alternative approach based on the notion of intertextual transference.

The first level refers to the psychological encounter between the two sides of Pai-chang. The identity of the "former master" of Mount Pai-chang should not be reduced to a purely imaginary entity or to an al-legorical figment; it should be considered a projection of the "current master's" encounter with conflicting aspects symbolized by the wild fox. From this standpoint the current Pai-chang—in a timeless moment or a time that lasts five moments but seems like five hundred lifetimes—is in dialogue with himself and liberating himself (or that morally deficient segment symbolized by fox possession) and Huang-po's slap completes and confirms an act of contrition for his misunderstanding. This interpre-tation is supported by the drawing in Figure 3 (Chapter 1) that shows Pai-chang rising or emanating out of the vulpine corpse even as he per-forms an exorcistic mudra over the fox body. Pai-chang is at once the victim of possession or retribution and the vehicle for generating exorcism and release. The function of the movement between boundaries in the interior dimension seems to correspond to the way images of mythical time and space representing illusions are evoked in numerous *setsuwa* tales (Yoshifuji's thirteen years and the dissolution of his mansion, for example, as well as similar episodes in *Jen-shih chuan* and *Ugetsu*). As in the narrative about two Ch'iens in *Wu-men kuan* case 35—which is based on a T'ang folktale of ill-fated lovers kept apart by their families yet united through the bilocation of the bride who is eventually restored to her true identity—this conceit allows for a displacement of the fundamental existential problem onto another person mythically portrayed. The effect enhances the cathartic function by detaching and resolving the interior event in terms of externalized circumstances in a way that accords with the role of exorcism in various Buddhist and non-Buddhist practices. But while Pai-chang's encounter is to some extent interior—dealing with his own attachments and sense of arrogance in presuming that as abbot he is somehow immune to karma—this is not the exclusive meaning of the episode. He can also be seen as confronting and eliminating the antinomian tendencies he finds in the Zen practice surrounding him or his temple compound, for example, which must be stifled by rules of expulsion. In both scenarios, the fox symbolizes wildness in the negative sense. But perhaps the former master is also a distorted image of wildness in the positive sense of an experiential realm that purposefully fosters the transgression of debilitating rules. This image of Pai-chang the fox represents the legitimate behavioral trends of unrestrained Zen masters—such as hermits dwelling in huts and meditating on Ta-hsiung Peak—that are easily misunderstood by Confucian rivals. Whether the wildness is positive or negative, the encounter between the two Pai-changs on some level draws attention away from the interior dimension and toward the significance of external factors.

The second level of conceptual movement pertains to Zen's intra- and intersectarian ideological exchange with other Buddhist, Taoist, Shinto, and folk religious sects and cults. By deploying the imagery of spirit possession, the kōan is at once able to usurp as well as dispel the animistic elements used by rival ideologies. This can be characterized as a process of hegemonic functionality in that Zen discourse establishes dominance by domesticating the otherness of local cults and showing its own superiority in controlling what is disruptive. Zen and indigenous religions coexist in a competitive relation—a kind of chess game in which the "winner" is often based on ritual efficacy (orthopraxy) rather than theological consistency (orthodoxy). One reason for using this criterion is that the various religious movements, in sharing a force field of common beliefs, often do not contest these beliefs. Rather, their sense of testing/contesting involves the use of correct practices, such as displays of supranormal powers that are situationally appropriate or efficacious, which is why in *setsuwa* sources there are often multiple kinds and degrees of exorcism/repentance. Using the notion of hegemonic functionality also explains how Pai-chang can be regarded as an accomplished exorcist as well as a master who would never dream of indulging in supernatural practices—a conjunction of seemingly contradictory ideologies symbolized by the juxtaposition of the two inscribed stones, the wild fox rock and the Vinaya rock, standing between the compound and Ta-hsiung Peak in the diagram of Mount Pai-chang (Figure 10).

In parallel fashion, Zen shares with Confucianism a view of patriarchal lineal transmission drawing from a force field of ancestor worship beliefs. The dispute between sects, then, primarily concerns the means of legitimating genealogies. The interaction between religious sectors is not necessarily a hostile competition—though hostility did break out rather dramatically in the 840s suppression and other instances—but an ongoing process of assimilation marked by compromise and accommodation as much as by conflict and contrast. Zen, like other forms of Buddhism, has had to learn to outplay indigenous cults at their own game rather than simply reject or disdain them. Thus Zen has taken on some of their features in adapting its own identity while also trying to indoctrinate followers with Zen Buddhist values.

Examining Diverse Methodologies Dealing with Hegemonic Functionality

Holmes Welch points out the problematic conventional two-tiered view in which "foreign writers on Chinese Buddhism have portrayed the *saṃgha* as divided into two camps: those who performed Buddhist services with the enthusiasm of greed or superstitious ignorance; and those who did so as a disagreeable necessity because they depended on it for livelihood."[1] Yet numerous scholars of East Asian Buddhism have been challenging the assumption that Zen leaders abhorred the necessity for superstition. They stress the need to overcome the trickle-down view of popular religion as something marginal, insignificant, or even deficient that at best represents a failure to evolve and at worse is a force that cannot help but contaminate elite religion. "But as long as Chinese religion is viewed from the top downward," Stephen Teiser argues in *The Ghost Festival in Medieval China,* "the most persistent forms of ritual activity will be relegated to the unchanging and lackluster heap of 'popular religion.'" In order to cast aside dichotomous and top-heavy assumptions, he argues, "we must address the enduring components of Chinese socioreligious life: mythology, ritual, cosmological conceptions, religious virtuosi, the ancestral cult."[2] Once Teiser's suggestion is acted upon and a hierarchical view is replaced by a horizontal model—with the basic dichotomy of structures preserved yet recast in a new light—the next question is how to evaluate the interaction between structures. Recent scholarship has evinced several attitudes toward evaluating the lines of continuity/discontinuity or compatibility/incompatibility that emerge in a consideration of medieval Zen's hegemonic functionality. These recent approaches have stressed: an epistemological gap between elite and popular religions; a seamless continuity between traditions; a view that the traditions represent separate but parallel paradigms; and an emphasis on the way the monastic institution absorbs popular religious elements.[3] Although innovatively executed by eminent scholars, these approaches often tend to recreate unwittingly a two-tiered model. After critically discussing these attitudes, I explore an alternative standpoint that seeks to overcome the methodological impasse the trickle-down model tends to create.

The first approach—stressing epistemological inconsistency—is best exemplified in books and articles by Bernard Faure: *The Rhetoric of Immediacy, Chan Insights and Oversights,* and *Visions of Power* combine a masterful command of original sources with a variety of poststructuralist literary and critical theories to provide a wide-ranging cultural and epistemological critique of the Zen tradition. In Foucauldian fashion, but with an additional "Californian obsession," Faure focuses on what he refers to as the "fault line" (rather than the image of "boundary" used in *Jen-shih chuan*) between the ideology of immediacy—which stresses a uniform, idealized, utopian vision—and the ritual of mediation, which gives rise to multiple factors of religious practice, many of which seem to disregard or violate the basic ideal of purity.[4] In the conclusion of *The Rhetoric of Immediacy,* he argues: "This fault line, which I followed throughout representations of Chan attitudes toward dreams, thaumaturgy, death, relics, ritual, and gods, has been usually silenced or explained away—by notions such as the Two Truths."[5] One of the two main victims of the silencing of popular religion by the mainstream philosophical tradition, which evokes the doctrine of the identity of absolute and relative truths, are the "inner dialogues" of Zen. This refers to the intrasectarian disputes about the orthopraxic efficacy of rites and symbols that philosophers conceal in order to portray a unified front. The other factor concealed is the syncretic elements in Zen. These Faure categorizes as either "militant syncretism," which opposes and seeks to overcome opposing cults, or "popular syncretism," which attempts to fuse with rivals in adapting an "if you can't lick 'em, join 'em" outlook.[6] Yet Faure shows that underlying and continually breaking through the facade of univocality is a pervasive multivocality. Thus in an individual thinker or in a single text there coexist various voices causing repeated distances, discrepancies, and dislocations to reverberate on diverse discursive layers. There are three primary discursive layers: theoretical discourse, or the mainstream demythologizing philosophy striving for pristine purity; practical logic, which contradicts pure theory through a plurality of mediating forces that are oblivious to charges of impurity; and the collusion of the theoretical and practical, which occurs by reconciling their very contradiction.[7]

Faure's approach is itself complex and multifaceted. In addition to nearly revolutionizing the field with his relentless focus on the role of popular religion in relation to Zen iconoclasm, he displays a consistently probing attitude characterized by a remarkable degree of methodological flexibility and self-reflective criticism about the limitations of whatever hermeneutic angle he develops. Over the course of his writings, there emerge overtones of skeptical doubt concerning the ability of Zen discourse to reconcile its contradictory elements—or even sharp criticism of the tradition in a manner that seems to imply a hierarchical evaluation and critique of contamination caused by the practical logic of popular religion. Moreover, there are undertones of a theme of depicting the multiple layers of Zen discourse in a way that, devoid of judgment or criticism, attempts a neutral inquiry into the tradition. The tension between the overtones and undertones in Faure's approach is evident, for example, in his interpretation of the relation between the discourses concerning sacred space in Zen iconoclastic philosophy and sacramental religiosity. In this case, Faure's undertone hermeneutic suggests a descriptive approach that refrains from imposing a hierarchical evaluation. "We have here," he explains in his analysis of Keizan, the fourth patriarch of Sōtō

Zen in Japan, who was largely responsibile for the sect's pattern of the assimilation of estoric rites and indigenous deities, "a confrontation between two incompatible worldviews (even though they do coexist in practice): the utopian, unlocalized, and universalist conception derived from Buddhism, and the 'locative' and localized conception of local religion—two visions of space, two different anthropologies. Paradoxically, the utopian view is actualized spatially in architectural layouts, and temporally in the structure of ritual."[8]

Yet it is clear that Faure is also at times distressed by Zen's use of the Two Truths theory to mask its unsettling compromises with indigenous traditions, although his concerns in this regard are quite different from similar objections raised by Critical Buddhism.[9] Indeed, Faure's overtone implies a judgment when he points out that Zen discourse leads not "to an opposition between two juridically or socially distinct parties, but rather to what Lyotard would call a *différend* between incommensurable perceptions and unequal uses of the same space."[10] The overtone probably does not intend its reference to "unequal uses" to indicate hierarchy: it resembles Bourdieu's view of a "dual reading" of texts characterized by ambiguity as well as LaFleur's view of kōans and *setsuwa* as parallel but innately separate discourses. Yet in some ways Faure tends to recreate a two-tiered standpoint that sees Zen's interface with popular religion occurring along an epistemological fault line that represents the corruption of a supposedly incorruptible, *un*-popular religion.

Thus, for Faure, Zen's antisupernaturalist rhetoric suggests an evasiveness of the sect's origins whereby "Chan discourse proved *hybrid* in both senses of the term: its *hybris* led Chan to deny its hybridity in the name of pristine purity and to leave the solid ground of practice for the icy sphere of antinomian metaphysics."[11] This approach, if applied to the fox kōan, which Faure discusses in several instances, shows how popular religiosity was decoded and domesticated in the narrative of Pai-chang liberating the ancient monk. But it may not adequately describe how the muted structure contributes to the overall Zen view of karmic retribution and release, not so much by corrupting, but by enhancing it with its own sense of wisdom concerning the meaning of illusion and the mode of transforming ignorance through repentance. Faure's tendency to focus on the heterological dimension may overlook Derrida's notion of *différence* implying "to defer" as well as "to differ" (which he also cites)—which represents a different view of difference than Lyotard's notion of *différend,* one that leaves the door open to the intersecting aspects of, rather than the inevitable gap between, competing discourses.

The approach at the other end of the methodological spectrum—emphasizing a seamless continuity in that Zen and popular religiosity form a harmonious continuum without ideological conflict or compromise—is represented by William Bodiford's *Sōtō Zen in Medieval Japan*. This book does a highly commendable job of introducing and integrating a variety of traditional and modern materials about the post-Dōgen development of the sect. Bodiford, like Faure, is largely concerned with the various roles played by popular religion in shaping medieval Zen, including issues surrounding death, such as funerals, ghosts, revelatory dreams, and posthumous precepts. Moreover, both scholars are especially effective in explicating this theme by using the Muromachi-era esoteric kōan commentary materials known as *shōmono* or *kirigami*. The *kirigami*, which are among the main Sōtō documents available from the medieval period, reflect a creative use of traditional kōan records integrated with popular religious themes such as devotion to local gods and the exorcism of demonic spirits. Yet Bodiford's method is quite different from Faure's in that he sticks strictly to a Buddhist studies textual-historical approach without discussing contemporary history of religions, social scientific, or literary theoretical models. Apparently he thinks that a focus on theory would distract from an examination of religious texts.

Yet a lack of theoretical discussion does not mean there is no presupposing of a viewpoint or evaluation of popular religiosity vis-à-vis the elite structure. In this regard it is clear that Bodiford is nearly opposite to Faure in espousing a view that there is a profound compatibility and mutual enhancement of elite and popular religions generally lacking in conceptual tension or conflict. In dealing with the relation between the monastic ideal of indifference to material rewards and the practice of medieval Japanese Sōtō masters in rituals contributing directly to the pursuit of worldly benefits *(genze riyaku)* for the general populace, Bodiford argues that these elements may appear "somehow incompatible. However, the opposite can be just as true. In the eyes of rural laymen the power of Buddhist prayers was enhanced by the ritual and meditative practice of the monks."[12] This approach may suggest a "trickle-up" model that views the spiritual power *(zenjōriki)* of Zen leaders as an admixture of meditative and supranormal powers. But it does not attempt to generate a critical stance about the origins of and claims for this power. Still, the complexity of Bodiford's overall outlook is clear: he too expresses critical undertones. In a series of articles that deromanticize the idealized "Zen and the Art of . . ." syndrome, Bodiford focuses on the problem of discrimination in funeral rites in addition to other social shortcomings of the modern sect.[13]

Another approach to the relation between elite and popular religion in Sōtō Zen reaches conclusions that are nearly identical to Bodiford's seamless continuity by constructing a model based on the notion of "soteriological interdependence." Yamaoka Takaaki takes up the case of Saijōji temple located near Odawara City in Kanagawa prefecture on a mountain known as Mount Daiyūzan (C. Ta-hsiung-shan), named after the temple of Pai-chang, who is venerated with a large statue.[14] Saijōji has an especially interesting history and current style of practice revolving around bivalent images of the founder. The temple was founded in 1394 by Ryōan, a disciple of Tsūgen, who discovered the mountain when he was led to the site by an eagle—a messenger from the mountain's *bakemono* spirit or *tengu,* a long-nosed goblin. On the one hand, Ryōan is known for prolonged periods of meditation, like Pai-chang and Jui-yen in China, sitting on a "*zazen* stone" still located in the temple compound.[15] On the other hand, Ryōan is transmuted by the tradition into a supernatural figure who is enshrined in a form that combines human and *tengu* features referred to as Dōryōzon, or Dōryō-bodhisattva, "who is known to show his presence with mysterious occurrences and by his receptiveness to prayer."[16] In modern times, Saijōji has become both a training temple for monks under the auspices of Sōjiji temple in Yokohama—which along with Eiheiji is one of the two "head temples" *(honzan)* of the sect—and a prayer temple *(kitō jiin)* sponsoring numerous festivals for lay believers throughout the year. One of the main festivals is the sacred fire ceremony of late autumn—a nighttime rite in which the previous year's talismans are tossed into a sacred fire that is transported by monks blowing conch shells from the Dōryōzon shrine while worshipers, who pick up lucky beans during the procession, believe that their negative karma has been purified.

Yamaoka considers the two levels of religiosity that are operative at Saijōji: on one level is the monks' quest for tranquility through the self-discipline and self-negation of the ascetic practices of meditation and daily chores, or "world transcendence" (Skt. *lokattara*); on the other level is the lay believers' quest for worldly benefits through faith and a valorization of self seeking gains in the material realm, or "world affirmation" (Skt. *laukika*). According to Yamaoka, the two worldviews not only exist side-by-side. They are mutually supportive and interdependent in that the lay believers depend on the monks to receive their offerings and respond to their prayers and the elite monks are just as dependent on the lay believers through the process of extending their merit fields and delivering relief from suffering in order to demonstrate their realization of spiritual accomplishments. Neither of the two dimensions would be able to sustain itself without reference to the other. The intertwining of their soteriological claims culminates in the yearly cycle of ritual activities led by elite monks for the sake of the common folk. But Yamaoka's argument needs further support from two kinds of evidence that he fails to provide: documentation that the elite do not succumb to a cynical manipulation of the masses and evidence that the lay believers have a genuine understanding of the philosophical background of their participation in ritual.[17]

Neill McFarland's examination of the various roles played by images of Bodhidharma (C. Damo; J. Daruma) in Japanese society is similar to the seamless continuity approach taken by Bodiford and Yamaoka. In *Daruma: The Founder of Zen in Japanese Art and Popular Culture*, McFarland considers the question of how the first Chinese patriarch who epitomized Zen irreverence by criticizing the emperor and refusing to leave his meditation cave has come to be regarded as a talisman through the distribution of limbless Daruma dolls of various shapes, sizes, and degrees of craftmanship in temples and shrines throughout the country. Darumas rival *kitsune* icons in the pervasiveness and sheer variety of their appearances and uses. Of course, many features of the exaltation of Daruma were evident in the early hagiographic records—including reports of him losing his limbs during prolonged meditation and demanding that the second patriarch cut off his arm as a sign of determination, as well as the legend that in a fit of self-loathing for having fallen asleep during *zazen*, he tore off his eyebrows which then fell to the ground and sprouted tea leaves. There is also a degree of demythology built into certain rituals in which Darumas are routinely discarded or burned at the conclusion of a festival, somewhat resembling the treatment of kachinas in Native American rites. McFarland views Daruma as both a representative of sublime meditation and an object of affection and veneration—ranging from a charm for children to an inspirited recipient of devotion and prayers for relief from all manner of ailments and sorrow—and he finds continuity in the paradoxically linked mythical and demythical levels of discourse. He also considers the relation between sacred and secular appropriations of Daruma images, as in games or advertising, to be marked by an underlying ideological consistency.

McFarland deals especially with the intriguing issue of symbology, or symbolic uses of imagery, for in some cases Daruma dolls are large in size and elaborate in design but in iconoclastic images Bodhidharma is portrayed as a sketchy, hollow shape lacking human features or even as an empty circle. These images are barely recogizable as the first patriarch and seem entirely unrelated to the typical Daruma icons. According to McFarland's view of the consistency of images and nonimages of the first patriarch: "Thus, the conventional interpretation of Daruma, so rigidly stereotyped, is clearly an iconographic tradition; but it is not wholly an aberration. . . . It is an *iconoclastic iconography* or an *iconographic iconoclasm.*"[18] This approach, if applied to the fox kōan, stresses a homological compatibility between internal spirituality and exorcistic ritual. Yet by emphasizing that the high tradition uses popular religiosity to do its bidding, it may represent a two-tiered model that too readily reconciles contradictory materials. Like others in the seamless continuity approach, McFarland does not analyze fully the mutual transformation of divergent paradigms.

Two additional approaches attempt—from very different perspectives—to create a compromise between standpoints emphasizing the continuity or the discontinuity of discursive structures. One is William LaFleur's view, discussed in the previous chapter, dealing with the paradigms of transcendence in *setsuwa* literature and ludization in the fox kōan, among other forms of medieval Buddhist discourse. Yet in regarding these paradigms as separate and independent and by not examining the mutual influences and give-and-take between them, LaFleur falls short of developing a hermeneutic for understanding the formation of the kōan tradition. The other compromise approach is to be found in the works of Martin Collcutt and Griffith Foulk, who focus on the institutional operations of Zen monasticism, including the impact of political and economic forces and rivalries.[19] Collcutt and Foulk, like Bodiford, are buddhologists generally unconcerned with applying critical theory. The merit of their approach lies in a positivist historiography that creates its own demythologization by probing the limitations in traditional hagiographies, and both scholars are particularly forceful in questioning the tradition's claims about the role of Pai-chang's rules in shaping Zen monasticism. But they differ sharply from Bodiford in that they raise the issue of popular religiosity as it pertains to the monastic institution—as in mentioning the assimilation and veneration of indigenous local gods.[20] Thus the topic of popular religion—symbolized by the wild fox rock in addition to the Vinaya rock on Mount Pai-chang—does not receive sufficient attention for us to relate this approach to interpreting the origins of the fox kōan.

Intertextual Transference: From a Hierarchical to a Horizontal Model

Faure's approach, based on the presence of a fault line or epistemological gap, stresses heterological antithesis whereas Bodiford's approach based on continuity highlights homological synthesis. Another way of creating a compromise view that borrows from Faurean undertones emphasizes the role of different degrees of syncretism—understood as an unsystematic amalgamation of multiple perspectives encompassing shifting alliances and lines of divergence rather than a combination, harmonious or otherwise, of two different elements.[21] The starting point for this compromise position is an understanding that the coexistence of mythological and demythological elements opens up a discursive gap in Zen religiosity. This gap was not necessarily either evaded or sanctioned. But it was recognized as both problematic and inspirational by many thinkers in the formative period of the kōan tradition. Robert Gimello points in this direction when he comments on a Zen devotee's sense of inner turmoil about enjoying visionary experiences of Mañjuśrī and his celestial entourage on Mount Wu-t'ai, a practice treated with characteristic irony in several kōans, despite the *Lin-chi lu*'s admonitions against pilgrimages since the real bodhisattva is located not on the mountaintop but within the heart. According to Gimello: "The appearance of conflict between such things was noted widely during the Sung—for example, between the sober rationalism of literati culture or the disenchanting and demythologizing tendencies of Ch'an Buddhism, on the one hand, and the 'otherworldly,' visionary bent of those forms of Chinese Buddhism more characteristic of earlier times, on the other, or, just as often, between interior religious cultivation and exterior religious display."[22] Gimello's remarks can be coupled with Faure's focus on syncretism: "Chan adepts may find themselves on the threshold between learned and popular culture when they interpret in a 'spiritual' or 'allegorical' sense legends that they do not completely disbelieve." According to Faure: "Rather than an opposition—even if dialectical—or a fusion between Chan and local or popular religion, or between Chan and official religion, we can observe an intertwining of—or a transferential relationship among—antagonistic or analogous segments of each of these religious traditions."[23]

My approach extends the observations of Gimello concerning the tension between discourses and those of Faure concerning the suspension—or in some cases simply lack—of disbelief on the part of the elite. I argue that the compromise approach shows how Zen was affected by popular religion in that both derive from a common but dispersed and polysemous force field of fox imagery whereby one person or one text participates in two or more discourses or two or more discourses are simultaneously expressed in a single person or text.[24] Thus the debate between homological and heterological interpretations is resolvable in terms of seeing a third level of conceptual movement as an intertextual transference: a movement between fluid, interdependent texts rather than stiffened, independent sects that is in turn multileveled. The intertextual interaction of universal and local traditions forges an ideological compatibility and viability based on shared moral concerns. Yet intertextuality is also a critical, creative tension between discourses that does not culminate in either a *différend* or an unmediated continuum but is based, rather, on the continuing give-and-take that is at once mutually supportive and subversive. This is a process of accommodation/sublimation as well as distance/dislocation whereby Zen allows the folklore view to express itself while continually inverting and diverting its meaning.

The key is to develop an analysis not from the standpoint of how Zen trickles down to popular religion or how popular religion trickles up to Zen—both views fall into the pattern of a binary opposition—but in terms of the constant struggle between perspectives conceived on a horizontal playing field. According to James Berlin: "Rhetorics are usually born in conflict, representing formulations of competing ideological positions. Language is always a major arena of contention, with competing groups attempting to claim ownership of the 'true' methods of speaking and writing."[25] The topos of the intertextual encounter is language: the harbor and harbinger of meaning. The kōan—a linguistic snapshot of the ongoing process of recording oral dialogues that convey the encounter between traditions—reflects not just two but several levels of interconnected textual and metatextual (social and institutional) paradigms, at times overlapping or conflicting, that are contending for the meaning of the wild fox.

Gurevich and Bourdieu give prominence to the role of the muted structure—now highlighted not only as an equal partner in discursive exchange but as contributing to or even forming the force field of the dialogue at once generating and undermining the symbolism in the main structure. To use another analogy, the philosophical commentaries are the tip of an iceberg, the existence of which is predicated on a structure of popular religiosity that is foundational but submerged and thus hidden from view. The folklore structure must therefore be understood in a double sense. On one level, it is the opposite, secondary, somewhat suppressed end of a horizontal rather than vertical polarity with the main, overt philosophical structure. But on a deeper level, folklore ideology forms the reservoir of beliefs from which both structures emerge. Thus it helps shape the philosophical ambivalence that is reflective of supernatural bivalence in which the fox can be either, or both, an object of exorcism or a force for exorcism. From this perspective, it is possible to explain the problems of ambiguity in that the authors of medieval commentaries using fox imagery in ironic or duplicitous fashion thought they had no need to support or explain explicitly—though they could evoke indirectly—an idea in the force field that their readers already understood or took for granted without discussion. Or perhaps they were unwilling to take a strong stand in refuting what most people in the competitive religious environment already deeply believed, while at the same time giving the opposite signal about their outlook to the intellectual elite. In any case, the philosophical texts reveal an indebtedness to the force field—which, due to its contextual nature, is difficult to perceive and thus liable to be ignored or suppressed, disclosed only as a shadowy, muted discourse.

The polysemy of the term "wild fox spirit" is used on diverse levels reflecting rhetorical perspectives that, while at times conflicting, also depend upon and reinforce one another in continually referencing back to images of foxes as sacred mediators of transformation. Images of foxes, therefore, operate as a force field suggesting illusion, self-deception, or a dreamlike liminal realm in which the contours and boundaries of reality are called into question. The Zen kōan literary tradition seeking to establish its hegemony over local folk traditions in the formative T'ang period, as well as its credentials as a rational ideology in a Neo-Confucian environment in Sung China, as well as in a Tendai Buddhist context in Kamakura Japan, on one level selectively assimilates while at the same time actively dispelling and displacing the supernatural pattern of fox possession lore. Thus the philosophy of causality absorbs and is transformed by the supernaturalism it rejects in the very act of disdaining it. Encompassed by the force field, the relation between the paradigms of mythology and demythology is characterized by a homological dimension of convergence and complementarity in that both discourses highlight the problematics of delusion and the dynamics of attaining freedom. But it is also characterized by a heterological dimension—a notion that is especially clear in Bourdieu's theory of "doxa" underlying any conflict between orthodoxy and heterodoxy—of encounter and mutual subversion in that the philosophical view emphasizes an internal realization based on intellectual understanding and the folklore view emphasizes the external mechanics of exorcism. (For the positive side of bivalent fox iconography see Figure 18.)

The kōan does not merely reflect a state of being trapped in a discursive nexus it cannot control: it purposefully uses the backround of fox imagery for its moral impact. The imagery is not just descriptive or a substitute for literal description. Rather, it operates as a normative expression or as a driving force for a moral imperative by creating an atmosphere of embarrassment and revulsion. Many of the commentaries use indirect and ironic language. Such language neither accepts and en-

Figure 18. This maternal fox *(kitsune)* protecting her cub at the Toyokawa Inari/Myōgonji shrine/temple compound in Akasaka, Tokyo, illustrates the positive side of bivalent fox iconography. *Kitsune* is a protector of Dakini shinten (see Figure 6), whose image is kept hidden.

dorses nor refutes and dismisses the supernatural implications of the fox but prods the reader/disciple to overcome deficient karma and gain insight into reality. According to the opening section in the *Ts'ung-jung lu:* "If from the start you have even one word wrong in your heart you will go straight to hell like a flying arrow. This [monk] swallowed just a single drop of fox drool when he was thirty years old and he was never able to spit it out. This is not because heaven's commands are so harsh but because he was such a fool burdened by bad karma. How he must have transgressed in his previous lives!"[26] The final lines stress that the monk's karmic retribution does not occur because of a single misunderstanding or misstatement about causality: it derives from a profound degree of transgression building up to the moment when the punishment began. The monk's confession well may be disingenuous and perpetuate his self-deception, so that the term "a single drop of fox drool" becomes a call to action—to judge, reprimand, or punish the accused, whether oneself or others, as well as to repent and to elevate and purify one's actions. This notion is supported when the *Ts'ung-jung lu* commentary, which as a rule uses irony and humor to greater advantage than the *Wu-men kuan*, suggests: " 'Not falling,' 'not obscuring,' it is just a matter of words, / Too stubborn to stop drooling."[27]

The kōan embraces the following intertextually interactive elements: the rhetoric of antisupernaturalism, the legacy of exorcism, and the practice of amalgamation. In the first element, antisupernaturalism, philosophical commentaries often mock the claims of supernatural beliefs from a transcendental perspective and use the term "wild fox" as a rhetorical device indicating unenlightenment. The rhetorical level can be characterized as the "greatest" tradition (more or less corresponding to Faure's notion of the "theoretical layer") in the sense that it is the expression of supremely accomplished individual master/poets who seek to rise above the constraints of the institutionalized structure of the great tradition—the necessary but fundamentally delimiting social base that supports their transcendental outlook. The representatives of the greatest tradition are the individuals depicted in the commentaries who embody the fox in the positive sense of freedom and have appropriated the language of ritual purification for the purpose of disdaining the image of the wildness of the renegade priest. These figures refer to their rivals and to those who misrepresent the sect as foxes (in the negative sense). Yet they also call themselves and those they admire foxes (in the positive sense) in order to buffer themselves from the contemptible forces associated with the negative meaning. Yet they often delight in remaining ambivalent about the force field they refashion for the sake of edification, leaving it up to the audience to judge which meaning applies in a situation.

The intertextual element that appears to be the antithesis of the rhetorical level but continually interacts with it is the legacy of exorcistic trends—mixed with a tendency to assimilate local animistic religiosity at every stage—in which sacred images of the fox are seen as having a demonic, malevolent potential that, when improperly unleashed, requires a rite to purify and transform its power into a Buddhist framework. This element is the "littlest" tradition (corresponding to Faure's notion of "practical logic"). It represents pervasive ritual activity expressed in folklore literature existing beneath the structure yet often serving as the basis of the institutionalization of the little tradition. The great and little traditions can be defined in terms of the formation of institutional structures in relation to their respective claims for the salvific powers of icons and symbols. That is, the great tradition of Zen monasticism develops a centralizing institution based on a multibranched lineal transmission derived from the universal Buddha nature whereas the protean fox cults of the little tradition are regionally specific based on the bivalent function of vulpine images. Both traditions, great and little, create and support an institutional foundation for their practices that can intersect and become interdependent. The formula for the intersection seems to be this: the universal great tradition does not rely on but can embrace a variety of local deities; and the regional little tradition can symbiotically assimilate with a range of competing great tradition institutions. Therefore the greatest and littlest traditions are defined by *their shared concern with remaining unbound by an institutional structure*. The former—the eminent masters whose instructions are depicted in kōan dialogues—disdain the constraints of the monastery's social system by preferring to dwell in hermitages outside the compound gates. And the latter—the *fei-jen* and *jen* characters who populate spirit possession tales—are either unwilling to support only one creed in a search for the most efficacious mode of exorcism or are excluded from the mainstream community, which refuses to sanction their practices or dismisses them as superstition.

Embracing the interaction between the four dimensions of religious structure—the greatest and littlest traditions, which are at once polarized by the discrepancy between rhetorical excellence and ritual efficacy and bound by a noninstitutional structural link, and the great and little traditions, which disagree about universality versus localism but are bound by

Figure 19. This Tokugawa print of the "fox wedding" or "foxfire" *(kitsune-bi)* procession by Hiroshige is associated with another famous print of foxes gathered for the wedding under an *enoki* tree near Oji Inari shrine in Tokyo. According to legend, the foxes are eager to steal a groom in order to rob his life force and have one of their own disguise itself as his bride. In the drawing, the foxes are merrily leading off their victim in order to consummate the uncanny relationship. Today, a noodle restaurant stands near what was supposed to have been the original site of the fox wedding. This restaurant has a storehouse of fox masks, icons, and games from all over Japan and other parts of the world. One dish served is *kitsune-ken* (consisting of three foods symbolizing fox, hunter, lord—a takeoff on the children's game *jan-ken* (rock, paper, scissors).

an institutional structural link—is the practice of amalgamation (corresponding to Faure's notion of the "collusion" of the theoretical and practical). On this level, indigenous shape-shifting spirits like the fox, *nāga*, snake, tiger, or *tengu* are integrated into the mainstream religious and ritual structure by enshrinement in temple compounds and their images are woven into kōan narratives and other forms of literature and art, including exorcism tales, in order to craft a moral message. Amalgamation is the domain of the force field where great/little traditions commingle and define themselves in terms of their contrast—which is in turn shaped in the breach between rhetorical and exorcistic discursive realms. A prime example of the interaction on this level is Toyokawa Inari, the shrine where Zen and non-Buddhist forms of fox veneration compete and cooperate, so that the position of the primary and secondary icons may be continually alternated depending on festival cycles or the population sectors addressed in various rites. Although the images are defined hierarchically in Buddhist terms as *honzon* (main icon), *gongen* (avatar), and *chinjū* (monastery guardian), fox iconography appears on all levels simultaneously. The flying white fox carrying Dakini-shinten, for example, is the *honzon* concealed in an inner sanctum or holy of holies accessible only to specialized priests during a ritual performance; the fox statues with phallic tail and red bib guarding the torii as manifestations of the *gongen* are more openly displayed; and fox icons appearing in the memorial *reikozuka* (spirit-fox mound) serve as protective *chinjū*. Whereas the apparent diametrical opposites of greatest and littlest traditions actually have much in common—in not being tied to an institutional structure and in wanting to eliminate the fox—the domain of great/little traditions that stands in between yet encompasses their intersection seeks to uphold institutionalization by elevating and enshrining the fox, even if this sometimes involves an inverted form of demonization of one kind of shape-shifting in order to accentuate the veneration of a sacred fox.

In the intersection of discursive elements, shifting alliances between opposing standpoints mediated by the polysemy of bivalent imagery continually emerge and regress. (See Figure 20.) Antisupernaturalism and exorcism, for instance, which are opposed in epitomizing iconoclastic philosophy and sacramental religiosity, respectively, converge at the point of banishing the harmful effects of the demonic fox. Both are a form of domestication. And even though antisupernaturalism considers itself able to tame exorcism it does so in a way that is determined by the very structure it seeks to suppress, which is reflected in its alliance with

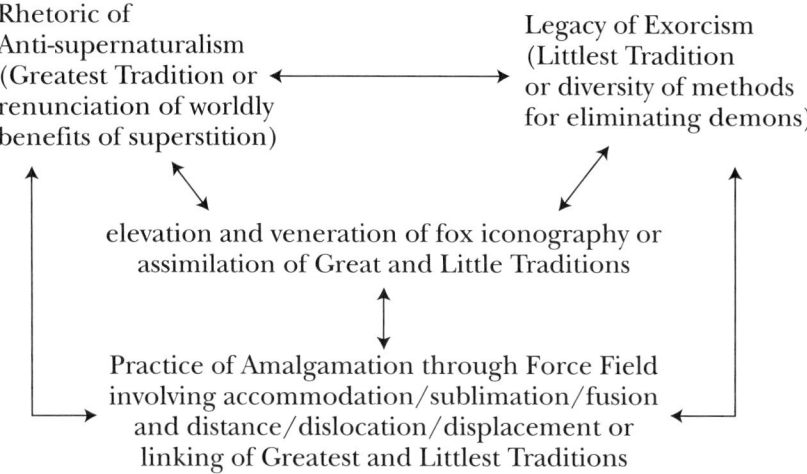

Figure 20. This diagram shows the intertextual interaction between discursive elements that are at once bound together and mutually repellent by virtue of being encompassed by the bivalent force field. The greatest and littlest traditions are polarized in practice yet linked in opposition to institutionalization, whereas great and little traditions form common institutional structures that compete for the veneration of fox iconography. The greatest and littlest traditions are connected through the practice of amalgamation despite the apparent polarity.

assimilationism. Furthermore, the philosophical paradigm embraces antisupernaturalism as well as assimilationism, and the popular religious paradigm encompasses exorcism and devotionalism; both share in amalgamation and distance themselves from it.

Therefore the phrase "wild fox" harboring a double structure—antisupernatural/supernatural and overt/muted—actually encompasses not just two but multiple levels of meaning. These levels include metaphysical paradox, in which the negative implications of wildness outweigh but are ultimately equalized with the positive implications of transcendence, and mythical bivalence, in which positivity and negativity coexist with the former transforming the latter which continually tries to undermine it. The term also contains an inverted structure, such as when it is evoked in a positive way that overrides the derisive implications (as in praise of someone's spiritual freedom or wildness); a reverse structure in that apparent heroes Pai-chang and Huang-po become the objects of criticism and ridicule rather than admiration so that negativity prevails; and a destructuring because the folktale of possession-exorcism contains the seeds of its own demythologization when understood as a process of cathartic displacement that defeats a fixation on either positive or negative meanings.

Poetic Epilogue

But in the end we must return to the kōan commentaries to understand the Zen view of the significance of the fox. Where do the commentators stand in regard to the issue of belief, suspension or lack of disbelief, or cynical compromise with supernaturalism? Or are they clever enough to avoid being pinned to a particular standpoint by always questioning the questioner or forcing those who would doubt to confront their own presuppositions and the undoubtedly biased source of their skepticism? On the one hand, the commentators emphasize that the way to overcome the fox-as-ignorance is to adapt a stance of nonattachment and nondiscrimination that views causality and noncausality from the standpoint of a paradoxical equality. On the other hand, they stress that the misuse or false sense of identity, which derives from a failure to discriminate causality and noncausality, results in nothing other than "wild fox Zen."[28] The following Sung-era verse echoes the opening section of the *Ts'ung-jung lu* commentary in suggesting that a single moment of indiscretion betrays a lifetime of ignorance plunging one into perpetual transmigrations:

> For five hundred lifetimes he was transfigured into a wild fox,
> Because the function of his mind was defiled by secular dust,
> One and only one word gave him away and caused this punishment,
> How his mind-ground endured such a show of stupidity![29]

The "one word" referred to here is *"lo"* or *"raku,"* which the current Pai-chang corrects by substituting *"mei"* or *"mai."* Despite the original purity of the mind-ground, the utterance of just a single word was all it took to create such a problem. The verse concludes with an ironic assertion suggesting that original enlightenment cannot be defiled. Or is the poet mocking this doctrine? Is one word really enough to correct the problem?

A *waka*-style commentary by Daikō sees the fox as a symbol of enlightenment:

> The thought
> Of renouncing the world
> Is awakened;
> But by the time this state has been attained,
> The fox still remains right there.[30]

Yet the verse is ambiguous due to the fundamental bivalence of supernatural imagery. It may be interpreted to mean that the fox is a perpetual threat that, like karmic causality, never vanishes even for an enlightened person. The aim of the commentaries is to remain noncommittal on the issue of supernaturalism while using the images of the fox spirit or fox drool ironically from the standpoint of an enlightenment experience that lies beyond and yet meaningfully explores the multiple implications of these terms.

The poetic comments on the fox kōan suggest that the ancient monk "was always of the fox body, right from the beginning, before he became a fox, after he became a fox, and after he returned from being a fox . . . only he did not realize it." And yet as soon as he was involved in causality he was vulnerable to transfiguration because "right and wrong is what makes foxes. Good and evil is what makes foxes. Cause and effect is what makes foxes."[31] These remarks along with the poems cited earlier demonstrate from different perspectives why the *setsuwa* view of the value of repentance, such that "one instance of repentance in their hearts will erase all those sins and free them from their punishments,"[32] becomes such an important ingredient in the Zen kōan case. Yet both views—the causal Zen view emphasizing plunging in an instant into transgression and the supernatural *setsuwa* view emphasizing arousing repentance in a single moment—can, in turn, point to the issue highlighted by Critical Buddhism: Zen seems to lack a genuine emphasis on making amends for transgressions. The kōan commentaries seem to aggravate this problem by eliminating the need for repentance in stressing either the inevitability of retribution or the idea that the problem itself is not real; *setsuwa* literature does so by making repentance seem too immediate and effective in a facile way.

Yet if pressed into a corner by contemporary methodological reflections, the representatives of the kōan tradition would likely offer that many of the levels of meaning of wild fox are at once contained and transcended in K'u-mu's verse commentary on the pivot word, *pu-mei yin-kuo*, "not falling into causality":

> On seeing a wild fox in person,
> Pai-chang granted his request most willingly;
> Now I have to ask my monks,
> Have you spit out fox drool or not?[33]

Another Sung verse creates a new level of paradoxicality between ignorance and wisdom (echoing a verse cited in the previous chapter which says that "not falling" and "not obscuring" are both mistakes): "Not falling, not obscuring, / You falsely accuse someone of the crime. / Not obscuring, not falling, / There is no rope, / So how can you tie yourself up? / Pity the willow leaves swirling in the spring wind, / Sometimes floating west, sometimes floating east."[34] An oral commentary indicates that the meaning of the natural imagery in the concluding lines supporting the references to "you falsely accuse" and "there is no rope" is this: there really was no trouble all along ("no rope"), but you looked and found some anyway!

As the *Wu-men kuan* rhetorically asks: "Now, tell me, what will you do?"

Appendix I

Translations of Fox Kōan Commentaries

The wild fox kōan or "Pai-chang and the wild fox" first appeared as a dialogue contained in the section on Pai-chang's life and teachings in the biohagiographic transmission of the lamp text, the *T'ien-sheng kuang-teng lu* (*chüan* 8) in 1036, which was the second main example of the genre of genealogical historical anecdotes following the groundbreaking *Ching-te ch'uan-teng lu* in 1004.[1] After this edition, the kōan text underwent considerable revision and change until eventually two main versions emerged: the *T'ien-sheng kuang-teng lu* (*TKL*) version, which appears with minor modifications in Pai-chang's recorded sayings text, the *Pai-chang yü-lu*, and a subsequent version with enhanced philosophical and folkloric elements appearing in the *Wu-men kuan* (*WMK*) version and other texts that has become the standard edition. In addition to its position in the *Wu-men kuan* collection of forty-eight cases, the fox kōan is cited, usually with prose and poetic commentary, in many historical records, kōan collections, and recorded sayings texts from Sung China and Kamakura Japan as well as subsequent periods, including the records of Pai-chang.

Some of the main texts containing the fox kōan include transmission of the lamp histories such as the *Tsung-men t'ung-yao chi* (1093, *chüan* 3, the primary source for what became the standard version), the *Tsung-men lien-teng hui-yao* (1163, *chüan* 4), the *Chia-t'ai p'u-teng lu* (1201), and the *Wu-teng hui-yüan* (1253). Another category of texts containing the case is kōan collections: in addition to the *Wu-men kuan*, the fox kōan is found in Ta-hui's *Cheng-fa yen-tsang* (1147) and the *Hung-chih sung-ku pai-tse* (1166, case 8), which were records of how leading masters selected and sometimes briefly commented on key dialogues. This category also includes the *Ts'ung-jung lu* (1224, case 8, plus a brief reference in case 80), which was based on Hung-chih's verse collection, as well as the comprehensive Ming-dynasty collection, the *Chih-yüeh lu* (vol. 8). Moreover, the case is cited in Dōgen's kōan collections—the *Mana Shōbōgenzo* (or *Shōbōgenzō sanbyakusoku*, 1235, case 102) and *Eihei kōroku juko* (1236, *chüan* 9 in the *Eihei kōroku*, case 77)—as well as the two *Shōbōgenzō* fascicles, "Daishugyō" and "Jinshin inga." A third category of Zen texts commenting on the kōan are the recorded sayings and poetry collections of numerous masters, who often gave formal *shang-t'ang* (J. *jōdō*) or informal *hsiao-ts'an* (J. *shōsan*) lectures on the case—many of which are contained in two twelfth-century collections, *Ch'an-tsung sung-ku lien-chu-t'ung tsi* (verses) and *Tsung-men nien-ku hui-tsi* (prose comments).

It is also important to note the texts that do not contain the fox kōan: the *Tsu-t'ang tsi* (952), a historical record that was an important antecedent to the transmission of the lamp genre, in addition to the *Ching-te ch'uan-teng lu*—despite the fact that these texts offer the earliest biographies of Pai-chang and frequently use "wild fox" terminology, including the sarcastic epithet "wild fox spirit" as terms of derision in other contexts. Nor does the kōan appear in such collections as the *Hsüeh-tou po-tse sung-ku* (1026)—which became the basis for the *Pi-yen lu* (1128)—and the *Chi-chieh lu*. The absence of the fox kōan from the *Pi-yen lu* and the *Chi-chieh lu* means that it was not cited in either of the two prominent collections compiled by Yüan-wu, Ta-hui's teacher, although he does include it in his own recorded sayings.

The *WMK* and *TKL* Versions

Following the translations is a textual comparison of the *WMK* and *TKL* versions.

Wu-men kuan Case 2 (T 48:293a–b)
(Also in the Tsung-men t'ung-yao chi, Tsung-men lien-teng hui-yao, and Wu-teng hui-yüan)

Main Case

Whenever Zen master [Huai-hai of Mount] Pai-chang [in Hung-chou][2] gave a lecture, an old man came to hear him expound the dharma along with the assembly of monks. When the assembly left [the Dharma Hall], the old man also left. One day, however, he stayed behind.

Pai-chang asked: "Who is this standing here before me?"

The old man responded: "I am really a nonhuman being (C. *fei-jen*; J. *hinin*).[3] A long time ago, in the age of Buddha Kāśyapa,[4] I was abbot of this very temple.[5] [But the change] happened when a disciple asked me: 'Does even a person of great cultivation (C. *ta-hsiu-hsing*; J. *daishugyō*)[6] fall into causality,[7] or not?' I answered: '[Such a person] does not fall into causality (C. *pu-lo yin-kuo*; J. *furaku inga*).' For five hundred lifetimes after that, I have been transfigured into a wild fox (C. *yeh-hu*; J. *yako*) body. Now, Master, may I ask you to express a pivot word (C. *i-chuan-yü*; J. *ittengo*)[8] that will turn my words around[9] and release me from this wild fox transfiguration?"

The old man then asked: "Does even a person of great cultivation fall into causality, or not?" The master answered: "Such a person does not obscure causality (C. *pu-mei yin-kuo*; J. *fumai inga*)."[10]

On hearing these words, the old man experienced a great awakening. He bowed and said: "I am now released from the wild fox transfiguration, and [my fox corpse] is already lying behind the gates of the temple compound. Master, may I dare to request that you bury it with the rites accorded a deceased monk?"

The master instructed the monk in charge of rules (or rector: C. *wei-na*; J. *ino*; Skt. *karmadāna*) to strike the clapper and announce to the assembly that a burial of a deceased monk would take place after the midday meal.[11] The puzzled monks discussing this instruction wondered: "Who could this be, as all of us are healthy and there is no one who has even been sick in the Nirvana Hall?"[12]

After the meal, the master led the assembly behind the temple gates where he used his staff to uncover the carcass of a wild fox lying under a large rock. The fox corpse was cremated in accord with the regulations [for Buddhist funeral rites].[13]

That evening during his sermon in the Dharma Hall, Pai-chang told the congregation the whole story concerning the debate about causality.[14] Thereupon Huang-po asked:[15] "The old man was transfigured into a wild fox for five hundred lifetimes because he used an incorrect pivot word. Suppose his pivot word had not been incorrect, then what would have happened?"

The master replied: "Come up here and I'll explain it to you." After hesitating, Huang-po approached Pai-chang and slapped him.

The master, clapping his hands and laughing, exclaimed: "I thought it was only the barbarian who had a red beard, but here is another red-bearded barbarian!"[16]

Prose Commentary

"Not falling into causality"—why was he transfigured into a wild fox? "Not obscuring causality"—why was he released from the fox body? If you can see this with a single eye,[17] you will understand how the former abbot of Pai-chang monastery cultivated his five hundred lifetimes of transfiguration.[18]

Verse Commentary

    Not falling, not obscuring:
    Two sides of the same coin.[19]
    Not obscuring, not falling:
    A thousand entanglements, ten thousand entanglements!

Tenshō Kōtōroku Version (T 135:656b–657a)
(Also in Pai-chang yü-lu)

Main Case

Every time Zen master [Pai-chang Huai-] Hai gave a lecture in the Dharma Hall,[20] an old man came to hear him expound the dharma along with the assembly of monks. He generally left [the lecture hall] with the others, but one day he stayed behind.

The master asked who he was, and the old man responded: "A long time ago, in the age of Buddha Kāśyapa, I was abbot of this very temple. A disciple asked me: 'Does even a person of great cultivation fall into causality, or not?' I answered: '[Such a person] does not fall into causality.' [Because of this] I have been transfigured into a wild fox body. Now, Master, may I ask you for a pivot word that will turn my words around?"

The master said: "Go ahead and ask." The old man then inquired:

"Does even a person of great cultivation fall into causality, or not?" The master answered: "[Such a person] does not obscure causality." On hearing these words, the old man experienced a great awakening. Bidding farewell to the master he said: "You have spared me from the wild fox transfigurations. [My fox corpse] is already lying behind the gates of the temple compound. Please make a burnt offering as at the funeral of a deceased monk."

Pai-chang instructed the monk in charge of rules to strike the clapper and announce that the assembly would participate in the practice of communal labor (C. *p'u-ch'ing;* J. *fusei*) by burying a deceased monk after the midday meal.[21] The monks were surprised to hear this. After the meal, the entire assembly went behind the temple gates and there they found the carcass of a wild fox lying among the rocks. They gathered some firewood and burned the fox corpse.

That evening during his sermon in the Dharma Hall, Pai-chang told the congregation the whole story concerning the debate about causality. Thereupon Huang-po asked: "The old man was transfigured into a wild fox because he used an incorrect pivot word. Now, his [mind] has been turned by a pivot word that is not incorrect. So what?"

The master replied: "Come up here and I'll tell you about it." Huang-po approached Pai-chang, and struck him a blow.

The master exclaimed:[22] "I thought it was only the barbarian who had a red beard, but here is another red-bearded barbarian."

Two Dialogical Commentaries

At that time, Kuei-shan was living in the *saṃgha* and working as chief cook. Ssu-ma the ascetic (Skt. *dhūta;* C. *t'ou-t'o;* J. *zuda*) cited the story of the wild fox and said: "Well, Cook, what do you say about that?" The cook grabbed the gate with his hands and shook it three times. Ssu-ma said: "Too coarse!"[23] The cook responded: "The Buddha Dharma is not based on a reason."

Sometime later, Kuei-shan cited the incident of Huang-po asking about the wild fox and queried Yang-shan about it. Yang-shan said: "Huang-po always uses this ability." Kuei-shan asked: "Did Huang-po gain it of his own accord, or was he instructed in it by someone else?" Yang-shan replied: "It is both an inheritance from his teacher and the result of his own thorough penetration of doctrine." Kuei-shan responded: "So it is, so it is."

Comparison of WMK and TKL Versions

A careful analysis of the texts from the formative period reveals that there are basically two versions of the case with minor but significant variations. The version that is most frequently cited because it serves as the basis of the *WMK* text as well as the *Shōbōgenzō* fascicles apparently was taken from the *Tsung-men t'ung-yao chi* transmission of the lamp text from 1093. The *Tsung-men t'ung-yao chi,* which became the precursor/model of the better-known *Tsung-men lien-teng hui-yao* but was lost until the recent discovery of medieval editions in Japan, was the first work in the transmission of the lamp genre to devise a new textual model. It skipped over the genealogical materials that preoccupied the other texts and presented a comprehensive yet convenient listing of kōans that could be easily adopted for instructional purposes. This text was therefore a primary influence on the major kōan collections. Although very similar in structure and content to the original *TKL* version, the *WMK* version deriving from the *Tsung-men t'ung-yao chi*—and also appearing with some discrepancies in the *Tsung-men lien-teng hui-yao* and the *Wu-teng hui-yüan*—contains some interesting details or embellishments from the standpoint of philosophy, ritual, and folklore. Some of these amplify the mythical elements of the narrative—such as describing the fox/monk as a *"fei-jen,"* a term typically used in folklore confession tales of foxes and other anomalous, shape-shifting beings, and making two references to the fox reincarnations lasting "five hundred lifetimes," which defies logical analysis and evokes the subjective even dreamlike nature of the perception of time. The use of the terms *"fei-jen"* and "five hundred lifetimes" does not appear in the *TKL* version, which does refer to the ancient monk's existence in the age of Kāśyapa.

Other changes in the *WMK* version enhance the ritual aspect of the narrative, such as explicit references to the monastic institutional structure (including the rank of functionaries like the abbot who carries the staff which uncovers the vulpine corpse or the role of buildings like the Nirvana Hall or infirmary); the sense of the etiquette of deference by junior disciples, including the fox/monk who bows to his superior, Pai-chang; and the cremation of the fox corpse taking place after the midday meal according to Buddhist rites. The references to the abbot's staff, to the bewilderment of the assembly about the fact that no monk has been sick in the Nirvana Hall, to the bowing by the *fei-jen,* and to the cremation do not appear in the *TKL* version. For example, the *TKL* version says that the fox/monk asked for a burnt offering, a typical ancestor prac-

Table 2. Different Syntax in *WMK* and *TKL* Versions

WMK Version	*TKL* Version	Discourse Factor
1. Lecture referred to as *"ts'an"*	Lecture referred to as *"shang-t'ang"*	Ritual (*TKL*)
2. Old man says he is a "fei-jen"	—	Myth (*WMK*)
3. Reference to "five hundred lifetimes"	—	Myth (*WMK*)
4. Master asks: "Who is this standing before me?"	Master asks who old man is	Formal (*WMK*)
5. —	Master says: "Go ahead and ask"	Formal (*TKL*)
6. Old man "released"	Old man "spared"	Ritual (*WMK*)
7. He "bows"	He "bids farewell"	Ritual (*WMK*)
8. Old man asks for "monk's funeral"	Old man asks for "burnt offering"	Ritual (*WMK*)
9. —	Reference to "universal labor"	Ritual (*TKL*)
10. Monks "wonder whose funeral it was as there was no one sick in the Nirvana Hall"	Monks are "surprised"	Ritual (*WMK*)
11. Abbot leads assembly behind the gates	—	Ritual (*WMK*)
12. Master uses staff to uncover dead fox "under a rock"	Monks find carcass "among the rocks"	Ritual (*WMK*)
13. Fox is "cremated"	Monks "collect firewood and burn" corpse	Ritual (*WMK*)
14. Reference to "five hundred lifetimes"	—	Myth (*WMK*)
15. Huang-po asks: "Suppose his pivot word had not been incorrect, then what would have happened?"	Huang-po asks: "Now, his [mind] has been turned by a pivot word that is not incorrect, so what?"	Formal (*TKL*)
16. Huang-po hesitates	—	Ritual (*WMK*)
17. Huang-po gives master a slap	Huang-po strikes master	Ritual (*WMK*)
18. Master claps hands and laughs	—	Ritual (*WMK*)

Note: This table outlines the main differences between the *WMK* and *TKL* versions. The third column indicates ritual, mythical, and formal discursive elements added in the later, *WMK* version. "Formal" refers to the atmosphere or tone created by the syntax, rather than substance. Elements 1, 5, and 9 are exceptions indicating ritual and formal factors deleted after the *TKL* version.

tice, but does not refer to a request for "Buddhist rites." It also indicates that other monks "gathered some firewood and burned the fox" without using the explicit term for "cremation" that implies a ceremonial performance. In addition, the *WMK* version makes a subtle but important alteration in the epilogue's dialogue between Huang-po and Pai-chang.

But the *TKL* version contains two important features that were deleted in the *WMK* version. First, it begins by referring to Pai-chang's lecture as a formal *shang-t'ang* lecture. Moreover, it says that "Pai-chang instructed the monk in charge of rules to strike the clapper and announce that the assembly would participate in the practice of communal labor by burying a deceased monk after the midday meal." This evokes a crucial requirement in Pai-chang's monastic rules text and suggests that the *TKL* version must not be overlooked but interpreted also with the *WMK* version. Second, the *TKL* version contains two additional dialogues that can be considered the first commentaries on the fox kōan; both involve one of Pai-chang's disciples, Kuei-shan, conversing with the ascetic Ssu-ma—who plays an important role in the background to *Wu-men kuan* case 40—and with his disciple Yang-shan. Table 2 highlights the main syntactic discrepancies between these two versions of the kōan text concerning the discursive elements of ritual, mythology, and formalism.

Translation of the *Ts'ung-jung Lu* Version

The fox kōan appears as the eighth case in the *Ts'ung-jung lu* kōan collection, which was created in 1224 by the Ts'ao-t'ung (J. Sōtō) priest Wan-sung by adding prose and verse commentary to one hundred cases selected with verse commentary by Hung-chih (J. Wanshi) in the *Hung-chih pai-tse sung-ku* (J. *Wanshi hyakusoku juko*) of 1166. Hung-chih was the leader of the twelfth-century revival of the Ts'ao-t'ung school who advocated silent meditation and was criticized by—though a personal friend of—Ta-hui (J. Daie), who led the Lin-chi school at this time. The *Ts'ung-jung lu* became one of the three main kōan collections in medieval Japanese Zen, along with the *Wu-men kuan* and the *Pi-yen lu* (which was created by Ta-hui's teacher, Yüan-wu (J. Engo), but does not contain the fox kōan). It closely resembles the multi-layered structure of the *Pi-yen lu*. Whereas the *Wu-men kuan* has three parts (the main case plus prose commentary and verse commentary by Wu-men), the *Ts'ung-jung lu* has seven parts: an introduction or pointer by Wan-sung; the main case selected by Hung-chih; capping verse commentary on the main case by Wan-sung; prose commentary on the main case by Wan-sung; a verse by Hung-chih; a capping verse on this verse by Wan-sung; and prose commentary on Hung-chih's verse by Wan-sung.

There are several differences in the discussions of the fox kōan in the *Wu-men kuan* and the *Ts'ung-jung lu*. First, the *Ts'ung-jung lu* contains more poetry—including one verse by Hung-chih, two capping verses and another brief verse by Wan-sung, and an additional Zen verse cited by Wan-sung in his prose commentary. Second, the main case cited here does not contain the epilogue featuring Huang-po's slap, although this is included in the prose commentary along with the second of the two dialogues involving Kuei-shan and Yang-shan mentioned in the *TKL* version. Perhaps the most significant difference is the extended ironic use of supernatural rhetoric throughout the *Ts'ung-jung lu* commentary—including references to "fox drool" in the capping verse on the main case; to "falling into ditches," "fishy skin," "red-bearded foxes," "living in a fox hole," the "tailbone showing," and Hung-chih's "claws and fangs" in the prose comments on the main case; to "harmonious babble" in Hung-chih's verse; and to being "too stubborn to stop drooling" in the capping verse on Hung-chih's verse—in addition to the way Wan-sung chides and corrects Hung-chih in the prose commentary on his verse by suggesting that he should have said that the Zen leaders "poked their heads into a fox den." Finally, the *Ts'ung-jung lu* makes at least a passing reference to the need for repentance in Wan-sung's capping verse on Hung-chih's poem. The *WMK* and *TJL* interpretations are quite similar, however, in supporting a paradoxical reading of the fox kōan and the relation between causality and noncausality. Although the *TJL* seems to give credence to a literal reading in some of Wan-sung's prose commentary on the main case, the various verses indicate support for the standpoint of the identification and equalization of apparent opposites.

Ts'ung-jung Lu Case 8 (T 48:231c–232b)

Introductory Comments (or Pointer)
If from the start there is even one wrong word in your heart you will go straight to hell like an arrow in flight. [The ancient fox/monk] swallowed just a single drop of wild fox drool when he was thirty years old and was never able to spit it out. This is not because heaven's commands are so harsh but because he was such a fool burdened by bad karma. How he must have transgressed in his previous lives![24]

Main Case with Capping Verse Commentary by Wan-sung
Whenever [Zen master] Pai-chang lectured in the Dharma Hall, an old man came to hear him expound the dharma along with the assembly of monks. When the assembly left [the lecture hall], the old man also left.

> Finding quiet in the midst of noise.

One day, however, he stayed behind.

> The other disciples must have doubted that he was really there.[25]

Pai-chang asked him: "Who is this standing before me?"

> Pai-chang may not have understood who he was, but when a guest arrives you must take care of him.

The old man responded: "Long ago, in the era of Buddha Kāśyapa, I was abbot of this very temple.

> Originally he was a member of the same family.

A disciple asked me: 'Does even a person of great cultivation fall into causality, or not?'

> Just do good things for the sake of doing good, not for the sake of a good return.[26]

I answered: 'Such a person does not fall into causality.'

> One correct sentence in the beginning and ten thousand truths are expressed with it.[27]

For five hundred lifetimes after this, I was transfigured into a wild fox body.

> This was because you said "not falling into causality."

Now, Master, may I ask you for a pivot word that will turn my words around?"

> What is the reason for my condition?

Pai-chang's answer: "[Such a person] does not obscure causality."

> You can bury both of them in a single ditch.

On hearing these words, the old man experienced a great awakening.

> But he still has fox drool![28]

Prose Commentary by Wan-sung
Whenever head priest T'ai-chi of Mount Pai-chang temple in Hung-chou prefecture gave a lecture, there was always an old man who came to hear him expound the dharma. Long ago, in the era of Buddha Kāśyapa, he was abbot of the very same temple. He had once used a mistaken pivot word in response to a student's query, and he was transfigured into a wild fox body. Just because he had leaned on a fence and knocked down a wall, he

caused others to fall into ditches. Seeing that Pai-chang's greater wisdom could pull out nails and draw out pegs, the old man gave himself over and asked Pai-chang for a pivot word. Pai-chang gave a fearless exposition that caused a turning of the way with great compassion: "There is no obscuring causality." On hearing these words [the old man] experienced a great awakening. [Pai-chang] expressed the true facts. Not falling into causality reflects the standpoint of denial, but not obscuring causality is a marvelous attainment of the universal flux.[29] Those who understand the teaching of the vehicles even slightly can see this clearly. But even though they have shed their hairy [fox] hide, they still have fishy skin.

Haven't you heard that when Zen master Tao-yüan stayed in the congregation of Zen master Nan's he heard two monks discussing this story? One monk said: "Even though he is not obscuring causality, why is he not yet released from the fox body?" The other monk responded: "As this itself is not falling into causality, when was he ever transfigured into a wild fox body?" The master was alarmed at this unusual discussion, and he went off to the hermitage in the bamboo forest on Mount Huang-po. Crossing a valley stream he experienced a great awakening. He told Master Nan what happened, but before even finishing the account tears were running down his face. Although Master Nan told him to sleep soundly on the attendant's bench, he suddenly arose and wrote a poem:

> Not falling, not obscuring,
> For monks or laypersons there are no taboos;
> The behavior of a commoner is the same as a king's,
> There is no enclosure or covering,
> A staff can be either horizontal or vertical—
> The wild fox enters the lair of the golden lion.

Master Nan had a big laugh. Looking at the situation in light of this verse, he commented that when asked for a pivot word the first time, if the ancient monk had not said, "there is no falling into causality," it would have spared novice disciples a great misunderstanding.

[According to the main case], later that evening during his sermon in the Dharma Hall, Pai-chang told the congregation the whole story concerning the debate about causality. Thereupon Huang Po asked: "The old man was transfigured into a wild fox for five hundred lifetimes because he used an incorrect pivot word. Suppose his pivot word had not been incorrect, then what would have happened?"

The master replied: "Come up here and I'll explain it to you."
Huang-po approached Pai-chang and struck him a blow. The master,
clapping his hands and laughing, exclaimed: "I thought it was only foxes
who had a red beard, but here is another red-bearded fox!"[30]

Yang-shan said: "Pai-chang expressed a great dynamism, and
Huang-po expressed a great ability. These masters did not get their
names without accomplishment."[31] In response to a question from
Kuei-shan, Yang-shan said: "Huang-po always uses this ability." Then
Kuei-shan asked: "Did Huang-po gain it of his own accord, or was he instructed in it by someone else?" Yang-shan replied: "It is both an inheritance from his teacher and the result of his own thorough penetration of
doctrine." Kuei-shan reponded: "So it is, so it is."

Think about Pai-chang, the father, and his son. They roam fearlessly
like kings of the jungle, so they are certainly able to live in a fox hole.
Wan-sung says: "My tailbone is showing more and more. Now I'll let
T'ien-t'ung [Hung-chih] ply his claws and fangs. Consider his verse (with
capping phrases)."

Verse Commentary by Hung-chih with Capping Phrases by Wan-Sung

A foot of water, a fathom of wave,
> Fortunately the rivers are naturally clear and the seas are calm.

For five hundred lifetimes of transfiguration, what could he do?
> If he knew then what he knows today, he would have repented
> that he wasn't careful from the beginning.

"Not falling," "not obscuring," they haggle,
> Too stubborn to stop their drooling.

Like poking their heads into tangled vines;
> Wrapping around their waist and entangling their thighs.

Ah, ha, ha![32]
> How utterly laughable, how utterly pitiable.

Get it?
> Like holding the head of the cow to make it eat grass.

If you are fully released,
> Like preventing bugs from chewing on wood.

You won't mind my babble *(ta-ta h'u-h'u)*;[33]
> But even so you will be confused.

The divine songs and sacred dances spontaneously create a harmony,
> The rhythm is there.

Let's clap our hands in the intervals and sing, "La de da."
Growing finer and finer.

Prose Commentary on Hung-chih's Verse by Wan-sung

The master [T'ien-t'ung Hung-chih] said of establishing practice and realization by distinguishing between cause and effect—this is "a foot of water, a fathom of wave." On transfiguring into a wild fox spirit "for five hundred lifetimes," Hung-chih suggests that even if the two monks at the hermitage in the bamboo forest had a great understanding, when we analyze their views it appears that they too have not yet avoided plunging into tangled vines. But in T'ien-t'ung's verse there are two words that do not sit right. Why doesn't he say, "Like poking their heads into a wild fox hole [instead of tangled vines]?" And "Ah, ha, ha!"—this phrasing illustrates Pai-chang's enlightenment. T'ien-t'ung especially reveals what is in his own heart in saying, "Get it?" But I wonder if perhaps he has not yet gotten it. "If you are fully released, you won't mind my babble"—he has a sense of responsibility, for there is nothing he would not do for others.

"Babble" *(ta-ta h'u-h'u)* is just baby talk, which means it is not real speech. According to a commentary on the *Lotus Sutra*, the syllable *"ta"* is a symbol of learning how to practice and *"h'u"* is a symbol of learning how to speak. The *Nirvana Sutra* refers to "practice to cure an illness" and "practice [to stop the crying] of babies."[34] Some texts also refer to "granny's talk" *(p'o-p'o h'u-h'u)*. Ch'an master Shan-tao of Shih-shih said that among the sixteen practices cited in the *Nirvana Sutra,* practice to stop the crying of babies is the best. When you say *"ta-ta h'u-h'u,"* it is the practice of someone studying the way and renouncing all attachments of the heart. This has the same meaning as "divine songs and sacred dances" in Hung-chih's verse cited earlier.

But what is the sound of the harmony?
It cannot be heard with the mind listening to ten thousand pipes;
Yet stand alone on a high cliff and you will recognize it even without using your ears.[35]

Wan-sung's Capping Verse on the Main Case (Restated)

Finding quiet in the midst of noise,
The other disciples must have doubted that he was really there;
Pai-chang may not have understood who he was, but when a guest arrives you must take care of him;
Originally he was a member of the same family;

Just do good things for the sake of doing good, not for the sake of a
good return,
One correct sentence in the beginning and ten thousand truths are
expressed with it;
This was because you said "not falling into causality";
What is the reason for my condition?
You can bury both of them in a single ditch,
But he still has fox drool!

Wan-sung's Capping Verse on Hung-chih's Verse (Restated)

Fortunately the rivers are naturally clear and the seas are calm,
If he knew then what he knows today, he would have repented that
he wasn't careful from the beginning;
Too stubborn to stop their drooling,
Wrapping around their waist and entangling their thighs;
How utterly laughable, how utterly pitiable,
Like holding the head of the cow to make it eat grass,
Like preventing bugs from chewing on wood;
But even so you will be confused,
The rhythm is there,
Growing finer and finer.

Translation of Dōgen's Verse Comments

Dōgen collected and commented on several hundred kōans in various
writings, including the *Shōbōgenzō,* the *Mana Shōbōgenzō* (or *Shōbōgenzō sanybakusoku,* containing three hundred cases), the *Shōbōgenzō
zuimonki,* and the *Eihei kōroku.* There is no question that the fox kōan
was one of the cases he considered most important as he discussed it extensively throughout his career. Dōgen's commentaries include: two fascicles in the *Shōbōgenzō,* "Daishugyō" in the early 75-fascicle text and
"Jinshin inga" in the later 12-fascicle text, both of which follow the *WMK*
version (although the former cites the *TKL*), in addition to citations in
"Raihaitokuzui" and "Ikka myōjū"; a citation in the *Mana Shōbōgenzō*
(case 102); a passage in the *Shōbōgenzō zuimonki* no. 2.4, which deals
primarily with the kōan of Nan-chüan cutting in half a cat that was disputed by his monks; five lengthy discussions in the sermons of the *Eihei
kōroku,* with over a dozen additional references to key terms like "fox
den," "red-bearded barbarian," or "Huang-po's slap"; and two verses in

the *Eihei kōroku juko* (*chüan* 9 of the *Eihei kōroku*, case 77).[36] A translation of the main case and two verses from *Eihei kōroku juko* follows.

Eihei Kōroku Juko Case 77 (DZZ 2:234–236)

Main Case

Whenever Zen master Pai-chang gave a lecture, an old man always came to hear him expound the dharma along with the assembly of monks. When the group left [the lecture hall], the old man also left. One day, however, he stayed behind.

Pai-chang asked: "Who is this standing before me?"

The old man responded: "I am really a nonhuman being. A long time ago, in the age of Buddha Kāśyapa, I was abbot of this very temple. It happened that one day a disciple asked me: 'Does even a person of great cultivation fall into causality, or not?' I answered: 'Such a person does not fall into causality.' For five hundred lifetimes after that, I have been transfigured into a wild fox body. Now, Master, may I ask you for a pivot word that will turn my words around and release me from this wild fox transfiguration?"

The old man then asked: "Does even a person of great cultivation fall into causality, or not?" The master answered: "Such a person does not obscure causality."

On hearing these words, the old man experienced a great awakening. He bowed and said: "I am now released from the wild fox transfiguration."

Two Verses

For saying, "A person of great cultivation does not fall into causality,"
He was transfigured into an anomalous spirit, but he was not just another old fox;[37]
On receiving a pivot word that released him from being an apparition,
The mountains and rivers were instantly transformed as confirmation of his liberated state.

What a pity that in the era of Kāśyapa Buddha
He was transfigured into a fox for five hundred lifetimes;
But when he heard the lion's roar of Master Pai-chang,
The endless yelping from his long drooling tongue ceased once and for all.[38]

Appendix II

Translation of "Pai-chang's Monastic Rules"

The *Ch'an-men kuei-shih* first appeared as a passage appended to the hagiography of Pai-chang in the *Ching-te ch'uan-teng lu*. Nearly all of the material in this version, however, is included though in different sequence in the section on Pai-chang in the monk biography text, the *Sung kao-seng chuan, chüan* 10, published sixteen years earlier.[1] The *Ch'an-men kuei-shih*, sometimes referred to by Dōgen and other commentators as the *Hyakujō shingi* (C. *Pai-chang ch'ing-kuei*) or *Hyakujō koshingi* (C. *Pai-chang ku-ch'ing-kuei*), apparently became the inspiration for the much lengthier sets of monastic codes: the *Ch'an-yüan ch'ing-kuei* (J. *Zen'en shingi*) of 1103 and the Yüan-dynasty rules text completed by Te-hui and others of Mount Pai-chang in 1338 (variously dated 1333), the *Ch'ih-hsiu Pai-chang ch'ing-kuei* (J. *Chokushū Hyakujō shingi*). (Pai-chang in this case, five centuries after the patriarch, refers to the mountain temple.) Although these texts, especially the latter, claim to have been modeled on the *Ch'an-men kuei-shih*, both contain much more detail meticulously defining and regulating the duties of the abbot and the daily functions of monks. Moreover, both texts reflect the absorption of certain elements of popular religiosity—including the rules for the enshrinement of local earth gods in the *Ch'an-yüan ch'ing-kuei* and tantric prayer formulas and explanations of cultic buildings in the *Ch'ih-hsiu pai-chang ch'ing-kuei*.

The *Ch'an-men kuei-shih* text may well be apocryphal. The picture of Pai-chang as the founder of the first pure Zen monastic system does not emerge in his biography in the *Tsu-t'ang chi* of 952, over a hundred years after his death, or even in the main section on his life in the *Ching-te ch'uan-teng lu*. The roots of the work can be traced to a couple of short texts produced at the Mount Pai-chang temple in the 880s that got integrated into the *Sung kao-seng-chuan* and then the *Ching-te ch'uan-teng lu* a century later. These late-ninth-century bridge texts seem to reflect a series of dramatic political upheavals affecting the temple—including its devastation during the severe suppression of the Hui-ch'ang era (841–846) at the hands of imperial authorities under Wu-tsung, followed by a rebuilding of the temple and the establishment of new, productive associations with the government administration.[2] Since the detailed instructions provided in the later rules texts are missing, it appears that significant parts of the text attributed to Pai-chang were either lost or anachronistic.

In any case, Pai-chang's rules advocate rituals that revolve around the deeds and words of "a spiritually insightful and morally superior" abbot who guides his disciples by exemplary behavior and a variety of instructional methods that target the needs of individual monks: formal sermons and open debates with the entire assembly in the Dharma Hall as well as individual pedagogy in the abbot's quarters. Several key aspects of Zen religious life are spelled out in the rules:

1. Zen Lineage: Zen declares its separateness and independence from the heretofore dominant Lü school—a term that literally means Vinaya but is used here and elsewhere to refer to private rather than public monastic lineages. The Zen regulations at once represent an admixture and transcendence of Hinayana and Mahayana precepts, although in actuality both sets of precepts were required in Zen in China and for the most part in Japan as well.

2. Charismatic Abbot: The abbot, or elder, as the living heir of the transmission process, is the "Honored One"—thus vitiating the need for a Buddha Hall with its icons, which was the centerpiece of other sects' temples (although in actuality Zen temples invariably used a Buddha Hall for ceremonial occasions). The abbot lives in a Vimalakīrtī-like "ten-foot-square" room (C. *fang-chang*; J. *hōjō*), to which he invites monks for personal instruction.

3. Dharma Hall: This becomes the most important site in the compound because it houses the abbot during convocations held twice daily. (In actuality, these events took place far less frequently.) During the abbot's formal sermons, which are recorded, the head monks and rank-and-file line the hall; time is allowed for informal discussion and debate (which is rarely recorded).

4. Monks' Hall: All monks reside together in the Monks' Hall—another of the major innovative features of the Zen monastic compound. Seniority is based on length of stay in the *saṃgha,* as in the early Vinaya. Each monk is assigned a site on the platform of the hall for keeping his possessions and for sleeping, which involves lying on the right side in "reclining meditation." Two vegetarian meals are eaten; the final meal is served at midday, as in the early Vinaya.

5. Communal Labor: Although mentioned here only briefly, the rule for universal, compulsory labor makes an association with several anecdotes from Pai-chang's recorded sayings—especially his saying, "A day without work is a day without eating."

6. Ten Officers: This spells out the main functionaries of the monastery (although the ten functions are not listed)—especially the rector or supervisor of the Monks' Hall, who has the authority to punish and expel anyone who commits an offense. The rector can begin the punishment, and the abbot will go on to flog miscreants with his staff, burn their belongings, and dispatch them through the side gate.

7. Excommunication: A large section of the rules text is devoted to explaining four kinds of rationale for banishing—rather than reprimanding—all offenders: preserving the faith of worthy monks; saving the reputation of the *saṃgha;* avoiding litigation; and keeping word of monastic misbehavior from spreading to the community at large. The last three reasons suggest a preoccupation with sidestepping any embarrassment that might invite harsh criticism from Confucian and other rivals.

In the following translation, the parentheses (except for citations of original-language terms) indicate passages that were probably later additions and emendations to the text. The brackets indicate my additions to the translation for the sake of clarity.

Ch'an-men Kuei-shih (T 51:250c–251b) "Monastic Rules of the Zen Lineage"

Zen master Pai-chang T'ai-chi[3] was aware that from the time of the founding of the sect by first patriarch Bodhidharma through the era of sixth patriarch Hui-neng and later, Zen monks for the most part resided in Lü-school [literally "Vinaya"] monasteries.[4] Although they had separate, quasi-independent cloisters [within the larger monastic compound], they did not adhere to a distinct set of rules concerning the preaching of the dharma by the abbot or the transmission of lineal authority.

Constantly troubled by this problem, Pai-chang declared: "I wish to see the way of the patriarchs spread and enlighten people limitlessly. We must consider what is the best way to conduct our practice in order to achieve this goal. (Why should our school be confined to following the practice of rules according to Hinayana teachings?")

A disciple asked: "The Mahayana precepts are explained in the *Yogācāryabhūmi śāstra* and the *P'u-sa ying-lo ching (Bodhisattva Garland Sutra)*. Why not adhere to and follow those rules?" Pai-chang replied: "For our sect the guiding principles should not follow strictly the rules according to either the Hinayana or Mahayana teachings; nor should they differ drastically from these. Rather, we must seek a middle ground that at once synthesizes the spirit of these approaches and lies beyond them in establishing regulations that are most appropriate to our style [of practice]."[5] In that way [Pai-chang] conceived the idea of instituting the first genuinely independent monasteries of the Zen sect.

The [Zen monastery's leader], who is revered as the "Honored One" (C. *ts'un;* J. *son*) for being spiritually insightful and morally superior,[6] is referred to as the abbot (C. *chang-lao;* J. *chōrō,* literally "elder"; Skt. *āyusmati*), just as virtuous or attained disciples in India were given the title Subhūti. As the embodiment of spiritual transformation, the abbot resides in a "ten-foot-square" room (C. *fang-chang;* J. *hōjō*).[7] This is not merely a private bedroom, but is the same as Vimalakīrti's room.[8] Thus there is no need for [a Zen monastery] to construct a Buddha Hall [as a place to enshrine an image or icon as an object of worship], but only to build a Dharma Hall (C. *fo-t'ang;* J. *hattō*) in order to honor the abbot as the legitimate living heir of the transmission of the buddhas and patriarchs.[9]

Regardless of whether their numbers are great or small, or whether they are of high or low social status, those who have joined the community as monks reside together in the Monks' (or Saṃgha) Hall (C.

seng-t'ang; J. *sōdō*), with rank based strictly on the number of summers since the time of their ordination. Platforms [for resting] are to be built along the side of the hall and should include a stand for each monk's robes and other belongings. The proper position is to lie on the right side—the position of the Buddha's final repose [at the time of entering *parinirvāṇa*]—with the headrest set at the edge of the platform and the hands used to support the head. The period of rest should be short even if it comes after a lengthy session of meditation. This is not considered a time for sleeping but for "reclining meditation." It is part of the practice of the four observances [of walking, standing, sitting, or lying down as forms of meditation].

Monks may request or be invited for personal interviews or instruction by entering into the abbot's room. Otherwise, each disciple is primarily responsible for regulating his own diligence or indolence [in making an effort at meditation], whether he is of senior or junior status. The entire assembly meets in the Dharma Hall twice a day for morning and evening convocations. On these occasions the abbot enters the hall (C. *shang-t'ang;* J. *jōdō*) and ascends the high seat.[10] The head monks and the rank-and-file disciples line up on either side of the hall to listen attentively to the abbot's sermon. This sermon is followed by an opportunity for a stimulating debate about the essential meaning of Zen doctrines which discloses how one must live in accord with the dharma.

The monks eat two simple vegetarian meals daily according to the routine schedule. These are prepared and served with utmost frugality to demonstrate that the activity of eating is an opportunity for realization of the dharma.

All members of the community must participate equally in carrying out the practice of communal labor (C. *p'u-ch'ing;* J. *fusei*).[11] Ten tasks for the regulation of the community are assigned to specific officers, each officer taking responsibility for the supervision and fulfillment of the duties assigned to his role. (For example, the monk who supervises rice is referred to as the Rice Steward and the monk who supervises vegetables is referred to as the Vegetable Steward.)

But anyone who makes a false claim of membership or is insincere or deceitful in his practice and abuses his office, or anyone who breaks the rules or otherwise stirs up trouble among the dedicated members of the monastic community, will be punished by the rector (C. *wei-na;* J. *ina;* Skt. *karmadāna*), who is to remove the impostor's possessions from the Monks' Hall and to expel and excommunicate him from the compound.[12]

This severe discipline serves as a warning to the other monks of the humiliation and disgrace that will ensue should a similar offense be committed. An offending monk will be flogged with the abbot's staff (C. *chu-chang;* J. *shujō*) and, after finding that his robes, bowl, and other belongings have been burned in front of the entire assembly, will be unceremoniously dispatched through the side gate.

This rule has four merits. First, the faith of the rank-and-file is not compromised by the incident but will continue to grow. (Those with evil karma in past, present, or future cannot be allowed to live in the monastery. According to the followers of the Vinaya rules, such offenders would be reprimanded. But we believe they must be excommunicated so that the rank-and-file monks can live with the peace of mind that the flourishing of their reverence and faith will no longer be disturbed.) Second, the reputation of the purity of Buddhist practice will not be besmirched. (Punishment [through excommunication] must be enforced. If transgressors are permitted to keep their Buddhist robe, this will necessarily become a matter of deep regret [among the faithful in the community].) Third, the dismissal avoids the need to seek out public litigation.

Finally, [the rule of excommunication means that] word of the incident will not spread outside the monastic compound in a way that would call into question the integrity of the sect. (When monks from all over the country come to reside together it is difficult to determine in advance who will turn out to be genuinely virtuous and who will not. Even in the Buddha's own day there were six evil monks [to whose improper conduct is attributed the laying down of laws by Buddha]. How could we possibly expect the complete absence of this behavior in these latter days of the Ages of the Semblance and Decline of the Dharma? There are monks who may see a colleague breaking the rules and thoughtlessly follow this example without realizing how such behavior significantly impedes the dharma. Today, even those monsteries that have little difficulty in dealing with troublemakers should adhere to the spirit of Pai-chang's monastic rules in swiftly settling any problems stemming from transgressions. Establishing detailed rules is a strong deterrent against wickedness. Do not allow a situation where offenses occur without having recourse to the appropriate punishments. One should reflect on the role of Zen master Pai-chang in protecting the dharma. How great it has been!)

It is important to remember and credit Pai-chang with the establishment of the independent status of Zen monasteries and, as well, to continue to recount the gist of his ideas.

Notes

Chapter 1 · Putting the Fox Back in the Fox Kōan

1. The main locations of the fox kōan text are: *WMK* no. 2, in *T* 48:293a–b; *TJL* no. 8, in *T* 48:231c–232b; and *MS* 102, in *DZZ* 5:178–180. (See also *Mana Shōbōgenzō goi sakuin*, ed. Sōtōshū shūgaku kenkyūjō (Tokyo: Sōtōshū shūgaku kenkyūjō, 1993), pp. 26–27.) The kōan is also included in many other texts; see Appendix I.

2. There is a discrepancy in traditional sources regarding the date of Pai-chang's birth. According to Ch'en Hsü's *Panegyrical Inscription*, which is followed by most modern scholars, Pai-chang died at the age of sixty-six. But the *CCL* and other hagiographies indicate that he died at the age of ninety-five, which would give him a birthdate of 720, although this is not supported by any other historiographical evidence. See Yi T'ao-tien, trans., "Records of the Life of Ch'an Master Pai-chang Huai-hai," *Eastern Buddhist* 8 (1975):42–73, especially p. 45, n. 4. Traditional sources for Pai-chang's biography include: *TTC, chüan* 14; *CCL, chüan* 6; *WTH, chüan* 3; *SKSC, chüan* 10.

3. For a discussion of Zen lineage systems encompassing the seven primordial buddhas see Yanagida Seizan, *Shoki Zenshū shisho no kenkyū* (Kyoto: Hōzōkan, 1967).

4. "Four houses" refers to the lineage of Ma-tsu, Pai-chang, Huang-po, and Lin-chi, whose texts of recorded sayings were collected in a single volume in the twelfth century. Ma-tsu's twisting of Pai-chang's nose and shouting in his ear are among the earliest instances of the use of physical abuse or intimidation in encounter dialogues. Pai-chang later gave and received the same treatment from Huang-po, who did the same with Lin-chi.

5. For the use of the twin phrases "the barbarian has a red beard, red-bearded barbarian"—which is a mouthful in Japanese pronunciation (*koshushaku shakushuko*)—in various kōan commentaries, especially Dōgen's,

see Suzuki Tetsuo, "Koshushaku to Shakushuko," *IBK* 44(3) (1996):720–727. It is interesting to note that Bodhidharma, known for his foreignness ethnically as well as culturally, was sometimes referred to as the "blue-eyed barbarian," though this was probably not one of his physical attributes. Moreover, in *WMK* case 4 Huo-an asks an inversion of the standard query, "Why has the barbarian from the west no beard?"

6. According to the basic Buddhist analysis of conditioned reality there are two types of causes for each and every phenomenon: the direct (Skt. *hetu;* C. *yin;* J. *in*) and the contributory (Skt. *pratītya;* C. *yüan;* J. *en*). The main point is that according to the doctrine of *pratītya-samutpāda* nothing exists independently—either without a prior cause and subsequent effect or with only a single cause minus the multiplicity of causal and conditioning factors. This raises the question of whether nirvana as the prime example of *asaṃskṛta-dharma* (unconditioned phenomena) can be considered either free from cause or the product of cause (the realm of *saṃskṛta-dharma* or conditioned phenomena, which is also analyzed in terms of the five aggregates and the doctrines of nonself and impermanence). Theoretically nirvana is both a product and transcendent of causality. Which is the correct view? Or is the doctrine of causality contradictory with regard to the status of noncausality?

7. But supernatural elements, such as revelatory dreams, bilocation, and magical practices, are prevalent in numerous cases (see Chapter 5).

8. This attitude may derive from a Confucian influence—as expressed in a famous passage in the *Analects* (11:11)—which negates the value of speculating on the afterlife. The absence of the motif in Zen may be considered an argument from silence in favor of such a view.

9. Originally the term apparently referred to a walking stick in Indian Buddhism for use by the old and sick. In China it came to refer to a stick carried by an itinerant monk who has traveled in the vast wilderness. See Robert Aitken, *The Gateless Barrier: The Wu-men Kuan (Mumonkan)* (San Francisco: North Point, 1990), p. 266. Aitken gives this a demythological interpretation in that cutting a stick in wild mountains is like shaping one's true nature or original Buddha nature. The staff is cited in *WMK* case 44, in which Pa-chia says to the assembly: "If you have a staff, I will give you a staff. If you have no staff, I will take a staff from you." In *WMK* case 43, Shou-shan holds up another kind of staff, a short bamboo stick, and says: "If you call this a staff, you are entangled. If you do not call this a staff, you ignore the fact. Tell me, what do you call it?"

10. *EK* 3.231, in *DZZ* 3:154; *EK* 7.510, in *DZZ* 4:90; Yün-men's saying appears in *PYL* no. 60.

11. The fox kōan is cited by Dōgen in *EK*, in *DZZ* (fascicle and paragraph, with the paragraphs numbered consecutively through seven fascicles of collected sermons) 1.62, 1.94, 3.205, 7.510, and 9.77 (which contains two verse commentaries, see Appendix I) or 3:42, 3:45–46, 3:138, 4:90, 4:234–236, respectively

(7.510 is the closest to "Jinshin inga"); and in *SZ*, 2.4 (which equates *fumai inga* with *fudō inga* or "immovable causality"), in *DZZ* 7:67–70. In addition, there are over a dozen other *EK* passages that cite a word or phrase from the *kōan*, such as "wild fox," "red-bearded barbarian," or "not obscuring causality." For a comparison of the "Jinshin inga" fascicle and other comments on the kōan, see Ishii Seijun, "Jūnikan *Shōbōgenzō* to *Eihei kōroku:* 'Hyakujō yako' no hanashi o chūshin toshite," *SK* 30 (1988):257–262.

12. The best source for the *shōmono* commentaries on the *WMK* is Nakao Ryōshin, *Mumonkan zenseki zenbon kochū shūsei* (Tokyo: Meicho fukyūkai, 1983); the fox kōan is included on pp. 40–51. This volume contains photo-facsimile versions of eight Sōtō *shōmono* commentaries—mostly from the seventeenth century but including the fifteenth through nineteenth centuries. The late Ishikawa Rikizan was the main authority on the overall development of the *shōmono* literature. Commonly used in medieval *rinka* ("forest") as opposed to *gozan* (Five Mountains) monasteries, this literature is now extensively studied by Japanese linguists for the role of colloquial language and its relation to other genres of medieval Buddhist writings. Ishikawa's many works on the topic include "Chūsei Zenshūshi kenkyū to Zenseki shōmono shiryō," in *Dōgen Zenji to Sōtōshū*, ed. Kawamura Kōdō and Ishikawa Rikizan (Tokyo: Yoshikawa kōbunkan, 1985), pp. 76–98; "Chūsei Sōtōshū ni okeru kirigami sōjō ni tsuite," *IBK* 30(2) (1982):742–746; and more than twenty publications of the texts in the *Komazawa Daigaku Bukkyōgakubu kenkyū kiyō* and other journals. For a discussion in English see William M. Bodiford, *Sōtō Zen in Medieval Japan* (Honolulu: University of Hawai'i Press, 1993), pp. 157–162. According to Ishikawa, "*Tōmon-shōmono*" is a generic term for Sōtō works in the late medieval and early modern periods that encompass *kirigami, monsan, daigoshō,* and *gorokushō* or *kikigakishō* collections (each kind has *kanbun* and *kana* varieties)—these all contain kōan commentaries known collectively as "*shōmono*." Furthermore, the *daigoshō, monsan,* and *kirigami* are a product of the union of the styles of kōan Zen and recorded sayings (*goroku*) commentaries: the first two represent instructional/conceptual devices and the third (*kirigami*) represents an esoteric or talismanic use of the language of kōans.

13. *TKL*, in *HTC* 135:656b–657a.

14. The *TTY* dating, once thought to be twelfth century, has been moved up according to Shiina Kōyū, " 'Shūmon tōyōshū' no shoshiteki kenkyū," *KDBR* 16 (1987):299–336.

15. For an interesting use of the image of five hundred lifetimes as an indicator of the immortality of a hermit (C. *hsien;* J. *sen*) see the verse by Hung-chih in the *HCKL, chüan* 9, in *T* 48:95c. As discussed in Appendix I, the *WMK* version alters the kōan epilogue's dialogue between Pai-chang and Huang-po.

16. On the history and theory of encounter dialogues see Yanagida Seizan, "The 'Recorded Sayings' Texts of Chinese Ch'an Buddhism," in *Early Ch'an in*

China and Tibet, ed. Whalen Lai and Lewis R. Lancaster (Berkeley: Berkeley Buddhist Studies Series, 1983), and Steven Heine, *Dōgen and the Kōan Tradition* (Albany: SUNY Press, 1994), pp. 183–186.

17. For the last three examples see *PYL* case 19; *WMK* case 3, which alludes to the previous case; and *WMK* case 46.

18. See W. Michael Kelsey, *Konjaku Monogatari-shū* (Boston: Twayne, 1982), pp. 96–97 and 164, n. 19. On the relation between Zen literature and popular Buddhism see Victor H. Mair, *Tun-Huang Popular Narratives* (Cambridge: Cambridge University Press, 1983), p. 24, who points out the Zen recorded sayings texts were among the earliest written examples of colloquial language in China. For a broad discussion of the rise of written vernacular literature see Victor H. Mair, "Buddhism and the Rise of the Written Vernacular in East Asia: The Making of National Languages," *Journal of Asian Studies* 53(3) (1994):707–751. Many of the *setsuwa* are at least indirectly influenced by early Buddhist *jātaka* tales, which generally refer to jackals rather than foxes. In some cases, however, the Sanskrit term is vague and indicates a four-legged hairy animal.

19. See Vladimir Propp, *Morphology of the Folktale,* trans. Lawrence Scott (Austin: University of Texas Press, 1968).

20. Rania Huntington notes two tales with this ending from the *T'ai-p'ing kuang-chi,* "Miss Jen" and "Li Nun," in "Tigers, Foxes, and the Margins of Humanity in Tang Chuanqi Fiction," *Papers in Chinese Literature* 1 (1993):59.

21. Alexander H. Krappe, "Far Eastern Fox Lore," *California Folklore Quarterly* 3(2) (1944):124–147, especially p. 136.

22. *TJL* case 8, in *T* 48:232a.

23. In Akizuki Ryūmin, *Zen mondō: kōan-e monogatari* (Tokyo: Chōbunsha, 1976), p. 128.

24. Cited in Yi, "Records of the Life of Ch'an Master Pai-chang Huai-hai," p. 49.

25. Huang-po remarks: "Had I known you were going to perform such miracles, I would have cut off your legs."

26. *EK* 7.510, in *DZZ* 4:90.

27. See Hirata Takashi, ed., *Mumonkan, Zen no goroku* 18 (Tokyo: Chikuma shobō, 1969), p. 24.

28. *CSLT,* in *HTC* 115:114a.

29. Kōun Yamada, trans., *Gateless Gate* (Tucson: University of Arizona Press, 1979), p. 20.

30. From the standpoint of a methodology he calls Critical Buddhism *(hihan Bukkyō)* Hakamaya Noriaki stresses that Dōgen underwent a profound change of heart in his later thinking. The later Dōgen, he says, emphasized a strict adherence to the law of karmic causality in a way that can inspire reform movements in modern Buddhism with regard to the social issues of nationalism and

discrimination. See *Dōgen to Bukkyō: Jūnikanbon Shōbōgenzō no Dōgen* (Tokyo: Daizō shuppan, 1992), pp. 289–334.

31. Kazuaki Tanahashi has translated a number of Dōgen's works including *Moon in a Dewdrop: Writings by Zen Master Dōgen* (San Francisco: North Point, 1985). He suggests a translation of "identification with causality" for this term and fascicle title.

32. *SH*, "Jinshin inga," in *DZZ* 2:390.

33. Hakamaya Noriaki, *Hihan Bukkyō* (Tokyo: Daizō Shuppan, 1990); and Matsumoto Shirō, *Engi to kū: Nyoraizō shisō hihan* (Tokyo: Daizō Shuppan, 1989). See also Steven Heine, "Critical Buddhism *(Hihan Bukkyō)* and the Debate Concerning the 75-Fascicle and 12-Fascicle Shōbōgenzō Texts," *Japanese Journal of Religious Studies* 21(1) (1994):37–72. Hakamaya's main colleague in Critical Buddhism, Matsumoto Shirō, supports the 12-fascicle text as well but with a lesser degree of certainty. Both scholars, while noting Dōgen's elitism, admire Hōnen and other Kamakura religious figures for their approach to Buddhist ethical issues. See also Jamie Hubbard and Paul L. Swanson, eds., *Pruning the Bodhi Tree: The Storm over Critical Buddhism* (Honolulu: University of Hawai'i Press, 1997).

34. Thomas Cleary, trans., *Sayings and Doings of Pai-chang* (Los Angeles: Center Publications, 1978), p. 95, n. 22.

35. *EK* 3.220, in *DZZ* 3:148.

36. See, for example, *PYL* case 93 for an extended, though ambivalent, use of fox imagery.

37. For a reference to "wild fox heretics" *(yeh-hu wai-tao;* J. *yako gedō)* in literary criticism see Chih-P'ing Chou, *Yüan Hung-tao and the Kung-an School* (Cambridge: Cambridge University Press, 1988), p. 38.

38. *LL*, in *RR*, p. 65; Sasaki, *The Recorded Sayings of Ch'an Master Lin-chi*, p. 16. See also Robert M. Gimello, "Chang Shang-ying on Wu-t'ai Shan," in *Pilgrims and Sacred Sites in China*, ed. Susan Naquin and Chun-fang Yü (Berkeley: University of California Press, 1992), p. 124.

39. *LL*, in *RR*, pp. 93–94; Sasaki, *The Recorded Sayings of Ch'an Master Lin-chi*, p. 24. There are other passages in the *LL* that evoke the wild fox: "All have been [ghosts] dependent upon grasses or attached to leaves, souls of bamboos and trees, wild fox spirits. They recklessly gnaw on all kinds of dung clods" (*RR*, p. 98; Sasaki, p. 25); "[You] sons and daughters of good families, bewitched by this pack of wild foxes, lose your senses. Blind idiots! Some day you'll be made to pay up for the vittles you've eaten!" (*RR*, p. 43; Sasaki, p. 10).

40. *LL*, in *RR*, p. 89; Sasaki, *The Recorded Sayings of Ch'an Master Lin-chi*, p. 22.

41. Paul Reps, *Zen Flesh, Zen Bones* (Garden City: Anchor, 1961), p. 68.

42. Mishima Yukio, *The Temple of the Golden Pavilion (Kinkakuji)*, trans. Ivan Morris (New York: Perigee, 1959), p. 66. The "cat kōan" cited in this context

could be interpreted as an insightful comment on the absurdity and futility of war. Perhaps Mizoguchi is correct that the abbot is evasive; or perhaps, in his dementia, he misunderstands the abbot's point; but that is another issue.

43. In *Taishō* 48:255a. In these lines, the first phrase is part of Hung-chih's verse commentary and the second phrase is Wan-sung's "capping phrase" comment on the verse.

44. *EK* 3.244, in *DZZ* 3:164.

45. *LL*, in *RR*, pp. 78 and 80.

46. *JCYL*, p. 377.

47. *EK* 4.298, in *DZZ* 3:194.

48. *EK* 9.7, in *DZZ* 4:186.

49. *EK* 9.77, in *DZZ* 4:234–236.

50. On "disingenuous blasphemy" see Gimello, "Chang Shang-ying on Wu-t'ai Shan," p. 122.

51. *PYL* no. 1, in *T* 48:140a.

52. Norman Waddell, trans., *The Essential Teachings of Zen Master Hakuin* (Boston: Shambhala, 1994), p. 115, n. 3. Hakuin is known for his painting "The Running Fox," using a ludicrously well-dressed fox to highlight human foibles.

53. It is not my aim here to explore the rich folklore of foxes and similar shape-shifters in other cultures, including Celtic, Native American, and African beliefs. There are two main theories about the origins of supernatural foxes: a single-source theory traces the origins to the *Pañcātantra*, which was disseminated eastward through the vehicle of the *jātakas* and west through a variety of texts including Aesop's Fables, the Reynard Cycle, and the Tales of the Brothers Grimm; a theory of multiple autochthonic sources contends that even in East Asia there is tremendous diversity and dissimilarity between Mongolian, Ainu, southeast Chinese, and pre-Buddhist Japanese rites.

54. Another feature distinctive in East Asia is the predominantly anthropomorphic nature of transfiguration along with some prominent examples of theriomorphism—such as the retold *jātaka* tale of Indra being outsmarted by a fox that seems to be the manifestation of a bodhisattva teaching the deity a moral lesson. Buddhist preachers typically commented that the lesson of the story was simple: if even a fox could be compassionate and wise, how much more so a human. See Edward Kamens, trans., *The Three Jewels: A Study and Translation of Minamoto Tamenori's Sanbōe* (Ann Arbor: University of Michigan Press, 1988), p. 285. The tale is also cited in several texts including the *Fa-yüan chu-lin* (J. *Hō'en shurin*, *T* 53:882c), which is probably borrowed from the *Wei-tsēng-yu yin-yüan ching*, *chüan* 5 (J. *Mizōu innengyō*, *T* 17:577c), and it is alluded to in the *Mo-ho chih-kuan* (*T* 46:45b) and cited in Dōgen's "Kie Buppōsōbō" fascicle of the 12-fascicle *Shōbōgenzō* (in *DZZ* 2:383–386).

55. *SH*, "Raihaitokuzui," in *DZZ* 1:302.

56. On the remarkable degree of syncretistic temples and deities see Gorai

Shigeru, ed., *Inari shinkō no kenkyū* (Tokyo: Sanin shimbunsha, 1985), pp. 75–170 (on Buddhist sects generally) and pp. 541–638 (on Zen, especially Sōtō, temples). Sōtō Zen temples also have extensive syncretism with a variety of indigenous deities as well as deities imported from India, both Buddhist and Hindu; for a full list see Azuma Ryūshin, *Sōtōshū: waga ie no shūkyō* (Tokyo: Daihōrinkaku, 1993), pp. 82–88.

57. There are indications of this in some of the tales in the *TPKC* collection and in the writings of Ennin, the Japanese chronicler of Chinese Buddhism in the ninth century, as well as through archaeological evidence.

58. For a creative etymology of the term *"kitsune"* see the earliest *setsuwa* collection in Japan, the *Nihon ryōiki* no. 2, in Kyoko Motomichi Nakamura, trans., *Miraculous Stories from the Japanese Buddhist Tradition: The Nihon ryōiki of Monk Kyōkai* (Cambridge, Mass.: Harvard University Press, 1973), pp. 104–105. In this story a man looking for a wife one day meets an attractive woman. They marry and have a child, but the family dog (dogs according to *Jen-shih chuan* are the one animal foxes fear) barks at her one day and her vulpine shape appears, but the husband asks her to return and she continues to come and sleep with him. He names her "Kitsune" meaning "come (*kitsu*) and sleep (*ne*)" or "come (*ki*) always (*tsune*)". Another creative etymology is in Kiyoshi Nozaki, *Kitsune: Japan's Fox of Mystery, Romance, and Humor* (Tokyo: Hokuseido Press, 1961), p. 3, which suggests that *"kitsu"* is the yelping sound a fox makes and *"ne"* evokes an affectionate feeling. *Jen-shih chuan*, the earliest major example of Chinese fox folkore, was originally recorded in the T'ang *I-wen-chi* collection and is also included in the Sung encyclopediac collection, the *TPKC, chüan* 452; for an English translation see Y. W. Ma and Joseph S. M. Lau, eds., *Traditional Chinese Stories: Themes and Variations* (New York: Columbia University Press, 1978), pp. 339–345; translations below have been altered.

59. See Yasui Shirō, *Toyokawa Inari monogatari* (Toyohashi City: Mai-booku-chieen, 1986), pp. 221–231.

60. John Kieschnick notes the importance of spells for exorcising foxes in pre-Buddhist Chinese literature that influenced monk biography text accounts of Buddhist exorcists. See *The Eminent Monk: Buddhist Ideals in Medieval Chinese Hagiography* (Honolulu: University of Hawai'i Press, 1997), pp. 82–83.

61. See Anne-Marie Bouchy, "Le Renard, élément de la conception du monde dans la tradition japonaise," in Marie-Lise Befa and Roberte Hamayon, eds., *Le Renard, tours, détours, et retours*, special issue of *Etudes mongoles . . . et sibéeriennes* 15 (1984):9–70; Bodiford, *Sōtō Zen in Medieval Japan,* p. 173; and Faure, *Rhetoric of Immediacy,* p. 281. There are many such accounts in vols. 16 and 17 (*Shiden* 1 and 2) of *Sōtōshū zensho,* 20 vols. (Tokyo: Sōtōshū shūmuchō, 1970–1973), esp. 17:278a, as discussed in Hirose Ryōko, "Sōtō zensō ni okeru shinjin kado-akurei chin'atsu," *IBK* 21(2) (1983):233–236. In some versions of the story, Gennō either cut through the rock or made it disappear with an enor-

mous explosion of poisonous smoke. The supposed site of the rock exists today in Tochigi prefecture; high levels of arsenic have been reported in the surrounding area. See also Janet Goff, "Foxes in Japanese Culture," *Japan Quarterly* (April–June 1997):66–77.

62. In addition to sources cited earlier see Winston Davis, *Dojo: Magic and Exorcism in Modern Japan* (Stanford: Stanford University Press, 1980), pp. 115–160; Naoe Hiroji, ed., *Inari shinkō* (Tokyo: Yūzankaku shuppan, 1983), pp. 287–293; and Kondō Yoshiro, *Inari shinkō* (Tokyo: Hanawa shobō, 1978), pp. 176–178. An interesting example is reported in M. W. de Visser, "The Fox and Badger in Japanese Folklore," *Transactions of the Asiatic Society of Japan* 36(3) (1908):34—an abbot is startled helpless by foxes hoping to make him ill by eating abominable food, "but their magic power came suddenly to an end at the first stroke on the prayer bell." Carmen Blacker, in *The Catalpa Bow: A Study of Shamanistic Practices in Japan* (London: Allen & Unwin, 1975), tells of the picture of the Meiji emperor used as a nonhomeopathic exorcism device with immediate efficacy.

63. This discussion of the fox in East Asia disagrees somewhat with the view of animism suggested by I. M. Lewis, who comments on Mary Douglas' remarks that the real animal is not necessarily a key to understanding the symbolic animal. See I. M. Lewis, *Religion in Context: Cults and Charisma* (Cambridge: Cambridge University Press, 1986), p. 26.

64. Robert F. Campany, *Strange Writings: Anomaly Accounts in Early Medieval China* (Albany: SUNY Press, 1995), p. 7. Karen Smyers argues that in Japan, the fox (Inari) represents, in a culture dominated by the values of hierarchy, homogeneity, and uniformity, the possibility for personal expression based on equality, differentation, and individuality; see "My Own Inari: Personalization of the Deity in Inari Worship," *Japanese Journal of Religious Studies* 23(1–2) (1996):85–116.

65. Lowell W. Bloss, "The Buddha and the Nāga: A Study in Buddhist Folk Religiosity," *History of Religions* 13(1) (1973):36–51.

66. See Thanissaro Bhikkhu, *The Buddhist Monastic Code* (Valley Center, Calif.: Abbot Metta Forest Monastery, 1994), pp. 46–67, for a discussion of the issue of nonhumans in relation to the two *pārājika* of sexual offenses and killing.

67. Nathan Katz, *Buddhist Images of Human Perfection* (Delhi: Motila Banarsidass, 1982), pp. 10–11.

68. In *The Vinaya pitakam,* ed. Hermann Oldenberg, 5 vols. (London: Williams & Norgate, 1879), I:86–87, as cited in John S. Strong, ed., *The Experience of Buddhism: Sources and Interpretations* (Belmont, Calif.: Wadsworth, 1994), pp. 60–61. This story, suggesting a refutation of supernaturalism while accepting its existence, recalls the legend in which Northern School master P'u-chi exorcised the snake that was the shape-shifting apparition of the vengeful spirit of an angered monk, allowing it to be reborn once again in human form. There is a similar legend of Hui-neng exorcising and converting a dragon.

69. See Tyler, *Japanese Tales,* pp. 325–326.

70. The *tengu,* like the fox, is often converted into a bodhisattva. The most famous case, discussed here in Chapter 6, involves Ryōan, founder of the Sōtō Zen Saijōji temple in the fourteenth century. Ryōan was known for a performance of *zazen* but also came to be identified with the mountain spirit that led him to the temple site and is depicted with *tengu* features in iconography.

71. For a redaction of the *Ming-pao chi* see *T* 51:787b–802a.

72. On the *Liao-chai chih-i* title apparently suggested by P'u Sung-ling, see Herbert A. Giles, trans., *Strange Stories from a Chinese Studio* (New York: Paragon, 1960), p. xx.

73. Susan Napier, *The Fantastic in Modern Japanese Literature: The Subversion of Modernity* (London: Routledge, 1996).

74. Lafcadio Hearn, *Glimpses of Unfamiliar Japan* (Rutland, Vt.: Tuttle, rpt. 1966), p. 335.

75. Karen Smyers, "The Fox and the Jewel: A Study of Shared and Private Meanings in *Inari* Worship" (Ph.D. diss., Princeton University, 1993), pp. 247–260; James Melville, *A Haiku for Hanae* (New York: Ballantine, 1989), p. 135; and Karl S. Y. Yao, *Classical Chinese Tales of the Supernatural and Fantastic* (Bloomington: Indiana University Press, 1985), p. 8. As Archilochus says, "The fox knows many things"—and the second part of the sentence is that "the hedgehog knows one big thing." See Isaiah Berlin, *The Fox and the Hedgehog: An Essay on Tolstoy's View of History* (Chicago: Dee, 1978), p. 3.

76. Janet R. Goodwin, *Alms and Vagabonds: Buddhist Temples and Popular Patronage in Medieval Japan* (Honolulu: University of Hawai'i Press, 1994), p. 126. Also, see n. 58 above.

77. Nakamura, *Miraculous Stories,* p. 65.

78. Huntington, "Tigers, Foxes, and the Margins of Humanity," p. 43.

79. D. D. R. Owen, trans., *The Romance of Reynard the Fox* (Oxford: Oxford University Press, 1994), p. ix.

80. Daniel K. Gardner, "Zhu Xi on Spirit Beings," in *Religions of China in Practice,* ed. Donald S. Lopez Jr. (Princeton: Princeton University Press, 1996), p. 110.

81. Huntington, "Tigers, Foxes, and the Margins of Humanity," p. 43.

82. Hiroko Kobayashi, *The Human Comedy of Japan: A Study of the Secular Stories in the Twelfth-Century Collection of Tales, Konjaku Monogatarishū* (Tokyo: Centre for East Asian Cultural Studies, 1959), p. 259.

83. In Joan Piggott, *Japanese Mythology* (New York: Bedrick, rpt. 1982), p. 23.

84. Franz Kafka, *The Trial,* trans. Willa Muir and Edwin Muir (New York: Modern Library, rpt. 1964), p. 45. Another affinity is in Kafka's use of the shape-shifting theme from a moral standpoint in *Metamorphosis.*

85. In Stephen Addiss, *Japanese Ghosts and Demons* (New York: Braziller, 1985), p. 127 (from an exhibition at the Spencer Museum of Art, Kansas City).

86. Nozaki, *Kitsune*, p. 164.

87. Royall Tyler, ed., *Japanese Tales* (New York: Pantheon, 1987), p. 118 (*KM* no. 16.17, in *NKBT* 24:456–458).

88. Charles Yim-tze Kwong, *Tao Qian and the Chinese Poetic Tradition: The Quest for Cultural Identity* (Ann Arbor: University of Michigan Press, 1994), p. 54.

89. Aron Gurevich, *Medieval Popular Culture: Problems of Belief and Perception*, trans. Janas M. Bak and Paul A. Hollingsworth (Cambridge: Cambridge University Press, 1988).

Chapter 2 · The Kōan's Multivalent Discursive Structure

1. Cited in Itō Kokan, *Kōan Zen-wa: Zen, satori no mondō-shū* (Tokyo: Daihōrinkaku, 1976), p. 336. The definition is in Isshū Miura and Ruth Fuller Sasaki, *Zen Dust: The History of the Koan and Koan Study in Rinzai (Lin-Chi) Zen* (New York: Harcourt, Brace, 1966), pp. 4–7.

2. See Kenneth Kraft, *Eloquent Zen: Daitō and Early Japanese Zen* (Honolulu: University of Hawai'i Press, 1992), p. 42, for the first rendering of this term. On Hakuin's system of ranking, see Akizuki Ryūmin, ed., *Mumonkan o yomu* (Tokyo: Tōsho-insatsu, 1990), pp. 211–221. The ranks include *hōjin* (*dharmakāya*, true nature of reality), *kikan* (dynamism), *genzen* (verbal expression), *nantō* (difficult to pass through), and *kōjō* (nonattachment).

3. Aron Gurevich, *Medieval Popular Culture: Problems of Belief and Perception*, trans. Janas M. Bak and Paul A. Hollingsworth (Cambridge: Cambridge University Press, 1988), p. xvii.

4. Pierre Bourdieu, *The Political Ontology of Martin Heidegger*, trans. Peter Collier (Cambridge: Polity Press, 1991), p. 3.

5. In Judith T. Zeitlin, *Historian of the Strange: Pu Songling and the Chinese Classical Tale* (Stanford: Stanford University Press, 1993), p. 7.

6. Gurevich, *Medieval Popular Culture*, p. 24.

7. Bernard Faure, "Space and Place in Chinese Religious Traditions," *History of Religions* 26(4) (1987):350.

8. Paul Veyne, *Did the Greeks Believe in Their Myths? An Essay in the Constitutive Imagination*, trans. Paula Wissing (Chicago: University of Chicago Press, 1988).

9. Emiko Ohnuki-Tierney, *The Monkey as Mirror: Symbolic Transformations in Japanese History and Ritual* (Princeton: Princeton University Press, 1987), pp. 212–213, especially n. 2, citing work by Edwin Ardener and by Shirley Ardener, ed., *Perceiving Women* (London: Dent; New York: Wiley, 1975). This refers to the muted structure as the inarticulated and sometimes suppressed level of discourse containing its own inversion.

10. John C. H. Wu, *The Golden Age of Zen* (Taipei: United Publishing Center,

1975), p. 114; and Shibayama Zenkei, *Zen Comments on the Mumonkan*, trans. Sumiko Kudo (New York: Mentor, 1974), p. 34. Thomas Cleary, however, remarks that the "phantasmagoric nature of the event in [Pai-chang]'s story symbolizes the expedient nature of his teachings." See his translation of the *WMK: No Barrier: Unlocking the Zen Koan* (New York: Bantam, 1993), p. 13.

11. Holmes Welch reports that Buddhist monasteries in China regularly received itinerant priests who were quartered in the Wandering Monks' Hall. But the temples were wary of being deceived by "vagabonds" *(chiang-hu)* and "wild monks" *(yeh ho-shang),* some of whom were tonsured but had fortune-telling as their primary interest. See Holmes Welch, *The Practice of Chinese Buddhism 1900–1950* (Cambridge, Mass.: Harvard University Press, 1967), p. 16.

12. *TJL* no. 8, in *T* 48:232a.

13. Maxine Hong Kingston, *The Woman Warrior: Memoirs of a Girlhood Among Ghosts* (New York: Vintage, 1975), p. 163.

14. Gurevich, *Medieval Popular Culture*, p. 97.

15. Ibid., p. 81.

16. Jean-Claude Schmitt, *The Holy Greyhound: Guinefort, Healer of Children Since the Thirteenth Century*, trans. Martin Thom (Cambridge: Cambridge University Press, 1979), p. 16.

17. David Barnhill provides an insightful overview of the trends in scholarship—especially with regard to Bashō's religiosity that encompasses Shinto, folk, and Chinese elements. He also suggests an ecologically based model in "Folk Religion and Shinto in the Ecosystem of Bashō's Religious World" (paper presented at the Panel on Japanese Religions at the American Academy of Religion annual meeting, Chicago, November 1994).

18. See Bernard Faure, *Visions of Power: Imagining Medieval Japanese Buddhism*, trans. Phyllis Brooks (Princeton: Princeton University Press, 1996), dealing with works by and about fourth patriarch Keizan; and see William M. Bodiford, *Sōtō Zen in Medieval Japan* (Honolulu: University of Hawai'i Press, 1993), pp. 43–62, who gives an overview of different commentarial styles. Both works are indebted to the groundbreaking studies of Ishikawa Rikizan. The genre of *kirigami* (literally "paper strips" of interpretive materials)—a term also used in other medieval traditions that are based on an intense master/disciple apprenticeship relation—provides an esoteric interpretation of kōans that is part of the *shōmono* collections.

19. Whalen Lai, "The *Chan-ch'a ching:* Religion and Magic in Medieval China," in *Chinese Buddhist Apocrypha,* ed. Robert E. Buswell Jr. (Honolulu: University of Hawai'i Press, 1990), pp. 175–206, especially p. 175, which mentions criticisms of the two-tiered model by Peter Brown, *The Cult of the Saints: Its Rise and Function in Latin Christianity* (Chicago: University of Chicago Press, 1981), pp. 12–22.

20. Brown, *Cult of the Saints,* pp. 119–120.

21. Hsün Tzu, cited in Burton Watson, trans., *Basic Writings of Mo-tzu, Hsun-Tzu, Han Fei-tzu* (New York: Columbia University Press, 1967), p. 85.

22. Patricia Buckley Ebrey, "The Response of the Sung State to Popular Funeral Practices," in *Religion and Society in T'ang and Sung China*, ed. Patricia Buckley Ebrey and Peter N. Gregory (Honolulu: University of Hawai'i Press, 1993), pp. 209–239, especially p. 210.

23. *TJL* no. 10, in *T* 48:233a–c.

24. See Clifford Geertz, *The Interpretation of Cultures* (New York: Basic Books, 1973), on the notion of "thick description."

25. Ohnuki-Tierney, *The Monkey as Mirror*, p. 223.

26. Pierre Bourdieu, *Outline of a Theory of Practice*, trans. Richard Nice (Cambridge: Cambridge University Press, 1977), p. 168. Bourdieu's holistic social theory recalls Nishida Kitarō's view of the unity of opposites.

27. Gurevich, *Medieval Popular Culture*, p. 5.

28. Ibid., p. xx.

29. For a discussion of parallel issues in late medieval and early modern Judaism see J. H. Chajes, "Judgments Sweetened: Possession and Exorcism in Early Modern Jewish Culture," *Journal of Early Modern History* 1(2) (1997):124–169.

30. On the notion of "negative charisma" see I. M. Lewis, *Religion in Context* (Cambridge: Cambridge University Press, 1986), p. 5.

31. *CMKS, CCL, chüan* 6, in *T* 51:250c–251b. For a discussion of the authorship of the text see Ishii Shūdō, "Hyakujō shingi no kenkyū: 'Zenmon kishiki' to 'Hyakujō koshingi,'" *Komazawa Daigaku Zen kenkyūjō nempō* 6 (1995):15–53; and T. Griffith Foulk, "Myth, Ritual, and Monastic Practice in Sung Ch'an Buddhism," in *Religion and Society in T'ang and Sung China*, ed. Patricia Buckley Ebrey and Peter N. Gregory (Honolulu: University of Hawai'i Press, 1993), pp. 147–208, especially pp. 156–159.

32. Although the notion of communal labor is referred to in the *CMKS*, the maxim is not cited there. It first appeared in the earlier *TTC* biography and then later in the *PCYL*, in *HTC* 119:820b.

33. *PCYL*, in *HTC* 119:820b. Ikkyū's poetry is cited in Sonja Arntzen, *Ikkyū and the Crazy Cloud Anthology* (Tokyo: Tokyo University Press, 1986), pp. 124 and 156. See also Alexander Kabanoff, "Ikkyū and Kōans," in *The Kōan*, ed. Steven Heine and Dale S. Wright (New York: Oxford University Press, forthcoming).

34. In some versions, Pai-chang fasted till he died; in others, the followers hid his tools playfully because they wanted to test his dedication.

35. See Tso Sze-bong, "The Decline of Buddhist *Vinaya* in China from a Historical and Cultural Perspective," in *Buddhist Behavioral Codes and the Modern World*, ed. Charles Wei-hsun Fu and Sandra A. Wawrytko (Westport, Conn.: Greenwood Press, 1994), pp. 111–122.

36. The four form meditations: rapture from withdrawal; rapture of composure; equanimity and mindfulness; and a state of neither pleasure nor pain. The

four formless meditations: transcending perceptions; transcending the infinitude of space and thought; the sphere of nothingness; and the sphere of neither perception nor nonperception. A common interpretation contends that the supranormal powers occur on the borderline between form and formlessness.

37. T. W. Rhys Davids and William Stede, eds., *The Pali Text Society's Pali-English Dictionary* (London: Luzac, 1966), p. 64; the list of six categories is mentioned in a variety of places including *Majjihima Nikāya* 4.6.77 and *Anguttara Nikāya* 3.99. On the role of supranormal powers in the context of East Asian Buddhism see Stephen F. Teiser, *The Ghost Festival in Medieval China* (Princeton: Princeton University Press, 1988), pp. 148–150; and Bernard Faure, *The Rhetoric of Immediacy: A Cultural Critique of Chan/Zen Buddhism* (Princeton: Princeton University Press, 1991), pp. 102–111.

38. See Reginald Ray, *Buddhist Saints in India: A Study in Buddhist Values and Orientations* (New York: Oxford University Press, 1994), especially pp. 293–323 on forest ascetic practices. The traditional list of practices includes twelve items: wearing rags taken from a refuse heap; wearing three monastic robes; wearing wool garments; living on alms food; eating in one place; eating before noon; dwelling in the forest; living at the foot of a tree; living in the open air; living in cremation grounds [as do foxes!]; remaining in a sitting posture without lying down; and accepting any seat that may be offered. See also Charles A. Prebish, "Ideal Types in Indian Buddhism: A New Paradigm," *Journal of the American Oriental Society* 115(4) (1995):651–666.

39. Nakamura, *Miraculous Stories*, p. 78, n. 121.

40. Thanissaro Bhikkhu, *The Buddhist Monastic Code*, pp. 81–82; and Teiser, *The Ghost Festival in Medieval China*, pp. 155–157.

41. According to a Rinzai Zen tradition, one who has only intellectual understanding without experience is said to practice "wild fox Zen" (*yako-Zen*) and one who has only experience without intellectual understanding is a "Zen devil" (*Zen-temma*).

42. In *SKSC, T* 50:771a—the passage on Pai-chang's rules containing much of the material, though in different sequence, that is in the *CMKS*. See also *Tai Sung-seng-shih lueh, T* 54:240a–b, also by Tsan-ning. And see Albert Welter, "Zanning and Chan: The Changing Nature of Buddhism in Early Song China," *Journal of Chinese Religions* 23 (1995):105–140. As Faure notes, there was always a tendency in Zen that attacks "magical methods and insists on the contemplation of basic principles"; see Bernard Faure, *The Will to Orthodoxy: A Critical Genealogy of Northern Ch'an Buddhism*, trans. Phyllis Brooks (Stanford: Stanford University Press, 1997), p. 10. For Tsan-ning's role in compiling monk biographies and the context of mainstream Chinese society, see Kieschnick, *The Eminent Monk*, pp. 60–63, which notes that "the response was not to disband the clergy as a whole; rather it was to 'weed out' undesirable elements, to push orthodox monks back in their neatly defined social/political

roles." Kieschnick also remarks that Tsan-ning "could claim to have tamed the trickster. No longer a dangerous subversive figure of the popular imagination, viciously manipulated by enemies of the faith, [he became] an emblem of the spiritual elite whose activities and esoteric cultivation were not only to be permitted by the authorities, but to be sponsored by them."

43. An extreme literary example is the perverse, solitary mountain priest who devours flesh as depicted in the Edo-period, supernatural, *setsuwa*-like tales by Ueda Akinari. See Leon Zolbrod, trans., *Ugetsu monogatari: Tales of Moonlight and Rain* (Tokyo: Tuttle, rpt. 1977). In "The Blue Hood" ("Aozukin") the priest comments: "In desolate places like this evil things sometimes happen" (p. 190).

44. *WMK* case 11, in *T* 48:294; *WMK* case 31, in *T* 48:297. In both cases Chao-chou sets out to "test," "check out," or "investigate" (C. *k'an;* J. *kan*)—borrowing from legalese—irregular practitioners.

45. This recalls *WMK* case 26 in which two monks are ordered to roll up a blind in identical fashion while Master Fa-yen proclaims that "one's got it, the other does not."

46. *SH,* "Tajintsū," in *DZZ* 2:241–252. Dōgen refutes the typical interpretation that the first two answers are correct and only the silent answer in the third case is wrong. He also provides a verse commentary in *EK* 9.27, in *DZZ* 4:198–200. Ta-erh is a Tripitaka master described in *CCL, chüan* 5.

47. Arthur F. Wright, *Buddhism in Chinese History* (Stanford: Stanford University Press, 1959), p. 53.

48. Ibid., p. 54. According to Pei-yi Wu: "The proliferation of Buddhism in China during the early days was much facilitated by the wondrous skills and magic powers displayed by the proselytizing monks. Healing was one of the devices that drew crowds and won converts." See Pei-yi Wu, "Self-Examination and Confession of Sins in Traditional China," *Harvard Journal of Asiatic Studies* 39(1) (1979):12.

49. See Visser, "Fox and Badger in Japanese Folklore," pp. 1–159; and D. C. Buchanan, "Inari: Its Origins, Development, and Nature," *Transactions of the Asiatic Society of Japan,* 2nd series, 12 (1935):i–191. Foxes, often associated with barbarians, were also connected with the onset of the Age of Decline; see Jan Nattier, *Once Upon a Future Time: Studies in a Buddhist Prophecy of Decline* (Berkeley: Asian Humanities Press, 1991).

50. According to the Vinaya, banishment lasts for the number of days counting from the time of the transgression until the time of the confession. But if the period of days is not remembered, the banishment is counted since the time of ordination, even if that was many years before.

51. Brown, *Cult of the Saints,* p. 110.

52. Shiina Kōyū, "Pai-chang-shan no genkyō to Tōdai ni okeru shomondai," in *Chūgoku butsu-seki kenmonki* (Tokyo: Chūgoku Bukkyō shiseki sankan dan, 1984), pp. 52–57. This diagram is from the Ch'ing era (1624).

53. On the general importance of stones in Chinese mythology and literature influenced by folklore—which function "as an agent that facilitates communication between the human and the supernatural . . . [a]s a mediator between heaven and earth . . . written or oral"—see Jing Wang, *The Story of Stone: Intertextuality, Ancient Chinese Stone Lore, and the Stone Symbolism in Dream of the Red Chamber, Water Margin, and The Journey to the West* (Durham, N.C.: Duke University Press, 1992), pp. 92–93 and 251–268 (on "The Inscribed Stone Tablet"). For a Western view based on Greek and Heideggerian sources see John Sallis, *Stone* (Bloomington: Indiana University Press, 1994).

54. On the disregarding of rules, Dōgen writes in a Chinese verse: "Previously I obscured the precepts down to the minutest details / Like some kind of trained animal; / Now, even though I wear Śākyamuni's robe, / Everyone in heaven and on earth laughs and calls me an old rice bag." See *EK* 10.16, in *DZZ* 4:252. Some groups, however, combined various kinds of recluses with mainstream priests: the White Lotus Society on Mount Lu in Kiangsi province near Mount Pai-chang, the founding of which is attributed to Hui-yüan, included over a hundred distinguished Buddhists, Confucians, and Taoists.

55. For other examples of period drawings see Richard E. Strassberg, trans., *Inscribed Landscapes: Travel Writing from Imperial China* (Berkeley: University of California Press, 1994).

56. *PCYL*, in *HTC* 119:820b.

57. *PYL* no. 85, in *T* 48:210b–211b.

58. *PYL* no. 26, in *T* 48:166c–167b; *PCYL*, in *HTC* 119:818b. This case, which concludes with the disciple bowing and Pai-chang striking him, is a favorite of both Ju-ching and Dōgen—in fact, Dōgen cites his mentor in the *Shōbōgenzō* "Hatsu-u" fascicle and then reinterprets the kōan several times in the *EK* collection, including 5.378 and 6.443. According to Ju-ching's recasting of the dialogue, the most extraordinary thing is eating rice in the monastery on Mount T'ien-t'ung; for Dōgen it is his sermons at Eiheiji temple on Mount Kichijōzan.

Chapter 3 · Philosophical Paradigm of Paradoxicality

1. The slap is discussed in two supplemental encounter dialogues involving Kuei-shan that are included in the *TKL* but not the *WMK* version.

2. Shibayama, *Zen Comments on the Mumonkan,* p. 35.

3. *WMK,* in *T* 48:299a–b.

4. Walpola Rahula, *What the Buddha Taught* (New York: Grove, 1959), p. 53. Rahula also expresses this principle in the modern formula: "When A is, B is; / A arising, B arises; / When A is not, B is not; / A ceasing, B ceases."

5. Herman Hesse, *Siddhartha,* trans. Hilda Rosner (New York: Bantam, rpt. 1971), pp. 32–33. Gotama's response, after a period of motionless silence: "You have found a flaw. Think well about it again. Let me warn you, you who are

thirsty for knowledge, against the thicket of opinions and the conflict of words." He then denies that what Siddhartha expressed was his exact view.

6. Junjirō Takakusu, *The Essentials of Buddhist Philosophy* (Honolulu: University of Hawai'i Press, 1947), pp. 72–73. According to the Sarvāstivāda Abhidharma analysis there are seventy-two conditioned and three unconditioned dharmas (including space, extinction through intellectual power, and extinction not by knowledge but due to a natural lack of a productive cause). According to the Yogācāra analysis there are ninety-four conditioned and six unconditioned dharmas (including the foregoing three plus extinction by a motionless state of meditation, extinction by the stoppage of idea and sensation by an arhat, and true suchness or *tathatā*).

7. Takakusu explains a progression of Buddhist philosophy based on different conceptions of the fundamental notion of causality—ranging from action-influence (karma), to the ideation-store *(ālaya-vijñāna)*, the matrix of thusness *(tathāgatagarbha)*, and the universal principle *(dharma-dhātu)*. See Takakusu, *Essentials of Buddhist Philosophy*, pp. 29–41 and 113. Takakusu's view is highly problematic for its conflation of ideology and historical development; yet at the same time it does seem to reflect the East Asian Mahayana view that a literal conception of karma must be transcended.

8. David Kalupahana, trans., *Nāgārjuna: The Philosophy of the Middle Way* (Albany: SUNY Press, 1986), p. 339.

9. Takakusu, *Essentials of Buddhist Philosophy*, pp. 40–41.

10. Kalupahana, *Nāgārjuna*, p. 333.

11. Examples of this pattern include *WMK* cases 5, 14, 19, 23, 24, 32, 36, 40, 43, and 44. There are additional cases that can also be considered to heighten the conceptual impasse, but in these it is explicitly stated.

12. *WMK* case 32, in *T* 48:297a.

13. *WMK* case 43, in *T* 48:298b.

14. *WMK* case 19, in *T* 48:295b.

15. Mu-chou Tao-tsung refers to "a clear-cut case *(hsien-cheng kung-an;* J. *genjōkōan)*"—when someone is nabbed red-handed in the midst of a crime—yet adds, "but I absolve you of thirty blows" (or "the realization of the kōan relieves you of thirty blows"). See *T* 47.547a; App, *Master Yunmen*, p. 107, n. 4; and Foulk, "Myth, Ritual, and Monastic Practice," p. 204, n. 82. The saying is also attributed to Ch'en in *CCL*, *chüan* 12, and to Te-shan Hsüan-chien in *WTH*, *chüan* 7. The term *"genjōkōan"* is used in a somewhat different sense by Dōgen to signify continuing enlightenment or the kōan realized in everyday practice.

16. *PYL* cases 70–72, in *T* 48:199b–200c.

17. *WMK* case 6, in *T* 48:293c.

18. *TJL* case 8, in *T* 48:232a.

19. Suzuki Tetsuo, "Koshushaku to shakushuko," examines a variety of

sources in Dōgen, including citations from *EK* and *SH,* in regard to the notion of *shushō-ittō.*

20. This comparison is suggested by Akizuki, *Zen mondō,* p. 131.

21. *WMK* case 4, in *T* 48:293b–c.

22. *CMKS,* in *T* 51:251a.

23. *T* 50:770c–771a; a verse commentary on the *CMKS* by Tsung-tse is included at the end of the *CYCK,* pp. 340–352.

24. Dōgen's references are unclear. Perhaps he is referring to the *CMKS,* which was probably unavailable to him (at least according to a theory that the text was inserted into *CCL, chüan* 6, in the fourteenth century). Or perhaps he is citing one of the earlier texts that formed the basis for the *CMKS.* See the discussion in Ishii Shūdō, "Hyakujō shingi no kenkyū."

25. Ibid., pp. 43–53.

26. John R. McRae, "Shen-hui and the Teaching of Sudden Enlightenment in Early Ch'an Buddhism," in *Sudden and Gradual: Approaches to Enlightenment in Chinese Thought,* ed. Peter N. Gregory (Honolulu: University of Hawai'i Press, 1987), p. 230.

27. Kenneth K. S. Ch'en, *Buddhism in China: A Historical Survey* (Princeton: Princeton University Press, 1964), pp. 226–233; and Stanley Weinstein, *Buddhism Under the T'ang* (New York: Cambridge University Press, 1987), pp. 114–136.

28. Wu, *Golden Age of Zen,* p. 111. For an interesting, though much more extreme, parallel see the description of Jean Chardin of a trip to Persia in which he encountered mendicants or dervishes who resembled monks but had no fixed abode and did not take holy orders: "the idle, wandering, bizarre beggars, dressed like theatrical buffoons . . . showing by their pretended poverty, and their contempt for the vanities of the world, mortification, loftiness of the spirit, struggles with sin and other different, pretended similar virtues." See Ronald W. Ferrier, trans. and ed., *A Journey to Persia: Jean Chardin's Portrait of a Seventeenth-Century Empire* (London: Tauris, 1996), p. 105. See also Kieschnick, *Eminent Monk,* pp. 67, 76, 93–94.

29. Wright, *Buddhism in Chinese History,* p. 60.

30. Jacques Gernet, *Buddhism in Chinese Society: An Economic History from the Fifth to the Tenth Centuries,* trans. Granciscus Verellen (New York: Columbia University Press, 1995), p. 249. See also Satō Tatsugen, "Dao-xuan and His Religious Precepts," in *Buddhist Behavioral Codes and the Modern World,* ed. Charles W. Fu and Sandra Wawrytko (Westport, Conn.: Greenwood Press, 1994), pp. 67–74.

31. Gernet, *Buddhism in Chinese Society,* p. 250.

32. Charles W. Fu, "Chu Hsi on Buddhism," in *Chu Hsi and Neo-Confucianism,* ed. Wing-tsit Chan (Honolulu: University of Hawai'i Press, 1986), p. 389; see also Wing-tsit Chan, *Chu Hsi: New Studies* (Honolulu: Univer-

sity of Hawai'i Press, 1989). Chu Hsi's approach is complex: in other passages he expressed a positive view of supernatural imagery.

33. *SH,* "Shisho," in *DZZ* 1:429. Dōgen's praise of his mentor may be taken as part of a sectarian polemic.

34. *SH,* "Shisho," in *DZZ* 1:429. The variety of discursive features in this fascicle may be related to partisan polemic: Dōgen laments the deterioration of Zen in the Age of Decline; describes a series of dreams that led him to find his mentor Ju-ching; and lambastes "remote followers" of both Lin-chi and Tung-shan.

35. In *T* 48:173b–174b.

36. Dōgen's *Eihei shingi* is ambivalent about the relative merits of begging and working. See Taigen Daniel Leighton and Shohaku Okumura, trans., *Dōgen's Pure Standards for the Zen Community* (Albany: SUNY Press, 1996), pp. 14–17.

37. Martin Collcutt, *Five Mountains: The Rinzai Monastic Institution in Medieval Japan* (Cambridge, Mass.: Harvard University Press, 1981), p. 8.

38. Ibid., p. 138.

39. Foulk, "Myth, Ritual, and Monastic Practice," pp. 158–159.

40. Welch, *Practice of Chinese Buddhism,* p. 105.

41. See Ishii Shūdō, *Chūgoku Zenshūshi hanashi* (Kyoto: Zen bunka kenkyūjō 1988), pp. 217–227.

42. Morten Schlütter, "When a Vinaya Monastery Is Not a Vinaya Monastery: Public and Hereditary Monasteries in the Song Dynasty (960–1279)" (paper presented at the panel on Buddhist Precepts in East Asia at the American Academy of Religion annual meeting, New Orleans, November 1996).

43. A third category includes "doctrinal schools" (C. *chiao-men;* J. *kyōmon*) such as the T'ien-t'ai, Hua-yen (or Avataṃsaka), and Yogācāra (or Dharma-lakṣaṇa) schools; see Welch, *Practice of Chinese Buddhism,* p. 398.

44. On the situation in India see Reginald Ray, *Buddhist Saints in India* (New York: Oxford University Press, 1994).

45. The schedules in the *CYCK* called for sermons delivered every five days. The daytime sermon or *shang-t'ang* was delivered on a "5–10" schedule (1st, 5th, 10th, 15th, 20th, and 25th days of the month); the evening sermon or *wan-ts'an,* discussed below, was delivered on a "3–8" schedule (3rd, 8th, 13th, 18th, 23rd, and 28th days of the month). There were sermons on other occasions, as well, such as the opening or closing of the three-month rainy season retreat, the winter solstice, and memorials and prayers for the well-being or installation of an emperor or other worthies. The ritual for the *shang-t'ang* style is carefully prescribed in terms of preparation, entry, bows, and departure. Furthermore, it is possible to distinguish between four types of sermon convocations *(ts'an)* in monastic settings: morning, evening, in the Dharma Hall, and in the abbot's room. The first and third and the second and fourth of these types often overlap.

46. The minor convocation, which was generally held outside the Dharma Hall, could in some cases be held in the morning, for example, and the evening

convocation was probably held only in the Dharma Hall. Yet both occasions are less formal than the major convocation.

47. In the *CYCK*, pp. 66–69, the procedure for requesting *ju-shih* is generally not spontaneous but, like all other aspects of monastic life, carefully regulated.

48. There are nine rites in the funeral ceremony for an abbot: placing the body in a coffin; transferring the coffin from the abbot's room to the Dharma Hall; closing the coffin; hanging a portrait of the deceased above the altar; having a wake; removing the coffin to the cremation ground; offering a libation of tea; then a libation of hot water; and lighting the funerary pyre. See *CYCK*, pp. 237–248, and Faure, *Rhetoric of Immediacy*, p. 193.

49. In the *PCYL* there is a brief anecdote in which a monk comes crying into the Dharma Hall and says: "My father and mother have both died; please choose a day for their funeral." The master reponds: "We will bury them first thing tomorrow morning." See *HTC* 119:818b. This passage is usually given a demythological interpretation in that the death of the parents can be taken to represent the casting off of the accumulated defilements and habits of ignorance and lust. Nonetheless it is certainly possible to read this passage as a way of introducing funerals for laypersons into the monastic routine (though in *SH*, "Daishugyō," Dōgen criticizes the practice of lay funerals).

50. Philip Kapleau recounts an anecdote based on a news story reported in both China and the international press in the 1930s. The story concerns the care and possible burial of a white fox, apparently thought to be of divine origin, in the manner of a person. One day a hunter found in his traps an unusually tame fox and thinking it strange gave it away to a man who was then directed in a dream to set it free in a certain monastery. There the fox bowed in the direction of the altar, and this made the abbot feel that it must have been a monk in another lifetime. The fox continued to pray, meditate, eat vegetarian food, and serve as a companion of the abbot. Kapleau speculates that it was undoubtedly given a funeral ceremony that would have included the reading of the *Heart Sutra*. See Philip Kapleau, *The Wheel of Life and Death: A Practical and Spiritual Guide* (New York: Doubleday, 1989), pp. 189–191.

51. William R. LaFleur, "Hungry Ghosts and Hungry People: Somaticity and Rationality in Medieval Japan," in *Fragments for a History of the Human Body, Part One*, ed. Michael Feber with Ramon Naddaft and Nadia Tuz (New York: Zone Books, 1989), p. 271.

52. *CMKS*, in *T* 51:251a.

53. The 12-fascicle text includes the following fascicles: "Shukke Kudoku"; "Jukai"; "Kesa Kudoku"; "Hotsubodaishin"; "Kuyō Shobutsu"; "Kie Buppōsōbō"; "Jinshin Inga"; "Sanjigo"; "Shime"; "Shizen Biku"; "Ippyakuhachihōmyōmon"; and "Hachidainingaku." For an English translation see Yūhō Yokoi, *Zen Master Dōgen: An Introduction with Selected Writings*, with Daizen Victoria (New York: Weatherhill, 1975).

54. Kawamura Kōdō, ed., *Shohon taikō Eihei kaisan Dōgen zenji gyōjō—Kenzeiki* (Tokyo: Taishūkan shoten, 1975), pp. 63–64; and Ōkubo Dōshū, *Dōgen zenji den no kenkyū* (Tokyo: Chikuma shobō, 1966), pp. 276–278. In an interesting discursive juxtaposition, probably the two main features of Dōgen's hagiography in the late period are the Gemmyō incident and an emphasis on the veneration of supernatural *rakan* (arhats) in his approach to lay religiosity.

55. *WMK* no. 12, in *T* 48:294c.

56. See Nakamura Eshin's note on this term in his modern Japanese translation of *Mumonkan* (Tokyo: Iwanami shoten, 1994), p. 64.

57. *TJL* no. 8, in *T* 48:232a. This version does not contain the second division of the kōan, but its commentary does cite similar dialogues and anecdotes.

58. Ibid.

59. Cited in Cleary, *No Barrier*, pp. 11 and 17. The poem also says: "With an opposing wind [Pai-chang] shouted him around, so the thunder's rumble died, / Shutting up, the fox returned to his home to hide his disgraceful ineptness."

60. *CSLT*, in *HTC* 115:112b.

61. See Chang Chung-yuan, trans., *Original Teachings of Ch'an Buddhism* (New York: Vintage, 1971), pp. 296–299, based on *CCL, chüan* 23.

62. Sasaki, *Recorded Sayings of Ch'an Master Lin-chi*, p. 82, n. 174. The term is used by Lin-chi in *RR*, p. 149; by Dōgen in the passage on the fox kōan in *SZ* 2.4 (as well as in several *SH* fascicles); and also by Hung-chih in a letter to a lay disciple (see Ishii Shūdō, *Sōdai Zenshūshi no kenkyū*, p. 302). See also *PYL* no. 96 on Chao-chou's three turning words.

63. See Yanagida, "The 'Recorded Sayings' Texts of Chinese Ch'an Buddhism"; and Whalen Lai, "Ma-tsu Tao-i and the Unfolding of Southern Zen," *Japanese Journal of Religious Studies* 12(2–3) (1985):181.

64. *EK* 9.77, in *DZZ* 4:236.

65. A variant reading is that he was a nonfox.

66. The last line recalls a passage in *SH*, "Daishugyō."

67. *SH*, "Daishugyō," in *DZZ* 2:187.

68. *PCYL*, in *HTC* 119:817b; also included in *MS* no. 152.

69. *PCYL*, in *HTC* 119:818a.

70. Shibayama, *Zen Comments on the Mumonkan*, p. 39.

71. *WMK* no. 2, in *T* 48:293b.

72. *TJL* no. 8, in *T* 48:231c.

73. Norman Waddell, trans., *The Unborn: The Life and Teaching of Zen Master Bankei, 1622–1693* (San Francisco: North Point, 1984), pp. 69–70. Bankei's point is twofold: teaching the doctrine of the "unborn" (*fushō*) is beyond words and texts; and what was appropriate for T'ang masters in the golden age does not easily transfer; thus all the kōans are unnecessary.

74. *CSLT*, in *HTC* 115:113b–114c.

75. Rahula, *What the Buddha Taught*, p. 40.

76. As cited in *SH*, "Jinshin inga," in *DZZ* 2:392.

77. *WMK* no. 2, in *T* 48:293b.

78. See Harada Kōdō, "'Shōyōroku hyaku monogatari': Hyakujō yako," *Chōryū* (1995):10.

79. Charles Luk, trans., *The Vimalakirti Nirdesa Sūtra* (Berkeley: Shambhala, 1972), p. 81. Concerning Ikkyū, his poetry alluding to the fox kōan also "speaks of his fear that his own Zen [marked by licentious behavior] was one that ignored karma," according to Arntzen, *Ikkyū and the Crazy Cloud Anthology*, p. 34.

80. *LL* in *RR*, p. 52; Sasaki, *Recorded Sayings of Ch'an Master Lin-chi*, p. 12.

81. Masao Abe, *A Study of Dōgen: His Philosophy and Religion*, ed. Steven Heine (Albany: SUNY Press, 1992), p. 220.

Chapter 4 · Deep Faith in Causality

1. *SH*, "Daishugyō," in *DZZ* 2:189. Dōgen is apparently influenced by his Chinese mentor, Ju-ching, also known for his strict adherence to *zazen* and discipline and his rejection of pomp and ceremony. In the record of their discussions, *Hōkyōki*, Dōgen notes Ju-ching's strong critique of any view that denies causality.

2. *SH*, "Daishugyō," first written in 1244, no. 68 in the 75-fascicle text, was apparently rewritten as *SH*, "Jinshin inga," compiled by Ejō in 1255, no. 7 in the 12-fascicle text (no. 26 in the 28-fascicle *Shōbōgenzō* text with "Daishugyō" no. 17); see *JSS*.

3. *SH*, "Jinshin inga," in *DZZ* 2:392, 394.

4. *SH*, "Jinshin inga," in *DZZ* 2:390.

5. The founder of the Daruma-shū sect, Dainichi Nōnin, unlike Dōgen and other leaders of early Japanese Zen, never visited China. He did send two disciples, however, to gain transmission from Te-kuang in the Ta-hui lineage. See Carl Bielefeldt, "Recarving the Dragon: History and Dogma in the Study of Dōgen," in *Dōgen Studies*, ed. William R. LaFleur (Honolulu: University of Hawai'i Press, 1985), pp. 21–53.

6. *SH*, "Jinshin inga," in *DZZ* 2:392.

7. *SH*, "Jinshin inga," in *DZZ* 2:393.

8. *SH*, "Jinshin inga," in *DZZ* 2:393.

9. Miriam Levering, "Ch'an Enlightenment for Laymen: Ta-hui and the New Religious Culture of the Sung," in *Buddhist and Taoist Practice in Medieval Chinese Society: Buddhist and Taoist Studies II*, ed. David W. Chappell (Honolulu: University of Hawai'i Press, 1987), pp. 181–209, especially p. 196.

10. The 12-fascicle *Shōbōgenzō* does cite earlier Buddhist texts more frequently than Zen transmission and recorded sayings texts. See Ikeda Rōsan, "Shinsō 'Jūnikanbon Shōbōgenzō' no kōzō to kadai," in *JSS*, pp. 297–318, espe-

cially pp. 297–304, on the citations of earlier and Zen works in the rewritten fascicles of the 12-fascicle text.

11. Kawamura Kōdo, "Jūnikanbon o meguru shosetsu," in *Budda kara Dōgen e*, ed. Nara Yasuaki (Tokyo: Tokyo shoseki, 1992), p. 231. See also David Putney, "Some Problems in Interpretation: The Early and Late Writings of Dōgen," *Philosophy East and West* 46(4) (1996):497–531.

12. In the colophon at the conclusion of this version of the "Hachidainingaku" fascicle, the final section of the 12-fascicle *SH*, Ejō explains that Dōgen wanted to create a 100-fascicle text. Ejō seems to suggest that the 12-fascicle edition including the rewritten fascicles was the start of this uncompleted project. Although he mentions the need to revere the 12 fascicles, the phrasing is ambiguous and could be interpreted to mean the "twelfth fascicle"; see *SH*, "Hachidainingaku," in *DZZ* 2:458.

13. William M. Bodiford, "Zen and the Art of Religious Prejudice: Efforts to Reform a Tradition of Social Discrimination," *Japanese Journal of Religious Studies* 23(1–2) (1996):1–27.

14. Part of the impetus behind Critical Buddhism and other reform movements within the Sōtō sect was a widespread sense of disappointment with the "Machida Incident"—a 1979 lecture at a world religions congress by Machida Muneo, then head of the Sōtō sect, in which he denied that there was Buddhist discrimination against *burakumin* or "special status" (outcaste) community. This remark caused an uproar that reverberated into many levels of the Sōtō institution from scholarship to the ritual activities of priests. On the ritualized marginalization of the *burakumin* in Japanese society see Ohnuki-Tierney, *Monkey as Mirror.*

15. A fairly common example is the use by Buddhist priests, in bestowing a posthumous ordination name on a headstone, of two characters, *gen* and *da.* When written as a single character, this becomes *chiku*—or beasts in the six realms of samsara—as a kind of code to reveal the outcaste identity of the deceased. See Shimada Hiromi, *Kaimyō: naze shigo ni namae o kaeru no ka* (Kyoto: Hōzōkan, 1991), pp. 72–75. The history of the practice of posthumous Buddhist names in Japan and the roots of the discrimination problem is complex. According to Critical Buddhism it is based to a large extent on the Mahayana notion of universal original enlightenment, which excluded certain categories of people considered excessively defiled, as derived from the Hindu caste system's discrimination against untouchables or *caṇḍāla.* See also the four-volume study by Noma Hiroshi and Okiura Kazuteru, who befriended and wrote about the *burakumin* community, in *Sei to sen* (Kyoto: Ninbun shoin, 1992–1994). The *kaimyō* practice, which gains one a name based on the amount contributed to the temple, is not the only aspect of discrimination; other rituals, such as *nanoka-gyō*, which memorializes the deceased for forty-nine days after death, are similarly affected. For contemporary Sōtō sect official responses to this issue,

which acknowledge the existence of problems and seek ways of repenting for offenses that have been committed, see "Sendara mondai senmon i'inkai hōkoku," no. 10, *Sanshō* 606 (1994):8–31.

16. The existence of the *caṇḍāla* or outcaste/untouchable community in India was reported in China by the pilgrim Fa-hsien, who traveled in the early fifth century, as defined by certain impure occupations or by the marriage of a *śudra* to a *brahmin*. The existence of such a discriminated group was disputed by the Buddha (as well as by Jainism and some Brahmanists). Outcasts probably came to be taken over and legitimized in East Asia through Buddhist restrictions against hunters, butchers, leatherworkers, and others who handled flesh.

17. See Matsumoto Shirō, "Nyoraizō Shisō wa Bukkyō ni arazu," originally delivered in 1984, chap. 1 in *Engi to Kū*, pp. 1–8, for comments on *tathāgatagarbha* thought. For the argument that Zen is a form of religion but not a form of Buddhism, see Itō Takatoshi, "Zen to Bukkyō no honshitsu," in *Budda kara Dōgen e,* ed. Nara Yasuaki (Tokyo: Tokyo shoseki, 1992), pp. 143–155. See also the excellent article by Paul L. Swanson surveying the Critical Buddhist literature: "'Zen Is Not Buddhism'—Recent Critiques of Buddha-Nature," *Numen* 40(2) (1993):115–149. For a rebuttal on the issue of Zen see Yoshizu Yoshihide, "Heki no ningen-kan to mondō ni yoru satori," in *Budda kara Dōgen e,* ed. Nara, pp. 131–142. The article by Swanson on Critical Buddhism, along with other articles and translations of works by Hakamaya and Matsumoto, appear in Hubbard and Swanson, *Pruning the Bodhi Tree.*

18. Hakamaya Noriaki, *Hihan Bukkyō* (Tokyo: Daizō shuppan, 1990), pp. 47–92, contrasts the "critical" philosophy of true Buddhism with "topical" philosophies—such as the Kyoto school of Nishida Kitarō and Nishitani Keiji—which he considers disguised as Buddhist. For a similar use of the fox kōan in the context of a critique of Zen's affinities with nationalism and militarism written in the context of the Vietnam War, see Ichikawa Hakugen, *Zen to gendai shisō* (Tokyo: Tokuma shoten, 1967), pp. 172–174, 242–244.

19. For example, Richard DeMartino says that when he interviewed D. T. Suzuki in the mid-1960s for *The Asahi Journal* (March 14, 1965), Suzuki insisted that Buddhism practiced compassion based on "motherly love" but was unwilling to acknowledge a problematic side of Buddhism in society.

20. Sallie B. King, *Buddha Nature* (Albany: SUNY Press), p. 170.

21. Hakamaya Noriaki, *Hongaku shisō hihan* (Tokyo: Daizō shuppan, 1989), p. 142.

22. See Peter N. Dale, *The Myth of Japanese Uniqueness* (New York: St. Martin's, 1986); and James W. Heisig and John C. Maraldo, eds., *Rude Awakenings* (Honolulu: University of Hawai'i Press, 1995).

23. Abe, *Study of Dōgen;* Tamura Yoshirō, *Kamakura shin-Bukkyō shisō no kenkyū* (Kyoto: Heirakuji shoten, 1965); Tamura Yoshirō, "Critique of Original Awakening Thought in Shōshin and Dōgen," *Japanese Journal of Religious*

Studies 11(2–3) (1984):243–266; Yamauchi Shuny'ū, *Dōgen Zen to Tendai hōngaku hōmon* (Tokyo: Daizō shuppan, 1986); and Ikeda Rōsan, *Dōgengaku no yōran* (Tokyo: Daizō shuppan, 1991).

24. *SH*, "Daishugyō," is the main exception: it does criticize *hongaku*.

25. Hakamaya, *Dōgen to Bukkyō*, pp. 289–334.

26. Matsumoto, *Engi to kū*, p. 8.

27. There is no record of Dōgen's teaching in Kamakura other than twelve Japanese poems included in his *waka* collection. Several revisionist historians have conjectured that Dōgen made the trip at the request (or demand) of patrons who were summoned by the shogun to lead a new Zen temple (which became Kenchōji).

28. Carl Bielefeldt argues that Dōgen entered a period of decline at the time of his flight to Echizen. In "Recarving the Dragon," Bielefeldt cites works by Japanese Rinzai Zen scholars, including Furuta Shōkin, Imaeda Aishin, Yanagida Seizan, and Masutani Fumio.

29. *EK* 1.48, in *DZZ* 3:34; in some versions of the *EK* text, this passage is 1.1, the opening passage.

30. Ryōkan, *Great Fool: Zen Master Ryōkan Poems, Letter, and Other Writings,* trans. Ryūichi Abe and Peter Haskel (Honolulu: University of Hawai'i Press, 1996), p. 42.

31. Matsumoto, "Jinshin inga ni tsuite—Dōgen no Shisō ni Kansuru Shiken," *JSS*, p. 234.

32. Another way of framing the issue of Dōgen's relation to *nyoraizō* thought, suggested by Matsumoto, is to distinguish Dōgen's later view from three perspectives: (1) since all things have Buddha nature, one must practice but the goal appears unattainable; (2) since Buddha nature encompasses all things, one need not practice because the Buddha nature is already present; (3) since Buddha nature is actualized by practice, one must continue to practice. Dōgen's early standpoint is reflected in view (3) as a refutation of (1) and (2). But even this view does not sufficiently emphasize the retributive consequences of karmic conditioning; see Matsumoto, "Jinshin inga ni tsuite," pp. 209ff.

33. Ishii Seijun, "Jūnikanbon *Shōbōgenzō* to *Eihei kōroku*."

34. *Hōkyōki* no. 8, in *DZZ* 7:12–14. But recent scholarship has argued that even though this record seems to have been produced shortly after his return from China in the late 1220s or early 1230s, it may in fact have been a product of the later period after he received a copy of Ju-ching's recorded sayings text from China, which Dōgen considered a disappointing and unreliable account.

35. See Matsumoto Shirō, *Zen shisō no hihanteki kenkyū* (Tokyo: Daizō shuppan, 1994), pp. 235–410, for a sustained critique of Lin-chi; see pp. 579–630 for a discussion of Dōgen's "Jinshin inga" fascicle.

36. In early works like *SZ*, Dōgen seems to emphasize that adhering to the precepts is less important than *zazen* meditation. But in the 12-fascicle text *SH*,

"Jukai," in *DZZ* 2:294–299, he develops a distinctive system of sixteen precepts: the three refuges (Buddha, Dharma, Samgha), the three pure precepts (do no evil, do good, benefit all sentient beings), and the ten major precepts (no killing, no stealing, no sexual relations, no lies, no intoxicants, no faulting of bodhisattvas, praising others, no coveting, no anger, no disparagement of the three refuges—representing ten of the fifty-eight precepts in the Mahayana scripture, the *Bonmōkyō*).

37. This raises the issue of why and when syncretic tendencies with popular religions became prevalent in the Sōtō sect. See Ishikawa Rikizan, "Chūsei Zenshūshi kenkyū to Zenseki shōmono shiryō," in *Dōgen Zenji to Sōtōshū*, ed. Kawamura Kōdō and Ishikawa Rikizan (Tokyo: Yoshikawa kōbunkan, 1985), pp. 76–98. For a discussion of these matters supporting the role of popularization as a positive development in the sect's history, see Bodiford, *Sōtō Zen in Medieval Japan.*

38. *SH,* "Kie-buppōsōbō," in *DZZ* 2:375. This fascicle, which includes an endorsement of fox veneration, is mainly concerned with the equality of female clergy and contains an extended discussion filled with wordplay about the nun/teacher Mo-shan, who tells her male disciple that she is a real master and not just a wild fox.

39. In *DZZ* 7:286–295; see also *DZZ* 7:224.

40. *SH,* "Daishugyō, in *DZZ* 2:191.

41. *SH,* "Daishugyō," in *DZZ* 2:191.

42. *SH,* "Daishygyō," in *DZZ* 2:192.

43. *SH,* "Daishugyō," in *DZZ* 2:188.

44. On Hakuin's comments see Aitken, *Gateless Barrier,* p. 25.

45. On the role of funerals in Buddhism see Nagai Masashi, "Chūgoku Bukkyō seiritsu no issokumen: Chūgoku Zenshū ni okeru sōshiki girei no seiritsu to tenkai," *KDBR* 26 (1995):109–148; Patricia Buckley Ebrey, "Cremation in Sung China," *American Historical Review* 95(2) (1990):406–428; Alan Cole, "Upside Down/Right Side Up: A Revision History of Buddhist Funerals in China," *History of Religions* 35(4) (1996):306–338; James L. Watson and Evelyn S. Rawski, eds., *Death Ritual in Late Imperial and Modern China* (Berkeley: University of California Press, 1988); and Dickson Kazuo Yagi, "Protestant Perspectives on Ancestor Worship in Japanese Buddhism: The Funeral and the Buddhist Altar," *Buddhist-Christian Studies* 15 (1996):43–59.

46. See *CYCK,* pp. 237–248.

47. Nakaseko Shōdō, *Dōgen zenji den kenkyū* (Tokyo: Kokusho kankōkai, 1979), pp. 382–384. Whether Dōgen actually made the trip or sent ten *waka* poems as his message is also under debate in current scholarship.

48. *EK* no. 251, in *DZZ* 3:166–168.

49. This passage has also been cited to show that Dōgen's disciples were "furious" with him for preaching to lay followers while abandoning his monks (see

Bodiford, *Sōtō Zen in Medieval Japan,* pp. 30–31), but this seems to be an interpolation of psychological reactions that the sources do not actually state. Using typical Zen metaphors, Dōgen says that during his travels the "moon was in the sky, but now the clouds [monks] are happy." He concludes by reaffirming his love for the Echizen mountains (that is, Eiheiji).

50. *SZ* 2.2, in *DZZ* 7:66.

51. *EK* 6.437, in *DZZ* 4:24–26.

52. *EK* 7.498, in *DZZ* 4:82.

53. *EK* 5.390, in *DZZ* 3:260–262. Dōgen also cites Pai-chang's rules, referred to as "Hyakujō shingi" or "Hyakujō koshingi," as an exemplary model for Zen behavior; see *Fukanzazengi* (*DZZ* 5:12) and *Eihei shingi* (*DZZ* 6:74). For a discussion see Kagamishima Genryū, *Dōgen zenji to in'yō kyōten-goroku no kenkyū* (Tokyo: Mokujisha, 1985), pp. 181–192, and Leighton and Okumura, *Dōgen's Pure Standards for the Zen Community.*

54. *SH,* "Keisei-sanshoku," in *DZZ* 1:283–284. In a fascinating early article Faure argues that "not once in his *Shōbōgenzō* does Dōgen make any approving reference to Japanese popular beliefs" and emphasizes Keizan's role in fostering syncretism in Sōtō Zen; see Bernard Faure, "The Daruma-shū, Dōgen, and Sōtō Zen," *Monumenta Nipponica* 42(1) (1987):48. But in later works, especially *Visions of Power,* which focuses on Keizan, Faure tries to bring out popular religious elements that were already present in Dōgen's thought.

55. Hakamaya, *Dōgen to Bukkyō,* pp. 244–288, especially p. 249. Some of the Buddhist-derivative New Religions put an extreme emphasis on repentance rites, such as Ittōen's communal toilet-cleaning rite; see Winston Davis, *Japanese Religion and Society* (Albany: SUNY Press, 1992), pp. 189–225. The notion of repentance is also the centerpiece of Kyoto school philosopher Tanabe Hajime's postwar work about a sense of guilt for participation in extreme nationalist rhetoric, *Tetsugaku toshite no zangedō;* see Tanabe Hajime, *Philosophy as Metanoetics,* trans. Takeuchi Yoshinori with Valdo Viglielmo and James W. Heisig (Berkeley: University of California Press, 1986).

56. Hakamaya has a lengthy discussion of the role of *zange* in "Shushōgi," a summary of Dōgen's philosophy created by modern Sōtō priests, as well as in *Shōbōgenzō,* "Keisei-sanshoku." Dōgen's death *gāthā* is quite similar to that of his Chinese mentor, Ju-ching, except that Dōgen omits the phrase *"zaigo"* (karmic sins) that Ju-ching uses in referring to a recognition of his own evil karma. Dōgen does, however, discuss the role of repentance in light of evil karma in the 75-fascicle "Keisei-sanshoku."

57. Daniel Stevenson, "The Four Kinds of Samādhi in Early T'ien-t'ai Buddhism," in *Traditions of Meditation in Chinese Buddhism,* ed. Peter N. Gregory (Honolulu: University of Hawai'i Press, 1986), pp. 45–97.

58. This argument does not, however, necessarily imply the converse—that an emphasis on repentance leads to ethical responsibility. The Jōdo Shinshū

sect, which emphasizes devotional repentance, has shown more interest in the plight of *burakumin,* for example, but this might be mainly because the membership numbers are considerably higher since the time of the Tokugawa shogunate, which assigned this group to the sect in many areas, especially in Kansai.

59. *T* 27:592a–593b.

60. William R. LaFleur, *The Karma of Words: Buddhism and the Literary Arts in Medieval Japan* (Berkeley: University of California Press, 1983), pp. 34–35.

61. Nakamura, *Miraculous Stories,* p. 99.

62. Ibid., p. 101.

63. *SH,* "Kesa kudoku," in *DZZ* 2:314, which provides a long list of supernatural beings from Sanskrit Buddhism.

64. *SH,* "Kesa kudoku," in *DZZ* 2:331.

65. From the *Hyakunijussoku,* as cited in Kraft, *Eloquent Zen,* p. 116, originally in Hirano Sōjō, *Daitō Zen no tankyū* (Tokyo: Kyōiku shinchōsha, 1974), p. 61.

Chapter 5 · Folklore Mythology and the Issue of Repentance

1. See Kieschnick, *Eminent Monk,* pp. 41–45.

2. See William F. Powell, trans., *The Record of Tung-shan* (Honolulu: University of Hawaiʻi Press, 1986), pp. 5–6, contrasting the rustic, colloquial style of recorded sayings with the refined, baroque style of transmission of the lamp histories.

3. Nakamura, *Miraculous Stories,* p. 33. The *"hsien"* (J. *gen*) in *"hsien-pao"* (J. *genpō*) refers to retribution in the immediate or present life, but the principle also encompasses karmic effects in the three times including the next life and future lives.

4. Nozaki, *Kitsune,* p. 21.

5. LaFleur, *Karma of Words,* p. 54.

6. Ibid., pp. 56–57.

7. Marra, *Representations of Power,* p. 95.

8. Kraft, *Eloquent Zen,* p. 62. Kraft's comments refer specifically to a Kamakura-era kōan collection translated by Trevor Leggett in *The Warrior Kōans: Early Zen in Japan* (London: Routledge & Kegan Paul, 1985).

9. LaFleur, *Karma of Words,* p. 57.

10. This is Akizuki's approach in *Zen mondō;* see also Aitken, *Gateless Barrier,* p. 35.

11. Y. W. Ma, "Themes and Characterizations in the Lung-t'u Kung-an," *Toung Pao* 59 (1973):179–202.

12. John C. Maraldo, "Is There Historical Consciousness Within Ch'an?", *Japanese Journal of Religious Studies* 12(2–3) (1985):166.

13. Robert E. Buswell Jr., "The 'Short-Cut' Approach of *K'an-hua* Meditation: The Evolution of a Practical Subitism in Chinese Ch'an Buddhism," in *Sudden and Gradual: Approaches to Enlightenment in Chinese Thought,* ed. Peter N. Gregory (Honolulu: University of Hawai'i Press, 1987), p. 345.

14. Heinrich Dumoulin, *Zen Buddhism: A History,* trans. James W. Heisig and Paul Knitter, 2 vols. (New York: Macmillan, 1988–1990), 1:241 and 249.

15. Foulk, "Myth, Ritual, and Monastic Practice," p. 153.

16. *WMK,* in *T* 48:299a.

17. *WMK* case 35, in *T* 48:297b.

18. The *Li-hun chi* is discussed in Akizuki Ryūmin, ed., *Mumonkan o yomu* (Tokyo: Tōsho-insatsu, 1990), pp. 15–16; Hirata, *Mumonkan,* pp. 130–131; and Shibayama, *Zen Comments on the Mumonkan,* pp. 253–254.

19. Cited in Shibayama, *Zen Comments on the Mumonkan,* p. 257.

20. *WMK* case 40, in *T* 48:298a.

21. *CCL,* in *T* 51:264b–266b.

22. Carl Bielefeldt, *Dōgen's Manuals of Zen Meditation* (Berkeley: University of California Press, 1988), p. 71.

23. *SH,* "Gyōji, pt. I," in *DZZ* 1:160; also cited in *Mana Shōbōgenzō* no. 18 and *Eihei kōroku juko* no. 9.63. A story of Ma-tsu and the earth spirit is in *Baso goroku,* ed. Iriya Yoshitaka (Kyoto: Zen bunka kenkyūjō, 1974), pp. 120–129.

24. The main Zen monastic code, the *CYCK,* refers to the earth deity hall *t'u-ti-t'ang* (J. *dojidō*); see Kagamishima, *Yakuchū Zen'en shingi,* pp. 76, 77, 256. See also Foulk, "Myth, Ritual, and Monastic Practice," pp. 177–178.

25. This case, in which a lowly bodhisattva is successful with one snap of the finger, was originally in *Shobutsu yōshūkyō, chüan* 2, translated by Dharmaraksa. This and other Zen records on women are celebrated from a "feminist" standpoint by the twelfth-century Chinese master Ta-hui. See Miriam Levering, "Lin-chi (Rinzai) Ch'an and Gender: The Rhetoric of Equality and the Rhetoric of Heroism," in *Buddhism, Sexuality, and Gender,* ed. José Ignacio Cabezon (Albany: SUNY Press, 1992), pp. 137–156, especially pp. 149–150.

26. *WMK* case 31, in *T* 48:297a; *TJL* no. 10, in *T* 48:233c.

27. Abe Chōichi, *Zenshū shakai to shinkō: zoku Chūgoku Zenshūshi no kenkyū* (Tokyo: Kindai bungeisha, 1993); Chün-fang Yü, "P'u-t'o Shan: Pilgrimage and the Creation of the Chinese Potalaka," in *Pilgrims and Sacred Sites in China,* ed. Susan Naquin and Chun-fang Yü (Berkeley: University of California Press, 1992), pp. 190–245. The four sites and their bodhisattvas are Mount Wu-t'ai (C. Wen-shu; J. Monjū), Mount Omei (Pu-hsien, Fūgen), Mount P'u-t'o (Kuan-yin, Kannon), and Mount Chiu-hua (Ti-tsang, Jizō).

28. *PYL* no. 35, in *T* 48:173b–174b. To questions about the size of the congregation on Mount Wu-t'ai, Mañjuśrī responds: "In front three by three, in back three by three."

29. *WMK* case 23, in *T* 48:295c–296a.

30. Shibayama, *Zen Comments on the Mumonkan*, p. 176. Shibayama contends that there is no mention of this "because they have not gone through actual searching and training themselves."

31. Robert C. Ellwood, *Introducing Religion: From Inside and Outside* (Englewood Cliffs, N.J.: Prentice-Hall, 1983), p. 19.

32. Blake Morgan Young, *Ueda Akinari* (Vancouver: University of British Columbia Press, 1982), p. 61.

33. This conflict between Inari and Izumo recalls a mythic struggle in early Japanese mythology between Amaterasu, a Yamato deity, and her chaotic brother Susano, apparently a stigmatized Izumo deity.

34. Zolbrod, *Ugetsu Monogatari*, pp. 30–32 and apps. 4 and 5.

35. I am using this term in a sense parallel to the "magical realism" of contemporary Latin American fiction—especially the works of Gabriel Marquez (and Japanese authors such as Nobel laureate Ōe Kenzaburō)—but also to reflect the distinctive externalization of emotional states portrayed in East Asian art, such as Chinese ink paintings and the Noh chorus. See also Keiko McDonald, ed., *Ugetsu: Kenji Mizoguchi, Director* (New Brunswick, N.J.: Rutgers University Press, 1993), p. 11; and Kelsey, *Konjaku Monogatari-shū*, p. 155.

36. Robert F. Campany, "Demons, Gods, and Pilgrims: The Demonology of the *Hsi-yu Chi*," *CLEAR* 7 (1985):109.

37. W. Michael Kelsey, "Salvation of the Snake, the Snake of Salvation: Buddhist-Shinto Conflict and Resolution," *Japanese Journal of Religious Studies* 8(1–2) (1981):110.

38. Kelsey, *Konjaku Monogatari-shū*, pp. 90–91 (based on *KM* no. 27.41, in *NKBT* 25:535–538).

39. According to Bassui: "Though [buddhas and ordinary people] are not separated by as much as the width of a hair, because of the one mistaken thought—'I am ordinary'—they think that enlightenment is difficult to realize." See *Mud and Water: A Collection of Talks by the Zen Master Bassui*, trans. Arthur Braverman (San Francisco: North Point, 1988), p. 28. But Bankei rejects "worthless old documents."

40. Blacker, *Catalpa Bow*, pp. 208–234.

41. Kwong, *Tao Qian and the Chinese Poetic Tradition*, p. 109. Kwong points out that some folklore was even attributed to Tao Ch'ien because of the striking affinity with his writings. At the same time, some have claimed that "Peach Blossom Spring" is "not merely a fantasy utopia but a factual record of the mountain stronghold of fugitives from the tyrannous [Fu] Ch'in state." See Li Ch'i, "The

Changing Concept of the Recluse in Chinese Literature," *Harvard Journal of Asiatic Studies* 24 (1962–1963):239.

42. *CSLT*, in *HTC* 115:115b.

43. *CSLT*, in *HTC* 115:115a.

44. Tyler, *Japanese Tales*, p. 118 (*KM* no. 16.17, in *NKBT* 24:456–458).

45. Masato Mori, "*Konjaku Monogatari-shū*: Supernatural Creatures and Order," *Japanese Journal of Religious Studies* 9(2–3) (1982):165. *Jen-shih chuan* has a similar sequence.

46. *KM* no. 27.5, in *NKBT* 25:483–484.

47. Yao, *Classical Chinese Tales*, p. 36; in one tale, for example, a fox-scholar is eradicated when a thousand-year-old wooden post, symbolizing the fox's striving for immortality, is chopped down.

48. Kelsey, "Salvation of the Snake," p. 109.

49. Yao, *Classical Chinese Tales*, p. 104. This tale, based on "Father and the Fox" (*SSC* 18.422, which also appears in *Fa-yüan chu-lin* 42.498b), raises the issue of whether fox spiritism is evoked in order to rationalize patricide.

50. Kelsey, *Konjaku Monogatari-shū*, p. 67 (*KM* no. 7.21, in *NKBT* 23:147).

51. Davis, *Dojo*, p. 19.

52. Blacker, *Catalpa Bow*, pp. 53–54.

53. Davis, *Dojo*, p. 155.

54. Blacker, *Catalpa Bow*, p. 314. See Brown, *Cult of the Saints*, on the role of *praesentia* and *potentia* in exorcism in early medieval Christianity.

55. For an interesting contemporary illustration of the displacement process see Edward Albee's play *Who's Afraid of Virginia Woolf?* (New York: Signet, 1962). In the third act (called "The Exorcism") following the second act ("Walpurgisnacht"), two couples during an evening of drinking and shocking personal disclosures come to terms with their respective delusions—reflected by hysterical pregnancies and imaginary offspring that were generated as psychological compensations for infertility and sterility, which symbolize larger problems in postwar middle-class America.

56. Mohan Wijayaratna, *Buddhist Monastic Life: According to the Texts of the Theravāda Tradition*, trans. Claude Grangier and Steven Collins (Cambridge: Cambridge University Press, 1990), pp. 123–124.

57. Faure, *Rhetoric of Immediacy*, p. 238.

58. An example of the last is the case of Kume Heinai, enshrined at a subtemple of Sensōji temple in Asakusa, Tokyo, a samurai who repented for his life of killing by converting to Zen and practicing meditation. At his death he donated his *zazen* image for burial at the temple so that people could tread upon it before it was properly set up. Eventually, Heinai became a folk deity that people pray to in search of a future spouse by writing down their wish. (Both "treading upon" and "writing upon" are pronounced "*fumi-tsukeru.*")

59. *T* 46:949a–955c.

60. M. W. de Visser, *Ancient Buddhism in Japan,* 2 vols. (Leiden: Brill, 1935), I:249–409.

61. But according to Pei-yi Wu: "The confessions written in China . . . never disclose any specific sinful act, with particularities such as time, place, accomplices. The lack of specificity in self-disclosure was of course universal: in the West the admittance of particular deeds of which the author is really ashamed began only with the Puritans. St. Augustine was the sole exception. St. Theresa, in spite of lengthy examinations of the self, is vague when she writes about her sins." See Pei-yi Wu, "Self-Examination and Confession of Sins in Traditional China," *Harvard Journal of Asiatic Studies* 39(1) (1978):31. Wu suggests that this lack of candor in China is due to a Confucian overemphasis on shame as a matter of social control rather than guilt—an emotional attitude he thinks would be more beneficial in fostering self-reflection and reversing one's behavior. Nonetheless, Wu recognizes the rich variety of Chinese terms implying self-correction, such as *tzu-sung* (J. *jishō*) and *tzu-tse* (J. *jiseki*) among others; see especially p. 21.

62. In Philip B. Yampolsky, trans. *The Platform Sutra of the Sixth Patriarch: The Text of the Tun Huang Manuscript* (New York: Columbia University Press, 1967), pp. 144–145 (Chinese version, p. 10); translation altered and emphasis added.

63. Lewis Lancaster, "The Terminology of the *Platform Sūtra* in the Chinese Buddhist Canon," in *Report of the International Conference on Ch'an Buddhism* (Taipei: Fo Kuang Shan, 1990), p. 58; emphasis added.

64. In Yampolsky, *Platform Sutra,* p. 136 (Chinese version, p. 15); translation altered and emphasis added.

65. According to David Chappell, there are five kinds of repentance: communal repentance to the *saṃgha* to ensure monastic conformity; personal repentance of karmic history; mythological repentance to a supermundane Buddha; meditation repentance of incorrect perceptions and attachments; and philosophical repentance of wrong concepts and discrimination. See David Chappell, "Formless Repentance in Comparative Perspective," in *Report of the International Conference on Ch'an Buddhism* (Taipei: Fo Kuang Shan, 1990), p. 253.

66. Ibid., p. 255.

67. The passage appears in *SH,* "Bendōwa" and "Gyōji," as well as in *Hōkyōki* and *EK.* An exception to this view, cited earlier, is in *SH,* "Keisei-sanshoku."

68. In Azuma, *Sōtōshū,* pp. 147–149.

69. Wu, "Self-Examination and Confession of Sins," p. 13.

70. *EK* 9.5, in *DZZ* 4:186. This case, originally from *CCL, chüan* 3, also appears in Keizan's *Denkōroku.* See also "Shoaku makusa" in the 75-fascicle *Shōbōgenzō* on the issue of overcoming evil through philosophical thinking alone. Moreover, a Sōtō anecdote makes a similar point in a story that closely resembles the fox kōan. While Tsūgen is preaching at Yōtakuji temple, Ikkei sees a strange woman sneaking into the hall and asks who she is. The woman responds

that her karmic retribution caused her to be reborn as a snake and she now seeks release. Ikkei asks her, "Since retribution originally is emptiness *(kū)*, from what do you wish to be freed?" The snake/woman cannot give an answer, but Tsūgen steps in and administers the precepts. Immediately she regains her human identity and bows in thanks to the priests. See Bodiford, *Sōtō Zen in Medieval Japan*, pp. 176–178.

71. Dōgen's verse: "The innumerable sins are unobtainable, / For they are too numerous to obtain; / But when [the lay disciple] realizes this, / It is like feeling a cool, refreshing breeze blowing his way."

72. See Wu, "Self-Examination and Confession of Sins," p. 13; Faure, *Chan Insights and Oversights*, p. 259.

73. Kelsey, "Salvation of the Snake," p. 103 (*KM* no. 13.17, in *NKBT* 24:231–232).

74. For a profound discussion of repentance at the opening and conclusion of a tale of sexual ribaldry see the famous Ch'ing novel, *Jou pu tuan*, in Li Yu, *The Carnal Prayer Mat*, trans. Patrick Hanan (New York: Ballantine, 1990).

75. Yao, *Classical Chinese Tales*, p. 36, referring to "Chang Hua and the Fox" (in *SSC* 18.421 and *TPKC* 442.11).

76. For an example of the theme of the identification of the fox, friend or foe, see Tyler, *Japanese Tales*, pp. 303–304 (*KM* no. 27.37, in *NKBT* 25:529–530). In this tale a man goes off in the mountains to look for a stray horse. He sees a two-hundred-foot-tall cryptomeria tree, feels frightened, meets a spirit, shoots arrows, and runs away. But the next day he returns to find a fox lying dead with a branch in his jaws and pierced through the belly by two arrows.

77. Arntzen, *Ikkyū and the Crazy Cloud Anthology*, pp. 25 and 36 (Ikkyū: "Students who ignore karma are sunk").

78. Ibid., p. 34.

79. For a modern expression of the visionary experience see Banana Yoshimoto, *Kitchen*, trans. Megan Backus (New York: Grove, 1993), p. 147: "Some people can't see [the vision of a ghost or spirit] at all. The residual thoughts of a person who has died meet the sadness of someone left behind, and the vision is produced."

Chapter 6 · Unconcluding Methodological Reflections

1. Welch, *Practice of Chinese Buddhism*, p. 197.

2. Teiser, *Ghost Festival in Medieval China*, pp. 215, 217. See also Catherine Bell, "Religion and Chinese Culture: Toward an Assessment of 'Popular Religion,'" *History of Religions* 21(1) (1989):35–57.

3. This case relates to the discussion of great and little traditions in Theravada Buddhism by Terence P. Day, who examines works by Ames, Bechert, Brohm, Spiro, and Tambiah to demonstrate that there are many more than two or three so-

cial-historical levels functioning when one takes into account Mahayana and Brahmanistic influences in addition to varieties of local animism and fetishism as well as the impact of westernization/modernization in shaping a religion dependent on patronage from the state. See Terence P. Day, *Great Tradition and Little Tradition in Theravāda Buddhist Studies* (Lewiston/Queenston: Edwin Mellen, 1988), pp. 176–185.

4. Faure, *Rhetoric of Immediacy*, p. 311.

5. Ibid., p. 305.

6. Ibid., pp. 309, 94–95.

7. Faure, *Visions of Power*, p. 286.

8. Ibid., p. 179.

9. Faure is harshly critical of Hakamaya and Critical Buddhism. Among other problems, he thinks it suppresses, intolerantly yet unconsciously, the issue of the incorporation of popular religiosity. See Bernard Faure, "The Kyoto School and Reverse Orientalism," in *Japan in Traditional and Postmodern Perspectives,* ed. Charles Wei-hsun Fu and Steven Heine (Albany: SUNY Press, 1995), pp. 267–269.

10. Faure, *Chan Insights and Oversights*, p. 170; see also Faure, *Rhetoric of Immediacy,* p. 311.

11. Faure, *Rhetoric of Immediacy*, p. 308.

12. Bodiford, *Sōtō Zen in Medieval Japan*, p. 117.

13. In his earlier article, "Zen in the Art of Funerals: Ritual Salvation in Japanese Buddhism," *History of Religions* 32(2) (1992):146–164, Bodiford uses an intriguingly ironic title but tends to be less critical of traditional institutions than in "Zen and the Art of Religious Prejudice."

14. Yamaoka Takaaki, "Daiyūzan Saijōji ni okeru Bukkyōteki fukugō ni tsuite," *SK* 25 (1983):115–136.

15. This stone makes an interesting counterpoint to the memorial rocks on Ta-hsiung Peak in China as well as the wishing stones *(kakure gan ishi)* at many Inari shrines.

16. *Daiyūzan: Daiyūzan Saijōji kaisō roppyakunen hōzan* (Shinagawa-ken: Daiyūzan Saijōji kaisō roppyakunen hōzan jimuchō, 1994), p. 9.

17. A rationale sometimes articulated by modern Sōtō priests is that the *"genze"* (this-worldly) in the phrase *"genze riyaku"* is equivalent to the *"genjō"* in *"genjōkōan."* While this may be appropriate with regard to an emphasis on the realization of truth here-and-now, it implies an identification of the notions of *riyaku* (benefits) and kōan that seems problematic.

18. H. Neill McFarland, *Daruma: The Founder of Zen in Japanese Art and Popular Culture* (Tokyo: Kodansha, 1987), p. 50; on p. 109 he suggests that this pattern is not so unique in world religions.

19. For an examination of the modern period see Welch, *Practice of Chinese Buddhism.*

20. Collcutt, *Five Mountains,* p. 156; Foulk, "Myth, Ritual, and Monastic Practice," pp. 171–172.

21. On the difference between "synthesis" and "syncretism" see Walter L. Brenneman Jr. and Mary G. Brenneman, "Holy Water," *Earthwatch,* March/April 1995, pp. 6–8, based on their book *Crossing the Circle of the Holy Wells of Ireland* (Charlottesville: University of Virginia Press, 1994).

22. Gimello, "Chang Shan-ying on Wu-t'ai Shan," p. 119. For another interesting example of a methodology that seeks a compromise view see Wen-jie Qin, "Revisiting the Laughing Buddha: A Study of the Metamorphosis of Maitreya in China" (paper presented at the Association for Asian Studies annual meeting, Chicago, 1997). According to Qin's discussion of early Chinese Zen, the P'u-tai (J. Hotei) cult is not an example of degeneracy or corruption of the elite by popular religiosity. Rather, it represents a constructive cross-fertilization and mutual transformation made possible by favorable historical conditions of the elite tradition, which seeds popular religion with notions of antiritualism and self-power, and the folklore tradition, which contributes to the sense of spontaneous joy and solidarity with the wretched that is symbolized by the image of the laughing Buddha. Thus the extraordinary is revealed in the ordinary and the earthly becomes a vehicle for manifesting the transcendental. Yet this approach tends to defuse the tension that occurs in the encounter between traditions and thus in some ways approximates the seamless continuity approach.

23. Faure, *Rhetoric of Immediacy,* pp. 93, 95. In his works Faure considers, among other paradigms, a river model with tributaries flowing into a central source, as well as a rhizome model with multiple horizontal roots.

24. I recognize there are other methods for overcoming the two-tiered model—including an inversion of the conventional hierarchy and the addition of a third (perhaps intermediary) tier. Moreover, some social theorists as well as historians of East Asian religions argue for interpreting popular culture, or popular religion, as simply that—popular culture or religion—without presupposing a dichotomy and thus the superiority of the high traditions. See, for example, such diverse works as Michel de Certeau, *The Writing of History,* trans. Tom Conley (New York: Columbia University Press, 1988), p. 184, and Teiser, *Ghost Festival in Medieval China,* pp. 214–216. My aim, however, is to view the encounter between philosophy and popular religion as relation in a way that is fair to both sides. As Gurevich suggests: "For simply stating that paganism was fused with Christianity or that Christianity was superficially assimilated hardly explains the character of early medieval popular culture." See Gurevich, *Medieval Popular Culture,* p. 75.

25. James A. Berlin, "Postmodernism, Politics, and Histories of Rhetoric," *Pre/Text* 11(3–4) (1990):178.

26. *TJL* no. 8, in *T* 48:231c.

27. *TJL* no. 8, in *T* 48:232a; Yasutani Hakuun, ed., *Shōyōroku* (Tokyo:

Shunjūsha, 1973), p. 46. This version does not have the second division of the kōan revolving around Huang-po's slap—though the commentary does cite other dialogues and anecdotes that are similar—but it nevertheless strongly (though ironically) supports the paradoxical interpretation of the case.

28. Akizuki, *Mumonkan o yomu*, p. 183.

29. *CSLT,* in *HTC* 115:112b.

30. Cited in Yasutani Hakuun, ed., *Mumonkan* (Tokyo: Shunjūsha, 1965), p. 43.

31. John Daido Loori, *The Heart of Being: Moral and Ethical Teachings of Zen Buddhism* (Boston: Tuttle, 1996), pp. 204, 212.

32. Kamens, *The Three Jewels*, p. 338.

33. Cited in *SH*, "Daishugyō," in *DZZ* 2:193; also in *CSLT,* in *HTC* 115:113a.

34. *CSLT,* in *HTC* 115:115a.

Appendix I · Translations of Fox Kōan Commentaries

1. The title of the case in other collections is "Great Cultivation" or "Not Obscuring Causality."

2. Pai-chang's (720–814) traditional biography is contained in the following texts: *TTC, chüan* 14; *CCL, chüan* 6; *WTH, chüan* 3; and *Sung kao-seng-chuan* (J. *Sōkōsōden*), *chüan* 10. The disciple of Ma-tsu—the second-generation patriarch after sixth patriarch Hui-neng—Pai-chang was the teacher of Huang-po, who became Lin-chi's teacher. These four masters of the Hung-chou lineage, known as the "four houses" as recorded in the *Ssu-chia yü-lu*, constitute one of the most important lineages in the early period of Zen in China. Pai-chang's teachings are collected in two recorded sayings texts, and he is also credited with the first Zen monastic code: the *CMKS*.

3. This could also be rendered: "I am not really a human being." The term *"fei-jen"* (J. *hinin*) is the translation of the Sanskrit term for nonhuman beings, *amanuṣya*, and in Japanese it also refers to a shape-shifter or *bakemono*. The term has also long been used as an epithet for outcasts and marginal groups.

4. Kāśyapa is the sixth of seven primordial buddhas culminating in Śākyamuni, who is also considered the first patriarch of Zen. Thus his era refers to a mythical period prior to the historical Buddha—obviously long before Buddhism was ever actually preached on Mount Pai-chang in China.

5. The literal meaning is simply: "I once lived on this very temple."

6. The phrase refers to an enlightened person who continues to practice meditation diligently after the attainment of enlightenment.

7. Causality (C. *yin-kuo;* J. *inga*) is the Chinese translation of the Sanskrit *"hetu-phala,"* which refers to the universal principle of the necessary relation between original or root cause and end result. In Sino-Japanese Buddhism this

term also implies the moral process of karmic determination and retribution, whereby a good cause begets a good result and an evil cause begets an evil result.

8. The "turning word" is referred to in numerous places, including the *LL*, the records of Hung-chih, the *SZ*, and the *SH*, "Kenbutsu," "Kōkyō," and "Sanjūshichibodaibumpō." While never clearly defined in these texts, it seems to refer to the use of a terse utterance—a phrase or a single word—which can inspire a revolution in one's thinking that results in a liberation experience.

9. I have expanded the original wording by adding the phrase "turn my words around."

10. "Not obscuring causality" is the literal rendering that seems most effective here, but it could also be rendered as "not blind to causality" or turned into an affirmative construction such as "remains bound to causality." In the latter case, "not falling into causality" could be turned into a construction such as "becomes free from causality."

11. In the Zen monastic system, the monk in charge of rules for the *saṃgha* was one of six main officers who would strike an octagonal anvil with an octagonal hammer signifying an event about to take place in the institution.

12. This refers to the infirmary. The name makes an association between nirvana as the termination of mundane existence and illness/death as the end of life.

13. This passage highlights the importance of funeral rites in Zen monastic life as codified in the main text for rules: the *CYCK* of 1103.

14. I have expanded the wording based on the text's pun on the term "whole story," which can also mean "causality."

15. Huang-po (d. 850) is reported in the following texts: *TTC chüan* 16; *CCL, chüan* 9; and *Hsü kao-seng chuan* (J. *Zoku kōsōden*), *chüan* 20. The writings attributed to him include the *Chuan-hsin fa-yao* (J. *Denshin hōyō*).

16. The "red-bearded barbarian" generally refers to foreigners. In Zen rhetoric it implies the bearded Bodhidharma, the twenty-eighth Zen patriarch and first in China, who "came from the west (India)." The term is also used as a duplicitous insult/praise. The word for barbarian (C. *hu;* J. *ko*) is a homophone for fox, and the *TJL* version refers to "red-bearded fox."

17. The "single eye" is not corporeal, of course, but the eye of dharma or nondualistic insight.

18. In some translations there is a more explicit reference to the "enjoyment" of the fox incarnations.

19. This line can be rendered: "Odd and even are on one die" or "Two winning numbers, one roll of the dice."

20. The *TKL* version contains an explicit reference to the Dharma Hall.

21. This version specifically cites the famous phrase about universal communal labor found in the rules text, the *CMKS*, attributed to Pai-chang.

22. In this version the master does not "laugh and clap his hands." This word-

ing is contained in the *PCYL*, however, which otherwise is the same as the *TKL* version.

23. A typical Zen insult—as used in the *LL* in Lin-chi's dialogues with the irregular practitioner P'u-hua—that can also be reversed to represent a form of praise depending on the context.

24. This suggests that the retribution occurred, not just because of what the ancient monk said, but because of a long-term buildup of karma.

25. A nod to supernaturalism in suggesting that the other monks were unable to perceive the illusory apparition.

26. A clear statement of the karmic moral imperative.

27. This appears to contradict the emphasis on karma in the introductory comments.

28. A classic use of ironic supernatural rhetoric.

29. This passage shows the conceptual dilemma about the relation between causality and noncausality leading to the paradoxical conclusion in the poem that follows.

30. This phrasing makes a pun on "barbarian," which has the same pronunciation as "fox" *(hu)*.

31. This dialogue is taken from the *TKL* version of the kōan.

32. As the following prose commentary indicates, this evokes Pai-chang's laughing at Huang-po's slap.

33. This remark leads to an extended discussion of the wordless but meaningful quality of nonsensical sounds.

34. This statement of the provisional, pedagogical nature of expressions of the dharma was made famous by Pai-chang's teacher, Ma-tsu.

35. This brief verse recalls the expression of transcendence through responding to the sounds of the universe in the *Chuang Tzu*, especially the second chapter.

36. See Ishii Seijun, "Jūnikanbon *Shōbōgenzō* to *Eihei kōroku*: 'Hyakujō yako' no hanashi o chūshin toshite."

37. This phrasing could be interpreted to mean that the ancient monk was a "nonfox."

38. This epitomizes the ironic use of supernatural rhetoric.

Appendix II · Translation of "Pai-chang's Monastic Rules"

1. *T* 50:770c–771a. A verse commentary on the *CMKS* by Tsung-tse is included at the end of the *CYCK*, pp. 340–352.

2. Ishii Shūdō, "Hyakujō shingi no kenkyū," pp. 43–54.

3. T'ai-chi (J. Daichi), literally "Great Wisdom," was an honorific name; his given name was Huai-hai.

4. The Lü (J. Ritsu) school may have referred in some cases to Vinaya mon-

asteries, but generally the term indicated a private monastic lineage. One of the main meanings of the *CMKS* is that it establishes Zen as the main public-lineage monastic system.

5. Although this passage seems to suggest that Zen is unbound by either Hinayana or Mahayana precepts, in fact, like other forms of Chinese Buddhism, Zen adhered to both sets of precepts. At first only the Mahayana precepts were accepted in Japan, where Dōgen proposed a modified system of sixteen precepts in *SH*, "Jukai," but eventually the Zen school followed both sets of precepts.

6. A term generally reserved for a buddha or bodhisattva or an icon/image (not a living human being).

7. The abbot's room, whether or not literally ten-foot-square, was in a sense the crown of the monastery: it stood at the end of a row of buildings along the main axis of the compound including the main temple gate, Buddha Hall, and Dharma Hall.

8. It is a chamber for instructing disciples.

9. Although Zen monasteries did contain a Buddha Hall (despite this text's admonition), they shifted the focus of religious practice to the Dharma Hall, which was the venue, along with the abbot's quarters, for a variety of sermons, lectures, and other forms of instruction.

10. By the time of the *CYCK*, the daytime formal and evening informal sermons were conducted about six times a month each.

11. This admonition is perhaps the most famous passage in the text, whether or not it was ever carried out.

12. These recommendations seem to be much stronger than in the traditional Vinaya, which allows for various methods of confession, penance, and repentance for those who admit their transgressions and are reembraced by the community.

List of Sino-Japanese Terms

Japanese pronunciation is given in brackets for certain terms, names, and titles given first in Chinese.

Agonkyō 阿含經

Amida 阿彌陀

an 案

Azuma Ryūshin 東隆真

bakemono 化け物

Bankei 盤珪

Bashō 芭蕉

Bassui 拔隊

Bendōwa 辨道話

Benzaiten 辨財天

Bishamonten 毘沙門天

Bonten 梵天

bunreisho 分靈所

burakumin 部落民

Busshō 仏性

butsuzō 仏像

Ch'an [Zen] 禪

ch'an-hui [*zange*] 懺悔

Ch'an-men kuei-shih [*Zenmon kishiki*] 禪門規式

ch'an-shih [*zenji*] 禪師

Ch'an-tsung sung-ku lien-chu-t'ung tsi [*Zenshū juko renshutsū shū*] 禪門頌古聯珠通集

Ch'an-yüan ch'ing-kuei [*Zen'en shingi*] 禪苑清規

Chang-ch'ing 長慶

chang-lao [*chōrō*] 長老

Chao-chou [Jōshū] 趙州

cheng-fa [*shōbō*] 正法

Cheng-fa yen-tsang [*Shōbōgenzō*] 正法眼藏

Cheng-tao-ko [*Shōdōku*] 証道歌

chi [*ki*] 奇

Chi-chieh lu [*Gekisetsuroku*] 擊節録

chi-hsin shih-fa [*sokushinzebutsu*] 即心是仏

ch'i-yü ch'i hsing [*kigen kiko*] 奇言畸行

chi-yüan wen-ta [*kien-mondō*] 機緑問答

chiang-hu 江湖

chiao-wai pieh-chuan [*kyōge betsuden*] 教外別傳

ch'ieh-lan shen [*garanjin*] 伽藍神

Ch'ien [Senjō] 倩女

chien [*nii*] 聾

Chih-hsien 知読

261

Chih-hsiu Pai-chang ching-kuei [*Cho-kushū Hyakujō shingi*] 敕修白丈清規

Chih-i 智顗

Chih-yüeh lu 指月録

ching [*sei*] 精

Ching-ching 鏡清

Ch'ing-i lu [*Shinekiroku*] 請益録

ch'ing-kuei [*shingi*] 清規

Ching-te ch'uan-teng lu [*Keitoku den-tōroku*] 景徳傳燈録

Ching-ts'en 景岑

chinjū 鎮守

cho-yü [*jakugo*] 著語

Chōjū giga 鳥獣戯画

chu [*jō*] 杖

chu-chung [*shujō*] 拄杖

Chu Hsi 朱熹

Chu-hung 袾宏

Chuan-hsin-fa-yao [*Denshin hōyō*] 傳心法要

chüan 卷

chuan-teng [*dentō*] 傳燈録

Chung-feng Ming-pen [Chūhō Myōhon] 中峰明本

dai-inga 大因果

daigoshō 伐語抄

daihonden 大本殿

Daikokuten 大黒天

Daishugyō 大修行

Daitō 大燈

Dakini 荼吉尼

Dakini-ho 荼吉尼法

Dakini-shinten 荼吉尼真天

Damo [Daruma] 達磨

danka 檀家

Daruma: see Damo

Daruma-shū 達磨宗

Den'e 傳衣

Denkōroku 傳光録

Dōgen 道元

Dōgen zenji zenshū 道元禪師全集

Dōryōzon 道了尊

Dōryūroku 道樹録

e-kuei [*gaki*] 餓鬼

Eihei goroku 永平語録

Eihei kōroku 永平広録

Eihei kōroku juko 永平広録頌古

Eiheiji 永平寺

Enni Ben'en 圓爾辯圓

ennin 円因

Ennin 圓仁

Enryakuji 延暦寺

eta 穢多

Fa-hua san-mei ch'an-i 法華三昧懺儀

fang-chang [*hōjō*] 方丈

fang-pien [*hōben*] 方便

fei-jen [*hinin*] 非人

fei-tao [*hidō*] 非道

fo-t'ang [*hattō*] 法堂

fu-tzu [*hossu*] 拂子

Fudō Myōō: see Pu-ting Ming-wang

Fugen 普賢

fumi-tsukeru 文付/踏付

Furuta Shōkin 古田紹欽

Fushimi Inari 伏見稲荷

fushō 不生

gan kakare ishi 願掛石

Gasan Jōseki 峨山韶碩

Gemmyō 玄明

genjō 現成

Genjōkōan 現成公按

Gennō Shinshō 源翁心昭

gensō bungaku 幻想文学

genze riyaku 現世利益

genzen 言全

Giin 義尹

giri 義理

gongen 權現

gyakuten 逆転

Gyōji 行持

Hachiman 八幡

Hakamaya Noriaki 袴谷憲昭

Hakuin 白隠

Hakusan 白山

Hakusan Myōjin Daigongen 白山明神大權現

hatsumu inga 撥無因果

hattō: see *fo-t'ang*

henka 変化

hihan Bukkyō 批判仏教

hōjin 法身

Hōjō Tokiyori 北条時頼

Hōkyōki 寶慶記

honden 本殿

honji-suijaku 本地垂迹

hongaku shisō 本学思想

honshō 本性

honshō myōshū 本証妙修

honzan 本山

honzon 本尊

Hotsubodaishin 發菩提心

Hsi t'ang 西堂

Hsiao-k'ung [Shōkū] 小空

hsiao ts'an [*shōsan*] 小參

hsien [*sen*] 仙

hsien-pao 現報

hsien-pao shan-e [*genpō zen'aku*] 現報善惡

hsin-pu-hua-te [*shin-fukatoku*] 心不可得

Hsü kao-seng-chuan [*Zoku kōsōden*] 続高僧傳

Hsü tsang-ching [(*Nihon*) *zoku zōkyō*] 続藏經

Hsüan-chüeh 玄覚

Hsüan-sha 玄沙

Hsüan-tsung 宣宗

Hsüeh-feng 雪峰

Hsüeh-t'ou [Setchō] 雪寶

Hsüeh-t'ou sung-ku pai-tse [*Setchō juko hyakusoku*] 雪寶頌古百則

Hsün Tzu 荀子

hu [*ko*] (barbarian) 胡

hu [*ko*] (fox) 狐

hua [*bakasu*] 化

hua-hsin [*keshin*] 化身

Hua-lin 華林

hua-t'ou [*watō*] 話頭

Hua-yen [Kegon] 華厳

Huang-po [Ōbaku] 黄檗

Huang-po-shan 黄檗

Hui-chung 慧忠

Hui-k'o 慧可

Hui-neng 慧能

Hung-chih [Wanshi] 宏智

Hung-chih kuang-lu [*Wanshi kōroku*] 宏智広録

Hung-chih sung-ku pai-tse [*Wanshi juko hyakusoku*] 宏智頌古百則

Hung-chou 洪州

Huo-an 胡子

I-chang 義忠

i-chüan-yu [*ittengo*] 一轉語

i-jih-pu-tso i-jih-pu-shih [*ichinichi fusaku ichinichi fushoku*] 一日不作一日不食

I-wen chi 異聞集

Ichikawa Hakugen 市川白弦

Ikka myōjū 顆明珠

Ikkei 一徑

Ikkyū 一休

immo-jin 恁麼人

Inari 稲荷

Indogaku Bukkyōgaku kenkyū 印度学仏教学研究

ine-naru 稲成る

Ishii Seijun 石井清純

Ishii Shūdō 石井修道

Jenshi chuan 任氏傳

jigō-jitoku 自業自得

jinen 自然

jinen-gedō 自然外道

jinko 人狐

Jinshin inga 深信因果

jisan-inga-hatsumu-zen 自懺因果撥無禪

Jizō 地蔵

jōdō: see *shang-t'ang*

Ju-ching [Nyojō] 如淨

Ju-ching yü-lu [Nyojō goroku] 如淨
語録

ju-lai-tsang [nyoraizō] 如来蔵

Ju pu tuan 肉蒲團

ju-shih [nyūshitsu] 入室

Jui-yen [Zuigan] 瑞巌

Jukai 受戒

Jūnikanbon Shōbōgenzō no shomondai
十二卷本正法眼蔵の諸問題

Jūroku rakan genzuiki 十六羅漢現
瑞記

Kagamishima Genryū 鏡鳥元隆

kai-shan [kaisan] 開山

kaigen 開眼

kaimyō 戒名

kamigakari 神がかり

Kannon: see Kuan-yin

k'an [kan] 勘

k'an-pien [kanben] 勘弁

Kao-seng-chuan [Kōsōden] 高僧傳

Kattō shū 葛藤集

Kawamura Kōdō 河村孝道

Keisei-sanshoku 渓声山色

Keizan 瑩山

Kenninji 建仁寺

Kenzeiki 建撕記

Kesa kudoku 袈裟功得

Kie-buppōsōbō 帰依仏法僧宝

kikan 機関

kikigakishō 聞書抄

kinhin 經行

Kinkakuji 金閣寺

kirigami 切紙

kitō jiin 祈祷寺院

ki-tsune 來常

kitsu-ne 岐都示爾

kitsune 狐

kitsune-bi 狐火

kitsune-mochi 狐持

kitsune-nyōbō 狐女房

kitsune-tsuki 狐憑き

kitsune-yomeiri 狐嫁入

kōan: see *kung-an*

Kōin 公胤

Kojiki 古事記

kōjō 向上

Kokonchomonjū 古今著聞集

*Komazawa Daigaku Bukkyōgakubu ken-
kyū* 駒沢大学仏教学部研究

Konjaku monogatari shū 今昔物語集

Kōshōji 興聖寺

konshushaku shakushuko 胡鬚赤赤
鬚胡

Kōzen gokokuron 興禪護國論

K'u-mu 枯木

ku-ts'e kung-an [kosoku-kōan] 古則
公案

Ku-tsun-su-yü-yao [Kosonshuku goyō]
古尊宿語要

kuai [kai] 怪

Kuan-yin [Kannon] 觀音

kuang-ch'an [kyōzen] 拄禪

kuei 鬼

Kuei-shan 潙山

Kūkai 空海

kūkan 空間

kung-an [kōan] 公案

kūshū-genkyō 空手還郷

Kyōunshū 狂雲集

kyūbi-kitsune 九尾狐

kyūsō 旧草

Leng-ch'ieh shih-tzü chi 楞伽師資記

li (ritual) 禮

li [ri] (phenomena) 理

Li-hun chi [Rikonki] 離佳魂

Liao-chai chih-i 聊齋自誌

Lin-chi [Rinzai] 臨濟

Lin-chi lu [Rinzai roku] 臨濟録

liu-tao [rokudō] 六道

Lü [Ritsu] 律

Lu-k'ou　路口

Ma-tsu [Baso]　馬祖

Mahikari　真光

*Mana Shōbōgenzō (Shōbōgenzō sanbya-
　kusoku*）　真字正法眼蔵（三百則）

manga　満果

Matsumoto Shirō　松本史朗

mi-hsin [*meishin*]　迷信

Ming　明

ming-pao [*myōhō*]　冥報

Ming-pao chi [*Myōhōki*]　冥報記

Miroku　彌勒

miyage　土産

mo-fa [*mappō*]　未法

Mo-shan　未山

Monju　文殊

monsan　門參

Mu-chou　睦州

mujō-busshō　無常仏性

musha-e　武者絵

Myōgonji　妙嚴寺

Nan　南

Nan-chüan　南泉

nantō　難透

Nichiren　日蓮

nien-ku [*nenko*]　拈古

Nihon koten bungaku taikei　日本古
　典文学大系

Nihongi　日本記

nihonjinron　日本人論

Nihonkoku genpō zen'aku ryōiki
　日本國現報善惡霊異記

ninjō　人情

Noh　能

nyoraizō: see *ju-lai-tsang*

okiyome　御清め

Oku no hosomichi　奥の細道

oku no in　奥の院

oni　鬼

Onjōji (Miidera)　園城寺（三井寺）

Otogizōshi　御伽草子

Pai-chang Huai-hai (T'ai-chi) [Hyakujō
　Ekai (Daichi)]　白丈懷海（大智）

Pai-chang ku ching-kuei [*Hyakujō
　koshingi*]　白丈古清規

Pai-chang kuang-lu [*Hyakujō kōroku*]
　白丈広録

Pai-chang shan　白丈山

Pai-chang yü-lu [*Hyakujō goroku*]
　白丈語録

P'ang　龐

Pi-yen lu [*Hekiganroku*]　碧巌録

p'o-p'o h'u-h'u　婆婆和和

P'u-chi　普寂

p'u-ch'ing [*fusei*]　普清

P'u-hua　普化

pu-lo yin-ku [*furaku inga*]　不落因果

pu-mei yin-kuo [*fumai inga*]　不昧因果

P'u-tai [Hotei]　普袋

Pu-ting Ming-wang [Fudō Myōō]
　不動明王

Raihaitokuzui　礼拝得髄

rakan　羅漢

Rakan kūyō shikibun　羅漢供養式文

reiken　霊驗

reikozuka　霊狐塚

rekinen　歴然

rokudō: see *liu-tao*

rokudō-baku　六道縛

Ryōan　了庵

Ryōkan　良寛

sabetsu shisō　差別思想

Saigyō　西行

Saijōji　最乗寺

Sambō-e　三宝繪

Sanjigo　三時業

seishin-byō　精神病

sendara　旃陀羅

seng-t'ang [*sōdō*]　僧堂

Senmen　洗面

senni-gedō　先尼外道

sesshō seki 殺生石

setsuwa bungaku 説話文学

shakujō 錫杖

Shakuzon 釋尊

Shan-tao 善道

shang-t'ang [*jōdō*] 上堂

shen [*kami*] 神

Shen Chi-chi 沈既濟

shen-hsin t'o-lo [*shinjin datsuraku*] 身心脱茖

Shen-hsiu 神秀

shen-t'ang [*jinzū*] 神通

shen-tse 神則

Shichifukujin 七福神

shih [*ji*] 事

shih-ch'an-hui [*ri-zange*] 事懺悔

shih-shih wu-ai [*jiji muge*] 事事無礙

shinbutsu bunri 神仏分離

shinkō 信仰

shinsō 新草

Shisho 嗣書

shō 性

Shōbōgenzō 正法眼蔵

Shōbōgenzō zuimonki 正法眼蔵隋聞記

shōmono 抄物

shōtaichōyō 聖胎長養

shū 宗

Shūgaku kenkyū 宗学研究

shūkyō 宗教

shushō-ittō 修証一等

Shushōgi 修証義

Sōjiji 総持寺

Sōni-ryō 僧尼令

sōgi Bukkyō 葬儀仏教

Sōtō: see Ts'ao-t'ung

Sou-shen chi 捜神記

Sou-shen hou-chi 捜神後記

ssu-chia [*shike*] 四家

Ssu-chia yü-lu [*Shike goroku*] 四家語録

Ssu-ma 司馬

su-shin-yang [*zatsu shinkō*] 雑信仰

Sung kao-seng chuan [*Sōkōsōden*] 宋高僧傳

sung-ku [*juko*] 頌古

szu-pu-pien-ch'u [*nan-fu hen-ko*] 何不変去

ta no kami 田の神

T'a-chi [Daichi] 大智

Ta-erh 大耳

ta-hsiu hsing [*daishugyō*] 大修行

Ta-hsiung-shan [Daiyūzan] 大雄山

Ta-hui [Daie] 大慧

Ta-kuang 大光

Ta-kuei-shan 大潙山

Ta-k'ung [Daikū] 大空

Ta-sheng wu-sheng fang-p'ien men 大乗無生方便門

ta-ta h'u-h'u 哆哆和和

ta-ts'an [*daisan*] 大參

Ta-yü 大愚

tadashii Bukkyō 正しい仏教

T'ai-p'ing kuang-chi 太平広記

Taishō shinshū daizōkyō 大正新修大蔵經

Tajintsū 他心通

tanuki 狸

Tao-ch'ien (Tao Yüan-ming) 陶潜 (陶淵明)

Tao-hsüan 道宣

Tao-yüan 道園

Tao-yüan ching [Tōgenkyō] 桃源境

Te-hui 徳輝

Te-shan [Tokusan] 徳山

Te-shan Hsüan-chien 徳山宣鑑

Tendai: see T'ien-t'ai

tengu 天狗

tenko 天狐

t'ien-hsia ching-kuei [*tenka shingi*] 天下清規

T'ien-sheng kuang-teng lu [*Tenshō kōtōroku*] 天聖広燈録

T'ien-t'ai [Tendai] 天台

T'ien-t'ung [Tendō]　天童

Tōji　東寺

Tōkokuki　洞谷記

torii　鳥居

t'ou-t'o [*zuda*]　頭陀

Toyokawa　豊川

Ts'ao-t'ung [Sōtō]　曹洞

Tsu-t'ang chi [*Sōdōshū*]　祖堂集

tsu-tze [*jiseki*]　自責

Tsūgen　通幻

ts'un [*son*]　尊

Ts'ung-jung lu [*Shōyōroku*]　從容録

Tsung-men lien-teng hui-yao [*Shūmon rentōeyō*]　宗門聯燈会要

Tsung-men nien-ku hui-chi [*Shūmon nenko ishū*]　宗門拈古彙集

Tsung-men t'ung-yao chi [*Shūmon tōyōshū*]　宗門統要集

Tsung-tse　宗賾

Tsurigitsune　釣狐

tsukimono　憑物

t'u-ti-shen [*dojijin*]　土地神

Tung-shan Shou-ch'u　洞山守初

tzü-hsing [*jishō*]　自性

Ugetsu monogatari　雨月物語

uji　有時

Uji shūi monogatari　字治拾遺物語

Ukemochi　保食神

ukiyo-e　浮世絵

wa　和

Wan-sung　萬松

wan-ts'an [*bansan*]　晩參

watakushi nashi　私なし

wei-na [*ino*]　維那

wen-hsüan [*bungaku*]　文学

wen-tse　文則

wu　無

Wu-cho　無著

Wu-men kuan [*Mumonkan*]　無門関

Wu-t'ai-shan [Godaizan]　五台山

Wu-teng hui-yüan [*Gotō egen*]　五燈會元

Wu-tsu　五祖

Wu-tsung　武宗

yama no kami　山の神

yamabushi　山伏

Yamaoka Takaaki　山岡隆晃

Yanagida Seizan　柳田聖山

Yang-shan　仰山

Yasha ga ike　夜叉が池

yeh ho-shang　野和尚

yeh-hu [*yako*]　野狐

yeh-hu Ch'an [*yako-zen*]　野狐禪

yeh-hu ching [*yako-zei*]　野狐精

yeh-hu hsien [*yako-zen*]　野狐涎

yeh-hu wai-tao [*yako-gedō*]　野狐外道

yeh-hu yen [*yako gan*]　野狐岩

yeh-pao [*gōhō*]　業報

Yen-t'ou [Gantō]　巖頭

yin [*in*]　因

yin-kou [*inga*]　因果

Yōkōji　永興寺

Yōrō-ryō　養老令

Yoshitsune senbon zakura　義経千本桜

Yōtakuji　永澤寺

Yu-chou　幽州

yüan [*en*]　縁

yüan-chi [*engi*]　縁起

Yüan-wu [*Engo*]　圜悟

Yume　夢

Yün-men [Unmon]　雲門

zange metsuzai　懺每滅罪

zazen　坐禪

Zen-temma　禪天魔

zen'ichi buppō　全一仏法

zenjōriki　禪定力

zenshin　善神

zettai mujunteki jiko dōitsu　絶対予盾的自己同一

Bibliography

Collections and Reference Works

Buddhist Dictionary: Manual of Buddhist Terms and Doctrines. Edited by Nyanatiloka Mahothera. Reprint. Colombo: Frewin, 1972.

Buddhist Hybrid Sanskrit Dictionary. Edited by Franklin Edgerton. Delhi: Motilal Banarsidass, 1977.

Bukkyōgo dai jiten. Edited by Nakamura Hajime. Tokyo: Tokyo shoseki, 1981.

Dai Nihon Bukkyō zensho. Edited by Takakusu Junjirō et al. 750 vols. Tokyo: Dai Nihon Bukkyō zensho kankōkai, 1931.

A Dictionary of Chinese Buddhist Terms. Edited by William Edward Soothill and Lewis Hodous. Reprint. Taipei: Ch'eng wen, 1976.

Dōgen zenji zenshū. Edited by Kagamishima Genryū, Kawamura Kōdō, Suzuki Kakuzen, Kosaka Kiyū, et al. 7 vols. Tokyo: Shunjūsha, 1988–1993.

Dōgen zenji zenshū. Edited by Ōkubo Dōshū. 2 vols. Tokyo: Chikuma Shobō, 1969–1970.

Eihei Shōbōgenzō shūsho taisei. 25 vols. Tokyo: Taishūkan, 1974–1981.

Hsü tsang ching. [Reprint of *Nihon zoku zōkyō.*] Edited by Nakano Tatsue. 150 vols. Taipei: Shin wen fang, n.d.

I-wen chi. In *T'ang-jen hsiao-shuo yen-chiu,* ed. Wang Meng-ou. Taipei: I-wen yin-shu-kuan, 1973. Vol. II:107–254.

Japanese-English Buddhist Dictionary. Tokyo: Daitō shuppansha, 1965.

Kōjien. Edited by Shinmura Izuru. Tokyo: Iwanami shoten, 1980.

Liao-chai chih-i. Collated by Chang Yu-ho. 2 vols. Shanghai: Ku-chi ch'u-pan-shi, 1978.

Nihon koten bungaku taikei. Edited by Yamada Yoshio et al. 100 vols. Tokyo: Iwanami shoten, 1961–1963.

The Pali Text Society's Pali-English Dictionary. Edited by T. W. Rhys-Davids and William Stede. London: Luzac, 1966.

Sōtōshū zensho. 20 vols. Tokyo: Sōtōshū shūmuchō, 1970–1973.
Sou-shen chi. Edited by Wang Shao-ying. Beijing: Chung-hua shu-chü, 1979.
Sou-shen hou-chi. Edited by Wang Shao-ying. Beijing: Chung-hua shu-chü, 1981.
T'ai-p'ing kuang-chi. Edited by Wang Meng'ou. 500 *chüan.* Beijing: Chung-hua shu-chü, 1981.
Taishō shinshū daizōkyō. Edited by Takakusu Junjirō and Watanabe Kaigyoku. 100 vols. Tokyo: Taishō issaikyō kankōkai, 1924–1932.
Vinaya pitakam. Edited by Hermann Oldenberg. 5 vols. London: Williams & Norgate, 1879.
Zengaku daijiten. Edited by Zengaku daijiten hensanjo. Tokyo: Taishūkan, 1985.

Other Sources

Abe Chōichi. *Chūgoku Zenshūshi no kenkyū.* Tokyo: Seishin shobō, 1963.
———. *Zenshū shakai to shinkō: zoku Chūgoku Zenshūshi no kenkyū.* Tokyo: Kindai bungeisha, 1993.
Abe Masao. *A Study of Dōgen: His Philosophy and Religion.* Edited by Steven Heine. Albany: SUNY Press, 1992.
Abe, Ryūichi, and Peter Haskel, trans. *Great Fool: Zen Master Ryōkan Poems, Letter, and Other Writings.* Honolulu: University of Hawai'i Press, 1996.
Addiss, Stephen. *Japanese Ghosts and Demons: Art of the Supernatural.* New York: Braziller, 1985.
Aitken, Robert. *The Gateless Barrier: The Wu-men Kuan (Mumonkan).* San Francisco: North Point, 1990.
Akizuki Ryūmin, ed. *Mumonkan o yomu.* Tokyo: Tōsho-insatsu, 1990.
———. *New Mahāyāna: Buddhism for a Post-Modern World.* Translated by James W. Heisig and Paul L. Swanson. Berkeley: Asian Humanities Press, 1990.
———. *Zen mondō: kōan-e monogatari.* Tokyo: Chōbunsha, 1976.
Albee, Edward. *Who's Afraid of Virginia Woolf?* New York: Signet, 1962.
Algarin, Joanne P. *Japanese Folk Literature: A Core Collection and Reference Guide.* New York: Bowker, 1982.
Allan, Sarah, and Alvin P. Cohen, eds. *Legend, Lore, and Religion in China: Essays in Honor of Wolfram Eberhard.* San Francisco: Chinese Materials Center, 1979.
Amino Yoshihiko. *Muen, kugai, raku: Nihon chūsei no jiyū to heiwa.* Tokyo: Tokyo Daigaku shuppankai, 1978.
App, Urs, ed. and trans. *Master Yunmen: From the Record of the Chan Master "Gate of the Clouds."* New York: Kodansha, 1994.
Araki Kengo, ed. *Bukkyō to Jukyō: Chūgoku shisō o keiseisuru mono.* Kyoto: Heirakuji shoten, 1976.
———. *Daie sho, Zen no goroku* 17. Tokyo: Chikuma shobō, 1969.

Ardener, Shirley, ed. *Perceiving Women*. London: Dent; New York: Wiley, 1975.

Arntzen, Sonja. *Ikkyū and the Crazy Cloud Anthology: A Zen Poet of Medieval Japan*. Tokyo: Tokyo University Press, 1986.

Azuma Ryūshin. *Dōgen shō-jiten*. Tokyo: Shunjūsha, 1982.

————. *Sōtōshū: waga ie no shūkyō*. Tokyo: Daihōrinkaku, 1993.

Baker, Joan Stanley. *Japanese Art*. London: Thames & Hudson, 1988.

Banerjea, J. N. *The Development of Hindu Iconography*. 2nd ed. Calcutta: University of Calcutta Press, 1956.

Barnhill, David. "Folk Religion and Shinto in the Ecosystem of Bashō's Religious World." Paper presented at the Panel on Japanese Religions at the American Academy of Religion annual meeting, Chicago, 1994.

Barthes, Roland. *Mythologies*. Translated by Anette Lavers. New York: Hill & Wang, 1972.

Basham, A. L. *The Wonder That Was India*. New York: Grove, 1954.

Bell, Catherine. "Religion and Chinese Culture: Toward an Assessment of 'Popular Religion.' " *History of Religions* 29(1) (1989): 35–57.

Berlin, Isaiah. *The Fox and the Hedgehog: An Essay on Tolstoy's View of History*. Chicago: Dee, 1978.

Berlin, James A. "Postmodernism, Politics, and Histories of Rhetoric." *Pre/Text* 11(3–4) (1990):170–187.

Bielefeldt, Carl, trans. "A Discussion of Seated Zen." In *Buddhism in Practice*, ed. Donald S. Lopez Jr. Princeton: Princeton University Press, 1995.

————. *Dōgen's Manuals of Zen Meditation*. Berkeley: University of California Press, 1988.

————. "No-Mind and Sudden Awakening: Thoughts on the Soteriology of a Kamakura Zen Text." In *Paths to Liberation: The Mārga and Its Transformations in Buddhist Thought*, ed. Robert E. Buswell Jr. and Robert M. Gimello. Honolulu: University of Hawai'i Press, 1992.

————. "Recarving the Dragon: History and Dogma in the Study of Dōgen." In *Dōgen Studies*, ed. William R. LaFleur. Honolulu: University of Hawai'i Press, 1985.

Blacker, Carmen. *The Catalpa Bow: A Study of Shamanistic Practices in Japan*. London: Allen & Unwin, 1975.

Bloss, Lowell W. "The Buddha and the Nāga: A Study in Buddhist Folk Religiosity." *History of Religions* 13(1) (1973):36–51.

Bodde, Derk. "Some Chinese Tales of the Supernatural." *Harvard Journal of Asiatic Studies* 6 (1942):338–357.

Bodiford, William M. "The Enlightenment of Kami and Ghosts: Spirit Ordinations in Japanese Sōtō Zen." *Cahiers d'Extrême-Asie* 7 (1993–1994):267–282.

————. *Sōtō Zen in Medieval Japan*. Honolulu: University of Hawai'i Press, 1993.

————. "Zen and the Art of Religious Prejudice: Efforts to Reform a Tradition of Social Discrimination." *Japanese Journal of Religious Studies* 23(1–2) (1996):1–27.

———. "Zen in the Art of Funerals: Ritual Salvation in Japanese Buddhism." *History of Religions* 32(2) (1992):146–164.

Bouchy, Anne-Marie. "Le Renard, élément de la conception du monde dans la tradition japonaise." In *Le Renard, tours, détours, et retours,* ed. Marie-Lise Befa and Roberte Hamayon. Special issue of *Études mongoles . . . et sibéeriennes* 15 (1984):9–70.

Bourdieu, Pierre. *Outline of a Theory of Practice.* Translated by Richard Nice. Cambridge: Cambridge University Press, 1977.

———. *The Political Ontology of Martin Heidegger.* Translated by Peter Collier. Cambridge: Polity Press, 1991.

Braverman, Arthur, trans. *Mud and Water: A Collection of Talks by the Zen Master Bassui.* San Francisco: North Point, 1988.

Brenneman, Walter L., Jr., and Mary G. Brenneman. *Crossing the Circle of the Holy Wells of Ireland.* Charlottesville: University of Virginia Press, 1994.

———. "Holy Water." *Earthwatch,* March/April 1995, pp. 6–8.

Britton, Dorothy, trans. *A Haiku Journey: Bashō's Narrow Road to a Far Province.* Tokyo: Kodansha, 1980.

Brown, Peter. *The Cult of the Saints: Its Rise and Function in Latin Christianity.* Chicago: University of Chicago Press, 1981.

Buchanan, D. C. "Inari: Its Origins, Development, and Nature." *Transactions of the Asiatic Society of Japan,* 2nd series, 12 (1935):i–191.

Bukkyō, tokushū: sabetsu. 15/4 (1994).

Buswell, Robert E., Jr. "The 'Short-Cut' Approach of *K'an-hua* Meditation: The Evolution of a Practical Subitism in Chinese Ch'an Buddhism." In *Sudden and Gradual: Approaches to Enlightenment in Chinese Thought,* ed. Peter N. Gregory. Honolulu: University of Hawai'i Press, 1987.

Bynum, Caroline Walker. *Holy Feast, Holy Fast: The Significance of Food to Medieval Women.* Berkeley: University of California Press, 1987.

Campany, Robert F. "Demons, Gods, and Pilgrims: The Demonology of the *Hsi-yu Chi.*" *CLEAR* 7 (1985):95–115.

———. "Ghosts Matter: The Culture of Ghosts in Six Dynasties *Zhiguai.*" *CLEAR* 13 (1991):15–34.

———. *Strange Writings: Anomaly Accounts in Early Medieval China.* Albany: SUNY Press, 1995.

Carson, Robert C., James N. Butcher, and James C. Coleman. *Abnormal Psychology.* 8th ed. Glenview, Ill.: Scott, Foresman, 1990.

Casal, U. A. "The Goblin Fox and Badger and Other Witch Animals of Japan." *Folklore Studies* 18 (1959):1–93.

Certeau, Michel de. *The Writing of History.* Translated by Tom Conley. New York: Columbia University Press, 1988.

Chajes, J. H. "Judgments Sweetened: Possession and Exorcism in Early Modern Jewish Culture." *Journal of Early Modern History* 1(2) (1997):124–169.

Chan, Wing-tsit. *Chu Hsi: New Studies.* Honolulu: University of Hawai'i Press, 1989.

Chang Chung-yuan, trans. *Original Teachings of Ch'an Buddhism.* New York: Vintage, 1971.

Chappell, David. "Formless Repentance in Comparative Perspective." *Report of International Conference on Ch'an Buddhism.* Taipei: Fo Kuang Shan, 1990.

Ch'en, Kenneth K. S. *Buddhism in China: A Historical Survey.* Princeton: Princeton University Press, 1964.

Chih-P'ing Chou. *Yüan Hung-tao and the Kung-an School.* Cambridge: Cambridge University Press, 1988.

Childs, Margaret Helen. *Rethinking Sorrow: Revelatory Tales of Late Medieval Japan.* Ann Arbor: University of Michigan Press, 1991.

Cleary, Thomas, trans. *No Barrier: Unlocking the Zen Koan.* New York: Bantam, 1993.

———. *Sayings and Doings of Pai-chang.* Los Angeles: Center Publications, 1978.

Cole, Alan. "Upside Down/Right Side Up: A Revision History of Buddhist Funerals in China." *History of Religions* 35(4) (1996):306–338.

Collcutt, Martin. "The Early Ch'an Monastic Rule: *Ch'ing kuei* and the Shaping of Ch'an Community Life." In *Early Ch'an in China and Tibet,* eds. Whalen Lai and Lewis R. Lancaster. Berkeley: Asian Humanities Press, 1983.

———. *Five Mountains: The Rinzai Monastic Institution in Medieval Japan.* Cambridge, Mass.: Harvard University Press, 1981.

Culler, Jonathan. *The Pursuit of Signs: Semiotics, Literature, Deconstruction.* Ithaca: Cornell University Press, 1981.

Daiyūzan: Daiyūzan Saijōji kaisō roppyakunen hōzan. Shinagawa-ken: Daiyūzan Saijōji kaisō roppyakunen hōzan jimuchō, 1994.

Dale, Peter N. *The Myth of Japanese Uniqueness.* New York: St. Martin's Press, 1986.

Davis, Winston. *Dojo: Magic and Exorcism in Modern Japan.* Stanford: Stanford University Press, 1980.

———. *Japanese Religion and Society: Paradigms of Structure and Change.* Albany: SUNY Press, 1992.

Day, Terence P. *Great Tradition and Little Tradition in Theravāda Buddhist Studies.* Lewiston/Queenston: Edwin Mellen, 1988.

DeVos, George, and Hiroshi Wagatsuma. *Japan's Invisible Race: Caste in Culture and Personality.* Berkeley: University of California Press, 1966.

DeWoskin, Kenneth J. "The Six Dynasties *chih-kuai* and the Birth of Fiction." In *Chinese Narrative,* ed. Andrew Plaks. Princeton: Princeton University Press, 1977.

DeWoskin, Kenneth J., and J. I. Crump Jr., trans. *In Search of the Supernatural: The Written Record.* Stanford: Stanford University Press, 1996.

Dorfman, Diane. "The Spirits of Reform: Politics of Belief in Northern China." Paper presented at the Association for Asian Studies national meeting, April 1994.

Dorson, Richard M. *Folk Legends of Japan*. Rutland, Vt.: Tuttle, 1982.

Douglas, Mary. *Natural Symbols: Explorations in Cosmology*. Harmondsworth: Penguin, 1970.

———. *Purity and Danger: An Analysis of the Concepts of Pollution and Taboo*. London: Routledge & Kegan Paul, 1966.

Dreams (Yume). Directed by Kurosawa Akira. Japan, 1990.

Dumoulin, Heinrich. *Zen Buddhism: A History*. Translated by James W. Heisig and Paul Knitter. 2 vols. New York: Macmillan, 1988–1990.

Dutt, Sukumar. *Early Buddhist Monasticism*. New York: Dutton, 1960. Originally published in 1924.

Eberhard, Wolfram. *Chinese Fairy Tales and Folk Tales*. London: Kegan, Paul, 1937.

———. *A Dictionary of Chinese Symbols: Hidden Symbols in Chinese Life and Thought*. London: Routledge, 1986.

———. *Folktales of China*. Chicago: University of Chicago Press, 1968.

———. *Guilt and Sin in Traditional China*. Berkeley: University of California Press, 1967.

Ebrey, Patricia Buckley. "Cremation in Sung China." *American Historical Review* 95(2) (1990):406–428.

———. "The Response of the Sung State to Popular Funeral Practices." In *Religion and Society in T'ang and Sung China*, ed. Patricia Buckley Ebrey and Peter N. Gregory. Honolulu: University of Hawai'i Press, 1993.

Ellwood, Robert C. *Introducing Religion: From Inside and Outside*. Englewood Cliffs, N.J.: Prentice-Hall, 1983.

Faure, Bernard. *Chan Insights and Oversights: An Epistemological Critique of the Chan Tradition*. Princeton: Princeton University Press, 1993.

———. "The Daruma-shū, Dōgen, and Sōtō Zen." *Monumenta Nipponica* 42(1) (1987):25–55.

———. "The Kyoto School and Reverse Orientalism." In *Japan in Traditional and Postmodern Perspectives*, ed. Charles Wei-hsun Fu and Steven Heine. Albany: SUNY Press, 1995.

———. *The Rhetoric of Immediacy: A Cultural Critique of the Chan/Zen Buddhism*. Princeton: Princeton University Press, 1991.

———. "Space and Place in Chinese Religious Traditions." *History of Religions* 26(4) (1987):337–356.

———. *Visions of Power: Imagining Medieval Japanese Buddhism*. Translated by Phyllis Brooks. Princeton: Princeton University Press, 1996.

———. *The Will to Orthodoxy: A Critical Genealogy of Northern Ch'an Buddhism*. Translated by Phyllis Brooks. Stanford: Stanford University Press, 1997.

Faurot, Jeanette, ed. *Asian Pacific Folktales and Legends*. New York: Simon & Shuster, 1995.

Ferrier, Ronald W., trans. and ed. *A Journey to Persia: Jean Chardin's Portrait of a Seventeenth-Century Empire*. London: Tauris, 1996.

Foulk, T. Griffith. "The Ch'an *Tsung* in Medieval China: School." *Pacific World* 8 (1992):18–31.

———. "Myth, Ritual, and Monastic Practice in Sung Ch'an Buddhism." In *Religion and Society in T'ang and Sung China*, ed. Patricia Buckley Ebrey and Peter N. Gregory. Honolulu: University of Hawai'i Press, 1993.

Frazer, James. *The Golden Bough*. New York: Macmillan, 1922.

Fu, Charles Wei-hsun. "Chu Hsi on Buddhism." In *Chu Hsi and Neo-Confucianism*, ed. Wing-tsit Chan. Honolulu: University of Hawai'i Press, 1986.

Furuta Shōkin. *Nihon Bukkyō shisō shi no shomondai*. Tokyo: Shunjūsha, 1964.

———. *Rinzai roku no shisō*. Tokyo: Nigatsu insatsu, 1962.

Gardner, Daniel K. "Zhu Xi on Spirit Beings." In *Religions of China in Practice*, ed. Donald S. Lopez Jr. Princeton: Princeton University Press, 1996.

Geertz, Clifford. *The Interpretation of Cultures*. New York: Basic Books, 1973.

Gernet, Jacques. *Buddhism in Chinese Society: An Economic History from the Fifth to the Tenth Centuries*. Translated by Granciscus Verellen. New York: Columbia University Press, 1995.

Giles, Herbert A., trans. *Strange Stories from a Chinese Studio*. New York: Paragon, 1960.

Gimello, Robert M. "Chang Shang-ying on Wu-t'ai Shan." In *Pilgrims and Sacred Sites in China*, ed. Susan Naquin and Chun-fang Yü. Berkeley: University of California Press, 1992.

Gjertson, Donald Edward. "A Study and Translation of the *Ming-pao chi:* A T'ang Dynasty Collection of Buddhist Tales." Ph.D. diss., Stanford University, 1975.

Goff, Janet. "Foxes in Japanese Culture." *Japan Quarterly* (April–June 1997):66–77.

Goodwin, Janet R. *Alms and Vagabonds: Buddhist Temples and Popular Patronage in Medieval Japan*. Honolulu: University of Hawai'i Press, 1994.

Gorai Shigeru, ed. *Inari shinkō no kenkyū*. Tokyo: Sanin shimbunsha, 1985.

Graham, A. C., trans. *Poems of the Late T'ang*. New York: Penguin, 1965.

Grapard, Allan. *The Protocol of the Gods: A Study of the Kasuga Cult in Japanese History*. Berkeley: University of California Press, 1992.

Green, Miranda. *Animals in Celtic Life and Myth*. London: Routledge, 1992.

Gurevich, Aron. *Medieval Popular Culture: Problems of Belief and Perception*. Translated by Janas M. Bak and Paul A. Hollingsworth. Cambridge: Cambridge University Press, 1988.

Hakamaya Noriaki. "Dōgen ni okeru jūnikanbon no igi." In *Budda kara Dōgen e*, ed. Nara Yasuaki. Tokyo: Tokyo shoseki, 1992.

———. *Dōgen to Bukkyō: Jūnikanbon Shōbōgenzō no Dōgen*. Tokyo: Daizō shuppan, 1992.

———. *Hihan Bukkyō*. Tokyo: Daizō shuppan, 1990.

———. *Hongaku shisō hihan*. Tokyo: Daizō shuppan, 1989.

———. "Nihonjin to animizumu." *KDBR* 23 (1992):351–378.

Hansen, Valerie. "Gods on Walls: A Case of Indian Influence on Chinese Lay Religion?" In *Religion and Society in T'ang and Sung China*, ed. Patricia Buckley Ebrey and Peter N. Gregory. Honolulu: University of Hawai'i Press, 1993.

Harada Kōdō. "Chūsei Sōtōshū to rakan shinkō." *IBK* 37(1) (1988):232–238.

———. " 'Shōyōroku hyaku monogatari': Hyakujō yako." *Chōryū* (1995):6–10.

Hayami Tasuku. *Heian kizoku shakai to Bukkyō*. Tokyo: Yoshikawa kōbunkan, 1975.

Hearn, Lafcadio. *Glimpses of Unfamiliar Japan*. Reprint. Rutland, Vt.: Tuttle, 1966.

Heine, Steven. "Critical Buddhism *(Hihan Bukkyō)* and the Debate Concerning the 12-Fascicle and 75-Fascicle *Shōbōgenzō* Texts." *Japanese Journal of Religious Studies* 21(1) (1994):37–72.

———. *Dōgen and the Kōan Tradition: A Tale of Two Shōbōgenzō Texts*. Albany: SUNY Press, 1994.

———. "Putting the 'Fox' Back into the 'Wild Fox Kōan': The Intersection of Philosophical and Popular Religious Elements in the Ch'an/Zen Kōan Tradition." *Harvard Journal of Asiatic Studies* 56(2) (1996):257–317.

———. "Sōtō Zen and the Inari Cult: Symbiotic and Exorcistic Trends in Buddhist–Folk Religious Amalgamations." *Pacific World* 10 (1994):71–95.

———. *Verses from the Mountain of Eternal Peace: The Zen Poetry of Dōgen*. Boston: Tuttle, 1997.

Heisig, James W., and John C. Maraldo, eds. *Rude Awakenings: Zen, the Kyoto School, and the Question of Nationalism*. Honolulu: University of Hawai'i Press, 1995.

Henderson, John B. *Scripture, Canon, and Commentary: A Comparison of Confucian and Western Exegesis*. Princeton: Princeton University Press, 1991.

Hesse, Herman. *Siddhartha*. Translated by Hilda Rosner. Reprint. New York: Bantam, 1971.

Hirakawa Akira. *A History of Indian Buddhism: From Sākyamuni to Early Mahāyāna*. Translated by Paul Groner. Honolulu: University of Hawai'i Press, 1990.

Hirano Sōjō. *Daitō Zen no tankyū*. Tokyo: Kyōiku shinchōsha, 1974.

Hirata Takashi, ed. *Mumonkan, Zen no goroku* 18. Tokyo: Chikuma shobō, 1969.

Hiro Sachiya. *Bukkyō to Shintō*. Tokyo: Shinchō sensho, 1987.

Hirose Ryōko. "Sōtō zensō ni okeru shinjin kado-akurei chin'atsu." *IBK* 21(2) (1983):233–236.

Hori Ichirō. *Folk Religion in Japan: Continuity and Change*. Edited by Joseph M. Kitagawa and Alan L. Miller. Chicago: University of Chicago Press, 1968.

Hubbard, Jamie, and Paul L. Swanson, eds. *Pruning the Bodhi Tree: The Storm over Critical Buddhism*. Honolulu: University of Hawai'i Press, 1997.

Hunter, Brandon. *One Hundred Japanese Strange Creatures*. Tokyo: Tsukuba shobō, 1992.

Huntington, Rania. "Tigers, Foxes, and the Margins of Humanity in Tang Chuangi Fiction." *Papers on Chinese Literature* 1 (1993):40–64.

Ichikawa Hakugen. *Bukkyōsha no sensō-sekinin.* Tokyo: Shunjūsha, 1970.
———. *Zen to gendai shisō.* Tokyo: Tokuma shoten, 1967.
Ikeda Rōsan. *Dōgengaku no yōran.* Tokyo: Daizō shuppan, 1991.
———. "Shinsō 'Jūnikanbon Shōbōgenzō' no kōzō to kadai." *JSS,* pp. 297–318.
Imaeda Aishin. *Dōgen: zazen hitosuji no shamon.* NHK Books 255. Tokyo: Nihon hōsō shuppan kyōkai, 1976.
———. *Zenshū no rekishi. Nihon rekishi shinsho.* Tokyo: Shibundō, 1966.
Imaeda Aishin et al., eds. *Sōtōshū.* Tokyo: Shōgakkan, 1986.
"In a Computer Age, Shinto Devils Still Prowl." *New York Times,* October 15, 1995.
Inada, Kenneth, trans. *Nāgārjuna: A Translation of His Mūlamadhyamakārikā with an Introductory Essay.* Tokyo: Hokuseido Press, 1970.
Iriya Yoshitaka, ed. *Baso goroku.* Kyoto: Zen bunka kenkyūjō, 1974.
———. *Rinzai roku.* Tokyo: Iwanami shoten, 1991.
Iriya Yoshitaka et al., eds. *Hekiganroku.* 3 vols. Tokyo: Iwanami shoten, 1992–1996.
Ishii Seijun. "*Eihei kōroku*—Kenchō nenkan no jōdō ni tsuite." *SK* 29 (1987):91–94.
———. "Jūnikanbon *Shōbōgenzō* to *Eihei kōroku:* 'Hyakujō yako' no hanashi o chūshin toshite." *SK* 30 (1988):257–262.
———. "Jūnikanbon *Shōbōgenzō* honbun no seiritsu jigo ni tsuite." *KDBR* 22 (1991):236–260.
———. "Mana *Shōbōgenzō* no seiritsu kansuru isshiken: 'Eihei juko' and 'Kōshōji goroku' to no naiyō taihi o chūshin toshite." *Sōtōshū shūgaku kenkyūjō kiyō* 8 (1994):53–67.
Ishii Shūdō. *Chūgoku Zenshūshi hanashi: Mana Shōbōgenzō ni manabu.* Kyoto: Zen bunka kenkyūjō, 1988.
———. "Hyakujō shingi no kenkyū: 'Zenmon kishiki' to 'Hyakujō koshingi.'" *Komazawa Daigaku Zen kenkyūjō nempō* 6 (1995):15–53.
———. "Nishimura Eshin Yakuchū 'Mumonkan.'" *Hanazono Daigaku bungakubu kenkyūjō kiyō* 28 (1996):113–136.
———. "Recent Trends in Dōgen Studies." Translated by Albert Welter. *Komazawa Daigaku Zen kenkyūjō nenpō* 7 (1992):219–264.
———. "Saigo no Dōgen—Jūnikanbon *Shōbōgenzō* to 'Hōkyōki.'" *JSS,* pp. 319–374.
———. "Saigo no Dōgen zenji kenkyū ni omou." *Chūgoku Sōtōshū seinenkai isshiken dai-kai kōgi roku* 60 (1994):1–130.
———. *Sōdai Zenshūshi no kenkyū.* Tokyo: Daitō shuppansha, 1987.
Ishikawa Rikizan. "Chūsei Sōtōshū ni okeru kirigami sōjō ni tsuite." *IBK* 30(2) (1982):742–746.
———. "Chūsei Zenshū to shinbutsu shūgō: toku ni Sōtōshū no chihōteki tenkai to kirigami shiryō o chūshin ni shite." *Nihon Bukkyō* 60–61 (1984): 41–56.
———. "Chūsei Zenshūshi kenkyū to Zenseki shōmono shiryō." In *Dōgen Zenji*

to Sōtōshū, ed. Kawamura Kōdō and Ishikawa Rikizan. Tokyo: Yoshikawa kōbunkan, 1985.

Ishizuka Takatoshi. *Nihon no tsukimono.* Tokyo: Miraisha, 1971.

Isshū Miura and Ruth Fuller Sasaki. *Zen Dust: The History of the Koan and Koan Study in (Lin-chi) Zen.* New York: Harcourt Brace, 1966.

Itō Kokan. *Kōan Zen-wa: Zen-satori no mondōshū.* Tokyo: Daihōrinkaku, 1976.

Itō Shūken. "Jūnikanbon *Shōbōgenzō* no senjutsu to sono itō ni tsuite." *JSS,* pp. 375–404.

———. "Manabi jūnikanbon *Shōbōgenzō* ni tsuite." *IBK* 36(1) (1987): 194–201.

Itō Takatoshi. *Chūgoku Bukkyō no hihanteki kenkyū.* Tokyo: Daizō shuppan, 1992.

———. "Zen to Bukkyō no honshitsu." In *Budda kara Dōgen e,* ed. Nara Yasuaki. Tokyo: Tokyo shoseki, 1992.

Ives, Christopher. *Zen Awakening and Society.* Honolulu: University of Hawai'i Press, 1992.

Johnson, David. "Chinese Popular Literature and Its Contents." *CLEAR* 3(2) (1981):225–233.

Kabanoff, Alexander. "Ikkyū and Kōans." In *The Kōan,* ed. Steven Heine and Dale S. Wright. New York: Oxford University Press, 1999.

Kafka, Franz. *The Trial.* Translated by Willa Muir and Edwin Muir. New York: Modern Library, 1964.

Kagamishima Genryū. *Dōgen zenji to in'yō kyōten-goroku no kenkyū.* Tokyo: Mokujisha, 1965.

———. *Dōgen zenji to sono monryū.* Tokyo: Seishin shobō, 1961.

———. *Dōgen zenji to sono shūfū.* Tokyo: Shunjūsha, 1994.

———. *Dōgen zenji to sono shūhen.* Tokyo: Daitō shuppansha, 1985.

———. "Jūnikanbon *Shōbōgenzō* no ichi-zuke." *JSS,* pp. 3–30.

———. *Tendō Nyojō zenji no kenkyū.* Tokyo: Shunjūsha, 1983.

Kagamishima Genryū and Suzuki Kakuzen, eds. *Jūnikanbon Shōbōgenzō no shomondai.* Tokyo: Daizō shuppan, 1991.

Kagamishima Genryū, Satō Tatsugen, and Kosaka Kiyū, eds. *Yakuchū Zen'en shingi.* Tokyo: Sōtōshū shūmuchō, 1972.

Kalupahana, David J. *Causality: The Central Philosophy of Buddhism.* Honolulu: University of Hawai'i Press, 1975.

———, trans. *Nāgārjuna: The Philosophy of the Middle Way.* Albany: SUNY Press, 1986.

Kamens, Edward, trans. *The Three Jewels: A Study and Translation of Minamoto Tamenori's Sanbōe.* Ann Arbor: University of Michigan Press, 1988.

Kapleau, Philip. *The Wheel of Life and Death: A Practical and Spiritual Guide.* New York: Doubleday, 1989.

Kasulis, Thomas. "Researching the Strata of the Japanese Self." In *Self as Person in Asian Theory and Practice,* ed. Roger T. Ames, Wimal Dissanayake, and Thomas Kasulis. Albany: SUNY Press, 1994.

Katz, Nathan. *Buddhist Images of Human Perfection.* Delhi: Motilal Banarsidass, 1982.

Kawabata Yasunari zenshū. 35 vols. Tokyo: Shinchōsha, 1982.

Kawamura Kōdō. "Dōgen to *Shōbōgenzō*—Jūnikanbon to wa nanika." In *Budda kara Dōgen e,* ed. Nara Yasuaki. Tokyo: Tokyo shoseki, 1992.

———. "Jūnikanbon o meguru shosetsu." In *Budda kara Dōgen e,* ed. Nara Yasuaki. Tokyo: Tokyo shoseki, 1992.

———. "*Shōbōgenzō.*" In *Dōgen no chosaku,* ed. Kagamishima Genryō and Tamaki Kōshirō. Tokyo: Shunjūsha, 1980.

———. *Shōbōgenzō no seiritsu-shiteki no kenkyū.* Tokyo: Shunjūsha, 1986.

———. *Shohon taikō Eihei kaisan Dōgen zenji gyōjō—Kenzeiki.* Tokyo: Taishūkan shoten, 1975.

Kelsey, W. Michael. *Konjaku Monogatari-shū.* Boston: Twayne, 1982.

———. "Salvation of the Snake, the Snake of Salvation: Buddhist-Shinto Conflict and Resolution." *Japanese Journal of Religious Studies* 8(1–2) (1981):83–113.

Keown, Damien. *The Nature of Buddhist Ethics.* London: Macmillan, 1993.

Kieschnick, John. *The Eminent Monk: Buddhist Ideals in Medieval Chinese Hagiography.* Honolulu: University of Hawai'i Press, 1997.

Kim, Hee-Jin. *Dōgen Kigen—Mystical Realist.* Tucson: University of Arizona Press, 1975.

Kimura Kiyotaka. "Dōgen to Inari." *Fushimi Inari Taisha "Aka"* 38 (1995): 41–45.

Kimura Seiyū. "Koshingi kō." *Zen no kenkyū* 31 (1939):1–11.

King, Sallie B. *Buddha Nature.* Albany: SUNY Press, 1991.

Kingston, Maxine Hong. *The Woman Warrior: Memoirs of a Girlhood Among Ghosts.* New York: Vintage, 1975.

Kishizawa Ian. *Shōbōgenzō zenkō.* Tokyo: Daihōrinkaku, 1974.

Kobayashi, Hiroko. *The Human Comedy of Japan: A Study of the Secular Stories in the Twelfth-Century Collection of Tales, Konjaku Monogatarishū.* Tokyo: Centre for East Asian Cultural Studies, 1959.

Koizuka Minoru. *Kitsune monogatari.* Tokyo: Sanichi shobō, 1982.

Kondō Yoshirō. *Inari shinkō.* Tokyo: Hanawa shobō, 1978.

Konishi Jin'ichi. *Image and Ambiguity: The Impact of Zen Buddhism on Japanese Literature.* Program for Comparative Study on Japanese and Chinese Literatures. Tokyo: Tokyo University of Education, 1973.

———. *Nihon bungeishi.* 3 vols. Tokyo: Kodansha, 1986.

Kraft, Kenneth. *Eloquent Zen: Daitō and Early Japanese Zen.* Honolulu: University of Hawai'i Press, 1992.

Krappe, Alexander H. "Far Eastern Fox Lore." *California Folklore Quarterly* 3(2) (1944):124–147.

Kwong, Charles Yim-tze. *Tao Qian and the Chinese Poetic Tradition: The Quest for Cultural Identity.* Ann Arbor: University of Michigan Press, 1994.

LaFleur, William R. "Hungry Ghosts and Hungry People: Somaticity and Rationality in Medieval Japan." In *Fragments for a History of the Human Body, Part One,* ed. Michael Feber with Ramon Naddaft and Nadia Tuz, New York: Zone, 1989.

———. *The Karma of Words: Buddhism and the Literary Arts in Medieval Japan.* Berkeley: University of California Press, 1983.

Lai, Whalen. "The *Chan-ch'a ching:* Religion and Magic in Medieval China." In *Chinese Buddhist Apocrypha,* ed. Robert E. Buswell Jr. Honolulu: University of Hawai'i Press, 1990.

———. "From Protean Ape to Handsome Saint: The Monkey King." *Asian Folklore Studies* 53 (1992):29–65.

———. "Ma-tsu Tao-i and the Unfolding of Southern Zen." *Japanese Journal of Religious Studies* 12(2–3) (1985):173–192.

Lakoff, George, and Mark Johnson. *Metaphors We Live By.* Chicago: University of Chicago Press, 1980.

Lancaster, Lewis. "The Terminology of the *Platform Sūtra* in the Chinese Buddhist Canon." In *Report of the International Conference on Ch'an Buddhism.* Taipei: Fo Kuang Shan, 1990.

Leggett, Trevor. *The Warrior Kōans: Early Zen in Japan.* London: Routledge & Kegan Paul, 1985.

Leighton, Taigen Daniel, and Shohaku Okumura, trans. *Dōgen's Pure Standards for the Zen Community.* Albany: SUNY Press, 1996.

Levering, Miriam. "Ch'an Enlightenment for Laymen: Ta-hui and the New Religious Culture of the Sung." In *Buddhist and Taoist Practice in Medieval Chinese Society: Buddhist and Taoist Studies II,* ed. David W. Chappell. Honolulu: University of Hawai'i Press, 1987.

———. "The Dragon Girl and the Abbess of Mo-shan: Gender and Status in the Ch'an Buddhist Tradition." *Journal of the International Association of Buddhist Studies* 5(1) (1982):19–33.

———. "Lin-chi (Rinzai) Ch'an and Gender: The Rhetoric of Equality and the Rhetoric of Heroism." In *Buddhism, Sexuality, and Gender,* ed. José Ignacio Cabezon. Albany: SUNY Press, 1992.

Lewis, I. M. *Ecstatic Religion: A Study of Shamanism and Spirit Possession.* London: Routledge & Kegan Paul, 1971.

———. *Religion in Context: Cults and Charisma.* Cambridge: Cambridge University Press, 1986.

Li Ch'i. "The Changing Concept of the Recluse in Chinese Literature." *Harvard Journal of Asiatic Studies* 24 (1962–1963):234–247.

Li Yu. *The Carnal Prayer Mat.* Translation of *Jou pu tuan* by Patrick Hanan. New York: Ballantine, 1990.

Link, Howard A. *Waves and Plagues: The Art of Masami Teraoka.* San Francisco: Chronicle Books, 1988.

Loori, John Daido. *The Heart of Being: Moral and Ethical Teachings of Zen Buddhism.* Boston: Tuttle, 1996.

Luk, Charles, trans. *The Vimalakirti Nirdesa Sūtra.* Berkeley: Shambhala, 1972.

Ma, Y. W. "Fact and Fantasy in T'ang Tales." *CLEAR* 2 (1980):167–181.

———. "Themes and Characterizations in the L'ung-t'u Kung-an." *Toung Pao* 59 (1973):179–202.

Ma, Y. W., and Joseph S. M. Lau. *Traditional Chinese Stories: Themes and Variations.* New York: Columbia University Press, 1978.

Mair, Victor H. "Buddhism and the Rise of the Written Vernacular in East Asia: The Making of National Languages." *Journal of Asian Studies* 53(3) (1994):707–751.

———. *Tun-Huang Popular Narratives.* Cambridge: Cambridge University Press, 1983.

Mana Shōbōgenzō goi sakuin. Edited by Sōtōshū shūgaku kenkyūjō. Tokyo: Sōtōshū shūgaku kenkyūjō, 1993.

Maraldo, John C. "Is There Historical Consciousness Within Ch'an?" *Japanese Journal of Religious Studies* 12(2–3) (1985):141–172.

Marra, Michele. *Representations of Power: The Literary Politics of Medieval Japan.* Honolulu: University of Hawai'i Press, 1993.

Marriot, Alice, and Carol K. Rachlin. *American Indian Mythology.* New York: New American Library, 1968.

Masutani Fumio. *Rinzai to Dōgen.* Tokyo: Shunjūsha, 1971.

Matsumae Takeshi. *Inari myōjin.* Tokyo: Chikuma shobō, 1988.

Matsumoto Shirō. *Engi to kū—Nyoraizō shisō hihan.* Tokyo: Daizō shuppan, 1989.

———. "Jinshin inga ni tsuite—Dōgen no Shisō ni Kansuru Shiken." *JSS,* pp. 199–247.

———. *Zen shisō no hihanteki kenkyū.* Tokyo: Daizō shuppan, 1994.

Matsuoka Yukako. *Kobutsu Dōgen no shii.* Kyoto: Kokusai Zengaku kenkyūjō, 1995.

———. *Shōbōgenzō* jūnikanon no gendaiteki: Hakamaya Noriaki *Dōgen to Bukkyō* hihan." *Zen bunka kenkyūjō kiyō* 22 (1996):89–148.

Mayer, Fanny Hagin. "Religious Concepts in the Japanese Folk Tale." *Japanese Journal of Religious Studies* 1(1) (1974):73–101.

McDonald, Keiko, ed. *Ugetsu: Kenji Mizoguchi, Director.* New Brunswick, N.J.: Rutgers University Press, 1993.

McFarland, H. Neill. *Daruma: The Founder of Zen in Japanese Art and Popular Culture.* Tokyo: Kodansha, 1987.

McRae, John R. *The Northern School and the Formation of Early Ch'an Buddhism.* Honolulu: University of Hawai'i Press, 1986.

———. "Shen-hui and the Teaching of Sudden Enlightenment in Early Ch'an Buddhism." In *Sudden and Gradual: Approaches to Enlightenment in Chinese Thought,* ed. Peter N. Gregory. Honolulu: University of Hawai'i Press, 1987.

Melville, James. *A Haiku for Hanae.* New York: Ballantine, 1989.

Miller, Alan L. "Religions of Japan." *Religions of the World.* New York: St. Martin's, 1983.

Mishima Yukio. *The Temple of the Golden Pavilion (Kinkakuji)*. Translated by Ivan Morris. New York: Perigee, 1959.

Miura, Isshū, and Ruth Fuller Sasaki. *Zen Dust: The History of the Koan and Koan Study in Rinzai (Lin-Chi) Zen*. New York: Harcourt, Brace, 1966.

Mizuno Yaoko. *Jūnikanbon Shōbōgenzō no sekai*. Tokyo: Daizō shuppan, 1994.

Monschein, Ylva. *Der Zauber der Fuchsfee: Entstehung und Wandel eines Femme-fatale—Motivs in der chinesischen Literatur*. Frankfurt am Main: Haag & Herchen, 1988.

Mori Misao. *"Mu" no shisō*. Tokyo: Kodansha, 1987.

Mori, Masato. "*Konjaku Monogatari-shū:* Supernatural Creatures and Order." *Japanese Journal of Religious Studies* 9(2–3) (1982):147–170.

Morishige, Yumi. "Cultural Construction of Foxes." M.A. thesis, Cornell University, 1994.

Morley, Carolyn Anne. *Transformation, Miracles, and Mischief: The Mountain Priest Plays of Kyōgen*. Ithaca: Cornell East Asia Series, 1993.

Morrell, Robert E. *Sand and Pebbles (Shasekishū): The Tales of Mujū Ichien, a Voice for Pluralism in Kamakura Buddhism*. Albany: SUNY Press, 1985.

Morris, Ivan. *The World of the Shining Prince*. New York: Penguin, 1964.

Nagahara Keiji. "The Medieval Origins of the Eta-Hinin." *Journal of Japanese Studies* 5(2) (1979):385–403.

Nagai Masashi. "Chūgoku Bukkyō seiritsu no issokumen: Chūgoku Zenshū ni okeru sōshiki girei no seiritsu to tenkai." *KDBR* 26 (1995):109–148.

Nakamura Eshin. *Mumonkan*. Tokyo: Iwanami shoten, 1994.

Nakamura, Kyoko Motomochi, trans. *Miraculous Stories from the Japanese Buddhist Tradition: The Nihon ryōiki of the Monk Kyōkai*. Cambridge, Mass.: Harvard University Press, 1973.

Nakamura Naokatsu, ed. *O-Inari-san*. Tokyo: Asunaro sha, 1976.

Nakamura Teiri. *Nihonjin no dōbutsukan: henshintan no rekishi*. Tokyo: Kameisha, 1984.

Nakao Ryōshin. *Mumonkan zenseki zenbon kochū shūsei*. Tokyo: Meicho fukyūkai, 1983.

Nakao Shunbaku. *Bukkyō to sabetsu*. Kyoto: Nagata bunshōdō, 1985.

Nakaseko Shōdō. *Dōgen zenji den kenkyū*. Tokyo: Kokusho kankōkai, 1979.

Naoe Hiroji, ed. *Inari shinkō*. Tokyo: Yūzankaku shuppan, 1983.

Napier, Susan. *The Fantastic in Modern Japanese Literature: The Subversion of Modernity*. London: Routledge, 1996.

Nara Yasuaki, ed. *Budda kara Dōgen e*. Tokyo: Tokyo shoseki, 1992.

Natsume Sōseki. *The Three Cornered World*. Translated by Alan Turney. Reprint. Tokyo: Tuttle, 1968.

Nattier, Jan. *Once Upon a Future Time: Studies in a Buddhist Prophecy of Decline*. Berkeley: Asian Humanities Press, 1991.

Noma Hiroshi and Okiura Kazuteru. *Sei to sen*. 4 vols.: Ajia, Nihon no Chūsei, Kinsei, Kindai. Kyoto: Jinbun shoin, 1992.

Nozaki, Kiyoshi. *Kitsune: Japan's Fox of Mystery, Romance, and Humor.* Tokyo: Hokuseido Press, 1961.

Ohnuki-Tierney, Emiko. *The Monkey as Mirror: Symbolic Transformations in Japanese History and Ritual.* Princeton: Princeton University Press, 1987.

Okimoto Kokki. "Hyakujō koki." *Zen bunka kenkyūjō kiyō* 12 (1980):51–61.

Ōkubo Dōshū. *Dōgen zenji den no kenkyū.* Tokyo: Chikuma shobō, 1966.

Ōtani Teppu, ed. "Daijōji hihon 'Tōkokuki.'" *SK* 16 (1974):231–248.

———. "Dōgen zenji to sono monryū in okeru 'kami' no gainen." *Shinbutsu shugō shisō tenkai.* Tokyo: Kyūko shoin, 1996.

Otis, Paul. "Japanese Folklore and Kurosawa's *Dreams.*" *Education About Asia* 2(1) (1997):42–47.

Owen, D. D. R., trans. *The Romance of Reynard the Fox.* Oxford: Oxford University Press, 1994.

Pepper, Elizabeth, and John Wilcock. *Magical and Mystical Sites: Europe and the British Isles.* Grand Rapids: Phanes Press, 1993.

Piggott, Joan. *Japanese Mythology.* Reprint. New York: Peter Bedrick, 1982.

Porter, Bill. *Road to Heaven: Encounters with Chinese Hermits.* San Francisco: Mercury House, 1993.

Powell, William F., trans. *The Record of Tung-shan.* Honolulu: University of Hawai'i Press, 1986.

Prebish, Charles S. *Buddhist Monastic Discipline: The Sanskrit Prātimoksha Sūtras of the Mahāsāamghikas and Mūlasarvāstivādins.* University Park: Pennsylvania State University Press, 1975.

———. "Ideal Types in Indian Buddhism: A New Paradigm." *Journal of the American Oriental Society* 115(4) (1995):651–666.

Propp, Vladimir. *Morphology of the Folktale.* Translated by Lawrence Scott. 2nd ed. Austin: University of Texas Press, 1968.

Putney, David. "Some Problems in Interpretation: The Early and Late Writings of Dōgen." *Philosophy East and West* 46(4) (1996):497–531.

Qin, Wen-jie. "Revisiting the Laughing Buddha: A Study of the Metamorphosis of Maitreya in China." Paper presented at the Association for Asian Studies annual meeting, Chicago, 1997.

Quong, Rose, trans. *Chinese Ghost and Love Stories.* With an introduction by Martin Buber. New York: Pantheon, 1946.

Rahula, Walpola. *What the Buddha Taught.* New York: Grove, 1959.

Randall, Lilian M. C. *Images in the Margins of Gothic Manuscripts.* Berkeley: University of California Press, 1966.

Ray, Reginald. *Buddhist Saints in India: A Study in Buddhist Values and Orientations.* New York: Oxford University Press, 1994.

Reader, Ian. "Zazenless Zen? The Position of Zazen in Institutional Zen Buddhism." *Japanese Religions* 14(3) (1986):7–27.

Reischauer, Edwin O., trans. *Ennin's Diary: The Record of a Pilgrimage to China in Search of the Law.* New York: Ronald Press, 1955.

Reps, Paul. *Zen Flesh, Zen Bones.* Garden City: Anchor, 1961.

Ross, Catrien. *Supernatural and Mysterious Japan.* Tokyo: Yenbooks, 1996.

Said, Edward. *Orientalism.* New York: Vintage, 1978.

Sakai Tadao. *Chūgoku zensho no kenkyū.* Tokyo: Kōbundō, 1960.

Sakai Tokugen. *"Eihei kōroku."* In *Dōgen no chosaku,* ed. Kagamishima Genryū and Tamaki Kōshirō. Tokyo: Shunjūsha, 1980.

Sakurai Ōtake. *Dōgen zenji go-eden.* Tokyo: Yūgen kaisha, 1985.

Sallis, John. *Stone.* Bloomington: Indiana University Press, 1994.

Sasaki, Genjun H. "Fox Obsession in Japan: The Indian Background." *Shakti* 5(3) (1968):27–29.

Sasaki, Ruth Fuller, trans. *The Recorded Sayings of Ch'an Master Lin-chi Hui-chao of Chen Prefecture.* Kyoto: First Zen Institute, 1975.

Sasama Yoshihiko. *Benzaiten shinkō to zokushin.* Tokyo: Yūzankaku shuppan, 1991.

———. *Dakini shinkō to sono zokushin.* Tokyo: Daiichi shobō, 1988.

Satō Shunkō. " 'Hakusan' no isō: Sōtō-shū kyōdan shi kenkyū no isshikō." *KDBR* 19 (1988):343–360.

———. "Hakusan shinkō to Sōtō-shū kyōdan shi." 20 parts. *Sanshō* (1990–1991): 556–575.

Satō Tadao. *Kurosawa meikai dai.* Tokyo: Iwanami shoten, 1990.

Satō Tatsugen. "Dao-xuan and His Religious Precepts." In *Buddhist Behavioral Codes and the Modern World,* ed. Charles Wei-hsun Fu and Sandra Wawrytko. Westport, Conn.: Greenwood Press, 1994.

Sawada Mizuho. *Bukkyō to Chūgoku bungaku.* Tokyo: Kokusho kankōkai, 1978.

———. *Chūgoku dōbutsu dan.* Tokyo: Sōbundō, 1978.

Schafer, Edward H. "The Table of Contents of the *T'ai p'ing kuang chi.*" *CLEAR* 2(2) (1980):248–263.

Schlütter, Morten. "When a Vinaya Monastery Is Not a Vinaya Monastery: Public and Hereditary Monasteries in the Song Dynasty (960–1279)." Paper presented at the panel on Buddhist Precepts in East Asia at the American Academy of Religion annual meeting, New Orleans, 1996.

Schmitt, Jean-Claude. *The Holy Greyhound: Guinefort, Healer of Children Since the Thirteenth Century.* Translated by Martin Thom. Cambridge: Cambridge University Press, 1979.

Schopen, Gregory. *Bones, Stones, and Buddhist Monks: Collected Papers on the Archaeology, Epigraphy, and Texts of Monastic Buddhism in India.* Honolulu: University of Hawai'i Press, 1997.

Sekida Katsuki. *Two Zen Classics.* New York: Weatherhill, 1977.

"Sendara mondai senmon i'inkai hōkoku" (Report of the Research Group on the Problem of Candala). Edited by Eiheiji Sendara Mondai Senmon I'inkai. *Sanshō* 606 (1994):8–31.

Sharf, Robert H. "The Idolization of Enlightenment: On the Mummification of Ch'an Masters in Medieval China." *History of Religions* 32(1) (1992): 1–31.

Shibayama Zenkei. *Zen Comments on the Mumonkan*. Translated by Sumiko Kudo. New York: Mentor, 1974.

Shiina Kōyū. "Pai-chang-shan no genkyō to Tōdai ni okeru shomondai." In *Chūgoku butsu-seki kenmonki*. Tokyo: Chūgoku Bukkyō shiseki sankan dan, 1984.

———. " 'Shūmon tōyōshū' no shoshiteki kenkyū." *KDBR* 16 (1987):299–336.

Shimada Hiromi. *Kaimyō: naze shigo ni namae o kaeru no ka*. Kyoto: Hōzōkan, 1991.

Shinohara Koichi. "Buddhist Precepts in Medieval Chinese Biographies of Monks." In *Buddhist Behavioral Codes and the Modern World*, ed. C. W. Fu and Sandra Wawrytko. Westport, Conn.: Greenwood Press, 1994.

Smits, Ivo. "An Early Anthropologist? Ōe no Masafusa's *A Record of Fox Spirits*." In *Religion in Japan: Arrows to Heaven and Earth*, ed. P. F. Kornicki and I. J. McMullen. Cambridge: Cambridge University Press, 1996.

Smyers, Karen. "Of Foxes, Buddhas, and Shinto Kami: The Syncretic Nature of Inari Beliefs." *Japanese Religions* 16(3) (1991):62–64.

———. "The Fox and the Jewel: A Study of Shared and Private Meanings in *Inari* Worship." Ph.D. diss., Princeton University, 1993.

———. "My Own Inari: Personalization of the Deity in Inari Worship." *Japanese Journal of Religious Studies* 23(1–2) (1996):85–116.

Stevenson, Daniel. "The Four Kinds of Samādhi in Early T'ien-t'ai Buddhism." In *Traditions of Meditation in Chinese Buddhism*, ed. Peter N. Gregory. Honolulu: University of Hawai'i Press, 1986.

Strassberg, Richard E., trans. *Inscribed Landscapes: Travel Writing from Imperial China*. Berkeley: University of Caifornia Press, 1994.

Strong, John S., ed. *The Experience of Buddhism: Sources and Interpretations*. Belmont, Calif.: Wadsworth, 1994.

———. *The Legend and Cult of Upagupta: Sanskrit Buddhism in North India and Southeast Asia*. Princeton: Princeton University Press, 1992.

Sueki Fumihiko. *Nihon Bukkyōshi*. Tokyo: Shinchōbun, 1992.

———. "Two Seemingly Contradictory Aspects of the Teaching of Innate Enlightenment *(hongaku)* in Medieval Japan." *Japanese Journal of Religious Studies* 22(1–2) (1995):3–16.

Suganuma Akira. *Dōgen jiten*. Tokyo: Tokyodō shuppan, 1977.

Sugio Gen'yū. "Dōgen Zenji no jiko-tōdatsu no go-shōgai to *Shōbōgenzō* no shinka-Jūnikanbon ni yotte 'Ippaku-kan' o omou." *SK* 27 (1985):7–12.

———. "Nanajūgokanbon *Shōbōgenzō* no kihonteki kōsatsu." In *Dōgen zen no shisōteki kenkyū*, ed. Kurebayashi Kōdō. Tokyo: Shunjūsha, 1973.

Suzuki Tetsuo. "Koshushaku to shakushuko." *IBK* 44(3) (1996):720–727.

Swanson, Paul L. "Zen Is Not Buddhism—Recent Critiques of Buddha Nature." *Numen* 40(2) (1993):115–149.

Takakusu, Junjirō. *The Essentials of Buddhist Philosophy*. Honolulu: University of Hawai'i Press, 1947.

Takeuchi, Yoshinori. *The Heart of Buddhism: In Search of the Timeless Spirit of Primitive Buddhism*. New York: Crossroad, 1983.

Tamamuro Taijō. *Sōshiki Bukkyō.* Tokyo: Daihōrinkaku, 1963.

Tambiah, Stanley. *Culture, Thought, and Social Action.* Cambridge, Mass.: Harvard University Press, 1985.

Tampopo. Directed by Itami Jūzō. Japan, 1987.

Tamura Yoshirō. "Critique of Original Awakening Thought in Shōshin and Dōgen." *Japanese Journal of Religious Studies* 11(2–3) (1984):243–266.

———. *Kamakura shin-Bukkyō shisō no kenkyū.* Kyoto: Heirakuji Shoten, 1965.

Tanabe Hajime. *Philosophy as Metanoetics.* Translated by Takeuchi Yoshinori with Valdo Viglielmo and James W. Heisig. Berkeley: University of California Press, 1986.

Tanahashi, Kazuaki, trans. *Moon in a Dewdrop: Writings by Zen Master Dōgen.* San Francisco: North Point, 1985.

Tao Ch'ien [Yüan-ming]. *Tao Yüan-ming chi.* Edited by Lü Chin-li. Beijing: Chung-hua shu-chü, 1979.

Taylor, Mark C. *Erring: A Postmodern A/Theology.* Chicago: University of Chicago Press, 1984.

Teiser, Stephen F. *The Ghost Festival in Medieval China.* Princeton: Princeton University Press, 1988.

Thanissaro Bhikkhu. *The Buddhist Monastic Code: The Patimokkha Training Rules Translated and Explained.* Valley Center, Calif.: Abbot Metta Forest Monastery, 1994.

Thompson, Stith. *Motif Index of Folk Literature.* 6 vols. Bloomington: Indiana University Press, 1955–1958.

———. *Standard Dictionary of Folklore, Mythology, and Legend.* New York: Funk & Wagnalls, 1949.

———. *Tales of the North American Indians.* Bloomington: Indiana University Press, 1929.

Tso Sze-bong. "The Decline of Buddhist *Vinaya* in China from a Historical and Cultural Perspective." In *Buddhist Behavioral Codes and the Modern World,* ed. C. W. Fu and Sandra Wawrytko. Westport, Conn.: Greenwood Press, 1994.

Tsunoda Tairyū. "Kana *Shōbōgenzō* to Mana *Shōbōgenzō.*" *KDBR* 24 (1993):143–160.

Tsunoda Yasutaka. "Jūnikanbon *Shōbōgenzō* no kenkyū dōkō." *JSS,* pp. 458–472.

Tyler, Royall, ed. and trans. *Japanese Tales.* New York: Pantheon, 1987.

Ugetsu. Directed by Kenji Mizoguchi. Japan, 1953.

Umehara Takeshi. *Rakan: butsu no hito aida.* Tokyo: Kodansha, 1977.

Unno, Mark. "Divine Madness—Exploring the Boundaries of Modern Japanese Religion." *Zen Buddhism Today* 10 (1993):96–112.

Ury, Mirian Bloom. " 'Genko Shakusho,' Japan's First Comprehensive History of Buddhism: A Partial Translation, with Introduction and Notes." Ph.D. diss., University of California, 1970.

Veyne, Paul. *Did the Greeks Believe in Their Myths? An Essay in the Constitu-*

tive Imagination. Translated by Paula Wissing. Chicago: University of Chicago Press, 1988.

Victoria, Daizen. "Japanese Corporate Zen." In *The Other Japan: Postwar Realities,* ed. E. Patricia Tsurumi. Armonk, N.Y.: Sharpe, 1988.

Visser, M. W. de. *Ancient Buddhism in Japan.* 2 vols. Leiden: Brill, 1935.

————. "The Fox and Badger in Japanese Folklore." *Transactions of the Asiatic Society of Japan* 36(3) (1908):1–159.

Waddell, Norman, trans. *The Essential Teachings of Zen Master Hakuin.* Boston: Shambhala, 1994.

————. *The Unborn: The Life and Teaching of Zen Master Bankei, 1622–1693.* San Francisco: North Point, 1984.

Walthall, Anne. *Peasant Uprisings: A Critical Anthology of Peasant Histories.* Chicago: University of Chicago Press, 1991.

Wang, Jing. *The Story of Stone: Intertextuality, Ancient Chinese Stone Lore, and the Stone Symbolism in Dream of the Red Chamber, Water Margin, and The Journey to the West.* Durham, N.C.: Duke University Press, 1992.

Watanabe Shōhei. "Zenshū to minshū to no ni tsuite." *Sōtōshū kenkyūin kenkyūsei kenkyū kiyō* 12 (1975):148–161.

Watson, Burton, trans. *Basic Writings of Mo-tzu, Hsun-Tzu, Han Fei-tzu.* New York: Columbia University Press, 1967.

————. *Chinese Lyricism: Shih Poetry from the Second to the Twelfth Century.* New York: Columbia University Press, 1971.

Watson, James L., and Evelyn S. Rawski, eds. *Death Ritual in Late Imperial and Modern China.* Berkeley: University of California Press, 1988.

Weinstein, Stanley. *Buddhism Under the T'ang.* New York: Cambridge University Press, 1987.

Welch, Holmes. *The Practice of Chinese Buddhism 1900–1950.* Cambridge, Mass.: Harvard University Press, 1967.

Welch, Holmes, and Anna Seidel, eds. *Facets of Taoism.* New Haven: Yale University Press, 1979.

Welter, Albert. "Zanning and Chan: The Changing Nature of Buddhism in Early Song China." *Journal of Chinese Religions* 23 (1995):105–140.

White, David Gordon. *Myths of the Dog-Man.* Chicago: University of Chicago Press, 1991.

Wijayaratna, Mohan. *Buddhist Monastic Life: According to the Texts of the Theravāda Tradition.* Translated by Claude Grangier and Steven Collins. Cambridge: Cambridge University Press, 1990.

Wood, Denis. *The Power of Maps.* New York: Guilford Press, 1992.

Wright Arthur F. *Buddhism in Chinese History.* Stanford: Stanford University Press, 1959.

————. *Studies in Chinese Buddhism.* Edited by Robert M. Somers. New Haven: Yale University Press, 1990.

Wu, John C. H. *The Golden Age of Zen.* Taipei: United Publishing Center, 1975.

Wu, Pei-yi. "Self-Examination and Confession of Sins in Traditional China." *Harvard Journal of Asiatic Studies* 39(1) (1978):5–38.

Yagi, Dickson Kazuo. "Protestant Perspectives on Ancestor Worship in Japanese Buddhism: The Funeral and the Buddhist Altar." *Buddhist-Christian Studies* 15 (1996):43–59.

Yamada, Kōun, trans. *Gateless Gate.* Tucson: University of Arizona Press, 1979.

Yamaoka Takaaki. "Daiyūzan Saijōji ni okeru Bukkyōteki fukugō ni tsuite." *SK* 25 (1983):115–136.

Yamauchi Shuny'ū. *Dōgen Zen to Tendai hōngaku hōmon.* Tokyo: Daizō shuppan, 1986.

Yampolsky, Philip B., trans. *The Platform Sutra of the Sixth Patriarch: The Text of the Tun Huang Manuscript.* New York: Columbia University Press, 1967.

Yanagida Seizan. "Dōgen to Chūgoku Bukkyō." *Zen bunka kenkyūjō kiyō* 13 (1984):3–128.

———. "Dōgen to Rinzai." *Risō* 513 (1976):74–89.

———. "Goroku no rekishi: Zen bunken no seiritsu shiteki kenkyū." *Tōhō gakkō* 57 (1985):211–663.

———. "The Life of Lin-chi I-hsüan." *Eastern Buddhist* 5(2) (1972):70–94.

———. "The 'Recorded Sayings' Texts of Chinese Ch'an Buddhism." Translated by John R. McRae. In *Early Ch'an in China and Tibet,* ed. Whalen Lai and Lewis R. Lancaster. Berkeley: Berkeley Buddhist Studies Series, 1983.

———. *Shoki Zenshū shisho no kenkyū.* Kyoto: Hōzōkan, 1967.

———, ed. *Sōdōshū.* Kyoto: Chūbun shuppansha, 1974.

———. *Zen no yuige.* Tokyo: Chōbunsha, 1973.

Yao, Karl S.Y. *Classical Chinese Tales of the Supernatural and Fantastic.* Bloomington: Indiana University Press, 1985.

Yasui Shirō. *Toyokawa Inari monogatari.* Toyohashi City: Mai-booku-chieen, 1986.

Yasutani Hakuun, ed. *Mumonkan.* Tokyo: Shunjūsha, 1965.

———. *Shōyōroku.* Tokyo: Shunjūsha, 1973.

Yi T'ao-tien, trans. "Records of the Life of Ch'an Master Pai-chang Huai-hai." *Eastern Buddhist* 8 (1975):42–73.

Yokoi Yūhō, ed. *Eihei kōroku.* Tokyo: Sankibō busshorin, 1978.

Yokoi Yūhō and Daizen Victoria, eds. *Zen Master Dōgen: An Introduction with Selected Writings.* New York: Weatherhill, 1975.

Yoshida, Teigo. "Mystical Retribution, Spirit Possession, and Social Structure in a Japanese Village." *Ethnology* 6(3) (1967):237–262.

———. *Nihon no tsukimono: shakai jinruigakuteki kōsatsu.* Tokyo: Chūō-kōronsha, 1979.

Yoshikawa Taiyū. *Mumonkan shō: Tōmon shōmono to kokugo kenkyū.* Tokyo: Ōfūsha, 1976.

Yoshimoto Banana. *Kitchen.* Translated by Megan Backus. New York: Grove, 1993.

Yoshizu Yoshihide. "Heki no ningen-kan to mondō ni yoru satori." In *Budda kara Dōgen e*, ed. Nara Yasuaki. Tokyo: Tokyo shoseki, 1992. 131–142.

Young, Blake Morgan. *Ueda Akinari*. Vancouver: University of British Columbia Press, 1982.

Yu, Anthony C. " 'Rest, Rest, Perturbed Spirit!' Ghosts in Traditional Chinese Fiction." *Harvard Journal of Asiatic Studies* 47(2) (1987):397–434.

Yü, Chün-fang. "P'u-t'o Shan: Pilgrimage and the Creation of the Chinese Potalaka." In *Pilgrims and Sacred Sites in China,* ed. Susan Naquin and Chun-fang Yü. Berkeley: University of California Press, 1992.

———. *The Renewal of Buddhism in China: Chu-hung and the Late Ming Synthesis.* New York: Columbia University Press, 1990.

Zeitlin, Judith T. *Historian of the Strange: Pu Songling and the Chinese Classical Tale.* Stanford: Stanford University Press, 1993.

"Zen and the Art of Modernity." *Los Angeles Times,* May 21, 1993.

Zolbrod, Leon, trans. *Ugetsu monogatari: Tales of Moonlight and Rain.* Reprint. Tokyo: Tuttle, 1977.

Zürcher, Erik. *The Buddhist Conquest of China: The Spread and Adaptation of Buddhism in Early Medieval China.* 2 vols. Leiden: Brill, 1959.

Index

291